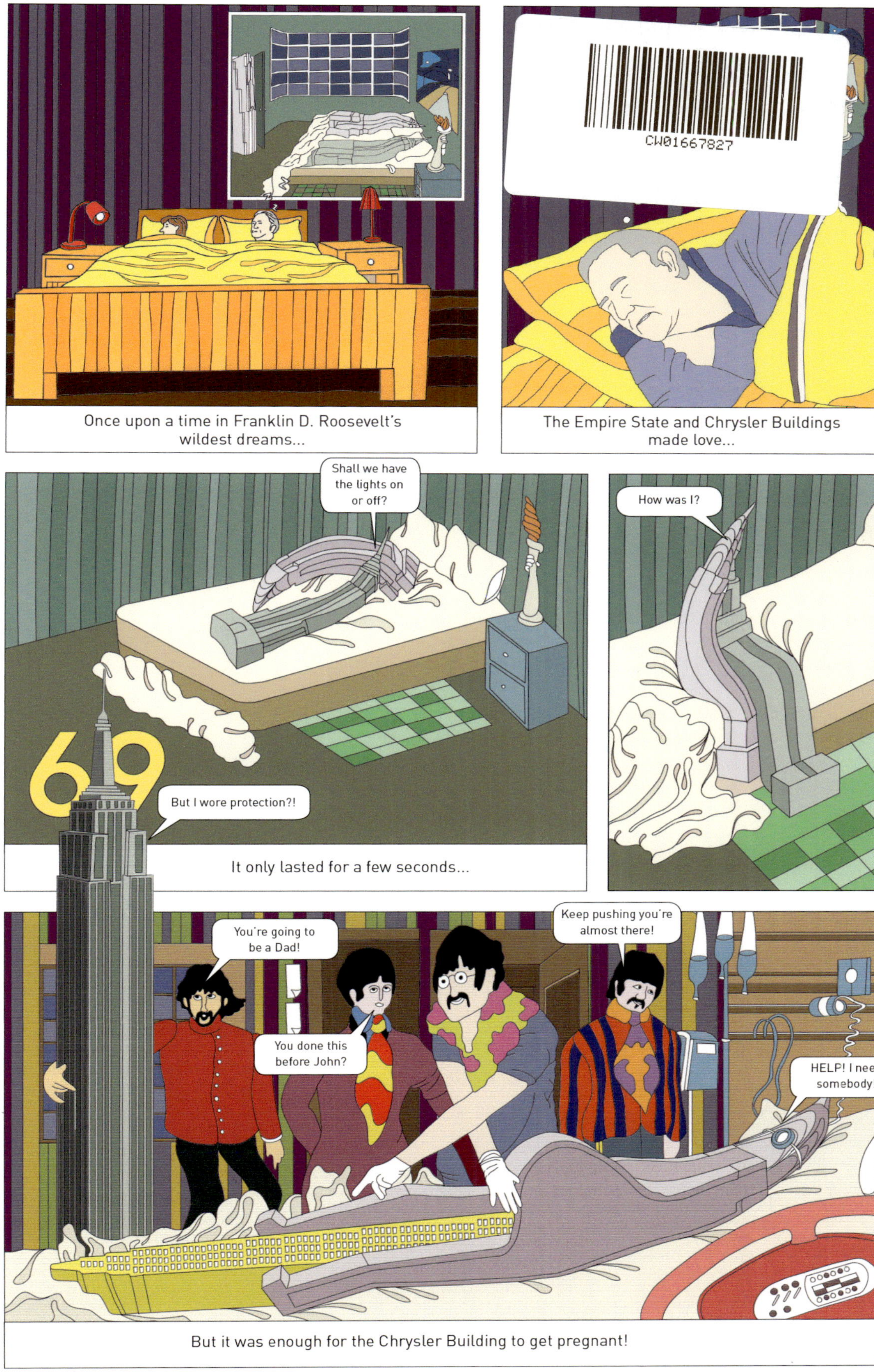

...to be continued on page 306

Dreams + Disillusions

Dedicated to Paul Allen

First published 2024
by Routledge
605 Third Avenue, New York, NY 10158

and by Routledge
4 Park Square, Milton Park, Abingdon, Oxon, OX14 4RN

Routledge is an imprint of the Taylor & Francis Group, an informa business

ISBN: 9780367075354 (hbk)
ISBN: 9780367075378 (pbk)
ISBN: 9780429021268 (ebk)
DOI: 10.4324/9780429021268

Designed cover image: © CJ Lim / Studio 8 Architects
Typeset in DIN by Studio 8 Architects

Publisher's note: This book has been prepared from camera-ready copy provided by the author.

Printed and bound in Great Britain by
TJ Books Limited, Padstow, Cornwall

FSC www.fsc.org MIX Paper from responsible sources FSC® C013056

CJ Lim + Luke Angers

Dreams + Disillusions

Routledge
Taylor & Francis Group
NEW YORK AND LONDON

Contents

DREAMS + DISILLUSIONS
book research team: CJ Lim, Luke Angers and Steve McCloy

Special Thanks
case studies research team: Xiaoliang Deng, Karen Tsang, Jess Yu and Hugh Kam

contents

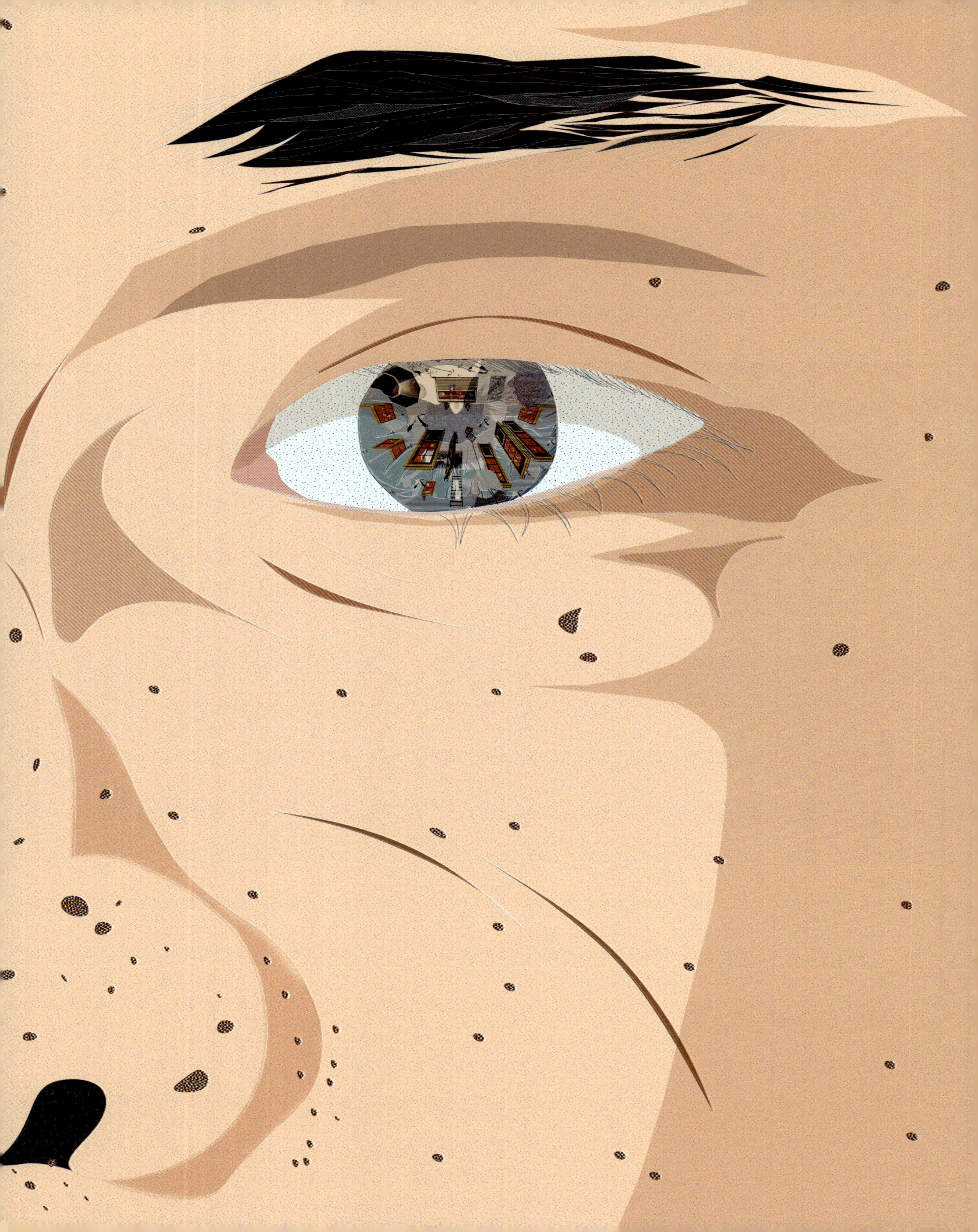

Preface

'Cities, like dreams, are made of desires and fears, even if the thread of their discourse is secret, their rules are absurd, their perspectives deceitful, and everything conceals something else... Cities also believe they are the work of the mind or of chance, but neither the one nor the other suffices to hold up the walls... You take delight not in a city's seven or seventy wonders, but in the answer it gives to a question of yours.'

– Italo Calvino, 'Invisible Cities', 1974

Interpreting dreams and disillusions, 'Invisible Cities' is a divine riddle for the imagination. The title alone evokes a world of unknown forces, psychological mysteries, and emotional depth. Set on relaxed terraces overlooking the balustrades of a vast palace, the conversations between Kublai Khan, Emperor of the Mongol Empire, and the Venetian explorer Marco Polo emphasise the need to master the arts of storytelling and listening. Calvino's book is at once explicit and implicit. It speaks abstractly and poetically of the agents that shape our experience of the built environment, both unseen and conspicuous. Free from superficiality and captivated by curiosity, it presents insights on a diversity of urban interpretations and improbable spatial delicacies.

One prominent Italian Senator, the architect Renzo Piano, cannot have escaped Invisible Cities and its influence. In 'Atlantis: A journey in search of beauty' (2020) the conversation between Renzo and his son Carlo contrasts fantasies with the cultural realities of cities, bringing to mind the enchanting passages exchanged by the two protagonists in Calvino's fiction. When asked whether the pair had found Atlantis on their various sailing trips around the world the elder Piano answers 'no', but alludes to the importance of narrative, metaphor, and speculation in support of his continuing belief. 'Everybody lives for Atlantis... Atlantis is beauty, it's the dream, it's spiritual. Life is not just about needs, it's also about desires, dreams, aspirations.'[1] For Carlo, the dreams that formed his father's career seem to be an affliction. 'All the water surrounding Punta Nave must be to blame for my father's burning desire for Atlantis. Maybe Atlantis has always hounded him. After all, what does an architect dream of if not the perfect city? For his entire life he had believed that a spirit of adventure was the essence of being an architect... the more I thought about it, the more this dream of chasing Atlantis seemed like a nightmare.'[2]

facing page: 'From now on, I'll describe the cities to you... in your journeys you will see if they exist.' – I Calvino, 'Invisible Cities', 1974

Human settlements, from the brilliant to the catastrophic, have been likened to living organisms that constantly adapt to evolving socio-political values and unpredictable environmental challenges. The very fabric of the city is a spatial library, a rich archive of built forms that has been layered over for hundreds or thousands of years of human life. From time-to-time, great dreams have carved heroic avenues or erected towering structures towards heaven. The Great Ziggurat of Ur was the zenith of the Neo-Sumerian Empire, which established its dynasty as a force of settlers to be feared and held in awe. It functioned as a shrine and administrative centre to a large temple complex, elevating the leaders of the city to high stature and one of its patrons, King Shulgi, even proclaimed himself a god. Many of the impressive ziggurats that stand along the mouth of the Euphrates today were almost lost to a succession of wars, rebuilt in the late 20th century on the orders of Iraq's infamous leader Saddam Hussein who was keen to write his own name into their legacy.[3]

1. R Piano, 'Interview for Europa Editions', 17 December 2020 [https://www.youtube.com/watch?v=MgOKa6d67Kk], retrieved 17 September 2022

2. R Piano & C Piano, 'Atlantis: A journey in search of beauty', Europa Editions, London, 2020, pp.15–23

3. J Marozzi, 'Lost Cities #1: Babylon – How war almost erased mankind's greatest heritage site', Guardian, 8 August 2016

Intertwined with ancient gods, myths and rituals, the lost dreams found in the remains of Luxor and Edfu 'Apollinopolis Magna', the Angkor Wat complex in Cambodia, the Aztec capital of Tenochtitlan, and the mountaintop Incan citadel of Machu Picchu offer insights into the historic fragility and fates of cities. Urban development and material wealth in London, Bristol and Liverpool came from the exploitations of the Victorian empire. The story is the same across many other cities in Britain, with street names, businesses, and institutions linked to undeniably dark histories. Investments into advanced infrastructure revolutionised life in the English capital – from Joseph Bazalgette's sewer system to the train stations of Euston, St Pancras, Paddington, Liverpool Street and Waterloo, and the numerous bridges knitting the two banks of the River Thames. At the same time, Britain famously exported its ideology of dense city living, imposing architecture, and transport infrastructure across the globe; all of which asserted British dominance and installed the supposed moral and economic values of Victorian society, and of the monarch.

Whether by bold gestures of power and wealth or by subtle attrition and guerrilla activities, cities are built on the dreams of princes and political leaders as well as the abstracted interpretations of countless planners, architects, authors, and citizens. For the keen observer, cities themselves can be read as encyclopedias of ideas and ideologies. They bequeath mysterious patterns for future urban archaeologists to decipher, from the role of civic spaces in ancient Greek cities or the importance of monumental buildings to ancient Egypt, to the repetitive efficiency of terraced workers' housing from industrial revolution-era England. Many layers of history, quirks and sub-cultures are at work simultaneously, not least within each of the ever-shifting economic and technological eras which often dictate priorities and urban form. Rome was not built in a day, but centuries later we have witnessed dozens of 21st-century Chinese cities assembled from scratch in just a few short years. Organic growth is often at odds with the commercial discipline of urban planning and the political aspirations of decision makers. Rapid changes in population and technology have overwhelmed and discarded our notion of the organic city, its old relationships torn or tangled, its future devolving into accelerated urban entropy. This process conjures thrilling and terrifying spatial consequences resembling anything but prosaic traditional ways of life.

We often get overly caught-up in dreams of illusory pasts or the promised futures of yesteryear when reflecting on our current urban situation and the possibility of radical societal change. Martin Pawley's 'The Private Future' (1972) predicts a chilling prospective civilisation where personal lives become increasingly private and social exchange is moved from the real world into a space of networked virtual communication. Referring to suburb-inhabiting city workers as 'shoals of anonymous commuters fed on sports reports and salacious advertising', Pawley inquires if such groupings of humanity can 'really be called communities'.[4] Corporate privatisation and personal isolation have progressively externalised costs, negatively impacting the unique social contracts and direct engagements which animate the built environment. The resulting disappearance of public space within cities leads to a dystopian form of undemocratic capitalism. In The Private Future, this process is seen as 'irreversible in the present circumstances of the Western world, and the allegiance of its peoples to the dreams so indiscriminately displayed within it will survive... this almost achieved dream represents the dead centre of the aspirations of the whole world'.[5]

Sometimes it is the collective reaction to an event that ultimately makes its mark on ways of life and modes of existence within the city. In early 2020, the quick spread of COVID-19 created a deadly pandemic which locked down borders and led governments to declare states of emergency. Almost overnight, the whole world witnessed extreme disillusionment and as humans hunkered down indoors, cities now considered 'high-risk' turned into never-before-seen ghostly environments with streets, parks and buildings abandoned. With much work being 'shifted out to more remote locations' urban theorist

Richard Florida warns that 'the pandemic will not only reshape cities but it's going to reshape suburbs and rural areas'.[6] As cities across the world witness the 'last gasp of the industrial revolution', the working-from-home economy is rapidly eroding the common culture of daily congregations in business districts, and hence the demand for large office towers. Whilst the post-COVID aftermath would see a dramatic fall in carbon emissions and the city greener, there are many other examples of more potent and fundamental influences which populaces have grown accustomed to, taken for granted, or never truly understood in their shaping of the human environment.

Urban accretions where coherent networks of huge infrastructure and giant buildings dominate could only ever be built and maintained by highly autocratic governments or exceedingly profitable private mega companies. In contrast to the perfection of a utopian dream, good science fiction reflects the present back to us through exaggerated and speculative visions of the future. For example, Ridley Scott's film 'Blade Runner' (1982) based on Philip K. Dick's book 'Do Androids Dream of Electric Sheep?' (1968), brought to life visions of a city with massive disparities between scales of urbanism, at once loaded with commercial megastructures and littered with micro-scale activities. The film was inspired by 1980s Hong Kong and portrays the imaginative means by which cities of such density have been inhabited. Journalist David Vetter argues that 'Blade Runner's world-building is perhaps most effective not in the grandness of its gloomy vistas, but in its imagining of humanity condensed. And Hong Kong, arguably more than anywhere else in the world, is a snapshot of exactly that. All the realms of human experience: young and old, rich and poor, living around and above and beneath one another.'[7] Vetter highlights the paradoxes of the movie's spatial environment – East meets West, technology meets tradition, affluence meets destitution – and how such dualities also define Hong Kong, a conduit between two worlds.

In Yevgeny Zamyatin's dystopian science fiction 'We' (1924) the paradoxical nature of communist society is projected to its logical conclusion. Zamyatin depicts a totalitarian future in conflict with the idiosyncrasies of human nature, governed by the ideals of rationalism and 'the great, divine, exact, wise straight line'.[8] Set in the glass-enclosed 'One State', a city-nation ruled over by the prophetic 'Benefactor', future citizens believe a world of perfect conformity to be the key to a harmonious existence. Under the strict scientific management of the panoptic One State, individuality is considered an affliction. '"You're in a bad way! Apparently, you have developed a soul." A soul? That strange, ancient, long-forgotten word.'[9] Mirroring the real-world anxieties of the time concerned with totalising systems, mass communication, and technological advancement, the narrative resolves in a return to the unfamiliar nature which the privileging of practicality had eliminated from the idealised systems of 20th-century planners.

In reality, post-revolutionary Soviet leadership was restructuring the era's social order based on a belief that communal living would replace the outdated nuclear family unit. This bottom-up change was to be accomplished, in part, through the coordinated deployment of town planners who were to play an important role in the creation of a new kind of collective city under an omnipresent government structure.[10] Filling the void left by the system of private enterprise, planners were made responsible for all manner of provisions including equal distribution of items for collective consumption, parallel development of industry and housing, and the construction of facilities for work, recreation, and

4 + 5. M Pawley, 'The Private Future', Pan Books, London, 1974, p.8 & p.203

6. V Romei & J Burn-Murdoch, 'From Peak City to Ghost Town: The urban centres hit hardest by Covid-19', Financial Times, 15 October 2020

7. D Vetter, 'Welcome To Ridleyville: How Hong Kong inspired "Blade Runner"', Cathay Pacific Magazine, 5 November 2019 [https://discovery.cathaypacific.com/welcome-ridleyville-hong-kong-inspired-blade-runner], retrieved 1 August 2022

8 + 9. Y Zamyatin, 'We', M Ginsburg (trans.), Viking Press, New York, 1972, p.2 & p.269

10 + 11. JH Bater, 'The Soviet City: Ideal and reality, explorations in urban analysis', Edward Arnold Publishers, London, 1980, p.22 & p.23

communal life. Not unlike Ebenezer Howard's 'Garden City' which was inspired by the utopian tract, 'Looking Backward: 2000–1887', by the American lawyer Edward Bellamy, the ideal socialist city was to have a relatively fixed number of approximately 50,000 inhabitants. It was believed that capping populations would prevent the cramped living conditions and associated social ills which arose in larger industrial urban centres. In fact, Soviet planners often placed more importance on the provision of nature than did Letchworth and Welwyn Garden City in the UK, proponents of Howard's concentric plan of open space, parkland and radial boulevards that carefully integrated housing, agriculture and industry.

Following the dictates of Marxist ideology in its distaste for industrial civilisation, the de-urbanist school advocated a radical approach with ribbon developments creating 'an essentially townless, socialist society in which the age-old contradiction between town and country would be abolished once and for all'.[11] Such an approach would, in theory, allow planners to disperse populations over all the habitable parts of a given state providing privacy for living quarters while employment nodes and centres of collective consumption would be incorporated continuously within a specified distance. Throughout the 20th-century Soviet cities slowly reversed these plans, ironically becoming synonymous with giant factories, power stations, and manufacturing plants. Communist leadership supplanted its own stated aims of harmonising town and country in favour of competition with the industrial power of capitalist America.

Leading the design of Frankfurt during the reign of the Weimar Republic, Ernst May later exported his ideas to the Soviet Union where he influenced the layouts of at least 20 cities through his principles of 'ideal' industrial planning. The remote steelwork capital of Magnitogorsk located in central Russia along the Ural mountain range is a prime example of how his experiments resulted in the unnavigable sprawl of the USSR's anomalous 'linear cities'.[12] In May's text 'The Structure of the Socialist City' (1931), he sets out a detailed vision of collective life realised through a belief in communist ideology, design, and sociological strategies. In such cities, it would be recognised as a waste of valuable time 'to see the function of woman in terms of lifelong cooking and dusting, when she should be contributing both physically and intellectually to the common good, using her free time to cultivate both body and mind. Regrets or no regrets, the fact remains that the traditional image of the family is in the process of extinction.'[13]

While the political dreams of the revolution may have been woefully misinformed, often creating more hardships and stumbling blocks than improvements in realising the promised worker's paradise, the creative thrust it generated allowed designers to speculate into the future as few had been liberated to do before. The resulting 'paper architecture' of the Constructivist movement provides countless images of compelling possibilities for urban life. Lasting less than a decade (1919–1928), it nonetheless exercises a profound and enduring impact on architectural and urban discourse through the manifestos and designs of its key figures including Alexander Rodchenko, El Lissitzky, Vladimir Tatlin, and Kazimir Malevich. Their life's work sought to break the mould, making noble use of their talents to pioneer new visions that would benefit coming generations rather than realise compromised buildings for a broken system.

There have always been those that unfairly criticise emerging creatives and thinkers who do not turn their dreams to concrete reality. Even so, it is the prominence of dreaming itself that has afforded many of the speculative and imaginative pursuits which shape the built environment of our cities. Before the hugely influential paper architects of Archigram, Superstudio and Yona Friedman, prominent architects such as John Soane and Christopher Wren were invested as much in their dreams, documented as drawings, paintings and writings, as their built work. The discourse of cities is not as simple as constructing the dream, but they should nonetheless be studied imaginatively. To a dreamer, the mundane inconvenience of not pouring concrete does little to stem the creative outpouring; process, sensibility, and repertoire may well emerge that will, when ready, change the world. Zaha Hadid was arguably one of the biggest stars in architecture, but hardly saw any of her later masterpieces completed. Projects such as the world's largest airport terminal in China, flagship stadium in Qatar, towers, concert halls, grand hotels, and unique urban spaces in the US, Europe and Asia have secured her name an unquestionable place in history. Hadid proudly stated, 'people always ask me why I haven't built earlier. I really believe that a project, irrespective of whether it is built or not, has as much importance. I think it has been my ambition and struggle for the past 20 years to achieve the theoretical project.'[14]

Creativity is important when interpreting dreams, and creativity carries risk. It is with good reason that dreams and disillusions are often bed fellows; there will always be a healthy dose of scepticism when something is exceptional. Architectural curator Mildred Friedman remembers the design process of Frank Gehry as 'a fascinating ten-year saga involving an idiosyncratic client who challenged the world's most daring architect... a laboratory of pure invention'.[15] While the Lewis Residence conceived during this period remains unbuilt, the fee for its commission brought a different dream to fruition by giving Gehry license to experiment in ways that otherwise would have been out-of-reach financially.[16] Through this process, his practice developed methodologies and made important technological innovations that would later redefine the urban identities of cities such as Bilbao, Chicago, and Los Angeles, and eventually transform the whole construction industry. Aerospace software would enable his design process to be captured and accurately documented for construction in a 3D virtual environment; the result was a demonstration of the radical benefits of new computational tools to realise ambitious buildings. These innovations brand Gehry as a creative genius and his clients, including the Disney family, as visionaries ready to place money and make marks wherever the dreams dictate.

Gehry's technological dream of creating awe through the reality of bleeding-edge construction methods, however, may not be completely suited to Walt Disney's design legacy of manufacturing illusions. Every one of Disney's theme park-cities has built upon a more covert tradition handed-down from historical architecture like Constantine's Aula Palatina, Borromini's Palazzo Spada, or most overtly in the Church of Santa Maria's apse in Milan – the visual trickery of forced perspective. Used extensively by 'imagineers' who assiduously fabricate 'the dream that you wish will come true',[17] this technique employs psychological and optical cues to make objects appear larger or farther away, creating immersive environments of unbelievable structures that would be impossible to build in reality. The Sleeping Beauty and Cinderella castles are exquisite examples of the trick in practice with intricate details, stepped-back structures, and ambiguously placed windows manipulating depth perception and creating the impression of soaring towers twice their actual size. On Disneyland's Main Street USA, the buildings are constructed to feign height by reducing the scale of second stories to 5/8ths normal size and third stories to half scale.[18] Being generally familiar with the heights of buildings and having the full-scale first floor as a visual reference, the human mind assumes that all three stories are the same size, and the upper floors appear smaller by virtue of their great distance from the ground rather than their design. Though it requires fewer physical resources, forced perspective is a fine art that demands incredible dedication to master as minor deviations can break the illusion of the city.

12. J Glancey, 'How to Read Towns & Cities: A crash course in urban architecture', Bloomsbury, London, 2019, p.146

13. E Lissitzky, 'Russia: An architecture for world revolution', E Dluhosch (trans.), Lund Humphries, London, 1970, pp.188–189

14. Z Hadid, 'New Work', Lecture, Architectural Association, London, 19 May 2003 [https://www.youtube.com/watch?v=5Fu3h5vr9I4], retrieved 17 September 2022

15. M Friedman, 'Frank Gehry: The houses', Rizzoli International Publications, New York, 2009, p.269

16. S Pollack, 'Sketches of Frank Gehry', Sony Picture Classics, 2006

17. N Washington & L Harline, 'When You Wish Upon a Star', 1940. Lyrics for the animated film 'Pinocchio' would go on to become the signature theme of the Walt Disney Company.

18. 'The Science of Forced Perspective at Disney Parks', Art of Engineering, 1 November 2020 [https://www.youtube.com/watch?v=yqefjmRVLTM], retrieved 26 August 2023

19. J Daly, 'Norman Foster: One's always chasing the end of the rainbow', Financial Times, 5 October 2021

20. N Foster, 'A tribute to Steve Jobs, by Lord Norman Foster', Archdaily, 6 October 2011 [https://www.archdaily.com/174212/a-tribute-to-steve-jobs-by-lord-norman-foster], retrieved 1 August 2022

21. 'Manchester IRA Bomb: Terror blast remembered 20 years on', BBC News, 15 June 2016 [https://www.bbc.com/news/uk-england-manchester-36474535], retrieved 1 August 2022

22 + 25. K Baxter, 'How Two Hollywood Stars Plan to Save a Team, and a Town, "Desperate for a Lifeline"', Los Angeles Times, 23 August 2022 [https://www.latimes.com/entertainment-arts/tv/story/2022-08-23/welcome-to-wrexham-ryan-reynolds-rob-mcelhenney-soccer-football], retrieved 30 August 2023

Disney's whimsical urban ideology still holds sway over the hearts and minds of many. The 1950s and 1960s 'world of tomorrow' generation it helped shape has now embarked on their pursuit of a technological and thoroughly capitalist dream. Like industrious company towns and university campuses before them, organisations such as Google, Apple and Facebook have become the latest client-visionaries able to afford commissions for state-of-the-art buildings, or even small cities in their ideological image. The impact of their investments divides opinions both popular and political, as the original identities of the locations they infiltrate are overrun by the economic and social influence of the techno-futurist dream. In 2009, Apple founder Steve Jobs hired Norman Foster to design the ultimate Californian corporate campus. The resulting project, a single 'city' shaped into a vast ring enclosing landscaped leisure gardens, opened in 2017 at the cost of approximately 5 billion US dollars. 'One's always chasing the end of the rainbow'[19] says the architect, who recalls that his demanding client 'was the ultimate perfectionist' and 'one of the truly great designers'.[20] In his youth, Foster's own dream of cities was fed by the great Victorian city of Manchester.

Since hollowed-out by the industrial revolution, central Manchester seized the devastation created by the 1996 IRA bombing as an opportunity to undergo urban revitalisation. The explosion was the biggest to occur on the UK mainland soil since World War II, and it decimated the old city centre; but remarkably 'the blast is now credited by some as kick-starting the city's regeneration'.[21] In its aftermath, hundreds of millions in private and public funding were invested in rebuilding efforts that attracted upmarket retailers to the renovated Arndale Centre, invigorating nearby entertainment venues and museums now connected by a new tram route. Surrounding neighbourhoods have also received significant investments and increases in population. In the past decades, the city has transformed into a cosmopolitan hub creating enough demand to spur the construction of a large tower block cluster nicknamed 'Manc-hattan'. Planned for future growth, its downtown is becoming the most radical dream for urban transformation of any UK city in recent memory.

Other struggling manufacturing towns have gone beyond the familiar dreams of designers to embrace the glamour of showbusiness. Purchased by pop-culture stars Ryan Reynolds and Rob McElhenney, Wrexham Football Club in Wales is bringing new life to a downtrodden region through Premier League aspirations, a docuseries on Disney+ and a newfound belief in the more polished exports of the entertainment industry. The former mining capital founded its historied club at the height of the Industrial Revolution 'and the fortunes of team and town have risen and fallen together ever since',[22] with recent years characterized by steep decline. By contrast, the series' debut episode appropriately titled 'Dream' sets the stage for a happy ending where 'It's Always Sunny in Wrexham', Hollywood saviours conjuring sporting success that extends to the surrounding city. Show and football club have risen to popular acclaim on both sides of the Atlantic, particularly in McElhenney's birthplace and muse, Philadelphia. The home of Rocky Balboa loves a good sporting fairytale,[23] but some question whether the North American takeover is a viable model for widespread urban regeneration.[24] While 'coal and steel built Wrexham, soccer has long sustained it'[25] – and paired with a sunny aesthetic, American dollar-backed optimism, and mass-media stardust, the town is poised to inspire further investments. It has even been suggested the feel-good factor of a successful football club can help reduce crime. Luton Town's rise through the league table has been credited for the community feeling both happier and safer, evidenced by a noticeable drop in reported violent crimes, damage, and anti-social behaviour. Yaqub Hanif, the Bedfordshire borough's mayor, believes that 'football is really the official religion of this country because it brings people together'.[26]

Sometimes ambitious dreams and revolutionary ideas are regrettably left consigned to the archives of unbuilt history, and London has its fair share. An airport runway built over the Thames next to the Houses of Parliament. A monorail with buses off the road and up in the air traversing Regent Street. A magnificent pyramid-shaped memorial instead of Nelson's Column in Trafalgar Square,[27] and, most radically, the straightening of the River Thames. In the late 18th century, there were at least four proposals by architect Willey Reveley to shorten time and simplify navigation of shipping goods up and down the waterway, all of which came to nothing. The grandest among these would form three new islands and as many wet docks by making the new channel take its course from Rotherhithe, through the Isle of Dogs and on to Greenwich.[28] If not for the failings of the risk-averse Parliament and unimaginative society, this audacious plan would have improved the river's flow, reduced water pollution and have radically transformed the city.

Not all dreams lead to iconic architecture or beautiful cities, and there is always a possibility of 'dream fatigue' where failures of imagination can lead to total abandonment of buildings, infrastructure and even whole cities. There is a mystery and eerie romance to a city swallowed-up by a jungle, or a mighty castle once used to defend positions in battle fallen into ruin during peacetime. Famously, the city of Detroit in the US has been in decline for decades due to loss of employment in the automotive industry and rapid suburbanisation. A hollowed-out downtown lacking wealth and political agency resulted in obsolete industrial remains returning to nature either by design or by neglect. Many of the 'Ghost Cities' in China seem to be waiting eternally for the bustling inhabitation of a future to come. Likewise the Renaissance Italian city of Palmanova was planned for 20,000 but has never attracted more than 5,000 inhabitants to this day.[29] Its design was so unpopular that in 1622, criminals were offered pardons to entice them to move to lodgings within the walled confines of the radial settlement. On critical reflection, some dreams are best left defeated and disillusioned as with the state-operated leisure city of Prora in Germany. One of the main holiday destinations in the Kraft durch Freude (KdF) organisation's portfolio in the 1930s, it functioned as architectural propaganda to promote the new societal concept of a 'Volksgemeinschaft' people's community. At its heart, KdF was a utopian idea, and as many as 10 million Germans took annual holidays there at its peak. Adolf Hitler had the German public in mind when conceiving the hubristic project and his vision, albeit dangerously misplaced, was one of hope.[30]

In Thomas Pynchon's novel 'Against the Day' (2006), hopes of finding Shambhala lead characters to Venice in search of the fabled Sfinciuno Itinerary, a map of post-Polo routes into Asia believed by many to contain its secret location.[31] Literally swallowed up by sand, the legendary city of the Tibetan Buddhist tradition is sometimes said to be buried deep beneath the Himalayas and inhabited by an enlightened technological civilisation that has achieved immortality. Indeed, one 'can dig till they're too blistered to dig anymore, and they still won't ever find it, not without the right equipment'[32] – the map and a proper mindset, like a form of architectural prayer, are necessary if seekers ever hope to enter the city's confines. Calvino elaborates that 'when a man rides a long time through wild regions he feels the desire for a city... the dreamed-of city contained him as a young man; he arrives in his old age'.[33] Perhaps this is an inevitable aspect of all cities, if, as he whispers, 'desires are already memories'.[34] They are products of humanity, or sometimes the lack of it, subject to the ebb and flow of the outward ambitions and secret devotions that underpin the stories of its citizens' lives. Cities, in the words of the great storyteller, can be better understood if we trace the dreams and disillusions that form their ideological foundations.

23. R Harries, 'How Hope Came Back to the People of a City Dying on Its Knees', WalesOnline, 25 February 2023 [https://www.walesonline.co.uk/news/wales-news/welcome-wrexham-how-football-club-26312558], retrieved 30 August 2023

24. A McDonald, 'Ryan Reynolds Has Transformed Wrexham. Who Will Save Britain's Other Struggling Towns?', Politico (blog), 30 August 2023 [https://www.politico.eu/article/britain-struggle-football-club-ryan-reynolds-save-wrexham], retrieved 30 August 2023

26. L Cawley, 'Luton Town: Did a football club's success help reduce crime?', BBC News, 30 September 2023 [https://www.bbc.co.uk/news/uk-england-beds-bucks-herts-66727829#], retrieved 2 October 2023

27. 'In Pictures: The London that could have been', Barratt London, 2 November 2018 [https://www.barratthomes.co.uk/new-homes/london/advice-and-inspiration/interactive/in-pictures-the-london-that-could-have-been], retrieved 18 July 2022

28. A Forrow, 'The Thames and Its Docks: A lecture', Spottiswoode & Co., London, 1877, p.42

29. H de la Croix, 'Military Considerations in City Planning: Fortifications', George Braziller Inc., New York, 1972, p.10

30. C Weller, 'Hitler's 3-mile-long Abandoned Nazi Resort is Transforming into a Luxury Getaway', Business Insider, 10 July 2017 [https://www.businessinsider.com/adolf-hitler-nazi-resort-prora-2017-7?r=US&IR=T], retrieved 3 October 2022

31 + 32. T Pynchon, 'Against the Day', Penguin Press, New York, 2006, p.273 & p.478

33 + 34. I Calvino, 'Invisible Cities', W Weaver (trans.), Secker & Warburg Ltd, London,1974, p.8

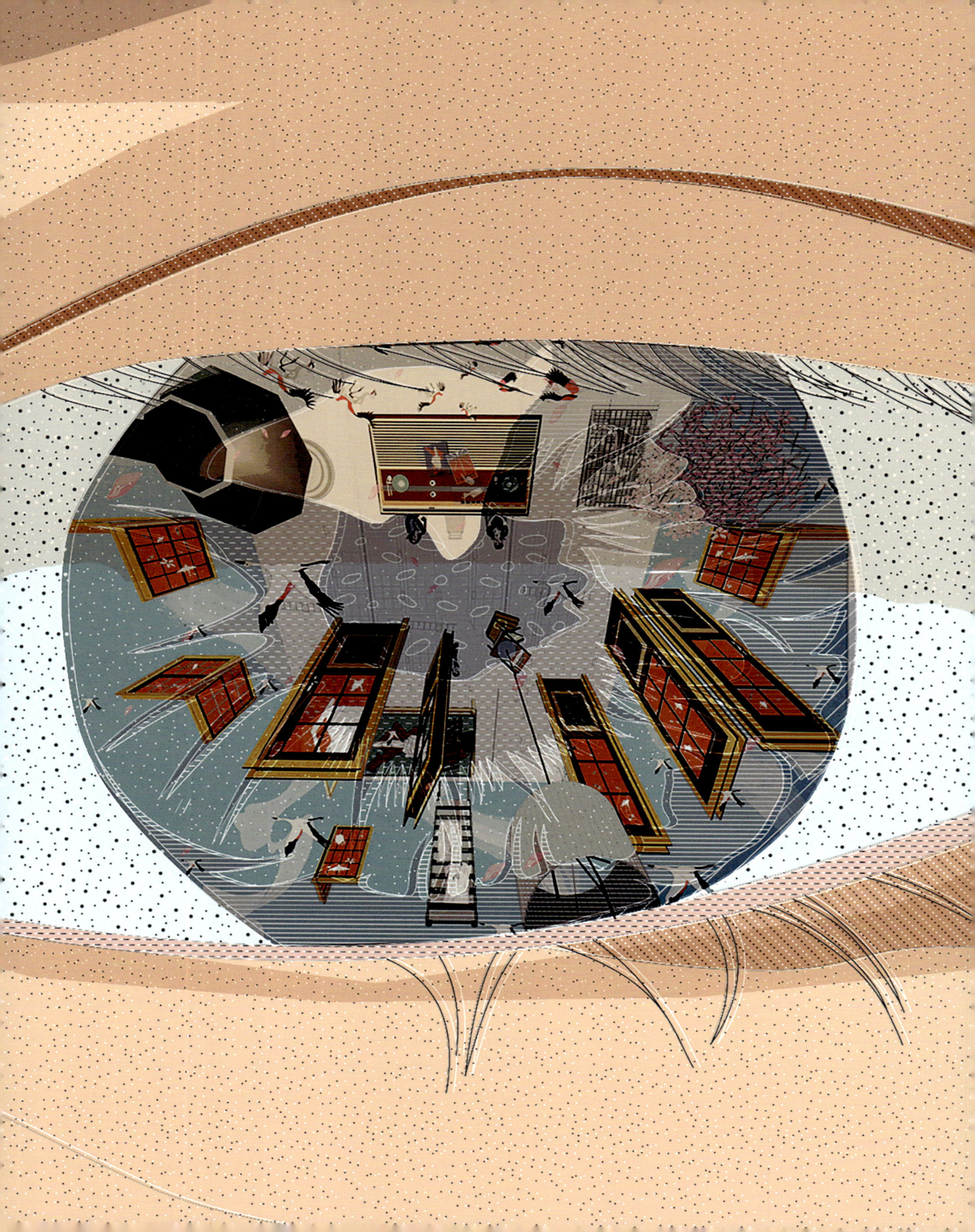

chapter one

Myth + Belief

'The value of a built environment, therefore, is a conglomerate of its actual physical existence and the historical memories and myths people attach to it, bring to it, and project on it... not simply a set of forms or of rules dealing directly with buildings.'

– Oleg Grabar, 'Why History: The meanings and uses of tradition', 1993

Although myths are usually consigned to the realm of literature and storytelling, a closer investigation of urban form, structures, and buildings can reveal a wealth of mythological symbolism suffused into many societies' space-making practices. Furthermore, the architecture represented in mythological narratives can be especially telling, distilling the most important values of a given culture through written descriptions of spaces real or imagined. There is immense authority in the words myth and belief. The latter allows individuals or collectives to fill-in, alter or obscure areas of knowledge, and often rejects uncertainty. Across the span of human civilisation, powerful political figures have been found re-writing history, imposing their own gods, and persecuting those who question the truth.

facing page: 'Your footsteps follow not what is outside the eyes, but what is within, buried, erased... Millions of eyes look up at windows, bridges, capers, and they might be scanning a blank page.' – I Calvino, 'Invisible Cities', 1974

It is certainly true that belief builds, sometimes at such great expense that it significantly weakens an entire civilisation. The inhabitants of Easter Island felled vast stretches of their limited forest to build almost 900 human figures with oversized heads to line their Pacific shores. Now famous for being a mysterious wonder of the world, the colossal stone 'Moai' were initially carved to represent deified ancestors. The ritual and religious devotion to the Pascuense mythology which called for their production along with other human-made and environmental factors effectively caused the extinction of the island's human population.[1] As one of the remotest inhabited areas in the world, this corner of the Polynesian Triangle was a unique anthropological petri-dish, a cogent demonstration of the ways in which such practices can shape the physical environment and even effect a society's chances of survival.

Enoch, the earliest mentioned human city in the Biblical corpus was built by the murderous firstborn of Adam and Eve (Genesis 4:17). 'Cain had relations with his wife and she conceived, and gave birth to Enoch; and he built a city, and called the name of the city Enoch, after the name of his son.' Religious scholars have commented on the fact that Cain being both the originator of city-building and the first artificer of violence provided an omen for the afflictions of urban dwelling.[2] Such speculations may be confirmed in a verse from the gospels of the New Testament (Matthew 10:15) where Christ deems the city a being of wickedness to be condemned on the day of judgement. The creation of the first city also represents 'man's fall from grace and the subsequent attempt to create a new order'.[3] As the theologian Jacques Ellul once noted 'Cain has built a city. For God's Eden he substitutes his own.'[4]

1. J Schalansky, 'Atlas of Remote Islands', Particular Books, London, 2010, p.100

2. J Byron, 'Cain and Abel in Text and Tradition: Jewish and Christian interpretations of the first sibling rivalry', Koninklijke Brill, Leiden, 2011, p.124

3. J Kotkin, 'The City: A global history', Modern Library, New York, 2005, p.12

4. J Ellul, 'The Meaning of the City', D Pardee (trans.), William B. Eerdmans, Grand Rapids, Mich.,1970, p.5

Taking inspiration from the Odyssey of Homer, a myth which parallels 'an old Indian tale in which the hero sets off to find the city of gold',[5] 'Ulysses' (1922) by James Joyce is the minute-by-minute account of 16 June 1904 in the city of Dublin. By transposing the earlier epic poem, which spans 10 years and journeys to strange, far-away lands – including the underworld – into the confines of ordinary encounters and meanderings about a handful of blocks on either side of Dublin Bay, Joyce reveals the intricate relationship between space and narrative that unfolds each day right under one's nose. With proper attention directed to the rhythmic activities of waking, eating breakfast, attending church, going to work, and so on, the domestic mundanities of everyday architecture transcend their unremarkable state to enter the greatest tragic and comedic realms of mythological storytelling.

Glamourous Paris is often mythologised as the city of love; but the first detective story to be published, Edgar Allan Poe's 'The Murders in the Rue Morgue' (1841), reveals its darker side. Following the mutations of the industrial revolution, Paris is framed in terms of the anonymity of urban life rather than the attractive backdrop for passion, all the while compared with the cautionary tale of the Tower of Babel (Genesis 11:1–9) in the subtext. The story 'reveals Paris to be a community of strangers, where – apart from commercial relationships – victims were largely unknown to their neighbours',[6] deeply alone in their urban existence. Nonetheless, subsequent literature fuelled the alter-ego of romanticism alongside a ceaseless barrage of cultural messaging, from projections in contemporary films to postcards featuring Henri Cartier-Bresson's black-and-white photos. Light plays an important role in this cultural identity, an ethereal maker of quality as much as a technological innovation. Being one of the first cities to illuminate entire streets like the Champs-Elysées, artificial light created a new form of nocturnal urban beauty. The many shimmering bridges reflected in the Seine afforded residents and visitors alike new opportunities for leisure and pleasure outside of standard working hours. In studies of cinema, a medium deeply associated with light and its attendant phenomena, the visual interweaving of betrayal, crime, lust and sensuous portrayals of the iconic city has created an independent belief. Existing only on screen and in the minds of its observers, Paris becomes a fictional amalgam of countless myths and 'love stories mapped onto the cityscape'.[7]

The mythical relationship between light and darkness is a fundamental element of the built environment, inseparable from the subjective experiences which shape its existence. Throughout the early 1900s, the radical introduction of electricity provided a new canvas on which architects and artists alike could project dreams of cities freed from cycles of darkness. Hugh Ferriss was inspired to produce his signature harshly lit renderings of New York high-rises, illuminated by spotlights against a black sky, images that could only be understood in the context of a society which had unlocked the secrets of light's optical behaviour. Edward Hopper used the advent of artificially lit environments as a device for 'highlighting a scene against a dark background, providing the viewer with a sense of sitting in a darkened theatre waiting for the drama to unfold'.[8] Like Ferriss before him, staging images as night scenes allowed Hopper to highlight key features while shrouding peripheral distractions. His quintessentially American style remains famous for its depiction of the changing constitution of cities in the 20th century, and his output might denote the character of Manhattan even better than Ferriss's towering monoliths. The power of the ubiquitous Hopper window scene, from 'Drugstore' (1927) to 'Nighthawks' (1942), 'crystallises superbly that momentary sense of the mystery and intensity of the thousands of lives pressing close to each other, all oblivious to the revelations of undrawn blinds, which spell New York more than the soaring spires of skyscrapers'.[9] The electricity which transformed Manhattan into a sleepless city seeped into other forms of media as well, as in the 1949 musical film 'On the Town', which takes place over the course of a single 24-hour day.[10] Here, any differentiation between waking daylight and nights restricted to dark slumber have been abolished in favour of a non-stop amusement ride glorifying endless urban activity.

Almost a century after illumination enabled such advances, the promises of modern planning practice and the social issues it purported to address were re-assessed in films like 'The Pruitt-Igoe Myth' (2011) by Chad Freidrichs. It considers the legacy of the titular St. Louis housing complex demolished on 15 July 1972 which is seen by many historians as the harbinger of modern architecture's descent. Upon closer inspection, the film reveals the forces which shaped Pruitt-Igoe as a scapegoat for the public imagination, taking the blame for an expansive confederacy of corrupt social structures, incompetent government agencies, and institutional decay. The popular conception of such projects in academic circles is 'that some silly architects had had a fantasy, which turned into the opposite' – but it is equally fanciful of such critics to believe 'that design alone can change things for the worse'.[11] Freidrichs has lamented the fact that when confronting the issues surrounding Pruitt-Igoe, architects 'often discuss it in terms of something that failed because of the style of architecture that it was built in... and so if this fails then the modern movement of architecture failed as a whole'.[12] But in reality 'the effects of architecture alone are rarely as significant as people think... politics, economics, and such things as the presence or absence of prejudice are what really change people's lives'.[13] The questions raised by Friedrichs prompt a reconsideration of the stories we have told ourselves about the past and, perhaps more importantly, how we are constructing the myths of our future built environment.

Circumambulation, Pilgrimage, and the Spatial Myths

In his late-life autobiography 'Memories, Dreams, Reflections' (1963), Carl Jung mused that 'the goal of psychic development is the self. There is no linear evolution; there is only a circumambulation of the self.'[14] This process is embodied in the footpaths of the great Buddhist Stupas of Madhya Pradesh, India, which follow processions of quadrants in a circular plan that, for the founder of analytical psychology, mirrored a metaphysical ascension to the centre of being.[15] Essential to the pilgrimages that have shaped the world's holy cities is the notion of circumambulation, an activity which involves believers in procession around a sacred space. Present in almost all religious architecture and even Freemasonic lodges, this idea was later reprised by Jung who applied it to his theories of psychological development.[16] Another example of this practice exists in Chartres Cathedral in France, whose architecture and religious ceremonies embody the idea of journeying to the promised land through a continual circling. The designers of Chartres further encapsulated the transformative experience of pilgrimage in a microcosm, taking the form of a labyrinth built into the central floor of the nave. Unlike a maze, there is only a single path through the circular stone walkway, which is split into quadrants representing the four corners of the world (NSEW). Upon entering, would-be pilgrims who perhaps lack the means of travelling abroad walk the path which covers the complete surface area of a single quadrant before entering the next, walking everywhere within the circle's territory before reaching their destination. At the centre of the labyrinth and, by extension, the cathedral, is a floral pattern in stone representing the true centre of the New Jerusalem where the saved are sent after the Last Judgement. Its perfect geometry reflects the account of the celestial city in the Book of Revelation, a localised axis mundi which reveals a connection between earth and heaven upon completion of the journey.[17]

According to P.D. Smith, 'sacred sites, like cities, are architectural palimpsests, rewritten by each generation'.[18] Sacred cities have powers that transcend those of everyday shrines, temples, and churches.

5. WR Lethaby, 'Architecture, Mysticism and Myth', Percival & Co., London, 1892, p.69

6 + 18. PD Smith, 'City: A guidebook for the urban age', Bloomsbury, New York, 2012, p.266 & p.130

7. B Mennel, '"Cities and Cinema", Critical Introductions to Urbanism and the City', Routledge, New York, 2008, p.63

8. JL Comey, 'Edward Hopper Hour of Darkness', Antiques & Fine Art, pp.153–157

9. M Morsell, 'Hopper Exhibition Clarifies a Phase of American Art', Art News 32, 4 November 1933, p.12

10. G Kelly, 'On The Town', Metro-Goldwyn-Mayer, 1949

11 + 13. R Moore, 'Pruitt-Igoe: Death of the American urban dream', Architecture, Observer, 26 February 2012

12. C Freidrichs, 'The Death of an Architectural Myth', PBS NewsHour, 5 March 2011 [https://www.pbs.org/video/pbs-newshour-the-death-of-an-architectural-myth], retrieved 13 June 2022

14, 15 + 16. CG Jung, 'Memories, Dreams, Reflections', A Jaffé (ed.) C Winston & R Winston (trans.), Collins, London, 1963, p.196, p.278 & p.197

17. J Glancey, 'How to Read Towns & Cities: A crash course in urban architecture', Bloomsbury, London, 2019, p.113

Their existence moves beyond the urban scale, able to attract visitors not only from surrounding areas but throughout the world through the tradition of pilgrimage. In these concentrated foci, myth and belief are subject to iteration and evolution – how many religions have disappeared to leave most of humanity believing in the current handful?

Located in western Saudi Arabia, Mecca is recognised as the holiest city in Islam. Nearly four million Muslims arrive at the city's enormous Masjid al-Haram Mosque around which large fragments of the surrounding urban fabric have been demolished to accommodate the annual Hajj pilgrimage.[19] According to The Quran (3:97) 'it is the duty of all men towards God to come to the House a pilgrim, if he is able to make his way there'. The birthplace of Mohammed, Mecca had theological significance even before the arrival of the prophet as the site of the Kaaba, 'a sacred shrine in the form of a stone cube that has long been thought of as the gateway between heaven and earth'.[20] Shrouded in a black veil, the Kaaba represents the final destination of the annual pilgrimage. Upon arrival, hajjis (pilgrims) perform a circumambulation, walking counterclockwise while praying and contemplating this 'House of God' for seven rotations. It is believed that the Kaaba was 'built by God for Adam', before being 'destroyed in the Flood and rebuilt by Abraham'.[21]

In Hindu, Jain, and Buddhist theology, the continuously inhabited ancient city of Varanasi in northern India is the preeminent destination among pilgrims. According to Mark Twain, its many temples appeared so timeworn as to be older than tradition itself.[22] Stone-stepped ghats lead directly to the shores of the sacred Ganges River whose waters can cleanse a lifetime of sins. Believing that passing in the holy city allows souls to escape the eternal cycle of samsara defined by life, death and reincarnation, many Hindus are brought far from home to have their remains burned on the riverbanks.[23] Beyond the funerial pyres and scattered ashes of these liberated souls, faithful pilgrims bathe in the waters and meditate on the significance of the holy site as they have done for thousands of years. Varanasi has held a mythological significance since the 5th century BC when Siddhartha Gautama delivered his first sermon as the Buddha close to its centre. Since that time the city's form has been dominated first by structures indebted to the Hindu pantheon, Shiva, Vishnu, Hanuman, Krishna and others, and then by those of Islam as invaders destroyed many earlier temples.[24]

Destination of the foremost Christian pilgrimage, Nazareth is first referenced as the childhood home of Jesus in the Gospels of the New Testament. Throughout the centuries, countless individuals have travelled on routes connecting the many religious sites of the city, each contributing to the urban form by defining paths which best facilitated their journey. Pilgrimages to the Holy Land are a tradition dating as far back as the 4th century when Christianity became the state religion of the Roman Empire and the practice was popularised by Church Fathers including Saint Jerome.[25] Sacred sites where Jesus is believed to have called his disciples and delivered much of his public ministry now connect Nazareth and the surrounding region of Galilee to a tradition that has been shaping cities for millennia.

Jerusalem holds significance in all three of the Abrahamic traditions and encompasses a variety of holy places. Temple Mount, the supposed site of Abraham's promised sacrifice of his first-born son Isaac before God stayed his hand, stands across from the remains of the perpetually destroyed and rebuilt Temple of Solomon. The first structure in Jerusalem according to the Hebrew Bible, the Temple once housed the itinerant Ark of the Covenant within the inner sanctuary of its tabernacle, a space known as the Holy of Holies. Since its disappearance, the Ark is believed either to be destroyed or reside in several speculative locations from Ethiopia to regions of Southern Africa. The Wailing Wall, part of the Temple's remains, is Judaism's most sacred site, while the Qubbat al-Sakhra (Dome of the Rock) on Temple Mount, like Mecca, was built with an ambulatory for pilgrims to circle the site and 'marks the spot where Muslims believe Muhammad ascended into heaven'.[26] As in Nazareth, Christian pilgrims to Jerusalem also follow in the footsteps of Christ, visiting key buildings which feature in accounts of his life from the Palace of Herod, the site of his trial by Pontius Pilate, to the Golden Gate through which he entered the city on a donkey. The Church of the Holy Sepulchre built under the reign of Constantine the Great stands on the site of the rock tomb where Christ was buried and resurrected. In the Christian tradition, this became the axis mundi, the absolute centre of the world, and thus marked the quintessential destination for pilgrimage. However, as the city would later come under control of Muslim leaders, much of the Christian population in Europe contrived new sites of devotion to journey to.

Chief among these was Santiago de Compostela, the destination of the Camino de Santiago pilgrimage whose spires were 'clearly visible above the surrounding buildings, beckoning pilgrims as they approached from many miles away'.[27] This cathedral is thought to be the burial site of one of the 12 Biblical apostles of Christ, Saint James. Pilgrim badges in the shape of scallop shells have been discovered throughout Europe demonstrating the pervasive capacity of this belief to spur its adherents on a sacred journey that persists to this day.[28] Intermingling with the surrounding secular life, the signposts and shrines which demarcate the path to Compostela serve as a surreptitious spatial reminder of the otherworldly on untold thousands of Spanish roads. Benedict XVI said of his own journey to the site that 'pilgrimage really means to step out of ourselves in order to encounter God where he has revealed himself... Christians go on pilgrimage to the Holy Land, to the places associated with the Lord's passion, death, and resurrection. They go to Rome, the city of the martyrdom of Peter and Paul, and also to Compostela, which, associated with the memory of Saint James, has welcomed pilgrims from throughout the world.'[29]

Collectivism

As Joel Kotkin identifies in his text 'The City: A global history' (2005), 'architects of the earliest imperial city were careful to build their legitimacy on the foundations and traditions of the earlier sacred places. Although the new rulers were Semites and not Sumerians, they maintained the old language for religious purposes, poetry, and mythological storytelling. In Mesopotamia, the tradition of respect for the old order by new conquerors persisted all the way through the Persian, Alexandrian, and Roman empires.'[30] Collective traditions are the true foundations upon which urban reality rests, with Rome, history's best-known metropolis, being a case in point. In early accounts, Rome was portrayed as a place of earthly sin and wickedness on which God would cast his scorn. However, by the 16th century, the 'Urbs Aeterna' (Eternal City)[31] had so developed its reputation as a site of pilgrimage that Pope Sixtus V led the reconfiguration of its street plan to accommodate more direct paths of travel between different holy sites. Following in the example of the emperor Charlemagne who sought to realise the Holy City described in St. Augustine's 'The City of God' (426 AD) through religious architecture, Pope Sixtus V set about the creation of the first urban environment to integrate sacred and state concerns into the life of its citizens. Rome was reimagined in the image of a shrine, where all the churches and basilicas which required visitation could be accessed within the span of a single day.[32] To accomplish such a feat, Sixtus employed methods like the 'widening of the streets which took place in the Hellenistic cities of the third century',[33] though the Greeks' ambitious urban changes were implemented to address military needs rather than Christian salvation.

19, 21, 23, 26 + 32. PD Smith, 'City: A guidebook for the urban age', Bloomsbury, New York, 2012, p.133, p.134, p.132 & p.135

20 + 28. J Glancey, 'How to Read Towns & Cities: A crash course in urban architecture', Bloomsbury, London, 2019, p.114 & p.116

22. M Twain, 'Following the Equator: A journey around the world', Floating Press, Auckland, 1897, p.461

24. M Juergensmeyer and WC Roof, 'Encyclopedia of Global Religion', vol.1, Sage Publications, 2012, p.115

25. A Cain, 'Jerome's Epitaphium Paulae: Hagiography, pilgrimage, and the cult of Saint Paula', Journal of Early Christian Studies vol.18, 1 March 2010, pp.105–139

27. DR McNamara, 'How to Read Churches: A crash course in ecclesiastical architecture', Rizzoli, New York, 2011, p.142

29. Pope Benedict XVI, 'Apostolic Journey to Santiago de Compostela and Barcelona', Cathedral of Santiago de Compostela, 6 November 2010 [https://www.vatican.va/content/benedict-xvi/en/speeches/2010/november/documents/hf_ben-xvi_spe_20101106_cattedrale-compostela.html], retrieved 9 June 2022

30. J Kotkin, 'The City: A global history', Modern Library, New York, 2005, p.41

31. Tibullus, 'The Complete Poems of Tibullus: An en face bilingual edition', University of California Press, Berkeley, 2012, pp.94–95

The great avenues extending from the Piazza del Popolo and carving into the city's heart set a precedent for similar future transformations based on an undeviating martial logic in the growing cores of other Renaissance cities. In Paris, Baron Haussmann's renovated boulevards doubled as a means of slum clearance and an exercise in military control, allowing better sightlines for riflemen and crews of cannon operators in the event of a peasant uprising.[34] It was this profound influence, emulated in the lines and traffic webs of countless modern cities that prompted the historian of architectural modernism Siegfried Gideon to label Sixtus V 'the first of the modern town planners'.[35]

Seat of power in the landlocked Vatican City-state situated on the west bank of the River Tiber in the centre of the Roman metropolis, The Holy See is no longer supported by a world empire but nonetheless remains an international religious power. Its relevance as a sovereign territory is supported by collective belief rather than any rational deduction based on geography or military might. It has been observed that 'the Vatican was the closest thing 12th-century Europe had to Silicon Valley'.[36] The Church created the first economic corporations through the spread of its monasteries, which introduced timekeeping, education, and advanced agricultural and administrative methods, all of which increased its shares in the currency of belief.

Strange then to think that such radical innovations were the product of a regime dominated by a city 'said to be founded by two brothers, Romulus and Remus, abandoned by the Tiber and raised by a she-wolf'.[37] But it is just this 'peculiar civic mythology and sense of divine mission'[38] that has proven the enduring source for Roman greatness. As the second major city of Christian pilgrimage, the effect of Rome is felt even more widely through the ideas, texts, and trends promulgated from it than the urban remnants and architecture which characterise the material city. Elements of Roman architecture were absorbed by many cultures during the reign of its empire and subsequently spread throughout the world in the form of infrastructure regardless of territorial and religious frontiers. Particularly in Western societies, whose cities have seen exponential expansion since the Renaissance, even seemingly secular buildings from banks to city halls take up the language of artistic developments and town planning founded on Roman soil.[39] 'York, London, Trier, Paris, Vienna, and Budapest', all 'owe their birthright to the urban genius born on the banks of the Tiber. Romanisation, in many senses, stood synonymous with the advance of urbanisation.'[40]

While the urban growth emanating from empires can be likened to an organism spreading its influence through a network of branching connections, decay likewise follows a natural model of struggle, death, and rebirth. 'Cities are like trees: once established, they must be destroyed to the roots before they cease to live: otherwise, even when the main stem is cut down, shoots will form about the base, as happened in Jerusalem.'[41] Indeed, transformations founded on long-established beliefs have not always been productive. Launched continuously throughout the 11th to 13th centuries, the Crusades to recapture the holy city of Jerusalem were based on the principle of adherence to God's will. The Christians who led these campaigns could cite the Bible for justification. In their eyes, it advocated the establishment of an undivided Jerusalem in II Chronicles 6:5–6, wherein King Solomon quotes God as saying, 'Since the day that I brought my people out of the land of Egypt, I chose no city in all the tribes of Israel in which to build a house, that my name might be there, and I chose no man as prince over my people Israel; but I have chosen Jerusalem that my name may be there and I have chosen David to be over my people Israel.' For those who joined, fighting, even dying, in the name of their God's word would be a ticket to paradise in heaven.[42] The iconoclastic destruction and looting which ensued was famously violent and contributed to the increasing layers of ruins upon which new structures, embodying new, more collaborative meanings, have been, or a still waiting to be rebuilt.

Closely associated with religious belief and especially the institution of the medieval Church is the academic system of the university. First emerging in Europe 'beginning with Bologna in 1100, Paris in 1150, Cambridge in 1229, and Salamanca in 1243 – though there were informal beginnings elsewhere in the cathedral schools of the 12th century – the university laid down a co-operative organisation of knowledge on an inter-regional basis'.[43] A unique cultural phenomenon elevating the pursuit of truth into an enduring raison d'être through its independence from singular groups of scholars, priests, and texts, the university nonetheless has its roots in the early guilds and craft associations formed under religious guidance. Oxford's 'dreaming spires'[44] reflect the symbolic association between the university's colleges and the ecclesiastical systems of architecture which preceded it. Designed by US President Thomas Jefferson, the University of Virginia and nearby Monticello plantation at Charlottesville were explicitly modelled on the city of Rome and the ideals of Romanitas, the political and cultural practices by which the Romans defined themselves, their city and place in history.[45] Others took inspiration from the earlier example of Plato's academy in Athens. Over time, the function of the university has become increasingly secular as belief in the value of religion has been overtaken by new beliefs in political knowledge and the supposedly value-free pursuit of science.

This change is reflected in the buildings added to campuses following the industrial revolution, a technological movement which the institutional prerogatives of the university helped to galvanise. In particular, the modern campus of MIT has, along with more recently established universities, forgone the religious associations present in Cambridge, Oxford, and older American schools like Harvard. Rather its buildings reflect a new form of faith in the redemptive power of technological advancement, employing all manner of modernist architects, from Alvar Aalto to Frank Gehry, I.M. Pei or Steven Holl, to add their own visions to the futuristic pastiche along the historic Charles River in East Cambridge, MA.

The trend has even been satirised in contemporary works of fiction, as in the maximalist Boston-based novel 'Infinite Jest' (1996) where Eduardo Catalano's existing brutalist Stratton Student Centre, destroyed in the Steven Pinker-led 'MIT Language Riots of 1997', is replaced by a new building on the corner of Ames and Memorial Drive described as 'one enormous cerebral cortex of reinforced concrete and polymer compounds'.[46] In a near-future where the countries of Mexico, Canada, and the US have merged into a continent-spanning superstate dubbed ONAN (Organization of North American Nations), the modern worship of human intellect above all is given physical form in a building which literally functions as an architectural brain. Described as the 'summum opus' design of topology expert A.Y. 'Vector-Field' Rickey, its 'walls are pink and laryngeally fissured' and its 'soft latex-polymer roof is cerebrally domed... everywhere textured, the bulging rooftop, with sulci and bulbous convolutions'.[47]

Future Myths and Evolving Beliefs in Cities

In his sociological critique of human relations ideology and behavioural codes, 'C. Wright Mills could still inventory the hierarchies within hierarchies embedded within the "enormous file" of the post-war office skyscraper, with a "row of clerks and a set of IBM equipment", while recording the extension of corporate power into the psychosocial realm of office "morale", which for him was still "the morale of cheerful robots".'[48] Hierarchies in today's cities have become ever more illusory and closed off, relegating past

33, 34, 41 + 43. L Mumford, 'The City in History: Its origins, its transformations and its prospects', Secker & Warburg Ltd, London, 1961, p.194, p.369, p.245 & p.276

35 + 39. S Giedion, 'Space, Time and Architecture: The growth of a new tradition', Harvard University Press, Cambridge, Mass., 1956, p.100 & p.73

36 + 42. YN Harari, 'Homo Deus: A brief history of tomorrow', Vintage, London, 2017, p.249 & p.136

37, 38 + 40. J Kotkin, 'The City: A global history', Modern Library, New York, 2005, p.61 & p.66

44. M Arnold, 'Poems By Matthew Arnold', Macmillan and Co., 1885, p.153

45. J Glancey, 'How to Read Towns & Cities: A crash course in urban architecture', Bloomsbury, London, 2019, p.27

46, 47 + 49. DF Wallace, 'Infinite Jest', Little, Brown and Company, Boston, Mass., 1996, p.184, p.186 & p.432

48. R Martin, 'The Organizational Complex: Architecture, media, and corporate space', MIT Press, Cambridge, Mass., 2003, p.120

obligations which the new world promises there will be no need for. Mechanically in thrall to 'the without-end pursuit of happiness' while having forgotten 'the old things which made happiness possible', these robots now 'stumble about in the dark, this confusion of permissions'.[49] The religious architectures of temples, cathedrals, mosques, and pyramids which once dominated the landscapes and imaginary dimensions of great cities have since been replaced by towering edifices for a social structure motivated by corporate capital. Unlike the modern skyscraper composed of sleek yet expressionless sheets of glass and steel, the earlier buildings 'suggested that the city was also a sacred place, connected directly to divine forces controlling the world'.[50] As urban theorist Kevin Lynch suggested, 'a striking landscape is the skeleton' in which city dwellers construct their 'socially important myths'.[51] In our own, so much more secularly oriented times, cities seek to recreate or replace the sense of sacredness through evocative structures dedicated to a culture of consumerism, whether in the form of massive stadia or miles of backlit storefronts and shopping arcades. Such sights inspire a sense of civic patriotism or awe, albeit without the comforting suggestion of divine guidance.

In examining the myths that build the modern metropolis, observers are inevitably confronted with the abstractions of high finance. Generically consistent across centres from Dubai in the Middle East, New York and Chicago in America, Tokyo and Shanghai in Asia, the architectural embodiment of these systems is found in the symbolically apt skyscraper. Their anonymous glass facades protect the by-products of quarterly reports, file storage, business records and contracts behind an impenetrable corporate identity. Here, the belief in bureaucratic mechanical process replaces the cooperative exchange of direct, unmediated human contact. The high-rise phenomenon is thoroughly interrogated in the 'Typical Plan' article of 'S,M,L,XL' (1995) where Rem Koolhaas reflects on the social and even anthropological ramifications of the seemingly endless multiplication of monotonous rectangular floor slabs. The repressive typical office block is here 'a place of worship' in distinct contrast to the religious buildings mentioned previously, 'a 20th century church without doctrine'.[52] In service to 'the first total abstract program', the towering financial centres of the world have created 'new territories for the smooth unfolding of new processes, in this case, ideal accommodation for business'.[53] Making no demands and thereby generating spaces devoid of form or identifiable values, Koolhaas speculates whether 'the plan without qualities created men without qualities', whether the synonymous programme of the modern office served as 'the incubator of the man in the gray flannel suit'.[54]

In a different configuration, the company towns which emerged in the 20th century represent a similar outgrowth of corporate belief and design ideology on the scale of an entire community as opposed to a single building. While financial centres are relegated to the downtown cores of larger metro areas, abandoned each evening for suburbs or more hospitable neighbourhoods, company towns were designed to encompass every aspect of their inhabitants' lives. From housing to retail, and of course the offices and workspaces themselves, every structure in places like Port Sunlight, Pullman, Fordlandia, Boulder City, Bournville, and Wolfsburg were created under the auspices of a single company. Ranging from bleak places of abuse to picturesque communities, thousands of company towns exist in the US alone. In the earliest manufacturing centres and the workers' housing which serviced them, poet William Blake saw only the soulless 'cogs tyrannic, moving by compulsion each other: not as those in Eden'.[55] Other, less perceptive souls envisioned these settlements of the industrial age as the harbinger of a glorious and prosperous future. Travelling in Leeds in 1835, Sir George Head was enamoured with the mechanised efficiency of the cloth factories, describing them as 'temples dedicated by man, grateful for the stupendous power that moved within, to Him who built the universe'.[56] For the industrialist, 'the 'hero of the age' was not the knight or aristocrat, but the 'hard-working mechanic, blackened by smoke, yet radiant in the light of intelligence'.[57]

The famous magnate responsible for the innovations of the assembly line, Henry Ford was one of the first to implement the company town model by importing American housing systems to the Brazilian Amazon starting in 1928. There, plantations established to supply the Ford Motor Company with rubber housed indigenous workers in a replica Detroit suburb hubristically titled 'Fordlandia'.[58] Though it offered free board, food, and healthcare, the top-down imposition of even the most utopian ideals under the command of one company proved to be antagonistic to the paradoxical realities of human existence. Bans on alcohol, sex, and all manner of unruly activities rendered the institution virtually unliveable and it was eventually abandoned. Similar failures continued to occur even when implementing such models in the familiar American context as in the cases of Pullman, Illinois, and numerous coal towns throughout the state of Virginia. The subtle paternalism which such settlements implemented in attempts to control workers was a particularly insidious form of social engineering. From the perspective of 19th-century businessmen, the company town offered a unique opportunity to advance society whilst furthering their own interests. However, the stifling emphasis on moral responsibility and religious obligation these environments foisted on their residents were inhumane and often times intolerable. Unfortunately, their legacy persists to this day, especially in more impoverished geographies such as Appalachia. 'Company Town' (2016) is a documentary film illustrating the plight of Crossett, Arkansas. Economically dependent on a Georgia-Pacific paper plant owned by the Koch Brothers, the community suffers horrific cancer rates attributed to the rampant pollution which the company has no incentives to prevent.[59]

Other models have paid closer attention to the intricacies of community well-being and urban planning, taking lessons from the Garden City model of Ebeneezer Howard as in Letchworth, the first town to be built explicitly following its guidelines. In contrast to company towns motivated by a scientific efficiency in the extraction of labour from its inhabitants, Garden Cities advocated 'a healthy, natural, and economic combination of town and country life, and this on land owned by the municipality'.[60] However, the diverse, community-led goals of these earliest attempts would be reformed with the paternalist leanings of the company town and its associated conflicts of interest.

Lever's Port Sunlight and Cadbury's Bournville combined certain aspects of the English Garden City model with greater employer control than had been initially intended by Howard and other reformers. Alfred Krupp's Margarethenhöhe outside Essen in Germany followed a similar approach. 'Like Howard's ideal Garden City, all three of these company towns incorporated significant green space and planned housing in a somewhat uniform but traditional style. A significant difference, though, was that occupancy of a home in Bournville, Port Sunlight, or Margarethenhohe was tied to employment at the respective factory and planning and ownership remained firmly the prerogatives of the industrialist in question.'[61] These towns, which were unfortunately held up as examples of Howard's ideas in practice, restricted workers' abilities to exercise independent political opinions by linking employment and tenancy to a single entity. Through such associations, the Garden City which originally emphasised freedom from any manner of ideological influence or moral education lost its former capacity as an agent of social reform.

A notable alternative to the planned company town exists in the example of Zlín, Czech Republic, where the Bata shoe company organically grew to dominate the industry of a pre-existing village at the turn of

50 + 57. J Kotkin, 'The City: A global history', Modern Library, New York, 2005, p.31 & p.123

51. K Lynch, 'The Image of the City', MIT Press, Cambridge, Mass., 1960, p.4

52, 53 + 54. R Koolhaas & B Mau, 'Small, Medium, Large, Extra-Large: Office for Metropolitan Architecture', J Sigler (ed.), Monacelli Press, New York, 1995, p.340, p.337 & p.346

55. W Blake, 'The Complete Poetry and Prose of William Blake' (revised ed.), University of California Press, Berkeley, 1982, p.329

56. A Lees, 'Cities Perceived: Urban society in European and American thought, 1820–1940', Columbia University Press, New York, 1985, pp.40–41

58 + 61. MJ Borges & SL Becerra Torres, 'Company Towns: Labor, space, and power relations across time and continents', Palgrave Macmillan, London, 2012, p.13 & p.46

59. N Kottke-Masocco & E Sardarian, 'Company Town', Penn Road Productions, 2016 [https://www.companytownfilm.com], retrieved 14 June 2022

60. E Howard, 'Garden Cities of To-Morrow', Dodo Press, 2009, p.2

the 19th century.[62] As it continued to expand its control over economic life, the company would go on to pioneer employee welfare and early urbanisation programs for social advancement including the construction of hospitals, schools, and thousands of flats. Following in the footsteps of his celebrated father, Tomáš J. Batá sought to transfer operations from Zlín to Canada as conditions in Europe became increasingly unfavourable due to German occupation in World War II. The resultant community of Batawa, Ontario, was, in contrast to Zlín, a true factory town, picked out of the vast wilderness based on land prices and proximity to water, rail, and road. Established in 1939, the village was almost entirely owned by the Bata company which controlled all aspects of life from accommodations to grocery stores and recreation halls. With many of the residents being immigrants from Bata's original homeland of Czechoslovakia, the community remained remarkably cohesive, and the factory continued to function until the year 2000 when reduced tariffs on Canadian shoe imports finally undermined its business viability.[63] As with any corporation that was to succeed in the globalising world, Bata had already expanded its brand to mirrored towns in places as disparate as Brazil (Batayporã), Pakistan (Batapur), India (Bataganj) and even Essex, UK (Bata-ville), continuing its legacy as one of the earliest and best-enduring multinational manufacturers. This trend finds sardonic expression in the lyrics of Tomáš J. Batá's personal theme song, 'It's a Small World', borrowed for use as his company's anthem from fellow corporate giant Disney.[64]

In a strange blending of company town and petro-capitalist utopia, the industrial steel belts of Germany have played host to some of the 20th-century's most successful car companies from Mercedes-Benz in Stuttgart to BMW and Porsche in Munich and Leipzig. Beginning under the Nazi state in Germany, Wolfsburg was initially formed in 1938 as the site for a purpose-built Volkswagen factory to assist in the war effort. Originally called 'Stadt des KdF Wagens' to commemorate the automaker, it was quickly transformed into a model village to house a growing workforce, becoming colloquially known as Wolfsburg which is now one of the largest cities in the state of Lower Saxony.[65] The city, also known for having one of the highest GDPs per capita in Germany, is helped by the fact that Volkswagen's massive headquarters and the world's largest car plant provide almost as many jobs as there are residents. The number is far higher than the actual working population, with the excess positions being filled by commuters whose lifestyles also serve to drive profits.[66] Regardless of whether Wolfsburg retains the title of richest city, its unusually high amounts of available capital and its blank slate potential as one of the few planned cities still being built in Europe's post-war period have made it a hotbed for architectural experimentation. Evidencing the productive efficiencies of the company town model, Alvar Aalto completed two churches as well as a cultural centre all within a few years of one another from 1962 to 1968.[67] Later, Zaha Hadid would create the Phaeno, a science centre whose 'underground urbanism of adjacent programs'[68] links the visitor's entry to the automotive plant with the city's train station, residential, and commercial districts. Integrating assembly lines into white-collar workspaces and complexes of exhibition and events venues, these buildings are incredibly popular tourist destinations where over three million annual visitors vie for the opportunity to be immersed in BMW's corporate culture.[69]

Multiple Beliefs: Nationalism, globalism, and pluralism

'Then, as this morning on the dock, again I saw, as if for the first time in my life, the impeccably straight streets, the glistening glass of the pavement, the divine parallelepipeds of the transparent dwellings, the square harmony of the grayish blue rows of Numbers. And it seemed to me that not past generations, but I myself, had won a victory over the old god and the old life.'[70] In the homogenised environment of this imaginary future in 'We' (1924), the ideals of science and rationality drive unanimity of form, materiality, urban organisation, and identity. But visions of unity are not a niche concept confined to the revolutionary rumblings of the 20th century. Especially in the current era, historians, intellectuals and powerful institutions more generally prize the virtues of tolerance and plurality. As such, the historical figure of Akbar the Great (1542–1605) is often lauded as a figure of symbolic unification, whose leadership spurred a flourishing of the arts which bonded a fragile collection of diverse and sprawling kingdoms in Northern India under the Mughal Empire.

During his conquest 'he championed a melding of Hinduism and Islam known as the din-i-ilahi' or the divine faith, and from this 'ethos of pluralism and tolerance that defined Akbar's age' arose 'the values of the modern republic of India'.[71] His material legacy remains in the Indian city of Fatehpur Sikri, former capital of the empire during his reign and built according to astronomical coordinates. Here, Akbar oversaw the construction of his crowning achievement, the Ibadat Khana (House of Worship). Within, a central dome covered an undivided main chamber which hosted assemblies of at least 150 religious authorities[72] from varying backgrounds including Hinduism, Buddhism, Islam, Zoroastrianism, Christianity and even Atheism for Akbar to indulge his theological curiosity. This commitment was so great as to require 'an edifice of no small size and pretensions, which needed the services of "skillful architects" to plan and of "clever builders" to erect'.[73] While the inter-faith dialogues which proceeded under his encouragement secured Akbar's modern-day legacy as a figurehead of peace and tolerance, his influence was short-lived. The rule of his great-grandson Aurangzeb, who re-instantiated a Muslim state, followed by the advent of British colonialism largely erased the cosmopolitan bohemia which historians of this period in India's past have extolled.

Like Akbar's pluralism which has been adapted by contemporary leaders in defining successful states, the concept of pilgrimage, despite its association with tradition, has proven flexible and updated itself in the modern era. The 'WASP Hajj' to Talladega Superspeedway, Alabama, is a pilgrimage held under the auspices of capitalism where average American consumers can express their commitment to an auto-centric oil-based economy. It is this new dedication that has shaped much of the urban development in New World cities around the harsh lines of the multi-lane highway. This trend was described by historian Lewis Mumford as the self-defeating 'religion of the motor car, which is ready to sacrifice the utilities and delights of city life for the development of space-eating facilities for getting in and out of town – though the very multiplication of such facilities reduces the effective speed of the traffic it seeks to promote'.[74] The street-widening tendency of militaristic societies combined with the democratisation of the individualistic motor car technology has, especially in North American cities, created disorder, ruin, and urban blight through widespread belief in the engineering marvels of the street grid and highway system. As Jane Jacobs observed as early as the 1960s, American downtowns are in the process of 'being witlessly murdered' by the policies and deliberate misapprehensions of designers severing potential connections with arterial highways and parking lots.[75] Unfortunately, this process has been emulated everywhere that sufficient resources existed to support car-faring populations and dreams of an ideal city, with the suburban community of Milton Keynes being one example from Britain.

This third-generation new town was established by a desperate 1960s UK government attempting to fix the implacable issues of housing. Wanting to address the lack of nature which characterised earlier planned communities, Milton Keynes' young architect-planner Derek Walker gave over 20 percent of its space to parkland on which millions of trees were planted. While the sentiment behind this edict was

62. MJ Borges & SL Becerra Torres, 'Company Towns: Labor, space, and power relations across time and continents', Palgrave Macmillan, London, 2012, p.7

63. J Gray, 'Way of Life Disappears with Factory in Batawa', Globe and Mail, 23 May 2000

64. D Gerrard, 'Enterprise: One Man's Multinational (Bata Shoe Company)', WGBH Educational Foundation, 1981 [https://www.youtube.com/watch?v=aT1Va4NgHuU], retrieved 12 July 2022

65 + 69. J Glancey, 'How to Read Towns & Cities: A crash course in urban architecture', Bloomsbury, London, 2019, p.148 & p.149

66. Editorial, 'Germany's Motown Is Country's Richest City', The Local, 29 July 2013 [https://www.thelocal.de/20130729/51105], retrieved 12 July 2022

67. K Fleig, E Aalto & A Alvar, 'Alvar Aalto – Das Gesamtwerk / L'oeuvre Complète / The Complete Work', Birkhauser, Basel/Berlin/Boston, 1990, p.17

68. Z Hadid, 'The Design of the Phaeno Centre, Wolfsburg', Lecture, Architecture Association, London, 28 February 2006 [https://www.youtube.com/watch?v=K9lKtpQio0U], retrieved 12 July 2022

70. Y Zamyatin, 'We', Mirra Ginsburg (trans.), Viking Press, New York, 1972, pp.4–5

71. I Tharoor, 'Top 25 Political Icons', Time Magazine, 4 February 2011 [http://content.time.com/time/specials/packages/article.html], retrieved 12 July 2022

72 + 73. VA Smith, 'Akbar's "House of Worship", or 'Ibadat-Khana', Journal of the Royal Asiatic Society of Great Britain and Ireland, 1917, pp.715–722

74. L Mumford, 'The City in History: Its origins, its transformations and its prospects', Secker & Warburg Ltd, London, 1961, p.443

75. J Jacobs, 'The Death and Life of Great American Cities', Random House, New York, 1961, p.184

admirable, the crippling homogeneity and low density of the sprawling development style intended to free inhabitants from the traditional conservatism of English domestic architecture resulted in an anti-human environment. 'Because the car was king in that decade of triumphant technological progress, Milton Keynes was laid out on a free-flowing grid of dual carriageways',[76] vehicles usurping the needs of pedestrians despite the designer's aspiration to address a lack of nature. The town unwittingly reinforced a new, and perhaps more destructive status-quo of total reliance on the automobile and the fossil fuels which powered them. In spite of such drawbacks, the paradoxical success of Milton Keynes lies in its fulfilment of a neoliberal promise which 'delivered to a broad swath of professionals, skilled workers, and even manual laborers a preferred "Englishness" of tidy homes and greenery that was once the exclusive province of the upper class'.[77]

Like many of the great nation-building projects of the 20th century, Brasília began with the dreams of erasing colonial history and re-imagining the identity of an entire country. However, these positive aspirations finally resulted in disillusion with the ability of modernism and its theories of urban planning to produce spatial cohesion, called into question by the city's many failures. Ironically, or perhaps poetically, Brasília was inaugurated on the same date as Rome on 21 April 1960.[78] Fully embracing the past century's belief in the redemptive abilities of technology, specifically the automobile, the city's designers shaped a layout completely reliant on the motorway. While many of its structures independently represent the positive aspects of modernism in their architectural refinement, the infrastructure linking these disparate elements demonstrated the inadequacy of beautiful buildings detached from successful planning. Informed by the deadening expressway belting of Robert Moses's Manhattan,[79] the multi-lane highways devoid of traffic lights or crosswalks in these connective areas disregard pedestrian life and the dynamic messiness essential to functioning urban centres.

From above, Oscar Niemeyer's masterplan appears as a curving line of similar blocks bending away from the artificial Lago Paranoa and bisected by a central promenade. This main axis hosts the commercial zone along with the dispersed diplomatic, political, and cultural icons the city is so well known for, while the outskirts are dotted with country clubs, embassies, and high-end restaurants.[80] This urban assemblage can only be appreciated from miles overhead in reality. Such perspectives are reserved for international visitors, or Brasília's elite diplomats and politicians as they fly to their homes in more desirable surrounding areas, leaving city-dwellers in confusion on the streets below. Despite its elaborate zoning, Brasília is also incapable of providing for the population growth it experiences as a diplomatic hub with a government-supported economy. In years past, favelas have continually cropped up in greenbelts of land intended for agriculture. Authorities allowed such misallocations to continue not out of benevolence but of necessity as 'from the favelas came the menial workers – cleaners, porters and security guards – without whom the city could not function'.[81] The ideological ambivalence of the modernist style it so assiduously employed may in fact be the project's politically defining feature, a fact often raised by proponents of classicism such as architect Leon Krier who 'correctly objects that there is no clear congruence between architectural form and ideological meaning. Washington, DC, he points out, has modern facades that would have been welcomed in Hitler's Berlin. Classicism, he thinks, has been unjustly tainted by association with fascism. At the other end of the spectrum, sleek modernist design was deployed under Mussolini and a forward-looking capital like Brasília, built to signify democratic openness, perfectly served Brazil's military regime.'[82]

It is perplexingly common for well-intended schemes aimed at improving the human condition to go tragically awry – indeed 'the history of Third World development is littered with the debris of huge agricultural schemes and new cities that have failed their residents'.[83] Other contentious national-capital planning projects conceived under the aegis of globalisation like New Delhi, Islamabad and Ankara, have prompted questions concerning the applicability of singular, centralised headquarters or urban systems to meet the demands of governance. Based on the explicit deficiencies of early organisations aimed at creating order like the League of Nations and the perceived failures of the post-war United Nations' effort, international and state interests have tended to disperse their spatial products in increasingly convoluted webs. Such trends have been analysed by Reinhold Martin on the architectural scale in 'The Organizational Complex' (2003), as well as by theorists Antonio Negri and Michael Hardt on the political, economic, and sociological levels in their work 'Empire' (2000). While the former emphasises the cybernetic, mechanical, and computerised architectural elements that have increasingly allowed for the exertion of power through even the most innocuous spaces,[84] the latter points to a larger apparatus wherein political influence encompasses and functions concomitantly with spaces of governance through information networks. Unlike previous models of political power where the architecture of parliaments and capitals served to display the performances of democratically elected leaders, in this new conception of Empire such functions are overtaken by the larger, diffuse webs of supranational and corporate institutions which increasingly permeate modern life through privatisation, surveillance, and mass-media. Contrary to narratives of increasing freedom, enlightened leaders, and breaking-off of archaic forms of political organisation, current 'elaborations of an international order could at most be recognised as a process of transition toward the new imperial power'.[85]

Following the threads of myth and belief as powerful agents in a city's evolution, it becomes increasingly apparent that architecture never exists apart from a philosophy or value system, whether subconscious or stated outright. No matter how opaque certain manifestations of a given programme, building style, or regime may seem, there is always some driving desire or aim beneath the surface, operating from the shadowy depths. While the systems for constructing cities have progressed from hierarchical to dispersed, rigid to fluid, and have become ever more coded and confused, one can always examine the irrational forces at play through the tangible results of built projects. Sol LeWitt once wrote 'irrational thoughts must be followed absolutely and logically'.[86] Heeding such advice leads one to the opposite of idealism, into the inherently contradictory nature of human creativity itself.

Human beings are ritualistic creatures living within the timeless structures provided by myth and belief. As such, we are partial to fertile quantities of irrationality, inefficiency, and imagination. From the religious capitals of bygone eras to the towering proliferations of consumer capital and their protracted existences in Hollywood productions – even in the minds of fiction writers – the objectives underlying the city are constantly propelled to new targets by the examination of watchful onlookers. A city founded on the disillusions of utopia will inevitably become saturated in contradictions and inconsistencies, but the dreams intrinsic to our current trajectory have found presageful summary in an interview between Rem Koolhaas and Wired magazine in 1996. 'The generic city, the general urban condition, is happening everywhere, and just the fact that it occurs in such enormous quantities must mean that it's habitable. Architecture can't do anything that the culture doesn't. We all complain that we are confronted by urban environments that are completely similar. We say we want to create beauty, identity, quality, singularity. And yet, maybe in truth these cities that we have are desired. Maybe their very characterlessness provides the best context for living.'[87]

76 + 80. J Glancey, 'How to Read Towns & Cities: A crash course in urban architecture', Bloomsbury, London, 2019, p.222 & pp.158–159

77. J Kotkin, 'The Human City: Urbanism for the rest of us', B2 Books, Chicago, 2016, p.144

78 + 81. PD Smith, 'City: A guidebook for the urban age', Bloomsbury, New York, 2012, p.68 & pp.170–171

79. B Schwarz, 'A Vision in Concrete', The Atlantic, 1 July 2008 [https://www.theatlantic.com/magazine/archive/2008/07/a-vision-in-concrete/306846], retrieved 12 July 2022

82. M Wise, 'Hitler's Words Into Stone: Can architecture itself be fascist?', Wall Street Journal, 12 April 2013 [https://online.wsj.com/article/SB10001424127887323296504578398542977265774.html], retrieved 12 June 2022

83. JC Scott, 'Seeing Like a State: How certain schemes to improve the human condition have failed', Yale University Press, New Haven, 1998, p.3

84. R Martin, 'The Organizational Complex: Architecture, media, and corporate space', MIT Press, Cambridge, Mass., 2003, p.17

85. M Hardt & A Negri, 'Empire', Harvard University Press, Cumberland, 2000, p.40

86. S LeWitt, 'Sentences on Conceptual Art', Art-Language, no.1, May 1969

87. K Heron, 'From Bauhaus to Koolhaas', Wired, vol.04, no.07, 1 July 1996 [https://www.wired.com/1996/07/Koolhaas], retrieved 10 July 2022

CLICK

The Spun Veil of Pyongyang

'Only in gossip can the true heart of this city be found. Gossip always muddles the senses. Starting with inconsequential things, it winds up trying to rewrite history. It leaves in its wake a chain of injustices... what makes gossip romantic is its unbridled imagination.'

– Anyi Wang, 'The Song of Everlasting Sorrow', 2008

'Gossip' is indeterminate, and the word can often be used interchangeably with 'rumour' and 'myth'. Spurious urban histories are carried across 'the silent electrical waves crisscrossing in the air above the city, like formless clouds' enshrouding it, 'intermixing right and wrong'.[1] Wang recognises the 'longtang' alleys of post-World War II Shanghai as lacking morality, places very conducive to the proliferation of gossip, rumours and myths which recruit complicit retailers to generate societies of their own imaginings. A comparable, if more Orwellian culture is 'inminban' in North Korea; Supreme Leader Kim Jong-un's totalitarian surveillance system is extremely adept at manufacturing disinformation and censoring susceptible local opinions. Here, under the watchful eyes of neighbors, 'if you want to keep a secret, you must also hide it from yourself'.[2] Sealed off from the outside world since 1953 and now existing in an internet-free vacuum, the North Korean gossip economy is booming. Each sensationalised rumour of defectors and 'expert' hearsay is worth billions of clicks.[3] Inferences and biases about such places should not exclusively rest on social media. In attempting to understand this context, however, an earnest overlay of half-truths, assumptions and misconceptions about the built environment prompt reflection on our own blind spots, becoming the basis of our longest lasting memories of the city depicted. Making truth out of fiction influences new forms of architecture, imbued with the courage to go against prevailing design opinions while attacking sanctimonious western perceptions. At least for now, one could attest that the undermentioned narrative of 'The Spun Veil of Pyongyang' is told in this spirit.

facing page: A mosaic of CCTV surveillance registers the productivity of various work units while delivering propaganda slogans exhorting the citizens to higher achievements.

following pages 30–33: There will be no emotions or love except the love and care of the Supreme Leader, experienced from each and every angle within the city.

There is no official city map of Pyongyang. Like most of North Korea's larger cities, it was progressively destroyed during the First Sino-Japanese War and later the Korean War. With assistance from the Soviet Union, urban spaces were often redeveloped with impermanent mediums in a socialist paradigm. Way-finding mechanisms employed verbal accounts, imaginative narrative geographies and mental diagramming, conceptualising places in the form of navigable ideas. In 'The Image of the City' (1960), urban theorist Kevin Lynch argues that city design is a temporal art. 'On different occasions and for different people, the sequences are reversed. Interrupted, abandoned, cut across. At every instant, there is more than the eye can see, more than the ear can hear, a setting or a view to be explored.'[4] Once you overcome the terror of staring into Kim Jong-un's eyes, one might find not the window to his soul but the mental map of Pyongyang with Lynch's pliable tropes: edges, districts, paths, nodes and landmarks.

1. A Wang, 'The Song of Everlasting Sorrow', Columbia University Press, 2008, p.8

2. G Orwell, 'Nineteen Eighty-Four', Penguin, 2008, p.283

3. A Broinowski, 'True or False: The 'kooky' North Korea stories they couldn't make up – but did', Guardian, 1 June 2015

4. K Lynch, 'The Image of The City', MIT Press, Cambridge, Mass., 1960, p.1

The outer edges of Pyongyang are draped by a 554.5-metre-high spun veil of 'vinylon', the exact height of South Korea's Lotte World Tower. With no oil reserves, North Korea instead makes vinylon from one commodity it has in abundance: gossip. Powering factories to manufacture this niche product is a story of self-reliance. When it rains, the material soaks up water, which clings to its skin like rumours and produces a vulgar smell. Not to be disillusioned by this inconsequential set-back, the use of vinylon is simply up-scaled to dress the entire perimeter of the city as a rainwater reservoir. As a matter of state loyalty, canteens, kindergartens, bicycle repair stands, and wired public telephone booths are appointed as whispering centres, fuelling gossips, myths, and even lies to power the ever-gullible spinning, weaving and dyeing machines. Vinylon production is now the largest part of the capital's light industry.

The Kims are obsessed with the number nine. Pyongyang has nine Special Environmental and Economic Districts (SEEDs) connected by nine urban paths, which are disguised as sheep pastures with rumour-fuelled micro-climates to combat severe winters for year-round lush grass cultivation. Amongst these districts 'you will find so-called No. 9 farms and No. 9 work details, specially assigned by the central party's financial administration department. Their produce is called No. 9 products.'[5] The number also influences the choice of date when the country makes international news with their impending rocket launches or nuclear tests. Armed with cyclists to continuously spin and weave gossip into No. 9 clouds with varying degrees of innocence and truth, the network of urban paths becomes a unique industrial loom. The clouds collectively seed the perfect daily propaganda of happiness while creating satellite camouflage for this notoriously secretive society, reaffirming the doctrine that its constituents 'aren't like Chinese factory workers who just work for the money. North Koreans have a different attitude – they believe they are working for their country, for their leader.'[6]

A recurring urban node of counter history, and an everyday social architecture, the nine housing towers are the eyes and ears of the authorities. In their function, they mirror the Panopticons dreamt up by Jeremy Bentham to propagate disciplinary forms of social engineering throughout Europe. In Pyongyang, the fear of being observed at any moment through each porous wall of the skeletal housing is enough to keep everyone in line, let alone the large teleportraits of the Supreme Leader smiling incongruously, which can detect 'a nervous tic, an unconscious look of anxiety, and the suggestion of abnormality of having something to hide'.[7] The brew of whispered gossips and embellished myths yield smells that drench the air with an inescapable putridness. With the national night-time curfew on electricity usage, the propaganda machine unwittingly betrays the malicious reach of recreational busybodies – the antithesis of Jane Jacobs's advocacy for increased safety when there are 'eyes on the street'.[8]

Provocations from urban planner Christopher de Gruben serve to illustrate the ambiguous moral fabric of the city, highlighting the treacheries of striking an ethical balance between totalitarian control and giving a free rein to market driven urbanism. 'Pyongyang has been completely planned with no community led organic growth, and has achieved what many other metropolitan centres of the world can only dream about. Surely a few sacrifices in individual liberties are worth it. The State knows best what's good for us... It is we the people, with our insatiable appetite for more, our constant demands for accountability, transparency and freedom of irrationality, that ruin the best laid plans.'[9]

facing page: The porous skeletal housing units make anonymity impossible, especially when gossip about others could become a weapon to defend one's own privacy.

following pages 36–37: Along the network of urban paths the army of cyclists spin and weave gossips into No.9 clouds, the perfect daily propaganda of happiness.

following pages 38–39: Someone to watch over his nine sheep pastures with rumour-fuelled micro-climates.

5. J Jang, 'In North Korea, Nine is the Magic Number', Guardian, 5 April 2013

6. Reuters API, 'North Korea Factories Humming with Made in China Clothes, Traders Say', Fashion Network, 14 August 2017 [https://ww.fashionnetwork.com/news/North-korea-factories-humming-with-made-in-china-clothes-traders-say,857848.html], retrieved 18 August 2022

7. G Orwell, 'Nineteen Eighty-Four', Penguin, 2008, p.41

8. J Jacobs, 'The Death and Life of Great American Cities', Random House, New York, 1961, p.45

9. C de Gruben, 'Pyongyang: The perfect city?', 9 January 2017 [http://www.degruben.com/pyongyang-the-perfect-city], retrieved 5 August 2022

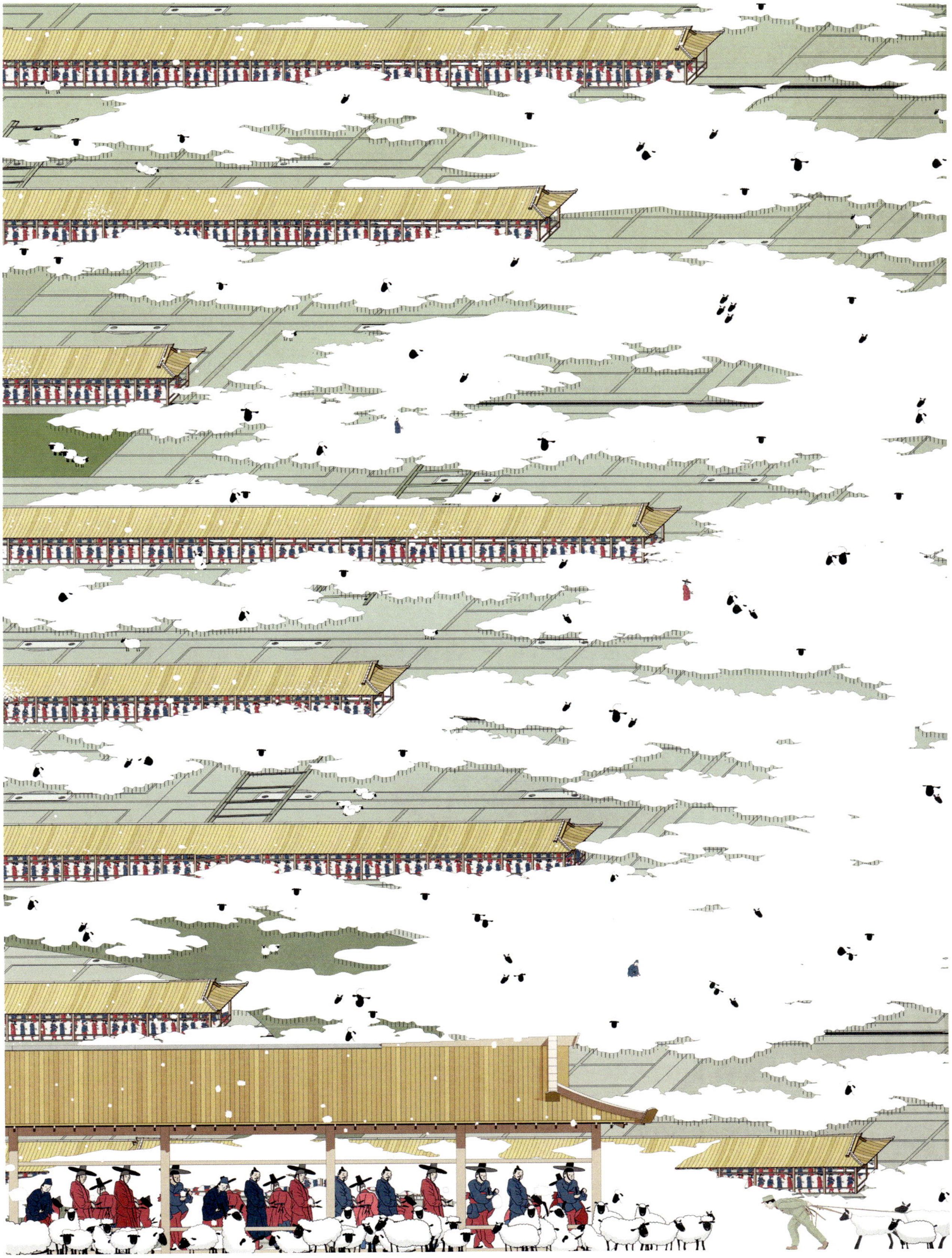

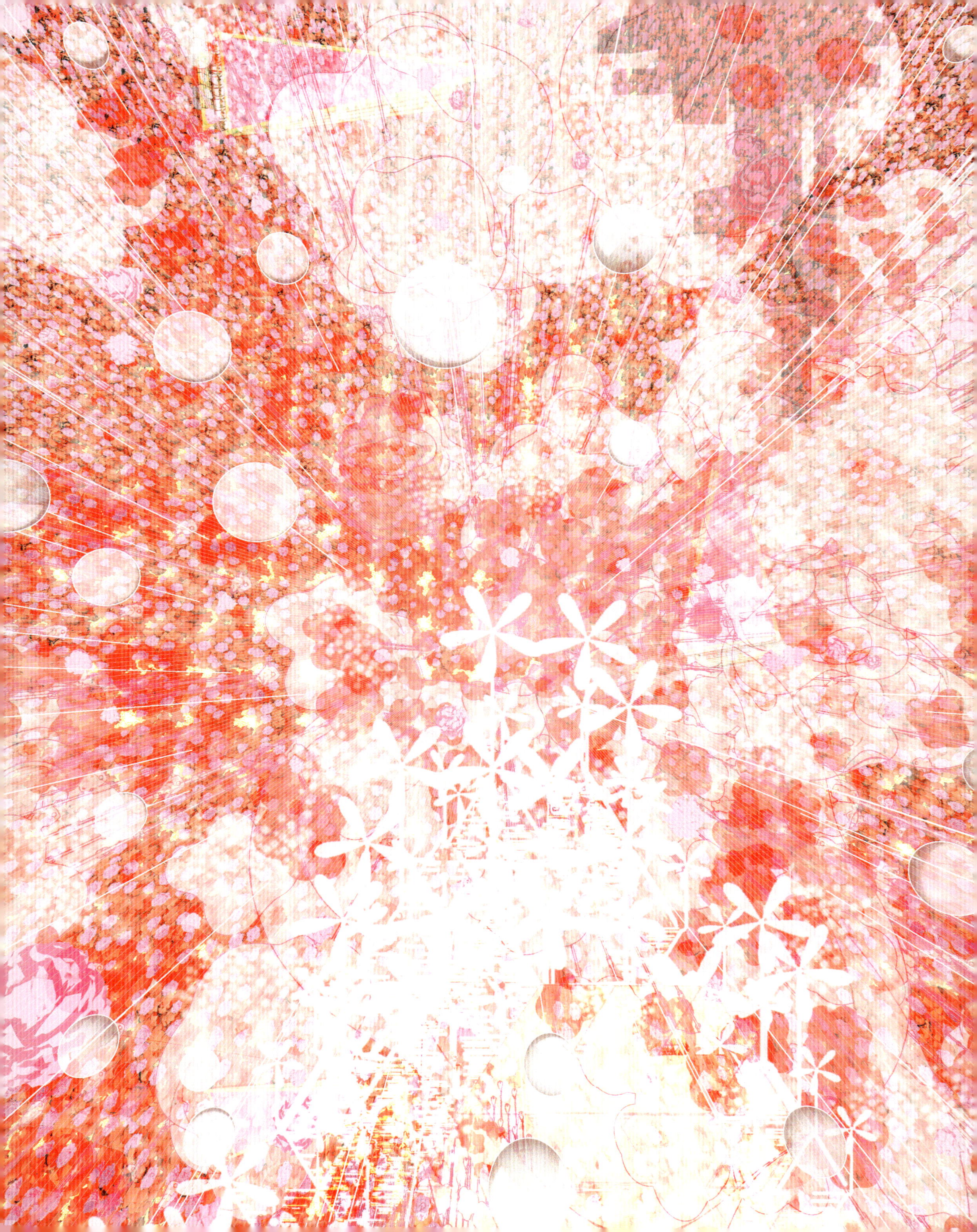

The Empress's Myth Blooms

'After Wu Zetian usurped the throne, the Jade Emperor was furious that a female would dare to rule and he punished China by withholding rain for three years. The rain-bringing dragon took pity and secretly ended the drought. The emperor was enraged, "The dragon has sinned, hence, he shall not be freed until golden beans bloom." On the second day of the second month one year, farmers found kernels and started to make popcorn, to let the golden beans bloom.'

– Lu Feiran, 'Spring Dragon Festival', Shanghai Daily, 12 March 2013

There is an ancient myth that it rains on the second day of the second month of the Chinese lunar calendar, because the dragon has awakened from his imprisonment. Myths and superstitions are contentious and are also believed to have demonised Wu Zetian – the only woman to have ever ruled in more than 3,000 years of Chinese history. Allegedly, she ruthlessly ordered the deaths of court rivals, ministers, and even members of her own family to secure authority. At the same time, she capitulated repeatedly to nepotism, elevated family members to high office, and maintained a harem in her old age. 'None of these actions, though, would have attracted criticism had she been a man',[1] Mike Dash writes in 'The Demonization of Empress Wu', pointing out the double standard that then existed – and still exists.

facing page: Myths of nature which played a large part in legitimising Wu Zetain's unprecedented ascent to power once again re-evaluate history to proffer more equitable perspectives.

following pages: The city adapts into a variety of sun-catching topographies, which feature a collection of peony gardens in full bloom throughout the year.

The majority of these allegations remain unsubstantiated. What is known for certain is that Wu was highly superstitious, and the nature-related myths which legitimised her unprecedented ascent to power once again re-evaluate history to proffer more equitable perspectives. Conversations between past and future begin with the overlapping of two urban frameworks in Luoyang, the capital of Wu's rule. The invisible legacy of the proto-feminist grid of the Tang Dynasty and the 21st-century industrial grid intertwine with the empress's mythical repertoire: the peony, the sunbird, and the phoenix deliver a series of otherworldly spatial phenomena. In the process, their efforts have erased divisions, blurred thresholds, and cultivated a new belief of urban unity and resilience.

'...I expect to see signs of spring. All flowers are ordered to blossom tonight'[2] demanded the Empress, and those that did not obey the imperial decree would have been punished. Even though it was snowing heavily, the imperial garden flowered with one exception – the peonies refused. Looking around now, Luoyang is a picturesque collection of peony gardens in full bloom throughout the year; gone are the coal-burning plants and industries that have dominated the city's landscape. The gardens' under-soil heating is a by-product of the new anaerobic digestion economy, which produces renewable energy while capturing methane emissions. When filled-up with biogas, the gardens adapt into a variety of sun-catching topographies. The myth of the peony has long been misunderstood considering that Wu's

1. M Dash, 'The Demonization of Empress Wu', Smithsonian Magazine, 10 August 2012 [https://www.smithsonianmag.com/history/the-demonization-of-empress-wu-20743091], retrieved 10 October 2022

2. M Yao, 'Tracing the First Empress in Grottoes and Peony Gardens', Shanghai Daily, 20 June 2009

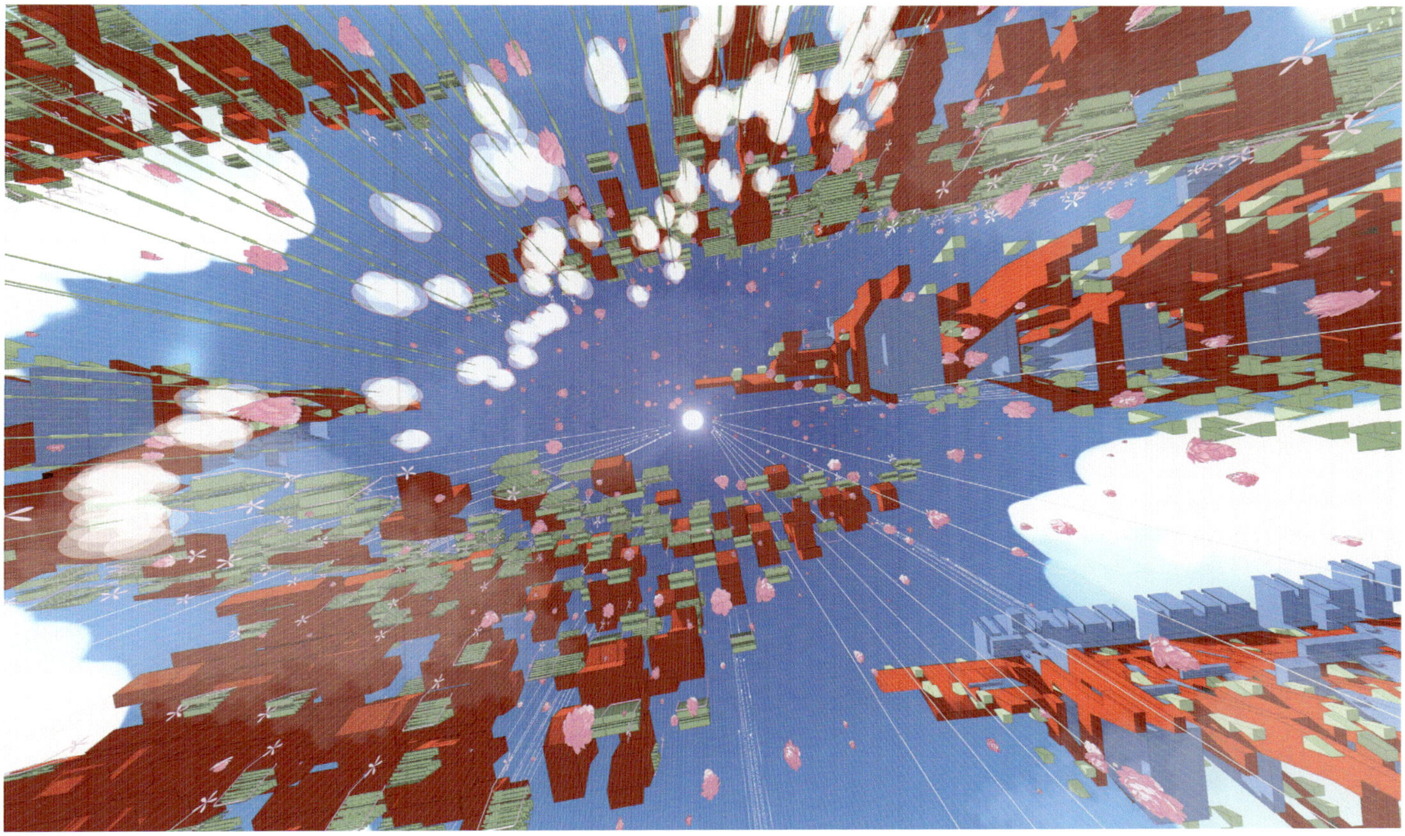

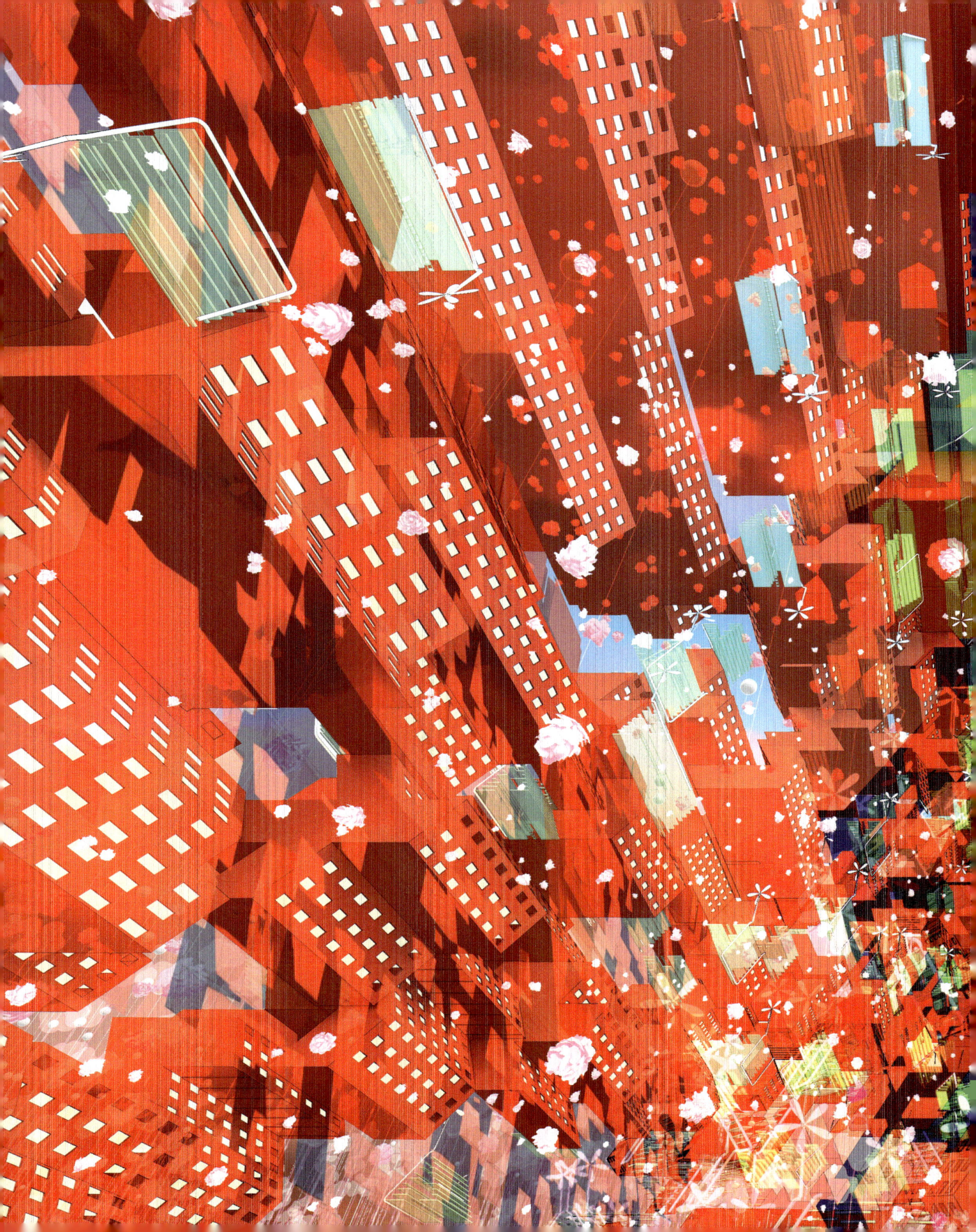

true intention, albeit harsh, was to cultivate courage and resilience in the face of severe hardship, a sentiment that seems aligned with many of today's urban climate responses.

Looking upwards, the sunbirds dart merrily between the golden clouds to address the energy and environmental crisis. The clouds compete to fly higher and higher, and as if they are energised by the rebel spirit of the rain-bringing dragon and the myth of the popcorn, they take advantage of the height difference to generate atmospheric electricity which also attracts pollutant particles to improve air quality. The unconventional sunbirds possess a third leg in the form of a tesla antenna which, upon meeting the clouds, transmits converted solar energy as affordable electricity to an appreciative population. Heading towards the suburbs, the astonishing lightning regularly strikes farmland to stimulate nitrogen uptake and improve crop yields, while purveying a metaphorical protest against male-dominated history. How times have changed – when Wu presented a similarly auspicious solar three-legged bird at court, she was depicted as a fraud who shamelessly sought to manipulate the mythical male emblem of the sun to reinforce her imperial persona and political authority.[3]

previous pages: The city actively seeks an ecological symbiosis between nature and built form to create diverse schemas of urban resilience.

facing page top + bottom: As if by magic, the mood of the city transforms into a spectacular spectrum of violet, magenta and purple as the phoenix spreads her wings to nurture domestic needs.

following pages: Energised by the various myths, there is a palpable sense of excitement and hope.

'The phoenix followed by hundreds of thousands of flocking rosefinches'[4] plays to the mythological grounding of Wu, the phoenix empress taking the throne and following God's will to bestow not only splendour but security to her people. Wu, unlike her male predecessors, realised that bringing 'gender equity to water'[5] would advance her reform agenda of poverty reduction while unlocking the potential of half of her people. She ordered the rivers, Yi and Luo, to be brought together to control Luoyang's seasonal drought and flood. With the new water management system cleansing landscapes as it circulates throughout the city, it brings housing closer to clean water access and the scattered pockets of natural habitats of lush flora and diverse wildlife in the vast network of wetlands. Wu also promoted the study of arts, and as part of her reform women are commissioned to paint the housing units in patterns of peony red and a vibrant blue to promote favourable associations with the red and blue feathers on the phoenix of harmony. The pigments of the peony and the blue butterfly pea flower are eco-friendly, and as if by magic, they can change the mood of the city into a spectacular spectrum of violet, magenta and purple with small additions of lemon juice.[6] There is a palpable sense of contentment and earnest hope for prosperous life – 'the phoenix spreads her wings' to nurture the domestic needs of the city, despite a rising population. Nonetheless, her many Confucian critics would view the metaphor as Wu's attempt to offset her feelings of guilt by applying softened language when ordering inhumane punishments.

Alas, much of Wu's achievements remain hidden beneath layers of bias and long-held superstitions. Social prejudices against the female gender reflect the Confucianism which dominates prevailing attitudes, imbued with patriarchal beliefs that impact perceptions and fuel injustice. What would Wu know about the bravery and liberation of women compared to the social justice historians of today? The rhetorical question withstanding, Wu's metaphor extends further into the discourse of modernity which has been equally unkind towards the application of myths and narratives in the practice of the built environment. Cities as vessels for humanity in every age, in every place, in every society have the responsibility to confess that their architecture and planning have to date been insufficiently attentive to this concept, and continuing to perpetuate obvious untruths only works to the detriment of all.

3. NH Rothschild, 'Wu Zhao's Remarkable Aviary', Southeast Review of Asian Studies, vol.27, 2005, pp.71–76

4. ZW Wu, SY Wu & SJ Yang , 'Phoenix Tree, Phoenix and Empress', American Journal of BioScience, vol.10, issue 1, January 2022, pp.1–9

5. 'Water and Gender', United Nations [https://www.unwater.org/water-facts/water-and-gender], retrieved 10 November 2022

6. GC Vidana Gamage, YY Lim & WS Choo, 'Anthocyanins From Clitoria Ternatea Flower: Biosynthesis Extraction Stability Antioxidant Activity and Applications', Frontiers in Plant Science, vol.12, 17 December 2021 [https://www.frontiersin.org/articles/10.3389/fpls.2021.792303/full], retrieved 10 October 2022

Another Myth of the Great Fire

'This is the myth that I hear people talking about most often. They may have read it in a children's book or heard it at school. The fire is supposed to have wiped out London's rats and fleas that spread the plague and burned down the insanitary houses which were a breeding ground for the disease. If anyone asks you about this, you can tell them that it's not true.'

– Meriel Jeater, 'Fire! Fire!', Museum of London, 2016

This is just one of the countless myths and misconceptions about London's Great Fire of 1666. From the calamity's origin to its reshaping of the city, there are a diverse set of facts, fictions and beliefs behind the fire's historical reality. A lesser-known myth holds that King Charles II vetoed the creation of the world's tallest isolated stone column, 'The Monument' to its memory which would have depicted him as saviour of the city. In fact, the immediate rebuilding of London, especially its homes, was the monarch's only priority and prayer in the fire's aftermath. At the same time, a group of intellectual elites saw a golden opportunity for London to break with the past, its old infrastructure no longer reflecting the ideals of the age. John Evelyn's plan elevated London's wealth, placing its most polluting elements away from the centre for trade to continue unencumbered. Robert Hooke's plan used a rectilinear grid of exact squares aligning due north to host markets and churches. Richard Newcourt's plan proposed a 'chessboard' of 64 urban blocks, each centring God with a church at the core. Christopher Wren's plan featured two diagonal boulevards that would cut across a grid of newly stone-fronted streets, leading to and from a grand Royal Exchange and an imposing St. Paul's Cathedral. The most controversial plan, authored by Valentine Knight, aimed to generate tax collected from a new commercial canal coursing the city to finance the reconstruction.[1]

facing page: With only a faint memory of St Paul's Cathedral, London adopts radical new forms as it rises from the ashes.

following pages: The new city embodies the ideological strategies of Evelyn, Hooke, Newcourt and Wren. The four architects' original plans become the structural exoskeletons of the bridges.

Befitting the magnanimity of the King, the final plan on which the rebuild came to pass was prophetic in its strategy. It drew only the most discerning virtues from the first four proposals, anticipating future growth and using urban systems whose implementation did not require protracted landownership negotiations. Knight's plan was totally ignored as the monarch was most offended by the suggestion that he could financially benefit from the fire.[2] The King's close relationship with France during his exile would almost certainly have influenced his decisions when determining the design of the new city. It looked to French boulevards and formal landscaping in its resolution between structure and nature, with the gardens of Versailles being of particular interest. This was a nod to Wren and certainly Evelyn, as the latter petitioned the monarch in 1661 regarding the addition of nature and especially trees to the urban fabric. New plantings would address the root cause of London's many health issues, combatting air pollution caused by the burning of coal and the manufacturing of soap, fabric dye and alcohol.

1. J Glancey, 'The London That Could Have Been', BBC Culture, 18 February 2016 [https://www.bbc.com/culture/article/20160217-the-london-that-could-have-been], retrieved 1 July 2022

2. A Forrest, 'How London Might Have Looked: Five masterplans after the Great Fire of 1666', Cities, Guardian, 25 January 2016

Extensive new forests of oak were planned in the outer suburbs of London to meet demand for the large quantities of timber required in the rebuilding effort. Felled and milled, this sustainable material would then be transported into the city on a new network of canals. The oak became a symbol for King Charles II, but also the country to which he was restored; it was believed that he found refuge in an oak tree in order to escape his enemies.[3] What is more, the monarch was determined to promote the benefits of locally sourced timber against the negative environmental impacts of the commonly preferred bricks. The 1667 Royal Rebuilding Act[4] ordered that 'all Buildings in and about the said City be henceforth made of controlled "charred" timber'. This ancient technique burns away cellulose, chemically restructuring wood to make it naturally resistant to flame and burrowing insects while minimising its reaction to changes in moisture.[5] The royal ritual of charring also commemorated the Great Fire, and reinforced the metaphor of refuge and protection for the King's people after so devastating a calamity.

During his exile in France, it was conceivable that King Charles read Nostradamus's prediction of the third calamity after the Plague and the Fire – the Flood would hit London when Mars, Jupiter and Saturn align in the year 2378![6] In a radical move to protect his people and the city's commerce, the monarch looked towards the Amsterdam model. Constructing a new myth against the agents of disaster, he would appoint not conventional builders but shipwrights with traditional knowledge of woodworking as the artisans of the new city's centrepiece – an interconnected series of inhabited bridges along the River Thames instead of Wren's St Paul's Cathedral. Following the ethos of a typical Amsterdam Grachtenhuis, the design of the inhabitable bridges unifies prototypical family homes above with commercial spaces below, giving citizens a stake in cultivating a more even distribution of wealth by intermingling districts of rich and poor, leisure and industry.

The King was eager to engage water in underpinning belief, well-being and community bonding. By hybridising Newcourt and Hooke's plans, 64 squares would act as filters, reservoirs and urban tidal pools, whilst providing access to clean water and assurance against the future threat of floods. The 'squares' on the Thames defined by the 12 inhabited bridges are designated religious hubs as the King recognised the role of water in the many rituals and social practices that come to shape the city. Each church, mosque, temple and synagogue acts as a pivot for transient social experiences, and the concept of time. When the tidal water reaches a predefined mark in the square, it denotes the time for prayer. As the winter sets in, bulwarks surrounding the piers of the bridges become wider, dramatically slowing the river's rate of flow and allowing the water to freeze. Beyond the merriment and spectacle of the Frost Fairs with football pitches, sledge rides, horse and coach races, and public houses for a pint or two, the firm ice would unite north and south London both physically and emotionally for over two months each year. During these times, social, economic and cultural disparities are forgotten, albeit temporarily.

The London of this myth is one of intimate yet proactive connections with her people, putting forward a resilient typology of architecture and urbanism that values care and cohesion under the framework of community. The alternative history is outward as well as forward looking, and unlike Wren's prioritisation of protected sightlines towards a single cathedral, King Charles' oak city offers diverse views, agencies and dreams of rebirth for each and every one.

previous page 54 top + bottom: Within the 12 inhabited bridges, the structures comprise accommodations interlaced with sky courtyards, and market halls and docks on the lower levels.

previous page 55: The vertical accommodation units are connected by water powered funicular transport systems.

facing page: An intimate physical and spiritual connection between inhabitants and the water feeds the growth of the city.

following pages: Public spaces reach out into the skies and punctuate the inclined streets within the inhabitable bridges.

3. P Seaward, 'Charles II', Oxford Dictionary of National Biography, 23 September 2004 [https://doi.org/10.1093/ref:odnb/5144], retrieved 1 July 2023

4. Parliamentary Archives, 'An Act for Rebuilding the City of London', UK Parliament, Catalogue no. HL/PO/PU/1/1666/18&19C2n14

5. 'Yakisugi (Shou Sugi Ban)', Japan Woodcraft Association [https://japanwoodcraftassociation.com/traditions/techniques/yakisugi-shou-sugi-ban], retrieved 1 July 2022

6. A Webber, 'Nostradamus on Floods in the 21st Century', www.nostradamus.com, 2013 [http://nostradamuscodes.com/Floods.html], retrieved 1 July 2022

chapter two

Tradition + Logic

'The new horizons before us will only recover the grand line of tradition by a complete revision of the methods in vogue and by the fixing of a new basis of construction established in logic. In architecture the old bases of construction are dead. We shall not rediscover the truths of architecture until new bases have established a logical ground for every architectural manifestation.'

– Le Corbusier, 'The City of To-Morrow and Its Planning', 1929

Not all cities are born from the application of wild dreams or extreme and abstract urbanisms which can result in unmitigated failures. The development of every successful human settlement has an underlying economic and social logic. Prosperous cities whose size and complexity can accumulate or adapt over time according to supply and demand often emphasise a vernacular response regarding climate, available resources, and culture. This unique process creates traditions with inventive evolutionary qualities and becomes a rich source of logical wisdom. But before the idea of vernacular could even be posited, notions of the ideal city and its architecture had to be set forth, a task taken up by many of the great thinkers and philosophers of the past.

facing page: In case study 4, 'Hometown Glory', Adele and her eye-lash parachutes shelter the skies and watch over us in the tradition of a secret Bond mission – emulating the celebrated 2012 Olympic double-act by Daniel Craig and Her Majesty Queen Elizabeth II.

Plato's 'Republic' is one of the earliest and most influential works of political theory. It involves a pragmatic discussion on the order and character of hypothetical city-states with the aim of discerning an optimal system. Starting with the 'City of Pigs'[1] in Book II, founded on the simplest cohesive character of mutual need, and progressing through examples of the legendary cities of Timaeus, Critias, and Atlantis, Plato's dialogue eventually arrives at his own creation, Callipolis. By taking elements from the previous examples, it is reasoned that Callipolis, under the rule of a philosopher-king employing the most logical systems of education, governance, and communal living, would possess an ideal and just structure. Whether this theoretical city could be realised is left ambiguous in the text. Because of this speculative quality, many have argued that this work is in fact positing the first example of a utopia. Taken to mean 'a description of an imagined society put forward by its author as better than any existing society, past or present',[2] the term would not be formalised for another two millennia through the writings of English statesman Thomas More.

Plato's student Aristotle was associated with another theoretician intent on realising the ideal city-state, Hippodamus of Miletus. Known as one of the earliest architects, Hippodamus was a polymath who 'invented the art of planning cities'[3] and appears in Aristotle's opus 'Politics' as 'the first non-statesman who made inquiries about the best form of government'.[4] He oversaw the building of two port cities, Miletus and Piraeus, based on rectilinear grids some 2300 years before the island of Manhattan was

1. Plato, 'Republic', C Rowe (trans.), Penguin Books, London, 2012, p.15

2 + 6. DR Morrison, 'The Utopian Character of Plato's Ideal City', in 'The Cambridge Companion to Plato's Republic', GRF Ferrari (ed.), Cambridge Companions to Philosophy, Cambridge University Press, 2007, p.232

3 + 4. Aristotle, 'Politics', RF Stalley (ed.), E Barker (trans.), Oxford World's Classics, Oxford University Press, 2020, p.37

planned. For Hippodamus, such designs reflected the practical philosophy of a city governed by democracy, dignity, and grace, 'creating an environment that expressed and nurtured the ideals of its citizens'.[5]

The quintessential rendering of an ideal city comes from the imagination of More, whose curious, sometimes ironic book 'Utopia' (1516) has imbued the word 'with a notoriously wide range of meanings'.[6] Being part polemic, part satire, it describes an island state of uniform cities ordered along ideal lines and without private property. Here, resident Utopians 'meet and eat together',[7] anyone 'may freely enter into any house whatsoever',[8] and 'all laws are promulgated for this end, that every man may know his duty; and, therefore, the plainest and most obvious sense of the words is that which ought to be put upon them'.[9] Another literary portrayal of a city obsessed by the virtues of logic is found in 'Gulliver's Travels' (1726) which satirises both human nature and its own genre, the travelers' tale. Jonathan Swift's Laputa is a floating island nation 'populated by astronomers, mathematicians, musicians, and technologists so lost in thought and ideals that they are unable to build in straight lines'.[10] This issue is rectified by architects who contrive 'a new method for building houses, by beginning at the roof and working downwards to the foundation'.[11]

As Oleg Grabar asserts, 'one can immediately see that tradition and development are often incompatible; development can proceed only when tradition is "forgotten". Nevertheless, it is only through traditions, real or fictitious relationships to half-forgotten and largely misunderstood pasts, that people recognise themselves.'[12] László Moholy-Nagy has likewise stated that 'tradition is man-made and must be constantly reevaluated, adhered to, or discarded'.[13] While ever accelerating developments often rely on logical approaches, opposing forces seeking solace in the tried-and-true methods of the past can temper against uncompromising excesses. Unlike the mortar, stone, and concrete piles beneath the buildings which make up its fabric, a city is also built upon the metaphysical substrate of ideals, traditions, and social patterns emerging over the course of time. Whether profound, idiosyncratic, or distasteful, the common thread connecting urbanism's driving factors is their emergence from human imagination. P.D. Smith believes that 'urban territory is leased to each generation. Residents and buildings are all temporary. What is permanent is the idea of the city.'[14] The drastic transformations required to create the urban environment clearly imply a set of powerful convictions. Motivated by foundational beliefs, humanity invested unthinkable effort into the earliest cities, ceaselessly creating traditions alongside physical dwellings.

Affirming long-held folklore, archaeological study shows that the first continuous settlements were born out of respect for the dead rather than a practical solution to the challenges of life, where humanity's fascination with the cyclical processes of survival and creation sought a fixed place for the 'powerful images of daylight fantasy and nightly dream'.[15] Lewis Mumford notes that 'the city of the dead antedates the city of the living. In one sense, indeed, the city of the dead is the forerunner, almost the core, of every living city.'[16] Traditions and rituals associated with the cemeteries of antiquity caused this greatest of civilisational transitions, inspiring nomadic hunter-gatherers to establish the sedentary agricultural societies necessary for the creation of permanent habitations. Once covered by olive trees, the mountains surrounding Jerusalem were turned white between the 9th and 7th centuries BC by the sea of stone tombs in the Silwan necropolis.[17] Similarly, the roads to many Greek and Roman cities were lined with rows of tombstones, reminding travellers of impermanence and the eventual, inevitable decay of the megalopolis into the necropolis. Even in the modern city, the illusory commitment to the past drives spatial evolution. For example, the exodus of buried remains from London to more desirable dwellings in the countryside has pre-empted the sprawling development of future boroughs. New buildings, too, inevitably deal with the city's past as they are 'raised up on the detritus of its long history'.[18]

Logic for a New Society

'The city of today is a dying thing because it is not geometrical. To build in the open would be to replace our present haphazard arrangements, which are all we have today, by a uniform layout. Unless we do this there is no salvation.'[19] Concerns about whether such generalisations were true or even accurate did little to lessen the ideological weight of Le Corbusier's dramatic edict. By the close of the 19th century with industrialisation well underway, expectations around technology had shifted so radically that changes in the design and construction of buildings were imminent. Modernism popularised the rhetoric of mass-produced architecture, borrowing ideas from the industrial revolution to solve the accelerating social problems its own processes were causing. Chief among these was the crowding driven by labour's mass-migration into cities which instigated a new typology of co-operative housing. To achieve the requisite density, this model challenged notions of domestic life and sought to maximise efficiency, replacing individualism with collectivism. Such desires found their apotheosis in Le Corbusier's 1914 Maison Dom-Ino,[20] a skeletal housing unit within which a multiplicity of decisions about wall and window placement could be accommodated. Despite emphasising spatial flexibility, this uncompromising logic of pure functionalism led to a proliferation of supremely austere, almost monastic dwellings.

In April of 1925, Le Corbusier submitted an influential proposal to Paris's International Exhibition of Modern Decorative and Industrial Arts, designing a space which embraced rational principles and utilitarian logic in the provision of housing for the new age. Called the 'Esprit Nouveau Pavilion', the controversial prototype broke with the tradition of decorative arts on which the exhibition was focused and instead 'explored the potential for standardisation and mass production in residential architecture'.[21] On top of this already contentious denouncement of contemporary practice and its licentious approach to building, the interior also showcased unprecedented urban proposals including the notorious 'Plan Voisin' for the reconstruction of Paris. Possessed of the simultaneous concerns that urban planners were resisting cars and the straight-lined spatial transformations they necessitated as well as the requirements for fresh air and tranquillity, Corbusier's plan sought a logical resolution to the conflicting elements of modern life. It claimed that the best path forward would be offered by vertical densification interspersed with a raised grid of motorways for the new modes of transportation, freeing the ground for open spaces and lush greenery. In 'The City of To-morrow' (1929) Corbusier defends the plan with logic and syllogisms, stating 'we must increase the open spaces and diminish the distances to be covered. Therefore the centre of the city must be constructed vertically.'[22]

While the proposal may have been a productive critique of squalid living conditions in city-centres at the time, its monomaniacal focus on the strict logic of clean-slate tower developments was not without its consequences. In fact, by emulating conditions in the significantly younger and still expanding cities across the Atlantic, Le Corbusier was advocating an approach which would 'obliterate one of the most complex and closely-detailed quarters of Paris in the interests of what he clearly conceived to be a Cartesian version of New York'.[23] Labouring under the delusion that population centres were being 'held back by the law of least resistance, lack of responsibility and respect for the past',[24] Corbusier was, through the moral justifications of supreme order and perfect geometry, creating a model that would wreak havoc on 20th-century cities even when applied in the expansive American context.

5. A Boyd, 'No. 2542: Hippodamus of Miletus', The Engines of Our Ingenuity, 2009 [https://uh.edu/engines/epi2542.htm], retrieved 20 July 2022

7, 8 + 9. T More, 'Utopia', G Burnet (trans.), Richard Chiswell, London, 1684, p.87, p.69 & p.134

10. J Glancey, 'How to Read Towns & Cities', Bloomsbury, London, 2019, p.171

11. J Swift, 'Gulliver's Travels', Everyman's Library, Dent, London, 1975, p.218

12. O Grabar, 'Why History: The meanings and uses of tradition', Traditional Dwellings and Settlements Review, vol. 4, no. 2, 1993, pp.19–26

13. L Moholy-Nagy, 'Vision in Motion', Paul Theobald, Chicago, 1947, p.14

14 + 18. PD Smith, 'City', Bloomsbury, New York, 2012, p.127

15 + 16. L Mumford, 'The City in History', Secker & Warburg Ltd, London, 1961, p.6 & p.7

17. D Ussishkin, 'The Necropolis from the Time of the Kingdom of Judah at Silwan, Jerusalem', The Biblical Archaeologist, vol.33, no.2, 1970, pp.34–46

19, 22, 27 + 32. Le Corbusier, 'The City of To-Morrow and Its Planning', F Etchells (trans.), Architectural Press, 1929, p.176, p.169, p.152 & p.173

20. E Farrelly, 'Shoebox or Gingerbread House?', Sydney Morning Herald, 31 December 2005

21 + 24. '31–Le Corbusier–5–Urbanism–Of Men & Asses', Listen Notes, 13 February 2018 [https://www.listennotes.com/podcasts/about-buildings/31-le-corbusier-5-urbanism-ihnC_ekXduY], retrieved 23 July 2022

23. C Rowe, 'The Present Urban Predicament: Some observations', Architectural Association Quarterly, vol.11, no.4, 1979, pp. 40–48

25. J Gehl, 'In Search of the Human Scale', TEDxKEA, 18 December 2015 [https://www.youtube.com/watch?v=Cgw9oHDfJ4k], retrieved 28 July 2022

Corbusier's Plan Voisin was only part of a longer tradition of radical urban transformation throughout Parisian neighbourhoods. The trend began in the mid-19th century with Baron Haussmann's so-called renovation which, in practice, was effectively a demolition focused on wholesale slum removal to accommodate widened avenues and boulevards, annexing dense housing to the surrounding suburbs. This represented an early step towards what Jan Gehl describes as the modern separation of streets from the 'human scale' in urban planning. Where the cities of 'the good old days' were 'geared to the actual senses of homo-sapiens' and 'built to suit the body',[25] Haussmannian Paris shaped an entirely new conception of public space at the expense of the populace, its streets serving 'as theatres for the urban flaneur as much as antidote against barricading mobs'.[26] Corbusier similarly proposed knocking down what remained of central Paris's old town to complete its modernisation, oblivious to the inevitable destruction of the city's prized character, informal recreation, and social networks that would be wrought by the imposition of a top-down urban form.

In Colin Rowe's analysis of the relationship between the classical and the modern, he often advocated for the approach of Corbusier through which he saw the early pretensions of modernism being undone by the retention of ideal forms. However, when it came to the realm of urbanism where Corbusier single-mindedly deferred to the laws of physics as 'the base of all human achievement',[27] the French radical proved to be beyond even Rowe's condonement. In his seminal text, 'Collage City' (1978), Rowe notes forthrightly that modernist urbanism spurred by the Plan Voisin and its ilk 'while professing to be scientific, displayed a wholly naive idealism' and 'professing to be humane, displayed a wholly unacceptable and sterile scientific rigour'.[28] Statements like these have increasingly impelled abstention from the intellectual arrogance bound up in certain forms of modernist planning, the ideology of its adherents well summarised as a dogma governed solely by standards. In Corbusier's own words, 'standards are a matter of logic, analysis and precise study. Standards are based on a problem which has been well stated. Architecture means plastic invention, intellectual speculation, higher mathematics.'[29] Rifts between the abstract ideals of the solitary architect and the practicalities which bound construction and broad participation in shared visions were proudly documented in articles like 'The New Spirit in Architecture' (1924). 'Suddenly, these men, who are involved in doing positive, logical, practical things, exclaimed: "So you want to spoil our cities! You barbarians! You are forgetting the rules of aesthetics!" ...they revealed that they were incapable of imagining the consequences of their work in any other field; they remained in the past...'[30]

Corbusier's process, summarised in 'Five Points Towards a New Architecture' (1926), became synonymous with the goals of the modern movement despite its rigid logic, fixed in history by the discourse of Rowe and other scholars. In the text, essential components of building construction are reduced to a precise list of elements, namely 1. pilotis (foundation columns), 2. roof garden, 3. free plan, 4. strip windows, and 5. free facade,[31] all of which are to be considered in turn when designing. These points were a powerful tool for rationalisation, creating a model that could be broadly emulated as well as an intellectual justification for Corbusier to pursue his own architectural agenda. Similarly reductive logics were later applied to the divergent and radically more complex practice of city planning. Disregarding the inability of inflexible systems to resolve projects whose scope exceeded single buildings, Corbusier and other modernists remained fixated by rationalism and designs whose arrangements would provide 'a spectacle of order and vitality'.[32]

A rare success in the portfolio of modern planning is the ideal city of Chandigarh, capital of East Punjab and one of the major works of Le Corbusier's later career. Initial plans were drawn up by Polish architect Maciej Nowicki and US planner Albert Mayer in 1947, and Corbusier would revise the layout to incorporate the gridiron of his unrealised Parisian proposals. While the significance of this geometry will be discussed further in a following section, it is worth noting that the grid 'proved subtle and adaptable'[33] in this context, combined with an emphasis on green spaces in a pedestrian-only city centre, and with sector layouts and modular elements considered in relation to the sun. After his first visit in 1952, Prime Minister of India Jawaharlal Nehru delivered a powerful statement on the dreams bound up in this new urbanism. 'Let this be a new town, symbolic of the freedom of India, unfettered by the traditions of the past – an expression of the nation's faith in the future.'[34]

Whilst examples of modernism's captivating logic have both good and bad points, a reiteration of William Morris's emphasis on the redemptive quality of craft could play an important role in addressing its excesses. Morris was a pioneer of the Arts and Crafts Movement which took up a reactionary stance against the mechanical insensitivities of the industrial revolution. It was not an exuberant style such as Rococo or High Gothic, but did have an aspect of the fairytale, the folkish and the quirky that recalled the eccentricities and forgotten logics of medieval times. In buildings and even cities as the case may be, the modernist tendency to separate the 'idea' from the process of construction has come to represent an era of architectural indifference and social alienation more generally. Intrinsically linked to industrialism and the totalising system of capital, this issue was only exacerbated by the neoliberal reforms that have privatised and anonymised the 21st-century city. As a counterpoint, 'craft' is defined as the creation and maintenance of real objects of utility rather than economic abstractions, as a practice with the potential to 'rehabilitate the entire capitalist enterprise away from exploitation and toward a more responsible system.'[35] Capitalism could be corralled as a tool to facilitate the invigorating praxis of craft traditions whilst bridging divides as 'to Westerners, creativity implies a break with tradition and a move beyond what exists, whereas to Easterners, creativity suggests the reinterpretation or rediscovery of tradition'.[36]

Dreams of the Logical Past

'Ought not the rational principle, which is wise, and has the care of the whole soul, to rule, and the passionate or spirited principle to be the subject and ally?'[37] This was the contention of Plato whose philosophy of politics has resounded for millennia, influencing countless thinkers to develop distinct theories for how power should be organised amongst people and within cities. But can a system that successfully navigates the messy realities of human existence be derived from purely logical grounds? Even in the first century BC, Vitruvius had recognised a duality in 'the building itself and an idea that its architect tried to express'.[38] 'The Ten Books on Architecture' outline a process dependent 'on Order, Arrangement, Eurythmy, Symmetry, Propriety, and Economy',[39] a series of elements which, like Corbusier's Five Points, are intended to give 'due measure to the members of a work considered separately, and symmetrical agreement to the proportions of the whole'.[40] The influence of Plato is pervasive throughout this first architectural treatise, an effect that would echo down the centuries in the works to follow. The notion that a realm of 'ideal forms' underlies the material reality in which architecture operates meant that, for Plato and his intellectual descendants, architecture would always be mediating between the perfect idea and the imperfections of a world 'subject to change and decay'.[41]

The relationship between geometric form and pristine idea was adopted by Le Corbusier, who reinvigorated the architectural obsession with primary shapes by combining appeals to Platonism with the machine aesthetic of his era. Corbusier's argument, clearly animated by the platonic realm of

26. R Kaput, 'Rethinking the Polis', Global Intellectual History, vol.7, no.1, 2022, pp.161–177

28. C Rowe & F Koetter, 'Collage City', MIT Press, Cambridge, 1978, p.6

29. Le Corbusier, 'Towards a New Architecture', F Etchells (trans.), Architectural Press, London, 1970, pp.145–148

30. Le Corbusier, 'The New Spirit in Architecture (1924)', C Benton, T Benton, et al. (trans.), 'Architecture and Design, 1890–1939: An international anthology of original articles', Whitney Library of Design, New York, NY, 1975, p.132

31. W Oechslin & W Wang, 'Les Cinq Points d'une Architecture Nouvelle', Assemblage, no.4, 1987, pp.83–93

33. J Glancey, 'How to Read Towns & Cities: A crash course in urban architecture', Bloomsbury, 2019, p.175

34. R Khosla, 'The New Metropolis: Nehru and the aftermath', Social Scientist, vol. 43, no. 3/4, 2015, pp.11–32

35. JP Morgan, 'Craft Theory And The Creation Of A New Capitalism', The New Polis, 18 November 2018 [https://thenewpolis.com/2018/11/18/craft-theory-and-the-creation-of-a-new-capitalism-jonathan-p-morgan], retrieved 27 July 2022

36. Y Shao et al.,'How Does Culture Shape Creativity? A Mini-Review', Front Psychol, vol.10, 28 May 2019 [https://www.frontiersin.org/articles/10.3389/fpsyg.2019.01219/full], retrieved 27 July 2022

37. Plato, 'Republic', C Rowe (trans.), Penguin Books, London, 2012, p.142

38. DR McNamara, 'How to Read Churches: A crash course in ecclesiastical architecture', Rizzoli, New York, 2011, p.6

39 + 40. Vitruvius, 'The Ten Books on Architecture', HL Warren (ed.), MH Morgan (trans.), Dover Publications, New York, 1960, p.27

41. J Hill, 'Immaterial Architecture', Routledge, London, 2006, p.39

perfect geometries, contends that the purpose of design is 'to map out in rhythmical quantities, animated by an even impulse, to bring life into the whole by means of a unifying and subtle relationship, to balance, to resolve the equation... with architecture which works by quantities. These quantities provide a mass of material as a basis for work; brought into measure, introduced into the equation, they result in rhythms, they speak to us of numbers, of relationships, of mind.'[42] This understanding of ideal forms and their self-evident superiority over 'any element that relates to the human countenance'[43] animated the work of Corbusier and his many acolytes. Enticed by perpendicular simplicity, they sought to transform cities along the lines of the gridiron and generate new architectures through the application of primal shapes. Put bluntly in 'The City of To-morrow', 'the right angle is the essential and sufficient implement of action, because it enables us to determine space with an absolute exactness'.[44]

On the grounds of conjectures like these, modernists advocated for the reordering of historic cities whose organic forms were inimical to inspection, quantification, and control. Despite traditionalist insistence that cities amenable to a high quality of life did not follow rigid grid designs, many urban planners insisted upon their utility as an ordering principle. Appeals to simplicity have only increased with the massive technological change demanded by swelling populations and debates over the suitability of grid layouts continue to this day. Mumford had early made the claim that 'the new gridiron plans were spectacular in their inefficiency and waste. By usually failing to discriminate sufficiently, in the first instance, between main traffic arteries and residential streets, the first were not made wide enough while the second were usually too wide for purely neighbourhood functions.'[45] The true problem, as other critics have pointed out, is an overreliance on car infrastructure implicit in even Mumford's worldview. The heavily intersected grid to which automobiles are ill-suited could, it is argued, easily accommodate other, more necessary urban functions. The logic of the grid in many cases actually makes for pedestrian streets easy to navigate on foot. It is rather the imposition of the motor car into these environments defined by plentiful intersections (as Corbusier notes, 'cross-roads are an enemy to traffic'[46]) and tightly knit blocks that causes issues which 'have nothing to do with grids'.[47] Equally, the fixation on right-angled perfection re Corbusier's insistence in 'The City of To-morrow' that the universal city's defining feature is the grid, has been treated with ambivalence alongside disavowals; 'it can be grid-like or it cannot be grid-like. It makes almost no difference.'[48]

The city of Barcelona is a good example of grid urbanism that was largely designed before the advent of the automobile and is today returning to its original civic vision. Ildefons Cerdà, who is credited with the invention of urbanism as a field of study, laid out the plan for Barcelona's district of L'Eixample in 1859 using a repetitive grid geometry to guide the even distribution of key infrastructures like hospitals and schools. Manhattan's grid first emerged in a proposal almost a half-century prior in 1811, though it would remain an ethereal idea until development could take place in reality – 'the land it divides, unoccupied; the population it describes, conjectural; the buildings it locates, phantoms; the activities it frames, nonexistent'.[49] Less speculatively, English Puritans in the remoter environs of New Haven, Connecticut employed the ordering principle of the grid to immediate effect in the jurisdiction of their theocratic government.[50] Cerdà's Barcelona plan also resulted in immediate consequences as its construction introduced the luxuries of good ventilation, natural lighting, greenery, and sanitation in the form of effective waste disposal to a real and growing population of city-dwellers.

Faced with serious air pollution problems in 2014, the modern city of Barcelona implemented a new urban mobility plan to reduce traffic and simultaneously address issues of noise and air quality. The proposal involves the creation of 'Superblocks', 400 by 400-metre conglomerates of three block lengths that are closed to through traffic, opening them to pedestrians and social programs like markets, public squares, and local retail.[51] The Cerdà Grid makes implementation of the practice on a city-wide scale feasible, with each neighbourhood implementing a more or less tailored approach while using the same underlying spatial tactics.[52]

Like Manhattan, Chicago takes the imposition of the urban grid to an extreme. It ranks even higher than its eastern counterpart in the spatial order and rigid configuration of its street network, a world-leading 0.9 on a scale from zero to one in its approximation of a perfect grid.[53] Because of this incredible monotony, Chicago is famous for having one of the most intuitive and organised road systems of any major metropolitan area, consistently ranking among the most walkable cities in the US.[54] This regularity also proved efficient from the standpoint of real-estate development as Chicago went from frontier settlement to the world's fastest-growing metropolis in a matter of decades, becoming one of the most populous urban centres of the early 20th century. Daniel Burnham, lead architect of the World's Columbian Exposition, proposed a series of diagonal breaks to the unchanging geometry in his 1909 'Plan of Chicago'. Most of these were never implemented, though realised suggestions to renovate, widen, and extend numerous avenues have contributed to the desirable pedestrian environment of the city. Inspired by the European trend of Haussmannisation, this project to create a 'Paris on the Prairie' is remembered equally for its intangible qualities, from stirring prose to the visual appeal of stunningly poetic illustrations, and Burnham's distinctly American exhortation to 'make no little plans'.[55]

When studying aerial photographs of African villages, researchers have noted a more intricate geometric logic governing their layouts, a fractal organisation characterising natural structures like fern leaves and believed only to have been formalised in human thought in the 20th century. The intentional self-similarity of patterns in the buildings of the Nankani society proves this assumption wrong. Composed of a series of scaling cylinders rotated about a central courtyard, their domestic architecture follows the life of an inhabitant where the 'first rite of passage is from mother's womb to the birthing room, next is to crawl into the courtyard, from the courtyard to the village as a whole, and finally from the village to the world'.[56] Recursions abound in the Ba-ila settlements in southern Zambia where rings of self-similar rings define habitable enclosures. At the enclosure's centre, a detached ring for the chief and his extended family creates an identical settlement within the settlement. At the back of this ring, sits the chief's own ring-shaped house and within this single house there is a microcosm of the detached ring, the household altar representing the settlement of ancestral spirits who, likewise, host miniature villages within their houses, in a pattern that repeats indefinitely.[57] Similarly, the architecture of Logone-Birni in Cameroon is an assemblage of rectangles within rectangles, from the urban scale to the individual buildings to the rooms within. Deep inside the city's central palace, the throne is accessed via a recursive 'golden' spiral of progressively smaller rectangles whose scale maps onto the requirement for polite behaviour until, 'by the time you arrive at the throne you are shoeless and speak with a very cultured formality'.[58] The streets of Cairo have also been shown to follow a branching fractal pattern through successive additions of smaller alleyways from larger roads. Elsewhere, ornaments in Islamic architecture display the complex properties of five-fold symmetry on walls constructed centuries before mathematical and material proofs for the existence of such geometrical structures were understood and formalised in textbooks.[59] Through its many unconventional expressions and techniques, the embodied wisdom found in vernacular building should thus be examined as one of humanity's most complex knowledge systems.

42 + 43. Le Corbusier, 'Towards a New Architecture', F Etchells (trans.), Architectural Press, 1970, p.186

44 + 46. Le Corbusier, 'The City of To-Morrow and Its Planning', F Etchells (trans.), Architectural Press, London, 1929, p.37 & p.171

45. L Mumford, 'The City in History: Its origins, its transformations and its prospects', Secker & Warburg Ltd, London, 1961, p.423

47. A Fisher, 'Grid Cities Are Fine, and OBF is a Copycat', The Armchair Urbanist, 2 July 2022 [https://www.youtube.com/watch?v=4QlZx1sjg4Y], retrieved 24 July 2022

48. '32–Le Corbusier–6–Urbanism–Let's Demolish Paris (Again)', About Buildings + Cities Podcast, Listen Notes, 5 March 2018 [https://www.listennotes.com/podcasts/about-buildings/32-le-corbusier-6-urbanism-Wj1rTasKdfN], retrieved 25 July 2022

49. R. Koolhaas, 'Delirious New York: A retroactive manifesto for Manhattan', Oxford University Press, New York, 1978, p.13

50. J Glancey, 'How to Read Towns & Cities: A crash course in urban architecture', Bloomsbury, London, 2019, p.173

51. C Haubursin & D Roberts, 'Superblocks', Vox, 27 September 2016 [https://www.youtube.com/watch?v=ZORzsubQA_M], retrieved 25 July 2022

52. R Postaria, 'Superblock (Superilla) Barcelona', Cities Forum, 31 May 2021 [https://www.citiesforum.org/news/superblock-superilla-barcelona-a-city-redefined], retrieved 25 July 2022

53. G Boeing, 'Urban Spatial Order', Applied Network Science, vol.4, no.1, 2019, pp.1–19

54. 'Chicago Neighborhoods on Walk Score', Walk Score [https://www.walkscore.com/IL/Chicago], retrieved 25 July 2022

55. CS Smith, 'The Plan of Chicago: Daniel Burnham and the remaking of the American city', Chicago Visions and Revisions, University of Chicago Press, Chicago, 2006, p.98

Agents of Tradition

'Behind every style of architecture there is an earlier style, in which the germ of every form is to be found; all architecture is one, when traced back through the stream of civilisations, as they followed or influenced one another.'[60] English architect W.R. Lethaby here echoes the time-honoured wisdom of Ecclesiastes 1:9 in his syncretic work 'Architecture, Mysticism and Myth' (1892). After all, 'What has been will be again, what has been done will be done again; there is nothing new under the sun'. Italo Calvino makes a similar argument, stating 'the city is redundant: it repeats itself so that something will stick in the mind'.[61] Architectures, like living organisms, can trace their genetic inheritance through time. Across continents and throughout historical periods, similar solutions are found to the eternal issues plaguing the built environment. The Taihedian, otherwise known as the Hall of Supreme Harmony in Beijing's Forbidden City, was protected as the tallest building in China during the Ming and Qing dynasties.[62] Building higher than the emperor was simply not permitted. In a modern context, towers on the island of Montreal are not allowed to rise higher than the peak of Mount Royal at its centre. According to local politicians and planners, this rule is upheld to respect views to and from the mountain and preserves the special character of the Montreal skyline[63] which has always featured the mountain alongside the illuminated cross on its south-eastern face. St Pauls Cathedral in London has a radiating effect on the form of the urban fabric surrounding it through a policy known as 'protected views'.[64] These conserve local sightlines from important locations including the South Bank, Thames bridges, Parliament Hill, King Henry VIII's Mound, and various other points by limiting the heights and geometries of potentially infringing buildings through planning controls. Similar planning requirements exist for view corridors to the State Capitol in Austin, Texas,[65] to New York Harbor from Green-Wood Cemetery,[66] and are taken to an extreme in San Francisco, whose incredibly restrictive laws have stalled densification causing an explosion in housing costs. Here the negative externalities of an over-reliance on cautious, conservation minded design principles to guide the logical shaping of cities becomes evident.

King Charles III has long held an interest in architecture and city planning, and since 1993 has been implementing his traditionalist design philosophy with the help of architect Leon Krier in an experimental urban extension to Dorchester. The resulting model town of Poundbury, still under development, emphasises connection to nature and pedestrian experience with heavily cross-programmed urban spaces. Maze-like streets are meant to discourage the use of cars, though surveys have documented increased car use in Poundbury relative to surrounding districts,[67] while the adjacent buildings host a mix of stores, cafes, offices, and private homes. Well intentioned as its ideas may be, Poundbury has evoked unpleasant comparison to the previous century's company towns, who were often maligned for their top-down, autocratic approach to managing the complex issues of urban life. In like fashion it has been criticised as 'fake, heartless, authoritarian and grimly cute',[68] a sort of artificial Disneyfication of earlier feudal societies driven by a nostalgic aristocracy. Nonetheless, Poundbury also has proponents who dispute the accuracy of such claims.

The late English philosopher Roger Scruton has defended Poundbury's pre-modern approach to aesthetics and organisation. In describing its virtues, he argues that 'this is not great or original architecture, nor does it try to be; it is a modest attempt to get things right by following patterns and examples laid down by tradition. This is not nostalgia, but knowledge passed on from age to age. Architecture that doesn't respect the past is not respecting the present, because it is not respecting people's primary need from architecture, which is to build a long-standing home.'[69] Mumford has similarly remarked on the positive elements of traditional planning when set against the scourge of capitalist urban economy. In his analysis of post-WWII redevelopment, he noted that 'where the new spirit was modified by an older ideology, more concerned with social and aesthetic norms, the results were conspicuously better'.[70]

Logical Urbanisms: Slums to skyscrapers

'The city is not a problem, the city is a solution'[71] is the tagline to Jamie Lerner's 2008 talk, 'Sing a Song of Sustainable Cities'. Combining architectural and spatial imagination with the practicalities of governance, leadership, and political will, Lerner is revered for his influence on the improvement of urban life in his south Brazilian state of Paraná and beyond. Throughout his career, he occupied a host of key political, strategic, economic, and social roles in the country, which is now seen as an incubator for new forms of intelligent social, ecological, and urban organisation, and made him a 'legend'[72] of the design and planning professions. A leading example of this process is his home city of Curitiba where he served as mayor for an unprecedented three terms and rapidly developed a sustainable urban fabric that has proved uncommonly successful despite the city's heavy industry base. Always an anomaly, Curitiba became a model for the renewal of industrial blight 'by defying the spirit of the time. In the late 1950s and early 1960s, urban developers throughout the world, influenced by Le Corbusier and his followers, were remodeling cities to facilitate the easy circulation of people in automobiles.'[73] While most cities were tearing down central neighbourhoods to make way for the logistical nightmares of the freeway and motor car, Lerner sought new methods that were more sceptical of individualistic, auto-centric culture: 'The car is like your mother-in-law – you have to have a good relationship with her, but she cannot command your life. When the only woman in your life is your mother-in-law, you have a problem.'[74]

The spread of multi-lane highways that plagued and even decimated similarly sized cities elsewhere in the world was addressed through Curitiba's innovation of 'bus rapid transit'. Paired with a reorganisation of the existing street network to allow efficient lanes for getting into and out of the city centre, the time-saving system still retained slower roads for circulating local traffic on either side. This is an example of one of Lerner's cardinal rules for logical organisation to maximise mobility in cities; separating different functions 'so they are never, never competing in the same space – you have to have each system feeding the other'.[75] Apart from having designated routes that allow buses to arrive in central stations almost every minute while transporting over 2.3 million passengers, more than the subway systems of larger cities like São Paulo and Rio de Janeiro,[76] stops are 'metronised' to make the boarding process more efficient and accessible. This is achieved by equipping them with 'boarding tubes' that function like the turnstiles of train stations, allowing passengers to pay beforehand and access the bus immediately upon arrival, drastically improving performance and efficiency. Curitiba's world-class transit has been emulated to notable success in Columbia's largest megalopolis, Bogotá, which underwent one of the greatest urban transformations of the last half-century. Lerner has also worked with more than 80 cities[77] worldwide to implement their own bus rapid transit networks, making him perhaps the most influential figure to address the problems of urban mobility since Robert Moses with his strategies of social stratification and highway belting – the difference being that Lerner has created some of the world's most desirable urban environments while Moses may have done the most to destroy them.

Curitiba, being sited on floodplains, also faced a geographic challenge which Lerner contrived to integrate with his masterplan through a set of characteristically unorthodox solutions. Rather than fight the problem with expensive and ineffective levees (see New Orleans p.158), the floodplains were allowed to remain as parks. Curitiba now has one of the highest per-capita park areas in the world, with

56. 'African Architecture', Culturally Situated Design Tool [https://csdt.org/culture/africanfractals/architecture.html], retrieved 9 August 2022

57 + 58. R Eglash, 'African Fractals', Rutgers University Press, New Brunswick, 1999, p.26 & p.24

59. 'The Rediscovery of Islamic Pattern Genius', The Radius Foundation [https://radiusfoundation.org/the-rediscovery-of-islamic-pattern-genius], retrieved 9 July 2022

60. WR Lethaby, 'Architecture, Mysticism and Myth', Percival & Co., London, 1892, p.11

61. I Calvino, 'Invisible Cities', W Weaver (trans.), Secker & Warburg, London, 1974, p.19

62. PD Smith, 'City: A guidebook for the urban age', Bloomsbury, New York, 2012, p.129

63. DJ Rowe, '232 Metres and No More', CTV News Montreal, 21 September 2021 [https://montreal.ctvnews.ca/1.5594618], retrieved 9 July 2022

64. 'Protected Views and Tall Buildings', City of London [https://www.cityoflondon.gov.uk/services/planning/planning-policy/protected-views-and-tall-buildings], retrieved 18 August 2022

65. 'How Do Capitol View Corridors Preserve Sights Of Austin's Most Famous Building?', KUT Radio, 2 February 2018 [https://www.kut.org/austin/2018-02-02/how-do-capitol-view-corridors-preserve-sights-of-austins-most-famous-building], retrieved 9 August 2022

66. 'Minerva Casts Curse on Brooklyn Development', The Architect's Newspaper, 13 September 2010 [https://www.archpaper.com/2010/09/minerva-casts-curse-on-brooklyn-development], retrieved 9 August 2022

67. G Watson et al., 'Learning from Poundbury', Research for the West Dorset District Council and the Duchy of Cornwall, 2004

68. S Bayley, 'I'll Show You a Real Carbuncle, Charles', Opinion, Guardian, 7 December 2008

lands maintained by 'municipal sheep' who serve the dual purpose of economical tractor mowers, keeping vegetation under control with their grazing, and community service as their wool funds programmes for local children who are taught about the importance of recycling and environmental protection. The United Nations has awarded Curitiba its highest environmental prize for a separate scheme integrated with the public education system, and which achieves an astounding recyclability rate of 70 percent for the city's waste.[78] For Lerner, the keys to a successful city are simple: 'One is mobility, the second is sustainability, and the third is identity. If every city could take care of these three main issues, we could have more hope in humankind.'[79] Due to its profusion of inventive and successful 'urban acupunctures',[80] signature projects constructed from salvaged telephone poles like the Wire Opera House, and the pedestrianisation of key blocks of its downtown, Curitiba remains one of the most desirable cities in all of Brazil, boasting an unprecedented quality of life and satisfied residents of whom '99 percent said they were happy with their city' and that 'they'd never leave'.[81]

Before their own bid for the Winter Olympics, Lerner proposed a solution for managing the financial strain and infrastructural problems associated with hosting the grand event in Russia, based on his own experience with the World Games of 1997. 'We organised in six months, 60 countries, 122 television channels. And we didn't spend one Rubel on stadiums or on arenas. The stadiums were nature, and the games were held according to this beautiful landscape.'[82] Here, Lerner's most radical characteristic becomes evident, namely the effective reuse or conversion of existing resources that allow his plans to function on substantially reduced budgets. Relying on this simple philosophy, Lerner righteously persuades jaded politicians that 'there is no place which is an ugly place. There is no frog that cannot be transformed into a prince, it depends on the kiss of the princess.'[83] Despite his dramatic successes, some criticise the uncompromising logic of Lerner by associating him with the military dictatorships that controlled Brazil and other South American countries for much of the 20th century. Indeed, the incredible reforms that have been a boon to Curitiba might have been impossible under the inherently slow-moving political system of democracy. While the results speak for themselves, it may still be relevant to ask what freedoms should be forfeit on the altar of ecology and central planning controls. Depending on one's perspective, Lerner can be interpreted as undercover authoritarian or devoted eco-warrior when he proclaims 'the idea that action should only be taken after all of the answers and the resources have been found is a sure recipe for paralysis. The planning of a city is a process that allows for corrections; it is supremely arrogant to believe that planning can be done only after every variable has been controlled.'[84] But regardless of the difficult questions raised by his Jekyll-and-Hyde political career the 'Architect of Curitiba' has generated important lessons in urbanism that could be usefully applied in countless contexts.

'No city is perfect. Urban reality never quite lives up to the dreams of the ideal city planners. There will always be urban slums because cities are magnets, attracting people in their thousands with the promise of better opportunities – education, healthcare – as well as greater freedom. But even the cities of the developed world have much to learn from slums.'[85] Indeed, subtle or unconventional uses of urbanism to improve lives are not limited only to central planners and architects. In terms of resilience, density and walkability; many self-assembled settlements achieve qualities that can only be dreamed about in wealthier cities, and using materials otherwise destined for the scrap heap. As Jane Jacobs notes in 'The Death and Life of Great American Cities' (1961), the social phenomenon of the slum which politicians are so eager to wipe away through clearance projects requires far more nuanced handling – Potemkin offerings never succeeded in addressing root causes. Often, the urban renewal policies of 'Fight Blight' campaigns simply shifted slums from here to there or, worse still, erased 'neighbourhoods where constructive and improving communities existed and where the situation called for encouragement rather than destruction'.[86] The paternalism and superficial imaging which continue to characterise efforts at improvement fail to regard inhabitants as capable actors who, when allowed to work in their own self-interest, could bring about necessary change. To address the social ills of slums in America, issues which extend to cities throughout the globe, Jacobs calls for a discernment of and respect for the 'forces for regeneration that exist in slums themselves, and that demonstrably work in real cities'.[87] When such forces are built upon and bolstered, slums have proven themselves capable of radical regeneration even against financial and official opposition.[88] A leading figure of the Situationist movement fighting against the architectural establishment in France, Alex Moscovitch also questioned the hygienic obsession which dominated modernisation efforts through rhetorically titled lectures like 'Are the Slums of Paris Sacred?'[89]

Urban theorist Mike Davis takes a more urgent if pessimistic tack when addressing the proliferation of slums, which are increasingly becoming synonymous with cities. Citing the Club of Rome's Malthusian perspective in their 'Limits of Growth' report (1972), Davis paints a bleak picture of 'the late-capitalist triage of humanity' where 'increasing numbers of poor people compete for the same informal scraps... just volcanoes waiting to erupt'.[90] These slums, whose official definition according to the UN are settlements characterised by overcrowding, poor or informal housing, inadequate access to safe water and sanitation, and insecurity of tenure,[91] present the greatest humanitarian crisis of the 21st century. The problems faced in these habitations are not limited to architecture. As 'insecurity of tenure' suggests, communities remain at risk of the wholesale clearances practiced so disastrously in earlier times. The historic removal and relocation of slum-dwellers has been a mainstay of history, from the reforms of Emperor Augustus in Rome to the evictions of large populations by Haussmann for his renewal of Paris, and now occur regularly in developing countries where new districts, satellite cities, and prestigious global gatherings or sporting events like the Olympics have forced untold thousands of relocations.

In 1950, more than 100,000 were evicted from informal housing in Hong Kong, and between 1965–1974 Rio de Janeiro relocated closer to 150,000.[92] More recently, Robert Mugabe's Operation Murambatsvina (Move the Rubbish) around Harare, Zimbabwe in 2005 influenced populations on the scale of millions.[93] Such effect sizes are only possible through the unimaginable density of human life concentrated within these areas. In Mumbai, Asia's largest slum Dharavi now has more than double the population density of the Victorian era slums that existed in Bombay and, for that matter, New York, which were believed to be 'the most crowded spots on earth'.[94] Contemporary mega-slums like Kibera (Nairobi) and Cité-Soleil (Port-au-Prince) have achieved even greater densities 'comparable to cattle feedlots: crowding more residents per acre into low-rise housing than there were in famous congested tenement districts such as the Lower East Side in the 1900s or in contemporary high-rise cores such as central Tokyo'.[95]

Demolished in 1993, Kowloon Walled City hosted some 50,000 people stacked vertically on a 2.6-hectare plot of land in British Hong Kong, making it the most densely populated place on Earth for a time.[96] The site was an enclave within the larger territory annexed by the British government, and while this made it an important mediating border between Kowloon and China, it also meant that a traditional authority structure was never put in place. Out of reach from the building policies of Britain and Hong Kong and abandoned by the People's Republic of China in the communist rise to power, the urban

69. R Scruton, 'Why Beauty Matters', 2009 [https://vimeo.com/549715999], retrieved 8 June 2022

70. L Mumford, 'The City in History: Its origins, its transformations and its prospects', Secker & Warburg Ltd, London, 1961, p.420

71 + 74. J Lerner, 'Sing a Song of Sustainable Cities', TEDTalks, 7 February 2008 [https://www.youtube.com/watch?v=haKh9mCk3xk], retrieved 22 July 2022

72, 75, 76 + 77. J Lerner, '04.14.2010 Sustainable City, Jaime Lerner', Lecture, GSAPP Columbia University, 2010 [https://www.youtube.com/watch?v=mqOY6Hmgm80], retrieved 22 July 2022

73 + 80. A Lubow, 'The Road to Curitiba', Magazine, New York Times, 20 May 2007

78. 'Sustainable Development in Brazil?', 25 February 2014 [https://www.youtube.com/watch?v=r4sumpEqnlY], retrieved 24 July 2022

79 + 81. O Rousset & R Tucker-Evans, 'City of Dreams', Journeyman Pictures, 2006 [https://www.journeyman.tv/film/3287], retrieved 22 July 2022

82 + 83. 'TEDxPerm – Jaime Lerner – 9/11/09', TEDx Talks, 11 November 2009 [https://www.youtube.com/watch?v=V6B0U37ONpI], retrieved 23 July 2022

84. M Lydon, A Garcia & A Duany, 'Tactical Urbanism: Short-term action for long-term change', Island Press, Washington DC., 2015, p.25

85. PD Smith, 'City: A guidebook for the urban age', Bloomsbury, New York, 2012, p.171

86, 87 + 88. J Jacobs, 'The Death and Life of Great American Cities', Random House, New York, 1961, p.287, p.288 & p.13

89. S Sadler, 'The Situationist City', MIT Press, Cambridge, 1998, p.62

90, 91, 92, 94, 95 + 101. M Davis, 'Planet of Slums', Verso, London, 2006, p.201, p.23, p.102, p.92 & p.36

settlement within its territorial borders came to be known as the 'triply neglected city'.[97] Growing organically within this footprint, Kowloon Walled City functioned both as political symbol and anarchic society, bypassing regulations for taxes and businesses while subverting social norms through eccentric communal spaces littered throughout the maze of fused buildings. The city became an important issue in the lead up to Hong Kong's return to China in 1997. Following the traditional approach in dealing with the predicaments raised by slums, demolition was announced, residents were removed, and entrances cordoned off.

Such approaches are exactly opposed to what Kevin Kelly sees as the natural, technological progression of the city. The author says that 'propagating slums is what cities do, and living in slums is how cities grow', and 'the majority of neighbourhoods in almost every modern city are merely successful former slums'.[98] Through a process where 'ad hoc shelters are upgraded over time, infrastructure is extended, and eventually makeshift services become official',[99] slums have the potential to metamorphose into the vibrant future urban districts, something which is already happening in Mumbai and Rio today. Describing slums as the 'skin' of a city, a permeable edge condition of extreme efficiency that can grow and shrink as seems fit, Kelly sees them as maximally generative areas producing new ideas and wealth by housing many of society's most industrious, productive people.[100] Research on Mumbai has revealed that, contrary to popular prejudice, of families living in these areas '97 percent have at least one breadwinner, and 70 percent have been in the city at least six years'.[101] Such statistics are hallmarks of fast progress, providing insights into the motivation for the creation of slums in the first place. As Suketu Mehta remarks in 'Maximum City' (2004), a book on the potential of Mumbai, many are incentivised to move to these productive environments 'so that someday your eldest son can buy two rooms on Mira Road. And the younger one can move beyond that, to New Jersey. Your discomfort is an investment.'[102] Such spaces also represent freedom, both financial and social, from the falsely idealised rural existence many are fleeing.

Activist Kavita Ramdas has remarked on the liberating potential found in the depredations of slum life when compared with the alternative: 'In the village, all there is for a woman is to obey her husband and relatives, pound millet, and sing. If she moves to town, she can get a job, start a business, and get education for her children.'[103] Likewise in the favelas of Rio first generation squatters are in pursuit of a better life not for themselves but for their children, 94 percent of whom become literate compared with the five percent[104] of their parents who were deprived of the miraculous cultural diffusions of the city. Mass exodus to Rio's La Rocinha has made it the largest favela in Brazil, housing a population in the hundreds of thousands. Recent projects focused on providing electricity, running water, shops, schools, and public services, are helping to bring life in the slum closer to that found in the city it overlooks.[105] A similar situation persists in São Paulo, the largest city in the southern hemisphere with a population twice as dense as Paris,[106] where an urban core bursting with skyscrapers is flanked by deeply deprived shanty towns. Architectural ingenuity can also help raise the quality of life as in the waterside settlement of Makoko in Lagos, where the Floating School (2012) by NLE was designed as a case study for dealing with the high winds and floods that affect its stilted informal housing.[107]

Slums are not only confined to developing areas. Various complications cause similar settlements to persist in even Europe's wealthiest countries, including England, Spain, and France, whose slumming Parisian outskirts have been faithfully documented in the filmic dramatisation of 'La Haine' (1995). As Jane Jacobs has recognised, these conditions have historically formed the underlying foundations of many of Americas most prosperous urban realms, Manhattan being no exception. Engraved at the base of the statue of liberty is a sonnet by Emma Lazarus which reads 'Give me your tired, your poor/Your huddled masses yearning to breathe free/The wretched refuse of your teeming shore/Send these, the homeless, tempest-tost to me.'[108] Following in credence of this promise, tides of refugees from Italy to Ireland along with less talked-about Asian populations washed into New York creating slums whose exploits have been immortalised in the films of Martin Scorsese, and have evolved into one of the most impressive and dynamic urban environments ever seen. Industrial infrastructure on docks along the Hudson marked the gateway to the fulfilment and disillusionment of many American dreams while also serving as a 'haunting expression of the way in which this great maritime city was the product of transatlantic trade and European culture'.[109]

There may be no end for the applications of logic to cities. Theorists now agree that the virtual processes of computer-aided design no longer work within the immutable, ordered world in which Corbusier situated his urban planning, and must contend with the constantly moving realm of information networks which underly digital reality. These new logics are tasked with integrating architecture's boundless considerations 'in a convergent, non-conflictual way',[110] naturalising change, relativising novelty, and maximising effectiveness and performance. Undulating waves in parametric facades may, in fact, represent a shift from the static worldview of modernism to one perpetually in flux.[111] On a broader scale, Antoine Picon has formalised the concept that the digital world is analogous to a new form of space, and thus presents new possibilities for the interpretation and experience of architecture. Whereas previous decades saw the realm of the computer and traditional reality as distinct, Picon forewarns that we are experiencing a complete break with this earlier mode of understanding, digital and physical realms becoming ever less discernible from one another.

William Mitchell in 'City of Bits' (1996) proposes that architects become the designers of the virtual world,[112] which is forecast to define the human experience of space in the near future. Whether in videogames, whose immersive environments have become increasingly associated with everyday experience while graphics undergo an exponential trend toward realism, or the simple pervasiveness of electronic media through technologies like the cell phone, 'the physical and the digital are not separate, but intimately linked'.[113] Can the complexities of humanity's most important and enduring invention really be computable? Or are the promises of the 'smart city' yet another illusion in a long line of logical but ultimately detrimental evolutions to the urban experience. When our conception of 'the real is defined as the computable, is there any room for something that is not computable?'[114]

The predominant logic of the present-day might prove irreconcilable with a traditional, 'old-world' spirit of romanticism. The pursuit of high-status careers and a well-tempered life in technologically controlled, precisely planned environments may always win out against the highs and lows of spontaneity, characteristic of past ways of life and their tumultuous freedoms. As Warren Chalk writes in an open letter to fellow Archigram member, David Greene, 'architecture is probably a hoax, a fantasy world brought about through a desire to locate, absorb and integrate into an overall obsession, a self-interpretation of the everyday world around us'.[115] The elaborate delusions of architectural logic can doubtless realise much value from an injection of tradition, whose understanding is likewise invigorated by the application of a logical approach. A healthy dose of both can mediate the delicate balance of multiplicities essential to the experience of the urban fabric.

93. M Bratton & E Masunungure, 'Popular Reactions to State Repression', African Affairs, vol.106, no.422, 2007, pp.21–45

96. D Nosowitz, 'Life Inside The Most Densely Populated Place On Earth [Infographic]', Popular Science, 19 April 2013 [https://www.popsci.com/technology/article/2013-04/life-inside-most-densely-populated-place-earth-infographic], retrieved 27 July 2022

97. TL Lui, 'A Triply Neglected City', in 'City of Darkness Revisited', I Lambot & G Girard (eds.), Watermark Publications (UK) Ltd, 2014, pp.218–223

98, 99, 100 + 104. K Kelly, 'What Technology Wants', Penguin Books, New York, 2011, p.83, p.84 & p.85

102. S Mehta, 'Maximum City: Bombay lost and found', Headline Review, London, 2005, p.504

103. S Brand, 'Whole Earth Discipline: An ecopragmatist manifesto', Atlantic Books, London, 2010, p.39

105, 106 + 109. J Glancey, 'How to Read Towns & Cities: A crash course in urban architecture', Bloomsbury, London, 2019, p.185, p.179 & p.123

107. NLE, 'Makoko Floating School', 2013 [https://nleworks.com/case/makoko-floating-school-2], retrieved 11 August 2022

108. E Lazarus, 'The Poems Of Emma Lazarus In Two Volumes', Houghton, Mifflin and Company, The Riverside Press, Cambridge, 1889, p.223

110. T Ireland & E Zaroukas, 'Actuating (Auto) Poiesis', Systema 3, 1 January 2015, pp.34–55

111, 113 + 114. A Picon, 'Atoms and Bits', EKA Conference 'Space and Digital Reality', 10 October 2019 [https://www.youtube.com/watch?v=pLS2tcnnnXU], retrieved 27 July 2022

112. WJ Mitchell, 'City of Bits: Space, place, and the infobahn', MIT Press, Cambridge Mass., 1996, p.44

115. Warren Chalk, 'Ghosts', Archigram, no.7, 1966

Hometown Glory

'Urban planning is not gender neutral. Though "gendering" still refers overwhelmingly to a female-male divide, today it is taking on an expanded range of meaning within the household and the city. To change this, vulnerable women must have the agency to advocate for themselves.'

– Saskia Sassen, 'Built Gendering', Harvard Design Magazine, 2015

Women possess superior common sense and acute thoughtfulness, qualities often lacking in the grandstanding professions of the built environment. A city designed by women for women is a logical strategy for everyone, irrelevant of gender, age, ethnicity, or socioeconomic status. In Barcelona, mayor Ada Colau has implemented 'superblocks', where pedestrian traffic and public spaces have reclaimed civic life, relegating cars to perimeter streets and cutting pollution. In Paris, mayor Anne Hidalgo has implemented the '15-minute city', whereby re-localising jobs and public services within walking distances give residents more time for social interaction and family life.[1] In Toronto's R.V. Burgess Park, the local Women's Committee implemented an inclusive market where marginalised individuals can collectively strengthen community by addressing socio-economic dislocation.[2] From municipally-driven gender audits of everyday life to teenagers making photographic urban diagnoses, not to mention the apps available that highlight digital maps where women typically experience vulnerability, initiatives to reclaim inclusive urban spaces have never had as much traction as they do today. The reconceptualisation of cities must start from first principles, from a gender-based perspective of space and time and the recognition that cities are more equitable if more female voices are heard, especially in policy making.

The post of mayor of London, since its inauguration in 2000, has been occupied by three men – therefore the 'One and Only' logical voice for the position is Adele! 'Yes, Adele Laurie Blue "Someone Like Youuu" Adkins. She's already "set fire to the rain", now it's time for her to set fire to the heaps of pointless paperwork stopping people from getting shit done at City Hall. She may not have oodles of political experience (okay, she has no political experience) but if she can single-handedly save a music industry – she should be able to do something about London's housing crisis. For example: "570 pcm to kip in a tent in the corner of a stranger's kitchen in Clapham? Fack off! Don't pay it, mate." No, she didn't say that, but you probably just thought she did',[3] campaigns the music journalist, Nick Levine. Adele is the Tottenham girl made good, and London wants to hear her no-nonsense voice of logic and empowerment.

'Hometown Glory'[4] adopts the EU and United Nations' 'gender mainstreaming',[5] explores its consequences for urban mobility from Adele's viewpoint, and parodies its concept through the lens of Tottenham, the fictional football capital of London. Living up to her lyric 'I have so much to tell you', Adele treats all

facing page: The one and only Adele Adkins as Mayor of London.

following page left: A daydreamer's aspiration, the heart shaped housing in the clouds becomes a possible endeavour towards better living environments.

following page right: Near the end of the Victoria line the everyday London commuter arrives at a renewed Tottenham, the mayor's symbol of imaginative provision and participation.

1 + 7. A Cundy, 'What Would A City Designed by Women Look Like?', Women in Business, Financial Times, 7 October 2020

2. V Philips, 'What Would A City Look Like If It Were Designed Entirely By And For Women?', Education, Forbes, 22 March 2021

3. N Levine, 'Why London Deserves Adele as Mayor', Time Out, 22 March 2016 [https://www.timeout.com/london/blog/why-london-deserves-adele-for-mayor-nick-levine-032116], retrieved 30 September 2022

4. A Adkins, 'Hometown Glory', debut single on her debut album '19', 2008

5. United Women, 'Gender Mainstreaming', United Nations [https://www.un.org/womenwatch/osagi/gendermainstreaming.html], retrieved 30 September 2022

ELECTION
=1LU

Londoners as if they are old friends with whom she wants to catch up on her strategic plans of a non-sexist city, transcending traditional definitions of home, workplace and neighbourhood in creating a collective future. This phenomenon is an incredibly pragmatic recognition of urbanist Dolores Hayden's 'material feminism', a model where socialised housework and care of children and elderly relatives become productive components of economic life.[6] Adele similarly affirms that female-friendly spaces are more urgent than ever. In keeping with the spirit of Queen Elizabeth II and James Bond's London Olympic opening stunt, eye-lash parachutes provide shelter on the off chance that changing climates let the 'sky fall when it crumbles', while balloons become part of a 'secret mission' to protect women from harassment. Female-friendly cities do not make guarantees on 'keeping everyone from harm', but it is reassuring when Adele's big, almond-shaped green balloons are watching over us.

Adele cites recent defiance of impossibility for her heart shaped housing tectonics in the clouds, offering day-care centres as the ultimate inhabitable endeavour of happy days. Housing security 'would be hard to chase but good to catch' murmurs the 'Daydreamer'. Adele muses over the possibility of her 'Make You Feel My Love' policy where Amazon(s) become the custodians of health, sending out donations and municipal supplies of love, energy and fresh food to every marginalised home. She proposes public allotments, cooperative kitchens and community dining halls amongst the housing to promote an economy for systematising collective processes which are otherwise conducted in a desultory way, wasteful of human resources. Economies of time and proximity to basic services and infrastructures for women are essential in an equitable city, if we recall Jane Jacob's writings in 'The Death and Life of great American Cities' (1961). When the balloons land, the whistles blow, prompting the sport gardeners to kick and unroll the green carpet which creates the new Tottenham Hotspur football pitch. As each chequered grid unravels, a sporting spirit of agriculture and baking permeates throughout London.

previous pages: When the balloons land and the whistle blows, the urban gardeners are 'Rolling in the Deep' to create the city's new green grid.

facing page: Sending Adele's love and charitable donations of energy and food supplies across the city.

following pages: The Tottenham Hotspur Football Club 'cockerels' travel around the city collecting public opinions before being rallied at the 'Hello Call Centre' to administer support.

'Rumour Has It' that Adele concurs wholeheartedly with Leslie Kern, author of 'Feminist City: Claiming Space in a Man-made World' (2019). 'The feminist vision is not just where we make all of the care work that women do easier to do more of, but about how we can make cities that make that care work more easily distributable.'[7] Cities need to cultivate support for women who devote more time to unpaid care work irrespective of their employment status, income or education. And Adele goes on to assure that what has been seen is but a foretaste of what is yet to come. 'Hello, it's me. How may I help you?'

Few leaders have the humility and fortitude to interact with a large audience on such a personal scale on socio-political urban issues. Promoting gender mainstreaming is not just a 'Chasing Pavements' improvement, it is a long, slow process, requiring advocacy, bravery and competence, reaffirming the 'ABCs' of care on many fronts over a long period of time. Though always well intentioned, solutions might run the risk of reinforcing stereotypes in characterising how men and women use urban spaces, rather than encouraging new behaviours.[8] 'Rolling in the Deep' together in the football capital, Adele reminds us of why we all love her – 'We will stand tall, face it all together' to shape society and the urban environment in bold, imaginative and logical ways! Patriotic red, white and blue confetti with her personalised handwritten 'thank you' notes cascade through the air in recognition of London's Hometown Glory.

6. D Hayden, 'The Grand Domestic Revolution: A history of feminist designs for America', MIT Press, Cambridge, Mass., 2000, pp.3–6

8. J Gardner & L Begault, 'How Better Urban Planning Can Improve Gender Equality', Behavioral Scientist, 9 April 2019 [https://behavioralscientist.org/how-better-urban-planning-can-improve-gender-equality], retrieved 30 September 2022

CHASING PAVEMENT
ROLLING IN THE DEEP
ALL CENTRE
ELLO C
ELLO CALL CENTRE
HELLO CALL CENTRE

HELLO CALL CENTRE

Greetings From Guantanamo
YOU ARE NOW ENTERING GUANTANAMO BAY
CAT

Reimagine Rebrand Rebirth

'Eden can play little direct role in mediating climate change or biodiversity loss. What Eden can do is ground the lightning of thinking about how to do that and demonstrate that humans can have agency. And I think part of what Eden needs to be is a shop window of hope.'

– Tim Smit, 'Eden Project's Mission', 2022

Smit believes in dreams that can change the world through nature and sustainability, and has reimagined a 160-year-old exhausted clay pit in one of the UK's toughest regions into a living theatre of ecology. The rebirth of Cornish landscapes and livelihoods for multiple generations failed by the state is now worth '£96.2 million annually, which translates into nearly 3,000 full-time equivalent jobs'.[1] Instead of adhering to existing histories or emulating irrelevant models, Bilbao was likewise a rough city in serious industrial decline before shaping its own unique narrative. Juan Ignacio Vidarte, director of its famed museum, explains that 'there were no previous examples of using cultural infrastructure as drivers of economic growth. Guggenheim Bilbao had two key elements at its origin... One is innovation, not being afraid to do things differently if you think that it will bring added value. Even though Bilbao is a small city, it must keep aiming for an international profile while never losing sight of its roots.'[2] More than just housing an art collection, the museum rebirthed its city's self-esteem and subsequent urban dreams – some Basques even believe the Guggenheim helped bring a ceasefire to the ETA terrorist campaigns.[3]

Unlike Bilbao which has become a model for cities without cultural tradition, Matera has its own enticing narrative of rebirth as one of Europe's oldest living settlements since the Palaeolithic era. Once shunned as the 'shame of Italy', the ancient Sassi city of cascading, warren-like cave dwellings has been rebranded as Europe's Capital of Culture 2019, in addition to gaining UNESCO World Heritage status. Formerly defined by overcrowded communities riddled with diseases and crippled by poverty and lack of natural light, electricity and potable water, Matera's tough history has helped rescue the present. Beyond the paraphernalia of underground swimming pools and a contemporary art museum, 'one cave complex is occupied by a computer software company with nearly 50 employees, and an enormous 16th-century cistern complex under the main plaza, with chambers some 50 feet deep and 240 feet long'.[4]

None of the aforementioned transformations were perceived as logical at their initial inception, and there are always some aspects of heritage and identity more worthy of sustaining than others. As the New York Times reports, 'President Trump said that "it's crazy" that the United States spends about $13 million a year for each terrorism suspect held at Guantanamo Bay, Cuba, and added that he would search for alternatives.'[5] This came after President Obama signed an executive order in 2009, mandating

facing page: The former Guantanamo Prison is reimagined, rebranded and rebirthed as 'Camp America', an ironic health 'punishment' for the gluttony, greed and sloth of Trump voters.

following pages: Saving money by outsourcing US Healthcare to Cuba, Americans are sent to Guantanamo on 'health holidays' as part of the Trumpcare reform.

1. CABI Case Study, 'Eden Project Boosts Cornish Economy', www.cabi.org [https://www.cabi.org/leisuretourism/news/15941], retrieved 19 October 2022

2. The Report Company, 'Interview with Juan Ignacio Vidarte, Managing Director of the Guggenheim Museum Bilbao', Guardian, 9 October 2014 [https://www.the-report.com/reports/basque-country/united-it-stands/interview-with-juan-ignacio-vidarte-managing-director-of-the-guggenheim-museum-bilbao], retrieved 18 October 2022

3. Arts, 'The Bilbao Effect: How 20 years of Gehry's Guggenheim transformed the city', BBC, 16 October 2017 [https://www.bbc.co.uk/programmes/articles/1HL3drXNNWQVq7tpC6pMRsJ/the-bilbao-effect-how-20-years-of-gehrys-guggenheim-transformed-the-city], retrieved 18 October 2022

Guantanamo
CUBA
← CUBA
USA →

NASCAR
NASCAR
NASCAR
NASCAR
NASCAR
NASCAR
NASCAR
NASCAR
Leche
Sal
Vegetales
SAL
SAL
SAL
SAL
SAL
ODF766
LECHE
SUGAR CANE
16

Club
JUGS
THE GIRLS NEVER STOP
Princess

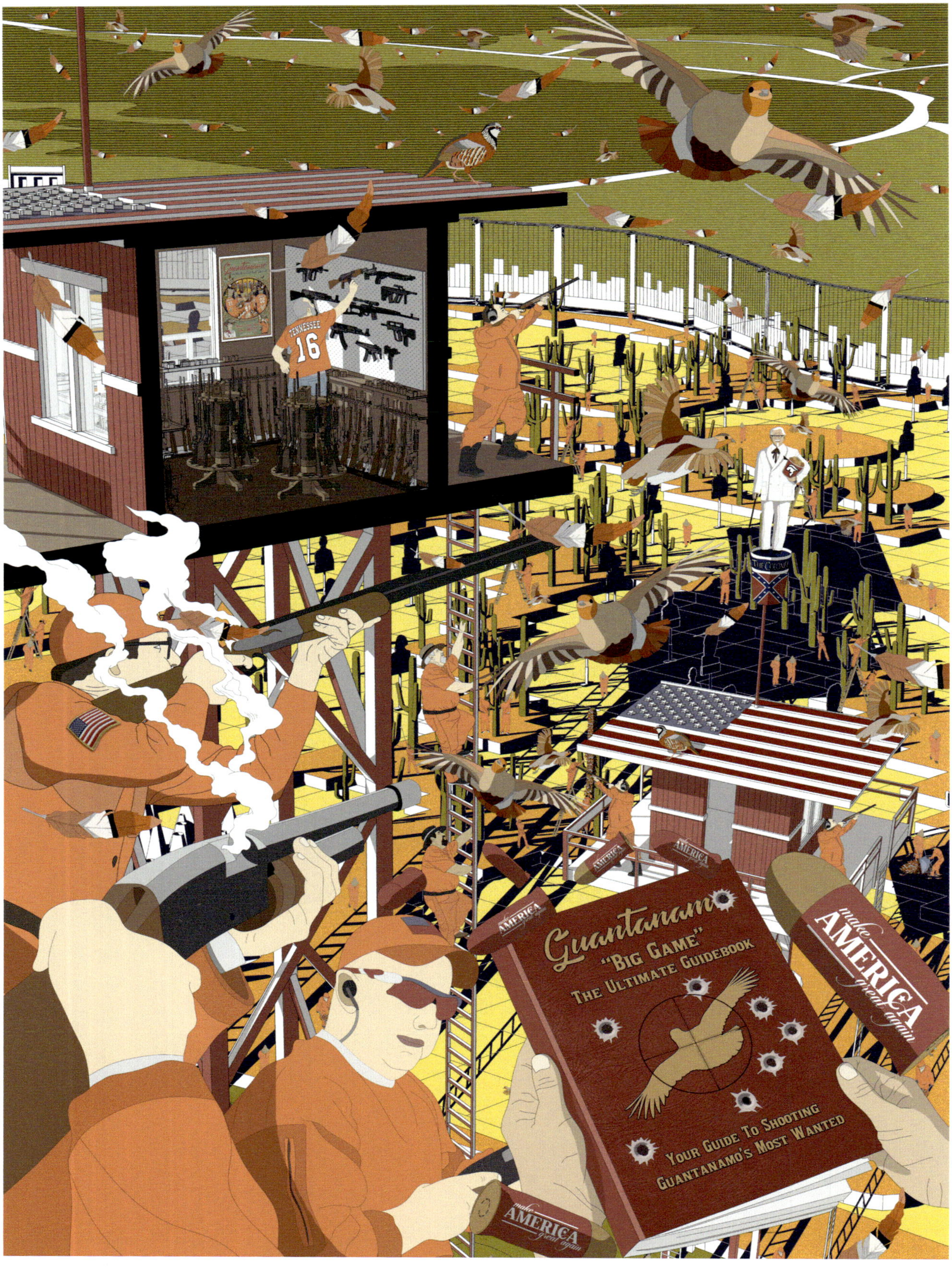
TENNESSEE
16
Guantanam
"BIG GAME"
THE ULTIMATE GUIDEBOOK
YOUR GUIDE TO SHOOTING
GUANTANAMO'S MOST WANTED
make
AMERICA
great again

the closing of its detention facilities. Trump is determined to end the extortionate economic torture at Guantanamo Bay and channel the savings to make human rights relating to healthcare a reality. The 'absurd yet possible' Trumpcare (American Health Care Act) incites all Americans to forgo the sofa and make a pilgrimage to the reimagined former detention centre as punishment for their health-related sins of greed, gluttony and sloth. The walk, not unlike the Camino de Santiago, might even be appealing to Democrats with its aims to discover well-being in life, to spiritually embrace nature, and to form a deep connection with the bastion of America's supremacy over the terrorism of ill health.

Besides the promise to 'repeal and replace Obamacare (Affordable Care Act) with something terrific',[6] outsourcing healthcare to Cuba is a shrewd strategy and would reduce a lot of the United States' federal spending. Fidel Castro launched the 'doctor diplomacy' policy after his 1959 revolution, partly to rebrand the communist image. The international outreach medical programme of highly trained healthcare workers has since become Cuba's most lucrative export, 'bringing in around $8.2bn annually. There are currently an estimated 55,000 Cuban medical professionals working across 67 countries.'[7] The US gets much needed medical expertise at non-American tariffs, and Cuba gets much needed cash plus a timely incentive to renegotiate the terms on the 1903 Guantanamo Bay Lease. Currently, while Cuba retains sovereignty, the US holds all control and jurisdiction over the territory.

Trump won big in the traditional ridings of the Bible Belt. The president, in turn, put his faith in their holy trinity of God, Bush, and Country & Western, to structure the reimagination of Guantanamo Bay. The Church of the Holy Spirit requires little description as it brews the best moonshine since the Prohibition era. The Church of Bush quilts the barren Cuban landscape in traditional tapestries of American patchwork, using cotton candy made from the sugar cane which Cuba has in abundance. Last but not least, the Church of Country & Western is all about familiarity and self-satisfaction: milk shakes at the Titty Bar, Kentucky Fried Partridge (KFP) from the Peep & Shoot Show, and sensual salting of the White Beach. Hunting for KFP is a healthy alternative for acquiring sustainable protein-rich food that serves the conservation of natural landscapes and the ethics of American gun laws. Trump's honest manipulations also call for increased 'torture' and 'waterboarding', code names for the intense exercise regimes within the health camp. Torturing the obese in hot tubs helps reduce weight and increases the output of sweat for salt production, creating the illusion of white sandy beaches in Cuba.

The logic of capitalising on honesty and integrity to place holds equal importance to the ubiquity of language used in rebranding cities – alas generations of deep social resentment and economically insecure communities have compelled Republicans to embrace Trump, his flaws and all his convenient theories. Reimagination can bring humanity to every place willing to plug into new beliefs, prompting the spontaneous rebirth of tough environments fraught with displaced populations, land misuse, and even oppressive regimes. Thought-provoking utopian challenges to redress the criticality of imagination can certainly pay big dividends – but there is a fine line between hope and hubris, and many cities have found themselves on the wrong side of this argument. There is no room for cynicism with the processes of rebirth and rebranding which, on their own, cannot discontinue poverty or pollution; instead, developing the humility to reimagine bold dreams with some logic in mind is a good place to begin.

previous page left: Trump supporters are led down the garden path of dairy farms to milk cows, thinking they are strip clubs.

previous page right: The Church of the Holy Spirit brews moonshine rum with local sugar cane, instead of the traditional corn used for Tennessee whiskey.

facing page: Existing surveillance infrastructures are re-appropriated for partridge hunting, which supplies sustainably sourced poultry for the making of KFP.

following pages: Sweat from soaking and sunbathing Americans is dried into salt, creating postcard illusions of the white sandy beaches which Cuba is famous for.

4. T Perrottet, 'How Matera Went from Ancient Civilization to Slum to a Hidden Gem', Smithsonian Magazine, February 2014 [https://www.smithsonianmag.com/travel/mater-went-from-ancient-civilization-slum-hidden-gem-180949445], retrieved 18 October 2022

5. P Baker, 'Trump Says "It's Crazy" to Spend $13 Million Per Inmate at Guantanamo', New York Times, 19 September 2019 [https://www.nytimes.com/2019/09/19/us/politics/trump-guantanamo.html], retrieved 19 October 2022

6. S Benen, 'Repeal and Replace With Something Terrific', MSNBC, 30 July 2015 [https://www.msnbc.com/rachel-maddow-show/repeal-and-replace-something-terrific-msna650576], retrieved 19 October 2022

7. R Waters, 'The Cuban Hustle: Doctors drive cabs and work abroad to make up for meager pay', STAT News, 8 February 2017 [https://time.com/5467742/cuba-doctors-export-brazil], retrieved 19 October 2022

Trumpcare
212-715-7290
call Donald
Get the special care you
deserve!
so much
winning

Guantanamo

Relocating Commonwealth

'Toni Morrison's "Beloved" powerfully evokes a past too painful to remember but which needs to be recovered through what she calls "re-memory" if that society is to reorient itself in such a way that it can come to terms with its own raced history. If such memories are not "re-membered" then they will haunt the social imagination and disrupt the present.'

– Catherine Hall, 'Histories, Empires and the Post-colonial Moment', 2002

The legacy of British colonialism has never been properly addressed, and it made an ignominious return to haunt the 2016 EU membership referendum. Conversely, hysteria about immigration statistics does not stand up to scrutiny. A regional head of the Bakers, Food and Allied Workers Union bemoans the racist rhetoric of the Brexit campaign – 'It's only the migrant labour that's keeping the food industry afloat. British jobs for British workers is a fantasy.'[1] Free movement within the EU has not harmed the pay, jobs or public services enjoyed by Britons but rather benefitted the British economy. It is 'far from being a "necessary evil" that we pay to get access to the greater trade and foreign investment generated by the EU single market'.[2] The economic plan for post-Brexit Britain orientates towards a revival of Commonwealth allies, irrespective of the illogic of geographical proximity. Prime Minister Theresa May, in her 2017 'Global Britain' speech, was desperate to reassure Britain of its 'unique and proud global relationships' with the Commonwealth, and the country's 'ambition to be a great, global trading nation'.[3]

Coveted industries and production facilities are satirised by overlaying the virtues of Commonwealth nations with the top Brexit Leave voting constituencies, forming four speculative New Districts: Canada in East Lindsey District, India in Boston District, Africa in South Holland District and Australia in Fenland District. In view of the UK's departure from the EU being driven primarily by questions of immigration and border control, the masterplan for 'Relocating Commonwealth' with the New Districts playing host to outsiders is one of illogicality, promoting the exact opposite of voting ambition. The absurd consequences of encircling represented by the square-shaped spatial arrangements underlines the 'blockhead' attributes of the population, so often regarded as conservative and inward looking. Meanwhile, each New District relates to a specific colour palette found in the respective relocated country.

The entrepreneurialism of the relocation exploits illogical, EU-incentivised stockpiling and bureaucratic regulatory madness. A coalition representing US dairy industries has warned that 'the European Commission must avoid dumping government-purchased skimmed milk powder and butter on the world market and implementing policies that undermine global dairy markets under the guise of protecting its farmers'.[4] The EU intervention of buying thousands of tons of butter each year at the taxpayers' expense

facing page: Knitted skies, hanging suns and radiator deer recreate a new micro-climate, the metaphor of a genuine force for progress and reconciliation.

following page left: Refrigerator buffaloes cool down the butter mountain landscape.

following page right: Hippos collect cotton from the hills to produce ropes, populating the orange sky of South Holland District with their wares.

1. J Chaffin, 'Businesses Fear Losing Polish Migrants After Brexit', Financial Times, 2 November 2016

2. A Travis, 'Are EU Migrants Really Taking British Jobs and Pushing Down Wages?', Guardian, 20 May 2016

3. T May, 'The Government's Negotiating Objectives for Exiting the EU: PM speech', Gov.UK, 17 January 2017 [https://www.gov.uk/government/speeches/the-governments-negotiating-objectives-for-exiting-the-eu-pm-speech], retrieved 30 August 2022

4. Editorial, 'The Government's Negotiating Objectives for Exiting the EU: PM speech', Dairy Industries International, 14 May 2020 [https://www.dairyindustries.com/news/34253/americas-ask-eu-not-to-intervene-in-smp-butter], retrieved 31 August 2022

FRAGILE
HANDLE WITH CARE
HANDLE WITH CARE
CE
CE
CE

began in the 1970s. Seizing this political opportunity, the unwanted dairy produce is reconsidered for the social and spatial imagination of the New Districts along with the imperfectly-shaped fruit and vegetables and appliances like vacuum cleaners which have not met EU consumer or energy efficiency standards. But are the accidental consequences of Brexit simply urban landscapes of false hope?

In East Lindsey District, EU-banned air conditioners choreograph snow of expanded polystyrene waste while the forever-red impression of the Canadian landscape is maintained by the continuous painting of maple leaf silhouettes. Vacuum-pumped forests and a sap-boiling industry are established to produce precious UK 'Made in Canada' maple syrup. In Boston District, heaters and humidifiers deemed 'too powerful' eagerly fabricate a hot, humid and tropical Indian climate while a green jungle is made from recycling electronic printed-circuit-boards. Banana cultivation, the key industry of the area, is designed to shore up public confidence in the UK's weakening food security after the upheavals of Brexit, COVID and the Russian invasion of Ukraine. In South Holland District, the sizzling dry African climate is manufactured with EU-banned radiators. Excess EU butter is moulded into pyramids and mountains – an illogical move that requires energy guzzling 'buffalo' refrigerators to stop the landscape from melting. Respite in the form of animated shadows comes from recycled cardboard waste tectonics inspired by African wildlife. On the slopes of the butter landscape are relocated vast vineyards and fruit orchards to counter wine and produce shortages. Finally, to experience life under the Australian seas, visit Fenland District; the marine atmosphere, albeit flipped into the skies, is akin to the Dieppe kite festival in France. A diverse assortment of aquatic, nature-inspired architectonics mingle with an array of inflatable fish made from plastic waste. Schools of light jellyfish made from EU-banned incandescent bulbs provide highly specified lighting conditions.

facing page: 'Jumping' flamingos press grapes for wine production, and generate energy to recharge the batteries of the refrigerator buffaloes.

following page left: Waste detecting owls look out for garbage to collect, building up the white sky from atop the maple trees.

following page right: Busy beavers paint everything in sight to recreate the red and white environment for East Lindsey District.

Relocating Commonwealth seems provocative and preposterous, but alongside the illogicality there grows a metaphor for celebrating cohesion and the collision of distinct social realities. Perhaps an analogy can be found in Beirut, Istanbul, Jerusalem, and Mumbai where churches, mosques and temples are concentrated within one square kilometre. In Berlin, the architects Kuehn Malvezzi referenced 'The City in the City'[5] (1977) with their 'House of One' which enables 'three monotheistic religions – related to one another, but also estranged – to engage with each other and with the secular urban communities'.[6] The utopian placebo of the relocation is not about identifying heroes and villains. Instead, it aims to 're-memory' the diverse perspectives of Britain's history. School teacher Dan Lyndon-Cohen successfully developed lessons about migration with his book 'Journeys: The story of migration to Britain' (2020) – children as young as five are able to show great empathy for the challenges that migrants face, and 'understanding how Empire has shaped our history is hugely beneficial in increasing tolerance and respect for our diverse communities. However, it is also a powerful tool for showing that whilst there has always been some opposition to migration, there are equally as many episodes of incredible solidarity and support between communities and a recognition that migrants have hugely enriched our lives.'[7] Illogical though it may be, the metaphor of Relocating Commonwealth can be a genuine force for progress and reconciliation if Britain can remember and acknowledge its legacy. Economic growth cannot take precedence over human conscience, and change should be guided by the traditional knowledge that it is best to avoid repeating mistakes by learning from them.

5. OM Ungers & R Koolhaas, 'The City in the City', F Hertweck & S Marot (eds.), Lars Muller Publishers, Zurich, 2013

6. MA Didero, 'Kuehn Malvezzi: Our architecture is anti-spectacular', Domus, 4 June 2021

7. N Morris, 'Children Must Learn About the British Empire at School to "Combat Racism and White Privilege"', Metro News, 17 March 2020

MAPLE
SYRUP

H2

facing page: Octopuses capture and distribute inflatable plastic to trap the multitudes of debris floating in the sea.

left: Electrolysis plants produce hydrogen while jellyfish light up the underwater environment of Fenland District.

following page left: In Boston District, scissor-like crocodiles cultivate a hot jungle environment by trimming electronic waste to capture solar heat.

following page right: APPLE monkeys jump from tree to tree, collecting bananas amongst the symphony of singing birds and other jungle creatures.

SHRUB
HUMIDI FLOWER
HUMIDI FLOWER
HUMIDI FLOWER
SOLAR LEAF
SOLAR LEAF
CRUNCH!
CRUNCH!
CHI CHI
HOO

MOTHERBOARD
FRESH
CPU
FRUIT
MOTHER
NATURE
APPLE

chapter three

Revolution + Marginalisation

'The ultimate hidden truth of the world is that it is something that we make and could just as easily make differently.'

– David Graeber, 'The Utopia of Rules', 2015

Guerrilla activities revolutionise and make unexpected use of urban spaces, implementing simple changes to reorder streetscapes. Marginalised groups, including but not limited to ethnic groups, form microcosms of culture and reimagine the city according to their specific needs, worldviews, and desires. From the inhabitation of Zuccotti Park in the 'Occupy Wall Street' movement to the various encampments which define sanctuaries and freetowns from Copenhagen to Los Angeles, guerrilla architecture has become an increasingly important aspect of 21st-century urban life. While its motivations and outcomes are topics for ongoing debate, such revolutionary tactics are doubtless effective in challenging the prevailing attitudes in space-making practices, providing crucial resistance to the often-blinkered pursuit of unsustainable 'progress'.

facing page: Guerrilla spiders are welding the broken electronics trimmings into tectonics which create resilience for the local community.

Though the work of starchitects may seem at odds with the inherently subversive agendas of true guerrilla architecture, they often share a disregard for expectations and authority, both surmounting perceived limitations to pursue alternate modes of organisation. Zaha Hadid's Galaxy SOHO development in Beijing and Frank Gehry's Guggenheim Bilbao have been dismissed as callously disrespectful to historic context but have simultaneously contributed to regeneration by improving economic prospects in their surroundings. Of course, the corporate capital that funded such icons was primarily monumentalising space for its own purposes – but, as the larger urban response bears out, aspects of these resources were subtly redirected by the purview of designers to benefit a larger cultural agenda. The stylistic tension between capitalist banality and avant-garde esotericism also reflects a balanced tension in political stances: conservative, market-driven traditionalism, and progressive liberalism, all of which are at play in the construction of dreams and disillusions. On the opposite end of the socio-economic spectrum exist more ephemeral and flexible architectures. Temporary refugee settlements, the slums of Mumbai, favelas of Latin America, and the Soweto township of Johannesburg are, out of necessity, founded on the shifting grounds of impermanence; where 'urbanism is not about grand vision, but about grand adjustment'.[1] Compared to a living organism, what urbanist Rahul Mehrotra calls the 'kinetic city'[2] is changing every day based on informal schedules emerging from the collective knowledge of a community rather than the dictates of top-down authority. In spite of scarcity, such environments still offer incredible opportunities for self-directed transformation with papier-mâché community halls forming in the voids of street corners over 10-day periods and wedding venues wrapping around cricket

1 + 2. R Mehrotra, 'The Architectural Wonder of Impermanent Cities', TED Talks, 29 August 2019 [https://www.youtube.com/watch?v=Kc6hkHGHQQc], retrieved 26 June 2022

3. PD Smith, 'City: A guidebook for the urban age', Bloomsbury, New York, 2012, p.169

pitches making temporary use of the city's public space. Such instantiations of elastic urban conditions may come even closer to realising Hadid's vision of buildings which are freed to move around the city than those by the architect herself.

Rather than creating permanent solutions for temporary problems, the practice of guerrilla architecture and urbanism can free resources from the static paradigms of conventional approaches, creating shared, moveable infrastructures more reminiscent of travelling fair grounds than stagnant swathes of suburbs. Such tactics are applicable in all levels of building practice and could address issues placing the greatest demands on finite resources, from the need for efficient housing to towering workspaces left disused. Even cultural amenities like Olympic grounds and university campuses that struggle to integrate with surrounding cityscapes stand to benefit from the innovations unlocked by guerrilla techniques. The World Bank has recognised potential in such approaches and funded work for ground-up improvements, providing water and sewage systems for millions in the slums of both Rio and Mumbai.[3] This move is reflective of a broader trend among established powers now opting for policies of incremental and flexible improvement rather than the clearance and redevelopment binary that characterised the previous century's response to difficult urban challenges.

Makeshift strategies relying on impermanence, speculative reuse and wit abound in difficult times. 'The BBC's radio transmissions to Germany contained not only news and comment but also drew on an unusual method of British psychological warfare, satire and humour, as a form of counter-propaganda. From mid-1940 until the very end of the war, pioneering satire feature programmes were written by German exiles under the close supervision of British authorities. They included Frau Wernecke – a sketch fronted by a fictional Berlin housewife, Kurt and Willi – a double act depicting two bungling Nazi propagandists, and other features pointing out inconsistencies in the Fuhrer's rhetoric.'[4] Inventive on-the-fly solutions were as essential in architecture as they were in media. After German bombing raids damaged Westminster's Parliamentary Chambers, Churchill quickly moved proceedings to the sturdier Church House, headquarters of the Church of England.[5] Just ten metres under nearby Downing Street can be found the subterranean network of spaces where much of the planning and organisation of Britain's World War II effort took place. Even with the mass of activity it hosted, the infrastructure's primary resource was, in fact, secrecy, as one direct hit would have wreaked havoc on operations had the enemy discovered the area's significance. Now covered by an unassuming parking lot, Hitler's Führerbunker played much the same role for the commanders of the Axis forces located in Berlin.[6] The city also houses more than 100 remaining bunkers and 25 miles of tunnels; while 90 percent of above-ground buildings and infrastructure were destroyed by the end of the conflict,[7] these hidden networks remain as a reminder of the alternative mirror-cities created by the construction efforts of wartime.

The clandestine city beneath Berlin finds a dark echo in Italo Calvino's imagination where Eusapia and its cadaverous twin play with similar subterranean poetics. 'To make the leap from life to death less abrupt, the inhabitants have constructed an identical copy of their city, underground... They say that this has not just now begun to happen: actually it was the dead who built the upper Eusapia, in the image of their city. They say that in the twin cities there is no longer any way of knowing who is alive and who is dead.'[8] Surreal built environments that are lifegiving rather than lethal are championed by the values of reconciliation and goodwill. Designed to function as a school of peace, the village of Neve Shalom in the Ayalon valley midway between Jerusalem and Tel Aviv seeks the protection of ordinary people marginalised by ongoing political conflicts in the region. Bringing together Arabic and Israeli-Jewish families under a co-operative framework of mutual understanding and collaboration, its founder Father Bruno Hussar has described the project as a dream to 'break down the walls of indifference or prejudice or misunderstanding' and 'build bridges of respect'[9] between the two communities. While retaining and incredible idealism and aspirations considered by many to be overly optimistic, residents are not unrealistic, impractical or naively utopian in their striving toward a better future. 'The Neve Shalom/Wahat Al-Salam experience humanises the conflict. It is called an oasis, but only as compared to other areas in the country. The village has many difficulties but at least we are not being broken. We do have personal squabbles as in any village, but we are living the conflict instead of fighting it.'[10] The growing dream of peace between countries historically marred by dispute was started here by a small group of citizens from both sides fantasising about coming together in harmony, creating a village 'to prove by its very existence that co-operation is possible'.[11] The emancipatory education it provides has since 'become a global role model of intercultural harmony, of teaching and learning to live together in peace'.[12] In 'Architecture of Peace' (2010), Aarjen Oosterman argues that such acts require bravery and determination, 'there are no guarantees and more disappointments ahead, but if we're serious about the global community, we better start finding out what architecture can help without introducing more or new conflict.'[13]

The power of transient inhabitants to transform the political and spatial dimensions of an area should not be underestimated. San Francisco is no exception as its relatively small population is the one most associated with the anti-establishment explosion of the 1960s, the advancement of LGBT rights, and the revolutions of the internet and personal computing. Harvey Milk, the first openly gay politician elected to public office in California, relied on the broad-minded atmosphere persisting in the city to act as a foothold in the movement he initiated. Beginning his political career campaigning for the Republican party as a devotee of free enterprise,[14] Milk was moved by the Castro District's coincidence of subcultures and hippie idealism which attracted a mass influx of gay populations, coming to realise that tight-knit neighbourhoods and cohesive commons were essential to the fabric of the city he wanted to create. By co-opting surrounding urban spaces and forging alliances with political minorities, seniors, working-class shop owners, and the Teamsters Union to accomplish mutual goals, he led a series of campaigns throughout the 1970s that would cement San Francisco as the liberal stronghold of American politics.[15]

Societal Revolutions

Being both radically transformative and recent enough to have not faded from society's collective memory, the American counterculture of the 1960s is the revolutionary movement which still holds the most sway over contemporary life. The attitude and values it stood for are summarised in 'The Graduate' (1967), a film where Dustin Hoffman playing a 21-year-old just back from college becomes disillusioned with his seemingly pre-ordained life. This character was a stand-in for a generation who had lost the thread of meaning binding previous times and sought alternatives to a commodified existence predicated on empty career pursuits in 'plastics'.[16] At the same time, trailblazers like Timothy Leary were popularising recreational use of newly-discovered psychedelics along with a message to 'turn on, tune in, and drop out'.[17] The diverse population that would become the hippies reprised past communal styles of living, reinvigorated with a new mission founded on music and the psychedelic vision. Haight-Ashbury became the focused gathering spot for their social experiment that would, in turn, be spread throughout the country by Ken Kesey and his band of Merry Pranksters, who delivered the counterculture gospel with new technologies like projectors, amplified recorders, and the informal shelters of geodesic domes.[18]

4. T Vermes, 'Beating Hitler with Humour', BBC Radio 4, August 2019 [https://www.bbc.co.uk/sounds/play/m00082zr?at_mid=iWWqGUTVDi&at_campaign=Archive_On_4_Beating_Hitler_With_Humour], retrieved 30 June 2022

5. House of Commons, 'Secret Session: Parliament in the air raids', UK Parliament, 17 September 1940 [https://www.parliament.uk/about/living-heritage/transformingsociety/private-lives/yourcountry/collections/churchillexhibition/churchill-and-ww2/secret-session], retrieved 30 June 2022

6. WL Shirer, 'The Rise and Fall of the Third Reich: A history of Nazi Germany', Secker & Warburg Ltd, London, 1960, p.1007

7. 'Hitler's Secret Berlin', National Geographic, 17 February 2009 [https://www.youtube.com/watch?v=xGGzSehAH-c], retrieved 30 June 2022

8. I Calvino, 'Invisible Cities', W Weaver (trans.), Secker & Warburg Ltd, London, 1974, pp.109–110

9, 10, 11 + 12. G Feuerverger, 'Oasis of Dreams: Teaching and learning peace in a Jewish-Palestinian village in Israel, Routledge, New York, 2001, p.124, p.141, p.124 & p.84

13. A Oosterman, 'Architecture of Peace', Volume, no.26, Stichting Archis, Amsterdam, 2010, p.12

14. R Shilts, 'The Mayor of Castro Street: The life and times of Harvey Milk', Atlantic Books, 1982, p.102

15. L Faderman & T Pichardo-Espaillat, 'Harvey Milk's Radical Vision of Equality', TED-Ed, 12 March 2019 [https://www.youtube.com/watch?v=wr3kUfW2fM0], retrieved 21 July 2022

16. M Nichols, 'The Graduate', Lawrence Turman Productions, 1967

17. M Pollan, 'How to Change Your Mind: The new science of psychedelics', Allen Lane, London, 2018, p.138

18. T Wolfe, 'The Electric Kool-Aid Acid Test', Bantam Books, New York, 1989, p.125

Also associated with the wealth of possibilities emerging from the psychedelic counterculture and the mental territories it unlocked was a new form of sci-fi inspired, future-oriented technological optimism. Buckminster Fuller was inspirational for a generation of thinkers and designers looking to embrace the tools of the future in the pursuit of a more sustainable world. Norman Foster, one of the many who looked up to Fuller as a mentor, said '(he) was the very essence of a moral conscience, forever warning about the fragility of the planet and man's responsibility to protect it. He was one of those individuals who fundamentally influence the way you view the world.'[19] Similarly Stewart Brand, creator of the 'Whole Earth Catalogs', admits to being a major if somewhat misguided evangelist for the growing environmentalist movement which widely popularised Fuller's efficient geodesic structures. In Brand's book 'How Buildings Learn' (1995), he reports 'with mixed chagrin and glee that they were a massive, total failure'.[20] Such setbacks did little to dampen enthusiasm for ingenious structures that would reduce ecological impacts by providing for densely populated human habitations.

Developed in tandem with the sci-fi imaginaries of writers like William Gibson, whose 'Neuromancer' (1984) envisions a cyberpunk future of self-contained cities, the Arcology movement has generated proposals for urban environments designed to operate with shared social resources. Unlike Neuromancer's 'vast cubes of corporate arcologies',[21] real-world implementation once again focusses on the efficient and environmentally sound geometry of the dome. To date, built programs in Arcology settlements have been limited to shared housing surrounded by vague arts-and-crafts studios and performance theaters, preserving the unrealised dreams of the original revolution.[22] Indeed, some have labeled the domed 'Arcosanti' prototype in the Arizona desert with the pejorative 'hippie design'[23] as it naively escapes from the harsh realities of urban life and agricultural production in an isolated setting reminiscent of Frank Lloyd Wright's 'Taliesin West' in nearby Scottsdale. In fact, Wright had proposed a similar model for a self-sustaining community decades earlier in his plans for 'Broadacre City'[24] which lamentably failed to account for the realities of population growth and other complexities arising from operating systems of commerce, agriculture, and transportation.

Buckminster Fuller's own 'Old Man River's City' project was an attempt to right 'the poverty-stricken, hopelessly obsolete city of East St. Louis'[25] by covering it with a mile-diameter domed megastructure, creating consistently pleasant weather for the homes, workspaces, and commercial thoroughfares occupied by its proposed 125,000 inhabitants. Incorporating advancements as varied as lattice-shell construction and psychedelics, the love for technology in such megastructural visions was presented, accepted, and engaged by a 'silent generation' about to be confronted by the Silent Spring. In the aftermath of the 1960s came 'a generation which realised that technology had to be integrated with metaphysics and culture, aesthetics and human anthropology – that indeed it was at the core of human anthropology and of the self-knowledge of man'.[26] The concept of 'spaceship earth', also popularised by Fuller, brought forward the necessity of harmonious existence with the broader environment, natural or constructed, extending the movement's utopian dream.

The counter-cultural vision of alternative city building also lives on, albeit in reduced capacity, through the annual 'Burning Man' festival. Supremely odd, dislocated from civil society and worshipping strange and wonderful forms of human expression, Burning Man is resurrected each year in a fully reversible encampment. Known as Black Rock City, the phenomenon exists for only a few weeks in the desolate Nevada desert. Built exclusively by participants in the shape of a pentagram with settlements arranged in a horseshoe formation around a central effigy, the camp 'alludes to ancient megalithic sites and city-states, as well as to Renaissance and mythic ideal cities'.[27] Fire, an agent of violent transformation in the urban context, here plays a role at the culmination of the festival where a 40-foot effigy of corporate authority, the eponymous 'Man',[28] is set aflame in a unique display of ongoing commitment to the consecrated revolutions of the 1960s. Here the practice of democracy and self-expression is facilitated through a bottom-up approach to design and an implicit recognition of the transformative potential of fire.

Fires and Monumental Changes

Perhaps the most electrifying account of urban conflagration belongs to Leo Tolstoy in his literary work 'War and Peace' (1869) and its description of Moscow's historic burning. 'The sounds of walls and ceilings breaking apart and crashing down; the sizzling hiss of the flames and the wild shouts of the crowd... flames licking up the walls in big, thick red sheaves or covering them with what looked like golden fishscales; the blistering heat, the choking smoke and the speed of everything roused Pierre in the way that only a huge fire can.'[29] Much like Tolstoy's revisionist retelling, London's fires have prompted speculations and continuous re-writings in the history books. Only a few years after the last bubonic plague pandemic had significantly lowered its population, The Great Fire of 1666 leveled between two-thirds and three-quarters of the city's fabric.[30] Urban displacement on such a scale would not be seen again in the English capital until the Luftwaffe blitzes of World War II. Like the post-war rebuilding efforts which elevated modernism to status-quo, the earlier coincidence of transformative catastrophes provided an unprecedented blank slate on which the architects and urbanists of the day could project brand-new possibilities for a city-spanning redesign. Though speculation abounds, historians generally agree that the fire which began on 2 September 1666 was of accidental origin. Starting from the house of baker Thomas Farriner on Pudding Lane, it quickly spread through to adjacent buildings whose upper stories were precariously cantilevered over the city's streets.[31] These wood and thatch overhangs extended upper floors until they all but touched the opposing buildings, devised by property owners to maximise the usable space on a given plot of land. While lawmakers in Westminster had banned the style of construction in preceding years specifically due to potential fire hazards, the ability and political will to enforce a prohibition was lacking on the side of London's independent authorities.[32] Despite the obvious mechanism for the fire's spread, a moral panic spurred on by anxieties around the ongoing Anglo-Dutch War engulfed London's stranded citizens. Blame was foisted on foreigners and Catholics, who were rumoured to be plotting an invasion and employing local incendiaries to feed the fire on purpose.[33]

Amongst the contentions and political jockeying which abounded in its aftermath, Royal Society founder and architect Christopher Wren used the fire as an opportunity to propose a revolutionary redesign. The plans for the new city which he presented to King Charles II were based on the earlier examples of Pope Sixtus V's axial plan for Rome and the formal layouts of the palace gardens at Versailles. By placing the Bank of England at the center of his proposal rather than St. Paul's, Wren illustrated an organic planning ideology in terms of a new order founded on rational exchange and capitalism, pre-empting London's evolution into a society where 'adventurous speculation and rapid turnover would become the key to great wealth'.[34] Concurrently, prominent writer and Royal Society member John Evelyn submitted three alternative proposals 'to restore London to far greater Beauty, Commodiousness and Magnificence'.[35]

To the dismay of Wren and other visionaries, city-wide schemes foundered due to issues of cost and practicality. Indeed, the strict organisation of the Baroque layouts which they proposed seemed at odds with the sensibilities of 17th-century London – Wren's plan was rejected by the king after a mere three

19. A Beard, 'Life's Work: Norman Foster', Harvard Business Review, 1 March 2011 [https://hbr.org/2011/03/lifes-work-norman-foster], retrieved 18 July 2022

20. S Brand, 'How Buildings Learn: What happens after they're built', Phoenix Illustrated, London, 1997, p.135

21. W Gibson, 'Neuromancer', Harper Collins, London, 1986, p.5

22. J Stein, 'The Sustainable City of the Desert of Arizona', FLORB, 6 March 2018 [https://www.youtube.com/watch?v=7UOONQ8Ewbw], retrieved 18 July 2022

23. C Skinner, 'Architecture Ahead of Its Time – The Paolo Soleri Amphitheater', TEDxABQ, 28 October 2014 [https://www.youtube.com/watch?v=AYnP_29xjrk], retrieved 18 July 2022

24. FL Wright, 'An Organic Architecture: The architecture of democracy', Lund Humphries, London, 2017, pp.349–361

25. J Baldwin, 'BuckyWorks: Buckminster Fuller's ideas for today', John Wileys & Sons, 1996, p.185

26. PF Drucke, 'Adventures of a Bystander', Routledge, New York, 2017, p.256

27 + 28. PD Smith, 'City: A guidebook for the urban age', Bloomsbury, New York, 2012, p.379 & p.377

29. L Tolstoy, 'War and Peace', A Briggs (trans.), Penguin Books, New York, 2006, p.1274

30, 31, 32 + 33. N Hanson, 'The Great Fire of London: In that apocalyptic year, 1666', John Wiley & Sons, Hoboken, NJ., 2002, p.169, p.179, p.32 & p.68

34, 35 + 39. L Mumford, 'The City in History: Its origins, its transformations and its prospects', Secker & Warburg Ltd, London, 1961, p.404, p.593 & p.220

days' consideration. The dissonance between the utopian plans generated in the fire's aftermath and the urban reality of London's characteristic disorderliness is best summarised by historian Sigfried Giedion who remarked that 'if any city can be accused of having grown irrationally, that city is London'.[36] Since London was not owned by any one person and the political apparatus of building controls had yet to be introduced, landowners largely conserved the geometry of its existing medieval streets, simply building upon the footprints of their incinerated properties.[37] Radical change was limited to the visual and material character of the city, as The Rebuilding of London Act 1666 nominally required architects to use brick and stone, banning the use of wood on exterior walls as well as jetties and overhangs to limit future catastrophes.[38] With the assistance of Nicholas Hawksmoor, however, Wren did gain the commission to rebuild London's 52 parish churches including St Paul's Cathedral which marked the new city's rise from the ashes.

Similar to the scapegoating which took place in reaction to London's fire, The Great Fire of Rome in 64 AD was rumoured to have been set by the Emperor Nero himself. Lewis Mumford went so far as to label it 'systematic slum clearance', a debacle which 'naturally increased the housing shortage and tightened the hold of rapacious landlords'.[39] The conflagration spread to at least 10 of Rome's 14 urban districts, and prompted Nero to expand plans for his ambitious Domus Transitoria by two-and-a-half square kilometres.[40] The palace was already massive enough to span two of Rome's seven hills, but after it was damaged in the fire Nero's ambitions for the ostentatious complex grew to engulf a third. Whether this expansion could have been a legitimate motive for starting the fire remains a topic of historical debate, though the fact the Nero could simply have requisitioned the necessary lands makes the argument unlikely.

Nonetheless, in the subsequent rebuilding 'Nero had the authority which, in similar circumstances, Wren lacked, and he was quick to seize his opportunity'.[41] Constructing neighbourhoods in the Greek style to which he was partial and instantiating a new set of rules for building to combat speculation, the effects of Nero's scheme can be discerned in Rome's layout to this day. The project generated significant architectural advancements through the coincidence of two circumstances, one of which was the blank slate provided by the fire's destruction, as in London which, through his individual buildings rather than overarching urban plan, secured the legacy of Wren. The other was a contemporaneous progression in both material and building techniques engendered by the volume of construction which ensued. Both would stimulate an unprecedented expansion in the fields of architecture and urbanism, described as a 'revolution in architectural technology and taste, of which Nero's buildings were the first public expression'.[42] Along with the imperial residences upon which so much money and attention was lavished, 'the time was ripe for the replacement of the ramshackle tenement houses of old Rome by the neat, orderly insulae which the newly developed concrete medium had made possible. The Great Fire furnished the occasion; and if it was, broadly speaking, a new Rome that rose from the ashes, Nero most certainly deserves a substantial share of the credit.'[43] While the motivating factors behind Rome's destruction and renewal during Nero's rule remain unclear and London's burning is widely thought to have resulted from a chance accident, fire has also been used as a deliberate tool of urban transformation.

In 1871, the Great Fire of Chicago would create an architectural revolution for a dawning modern age. The 'flimsily constructed boards'[44] comprising the barn where it started mirrored the era's largely wooden urban fabric, which after being burned away, made room for developments in radical technologies like the steel frame and elevator. In the fire's aftermath, figures as prominent as Frederick Law Olmsted criticised Chicago's poor building practices, accusing officials of allowing structures whose 'walls were thin, and were often overweighted with gross and coarse misornamentation'.[45] Standards were quickly rewritten to ensure higher quality in future construction, making Chicago a world leader in engineering and fireproofing innovations, creating the first skyscrapers and forever altering the perception of American metropolises. At the heart of the burgeoning social revolution 'was the image of the city in extremis, the urban creation of civilisation and progress, power and order, that was constantly prey to disruption and disaster'.[46]

Fire can also be used defensively, as in the 1812 French invasion of Russia. After suffering defeat in the Battle of Borodino, Russian troops evacuated Moscow along with remaining residents leaving the city empty when Napoleon and his Grande Armée arrived at its gates and proclaimed themselves conquerors. Expecting to be greeted by dignitaries formally offering Russia's surrender, Napoleon instead discovered an abandoned Kremlin where he would take up residence as small fires began to escalate out of control in surrounding neighbourhoods. City governor Fyodor Rostopchin was rumoured to have ordered the burning of key buildings, deliberately freeing criminals from Moscow's prisons for the task. Prior to the French occupation however, fires were being combatted by inhabitants almost daily and, lacking oversight, would have inevitably spread into a city-wide conflagration. Intentional or not, the destruction of the city's strategic infrastructure and food reserves proved invaluable from a military perspective, eventually causing Napoleon's voluntary retreat under the disastrous winter weather. As Napoleon insists in his memoirs, 'I had undertaken the expedition to fight against armed men, not against nature in the violence of her wrath. I defeated armies, but I could not conquer the flames, the frost, stupefaction, and death!'[47] Contingencies leading to the sacred site's destruction generated an incredible solution to the threat of conquest, the loss of beloved palaces and monuments ultimately strengthening the Russian cause. As Madame de Stael recognised, 'Moscow's very misfortune regenerated the Russian Empire, that holy city perished like a martyr, whose blood once shed grants new strength.'[48]

Fiction and Art: Identifying the enemy

'You would think the plumbers had finished their job and gone away before the bricklayers arrived; or else their hydraulic systems, indestructible, had survived a catastrophe, an earthquake, or the corrosion of termites.'[49] The city of Armilla resembles a forest of plumbing sprouting white porcelain fruits, composed only of 'water pipes that rise vertically where the houses should be and spread out horizontally where the floors should be'.[50] From its numerous 'Thin Cities' suspended between strings, ropes and catwalks, to Baucis, the inhabitation rising above a woodland and resting only on 'long flamingo legs',[51] Calvino's text makes palpable the tension between urban and natural environments. The poetic revolution of buildings without walls and ceilings foregrounds the overlooked and neglected elements which allow architecture to function. Much like these hidden service networks, there are minority activities and social realms accessible only to those in-the-know. In this sense, a city is really about the overlay of thousands of subtle maps, most of which are never drawn. Cartography has always been about editing and selectivity, used to understand contexts that have been marked out to tell certain, often convenient stories.

For better or worse, writer Ayn Rand holds claim to the most well-known portrayal of an architect in popular culture. Thought to be based on the personality of Frank Lloyd Wright, Howard Roark, architect and protagonist of 'The Fountainhead' (1943), has become synonymous with a certain brand of 'extremely reprehensible political messaging'.[52] The exceptionally polarising book has still found proponents

36. S Giedion, 'Space, Time and Architecture: The growth of a new tradition', Harvard University Press, Cambridge, Mass., 1956, p.618

37. K Downes, 'Sir Christopher Wren', Whitechapel Art Gallery, Trefoil Books, London, 1982, p.60

38. 'Charles II, 1666: An act for rebuilding the Citty of London', Statutes of the Realm, vol.5, Great Britain Record Commission, 1628–80, pp.603–612

40. 'Jul 18, 64 CE: Great Fire of Rome', Education, National Geographic Society, 28 September 2022 [https://education.nationalgeographic.org/resource/great-fire-rome], retrieved 16 July 2023

41, 42 + 43. JB Ward-Perkins & A Boëthius, 'Roman Imperial Architecture', 2nd integrated ed., The Pelican History of Art, Penguin, Harmondsworth, 1983, p.59, p.56 & p.61

44 + 46. CS Smith, 'Urban Disorder and the Shape of Belief: The Great Chicago Fire, the Haymarket bomb, and the model town of Pullman', University of Chicago Press, Chicago, 1995, p.19 & p.4

45. JJ Pauly, 'The Great Chicago Fire as a National Event', American Quarterly, vol.36, no.5, 1984, pp.668–683

47. EAD Las Cases, 'Memoirs of the Life, Exile, and Conversations of the Emperor Napoleon' (vol. III), Project Gutenberg, 17 January 2017 [https://www.gutenberg.org/files/53969/53969-h/53969-h.htm], retrieved 18 July 2022

48. Mdm de Staël, 'Ten Years' Exile', Project Gutenberg, 8 July 2005

49, 50 + 51. I Calvino, 'Invisible Cities', W Weaver (trans.), Secker & Warburg Ltd, London, 1974, p.49 & p.77

52. '13–Ayn Rand's "The Fountainhead"–1 of 2', About Buildings + Cities Podcast, Listen Notes, 30 January 2017 [https://www.listennotes.com/podcasts/about-buildings/13-ayn-rands-the-yo_sUv145-i], retrieved 26 June 2022

who revere Rand's ideology of objectivism, wholeheartedly embracing a worldview prizing self-reliance and individual accomplishment above all else. To the dismay of millions, modern US congressmen from Paul Ryan to Rand Paul follow in the footsteps of Ronald Reagan by citing the work as an influence. Roark has also popped up in discussions of the divisive Donald Trump,[53] even though lewdness and braggadocio are traits far removed from the Randian hero. Ellsworth Toohey, the novel's architecture critic antagonist was allegedly based on the real-life academic and historian Lewis Mumford,[54] while Henry Cameron, Roark's failed mentor, was inspired by the tribulations of Louis Sullivan. Lying on his deathbed the older architect laments the thought of his buildings fading into obscurity and encourages Roark, in the manner of 'The Graduate', to embrace the future wonder-material of plastics.[55] It seems that in times of great strain or emotional torment the heroes of capitalism must, like the wizened old businessman of the Hoffman film, talk about the petrochemicals industry. On top of this, the obsession with monetary measurement as a marker of absolute value have made the sentiments in 'The Fountainhead' farcical in a late-stage capitalist context, the questionable values entrenched by Rand's writings in post-war American life long ago identified and rebelled against by the counterculture movement.

Another spatial trend tailored to libertarian proponents of Ayn Rand's objectivist philosophy is the dream of a floating utopia, free from taxes and burdensome associations with the welfare state. An almost unrecognisable facsimile combining the opulence of the 'Titanic' with the floating megastructures of Buckminster Fuller and the Metabolists, modern instantiations of the sea-faring city forego the provision of honourable services as the UK's pirate radio stations and more grandiose masterplans once did, instead pandering to a wealthy elite seeking refuge from fiscal regulations. The 1960's self-sufficient 'Sea City' aspired to create a community of 30,000 off the Norfolk coast within a shared aerodynamic infrastructure, integrating housing and provisions for power, services for public life that included schools, hospitals, football fields, a marine zoo, and sluice gates to regulate water conditions.[56] Where Fuller's 'Triton City' was likewise concerned with practically combining social, economic, and environmental factors, avoiding exorbitant land costs to create a new form of affordable marine habitation,[57] 'Freedom Ship' almost exclusively advertises itself as a tax haven for those setting sail in the luxurious condominiums stacked onboard. The colossal late-20th-century cruise liner was projected to support 1,800 metres of free-floating urbanity as an integrated colony of libertarian seasteaders. But as easily as the proposal began to generate revenue, its reveries of water-borne freedom evaporated in a cloud of scandal and financial complications. As China Mieville points out in the text 'Floating Utopias', 'it is only one of countless recent dreams of a tax-free life on the ocean wave: advocates of seasteading are disproportionately adherents of one or other flavor of libertarianism, that peculiarly American philosophy of venal petite-bourgeois dissidence... It is a small schadenfreude to know these dreams will never come true. There are dangerous enemies, and there are jokes thrown up by history. The libertarian seasteaders are a joke.'[58] The insidious aimlessness of a supposedly utopic life on board even commercial cruise ships also provides occasion for comment. Advertised as the ultimate experience of freedom, the abdication of responsibility afforded by the environments of luxury craft produces, despite best efforts, a peculiarly modern atmosphere of anhedonia, 'a blend of relaxation and stimulation, stressless indulgence and frantic tourism, that special mix of servility and condescension that's marketed under configurations of the verb "to pamper"'.[59]

By contrast, filmmaker Jacques Tati's interpretation of the disproportionate indulgences afforded by modern urban life is highly sceptical. The wit of his critique first appeared in 'Monsieur Hulot's Holiday' (1953), set in a resort town with a series of characters escaping the metropolis in increasing desperation for refuge by the seaside. The urban condition only became the foreground in his following film, 'Mon Oncle' (1958) ostensibly analysing the fractured relationship between surviving city centres, post-war redevelopments, and their inhabitants. Opening on a group of dogs scrounging in the bins of a traditional European square, scenes progress out of the urban core past fields of concrete flats before arriving at a gated modern residence filled with uncomfortable designer furniture and all manner of impractical appliances. Circular windows resembling a pair of eyes are directed at the neighbouring yard and below a barred balcony creates the impression of a prison.[60] The film continues to critique the absurdities of technology and modern living through a series of clever spatial jokes. While his wife scours and dusts every prop that emerges, the company-man father drinks his coffee, lights his cigarette, dons his hat, driving gloves, and briefcase, retrieves his car from his purpose built shed and joins a line of traffic before depositing his son in a similar line to enter his factory-style schoolhouse. He finally arrives in a newly painted rectangular parking space at the antiseptic 'Plastac' hose factory, while the persistent buzzing and background humming of the mechanical environment is heard throughout.

As the story progresses, this style of living is contrasted with that of the older town centre where residents still shop at markets and sweep the streets by hand. Above this activity, Tati's character Monsieur Hulot, the fish-out-of-water uncle, must ascend a maze of staircases and clothes lines to reach his rooftop apartment in a flat-on elevation shot that Wes Andersen recently paid homage to in 'The French Dispatch' (2021). By the end of the film the traditional city is being torn down with jackhammers, mechanical implements of the modernist revolution, and Hulot departs from the old world in a shiny new sedan with his nephew and 'Plastac' employee brother-in-law – presumably following his example to become a company man of the future. In Tati's subsequent release 'Playtime' (1967), every aspect of the city's environment has been revolutionised. Glass skyscrapers have created a swathe of transparent barriers and the sprawling bureaucracy of the office cubicle has overtaken public parks and boulevards. From the travel posters advertising trips to London, Hawaii, Mexico, and Stockholm the same skyscrapers block the specificities of regional context, while the marble columns of antiquity have been co-opted for the design of a foot-operated trash can. Even the city being filmed, which turns out to be a heightened version of Paris, is rendered anonymous. The ornate Pont Alexandre III is entirely obscured by a grey office block and the Eifel tower is seen only in the reflection from a swinging glass door.[61] Every detail of the film subtly critiques the barriers and superstitions, anxieties, and follies of status-quo consumer society with exceptional lightness, always using a humorous touch and without stooping to cynicism.

Presciently, King Vidor's 'The Crowd' (1928) predicts the mass disillusionment created by an impersonal metropolis consisting of building upon building of endless office spaces, all filmed before the colossal influence of digital communication and computer networks could even be dreamed of. Hariton Pushwagner likewise explores the extremes of modern densification and conformity in 'Soft City' (2016). Taking the form of a graphic novel, the narrative thread of 'Soft City' depicts an urban entity dominated by oppressive grids of flat square windows, parking garages, and bumper-to-bumper multi-lane traffic all orchestrated in the service of the archetypal corporate workplace Soft Inc. Here, life has been simplified down to a series of rote tasks, aided by the comforts of 'Soft Consume' pills and under the watchful eye of the Boss who leads the endless sea of oblivious workers behind his massive surveillance-screened control panel. 'The machine is calling'[62] reads above the image of the Soft Electric clock as Baby Bingo rises and surveys the rows of identical windows of the surrounding city. The daily routine – 'get up, take a pill, kiss the baby, go to work, punch in, punch out, go home, kiss the baby, go to sleep' – allows for

53. M Harle, 'Trump at the Movies: Dismantling Ayn Rand's The Fountainhead', Cineaste Magazine, vol. XLII, no.3, September 2017 [https://www.cineaste.com/summer2017/trump-at-the-movies-ayn-rand-fountainhead], retrieved 1 July 2022

54. W Olson, 'The Writerly Rand', Reason Magazine, February 1998

55. A Rand, 'The Fountainhead', Signet, New York, 1993, p.295

56. 'Houses of the Future: British post-war architecture from modernism to futurism', National Science and Media Museum, 3 September 2021 [https://www.scienceandmediamuseum.org.uk/objects-and-stories/british-post-war-architecture-modernism-futurism], retrieved 17 October 2023

57. J Baldwin, 'BuckyWorks: Buckminster Fuller's ideas for today', John Wiley & Sons, 1996, p.186

58. C Mieville, 'Floating Utopias: Freedom and unfreedom of the seas', in 'Evil Paradises: Dreamworlds of Neoliberalism', M Davis & DB Monk (eds.), The New Press, New York, 2008, pp.330–343

59. DF Wallace, 'A Supposedly Fun Thing I'll Never Do Again: Essays and Arguments', Abacus, London, 1998, p.272

60. J Tati, 'Mon Oncle', Gaumont Film Company, 1958

61. J Tati, 'Playtime', Specta Films, 1967

62. KL Green, 'I Can't Help It: I've got a military-industrial complex', comiXology, 2010

no deviation and 'everyone frog marches to the same rhythm, ruled by the clock (if you're late, you're fired)'.[63] Repetitive, unchanging, uninflected, and uniform, Pushwagner's future city inspires far less joie de vivre than the previous examples.

Other conjectures about existence confined to a perfectly devised, uniform architecture abound in post-war-era writings. Increasing population, new construction technologies, emptying countryside and subsequently densified cities led to never-before-seen forms of housing. 'A new social type was being created by the apartment building, a cool, unemotional personality impervious to the psychological pressures of high-rise life, with minimal needs for privacy, who thrived like an advanced species of machine in the neutral atmosphere.'[64] The opening sentence of J.G. Ballard's 'High-Rise' (1975) describes the novel's protagonist eating dog meat on his modernist balcony, an image whose juxtapositions provide limitless fodder for speculative imaginations. For Ballard, the character of the architect residing on the penthouse floor of his eponymous tower is best suited for the role of manipulative anti-hero rather than angelic Randian saviour. The archetypal English apartment block, product of incredible innovation, becomes a microcosm of the city and its social structures. Wealthy dog-owners, who show disregard and distain for the building's public areas by allowing their pets to ruin them, live on the upper floors accessed by private elevators while struggling families are relegated below. Parallel examples can be found in films like 'Snowpiercer' (2013), where the spatial metaphor of a socially stratified city is extended horizontally, rather than vertically, across the compartments of a train that never stops. A world made uninhabitable by the hubris of human tampering is condensed into a single vehicle that must traverse the earth while providing shelter for its remaining population. Fueled by an exploited underclass, the technological masterminds of the train's perpetual engine seek to preserve the social patterns which facilitate their opulent lifestyles. 'Parasite' (2020) also explores the intricacies of social class and relations between groups stratified by wealth. The family home of an affluent businessman is employed as a spatial metaphor with its levels conveying different meanings and eliciting different behaviours from workers in their attempts at invasion, a striking filmic portrayal of the ideas expounded in Ballard's writing.

This increasingly pessimistic oeuvre, from Tati to Ballard, represents growing anxieties about how power is exercised over populations using contemporary tools of space-making. Such themes have grown in importance since the industrial revolution drastically altered the interface between human and machine, while the lack of moral direction provided by technological advances are key to their functioning in the world today. Though technology's fruits have increased certain qualities of life, primarily in the material realm, certain trade-offs always loom in the background, especially when changes are systemically implemented through institutions. While Pushwagner locates the corrupting influence over the modern metropolis in 'The Boss', a symbol of political autocracy and the network which Eisenhower referred to as 'the military-industrial complex',[65] other thinkers have speculated on the truly distributed nature of the city's repressive elements. The control that seeks uniformity at all costs, while remaining its own entity, could be distributed across a broad span of interacting elements; and indeed be located in the choices, actions and dreams of every individual contributing to the complex social patterns which define totalitarian, technocratic, and even democratic regimes.

Silicon Valley philosopher Kevin Kelly's pet notion sees technology as having its own mind and its own purpose, using humankind to create new entities through a networked web which he calls 'the technium'. This web, he predicts, will grow into something self-aware and independent of its human creators, working as an organising force for new kinds of deeply connected urban complexity. As Kelly explains in 'What Technology Wants' (2010), 'the technium is increasing the transparency of its roots, compiling more camera eyes, more communication neurons, more tracking technologies that reveal its own complicated processes... Cities are technological artifacts, the largest technology we make. With their sprawling, rapacious appetites for energy, materials, and attention, they seem like machines eating the wilderness, and many people wonder if they are eating us as well.'[66] From Mumford with his 'technics'[67] to recent thinkers who generalise technological forces in abstractions like 'Moloch' or 'The Machine', theories of the future city all seem to point in the same direction. Robert Pirsig has made especially cogent observations on the nature of increasing technological organisation in the megalopolis. While most individuals will 'never know how to fix one of these systems of wire and tubes down below the ground'[68] that keep it running, the urban system is nonetheless capable of maintaining itself through a form of distributed intelligence. This cohesive force holding the city's many systems together is termed 'the Giant', a social pattern which people look upon 'the same way cows and horses look upon a farmer; different from themselves, incomprehensible, but benevolent and appealing. Yet the social pattern of the city devours their lives for its own purposes just as surely as farmers devour the flesh of farm animals.'[69]

Marginalisation and the Public-Private Divide

As Thomas Hardy recognised in his late Victorian masterwork of class struggle, conjugal conduct and propriety 'Tess of the d'Urbervilles' (1891), 'every village has its idiosyncrasy, its constitution, often its own code of morality.'[70] This situation has seldom changed in the supposedly less repressive context of a free USA, a fact broadcast in subtle media messages dissenting against the conformity of stateside lifestyles at the height of their cultural influence. Things start off promising for Ned in the surprisingly subversive Hollywood film 'The Swimmer' (1968); he has a goal of swimming across town and it is a beautiful day. He has a dream, an American dream even. But as the film progresses, subtle hints begin to compile suggesting that all may not be as it seems. 'Well how goes it in never never land... Has the ideal All-American family found happiness on the hill?'[71] Ned's dream of the Lucinda River upturns the traditional expectations of the inhabitants of the gated Connecticut estates where the story is set. Connecting each of his neighbor's backyard pools, Ned attempts to swim his way to paradise before the illusion of suburban sublimity is broken: 'I'm an explorer... swimming home along a river of sapphire.'[72]

An event named after the fabled river has become a winter tradition in London, of all times and places, where a community group connects a series of water bodies from the north to the south of the city. Rising before 5 a.m. on a Saturday, participants connect Hampstead to Herne Hill through the disjointed ponds and pools they pass. As the runners-turned-swimmers connect the pieces of this unconventional water formation during an unlikely time of the year, the experience is described as an 'awakening' to the possibilities which the city holds, discovered from the inside-out while the population rises around them. The disparate green spaces of densely packed London, become, through their actions and imaginations, an illusory path that reflects 'the sense of serenity they find amid the calamity of the capital'.[73] Like the path of suburban pools in 'The Swimmer' along which Ned reconstructs the shambles of his own dreams, defiance of convention in the urban context is adopted to provide for the desires of numerous city-dwellers. Here the resources of the metropolis undergo an unconventional twist which, paradoxically, makes them more accessible to the residents they provide for. In opposition to the accommodations offered by London's green spaces, 'Hostile Design' is a contemptible trend characterised by floor spikes and slanted benches; simply put an approach to design that makes life in the city as uncomfortable as possible for a certain subset of people. Defined by elements that are intentionally introduced to restrict

63. S Sherwin, 'Artist of the Week 202: Hariton Pushwagner', Art & Design, Guardian, 9 August 2012

64. JG Ballard, 'High-Rise', Fourth Estate, London, 1975, p.34

65. DD Eisenhower, 'Military-Industrial Complex Speech', Avalon Project, 1961 [https://avalon.law.yale.edu/20th_century/eisenhower001.asp], retrieved 20 July 2022

66. K Kelly, 'What Technology Wants', Penguin Books, New York, 2011, pp.79–82

67. L Mumford, 'Technics and Human Development: The myth of the machine, vol.1', Harcourt, Brace & World, New York,1967

68 + 69. RM Pirsig, 'Lila: An inquiry into morals', Bantam Press, London, 1991 & pp.103–104

70. T Hardy, 'Tess of the d'Urbervilles', Cambridge University Press, Cambridge, 1891, p.48

71 + 72. F Perry, 'The Swimmer', Horizon Pictures, 1968

73. P Wood, 'Lucinda River', 2015 [https://www.youtube.com/watch?v=PcSCbQ8AC-o], retrieved 18 July 2022

74, 76 + 77. I Borden, 'Skateboarding and the City: A complete history', Bloomsbury, London, 2019, p.2, p.104 & p.102

or coerce behaviour in preventing deviation from socially accepted norms, such architecture specifically targets people who rely on the use of public spaces. For marginalised individuals, and those sleeping rough, hostile designs discourage or make impossible conventional or even necessary activities from 'loitering', remaining somewhere for all but the most transient periods of time, to skateboarding, graffiti or any remotely creative or subversive use of space.

For Iain Borden, the skateboard is an important tool for interacting with the city and its architecture. By challenging societal conventions skateboarding helps open spaces in the city to everyone, regardless of intended use. Borden notes how the disorderliness and irrationality of skating makes it a distinctive activity in the city's social fabric. Unlike more regulated spaces for conventional sports, the subculture of skateboarding benefits from a disruptive ambiguity which 'introduces tactics of appropriation and colonisation'.[74] Skateboards work as spatial technologies which disregard and transcend standard interpretations of the built environment. As with steam and combustion engines, indeed any technological advance, the revolutionary abilities bestowed are morally ambiguous – they can be used for good or ill as the case may be. It is useful to remember Marshall McLuhan's adage that 'the medium is the message'.[75] Just as the automobile could only arise in a culture that prizes material-laden individualism and freedom of movement like the United States, the skateboard, through its emphasis on autonomy and independence in action and thought, carries in its form a uniquely subversive social critique of public space and its conventions. Innovative uses of the urban realm have inspired parallel advances in hostile design, but even the most unaccommodating architectures can still be outwitted by the continuously evolving process behind skateboarding's abiding appeal, transforming the massive concrete of billion-dollar infrastructure projects into an 'unconquered frontier'[76] for seemingly impossible maneuvers and turning the widely emulated kidney-pools of Alvar Aalto, emptied by droughts, into arenas for perpetual movement. In more public facing areas, skateboards are ideal for 'inserting mobile euphoria into mundane urbanism'.[77]

Squatting can also be used as a form of political expression and community building. Originating from common law tradition in England, squatter's rights, also known as adverse possession, allow individuals to possess unoccupied properties after a given period.[78] While laws protecting squats were first codified in industrialised countries, expediting the freespaces of Denmark or the communes of Germany and the United States, squatting is global and undoubtedly has its largest effect in underdeveloped and marginalised contexts. After all, what now stands on the San Francisco Bay Area was effectively built by squatters. One survey in 1855 estimated that '95 percent of the property holders would not be able to produce a bona fide legal title to their land', and 'where there was a vacant piece of ground one day, the next saw it covered with half a dozen tents or shanties'[79] with squatters residing anywhere from marshes and military bunkers to sand dunes. In the UK where homelessness has risen drastically over the past decade and more than 200,000 residences have been empty for longer than six months,[80] the London-based Autonomous Nation of Anarchist Libertarians (ANAL) have taken matters into their own hands. By systematically identifying empty high-end properties and using the legal framework of squatter's rights, they have opened over 30 disused buildings to those who would otherwise be homeless.[81]

Marginalised urban areas from Latin America to India are composed largely of informal slums, often beginning as squatted settlements. It has been observed that 'every beautiful city begins as a slum... It doesn't matter in what century or in which country; Babylon, London, and New York all had teeming ghettos of unwanted settlers erecting shoddy shelters with inadequate hygiene and engaging in dodgy dealings... A century ago Manhattan was home to 20,000 squatters in self-made housing. Slab City alone, in Brooklyn, contained 10,000 residents.'[82] Its namesake in California's Sonoran Desert is a small squatter community made-up of tents, trailers and shacks with no running water, electricity or plumbing. This 'Last Free Place in America' has a transient population of more than 4,000 anarchists and outcasts in winter, shrinking to less than 150 in summer when temperatures hit 100 degrees or hotter.[83] Photographer Donovan Wylie notes that these 'are clearly people who don't want to be found, so there's something about disappearing, and the desert offers that kind of opportunity'.[84]

'A nation is the same people living in the same place – or also living in different places.'[85] The renowned remark of Leopold Bloom in James Joyce's 'Ulysses' (1922) has only increased in relevance since being penned more than a century ago. Setting the stage for a coming world of both incredible mobility and destructive displacement, this quote and the book speak to the timeless issues of social differences and the discontents of the societies they shape. In similar fashion, 'The Vanity of Small Differences' (2012) endeavors to critique close-mindedness as well as class structure by illustrating an ascent of the socio-economic ladder. Its meticulous tapestries examine the uniquely class-centric life in Britain while its artist, Grayson Perry, likewise embodies the task of challenging cultural expectations and gender roles by publicly presenting a fluid identity. Perry has also used the medium of television to critique model neighbourhoods like Royal Tunbridge Wells in Kent,[86] whose stultifying societal structures are reminiscent of the snobbery depicted in 'High-Rise'. Working in a context where social position is heavily internalised through language, possessions, and petty details, Perry interrogates the 'small differences' that serve to cohere or ossify groups of people and their perspectives.

The marginalisation and migration of cultures remain highly relevant to the fabric of many cities today. Following the colonial wars of the 19th century, a great Chinese diaspora saw massive numbers of people emigrate to surrounding countries and overseas due to poverty and ruin. As in the precedent set by Binondo, the world's oldest existing Chinatown in the Philippines,[87] newly opened seaports throughout Southeast Asia were the commonest destination. Districts or parcels of land would be granted as foreign settlement areas for working immigrants and traders, quickly developing into ethnic enclaves where cultural practices could be carried out freely. The neighbouring countries of Thailand, Malaysia and Singapore have the largest populations of overseas Chinese today,[88] closely followed by the United States where San Francisco's Chinatown began a trend of Disneyfication, commercialising Chinese culture and accommodating settlement areas to the skewed expectations of locals.[89] Chinatowns in Japan have also followed a 'theme-park' trajectory, 'from historical Chinatown, tourist Chinatown to just a concentration of Chinese stores'.[90] The Yokohama Chinatown in the south of Tokyo is a case in point with a proliferation of 250 themed shops and restaurants but few Chinese people actually living within and no community to speak of.

In this tradition, the city can straightforwardly be seen as a series of revolutions directed as often by its privileged and powerful leaders as by vast numbers of everyday citizens, or well-organised but marginalised groups holding fringe viewpoints. Dreams of alternative pasts and radical futures held in the minds of every individual play themselves out on the urban stage in daily dramas and nightly reveries. Relentless, ever-shifting activities give way to a stable form – the city – where, as often as not, promises of change reveal themselves to be mere illusions. In the words of humorist Terry Pratchett, the thing about revolutions is that they go all the way around.

75. M McLuhan, 'Understanding Media', WT Gordon (ed.), Gingko Press, New York, 2013, p.7

78. N Cobb & L Fox, 'Living Outside the System? The (Im)Morality of Urban Squatting After the Land Registration Act 2002', Legal Studies 27, no.2, 2007, pp.236–260

79. R Neuwirth, 'Shadow Cities: A billion squatters, a new urban world', Taylor & Francis Group, London, 2004, pp.197–198

80 + 81. 'The London Anarchist Group Squatting Mansions to Fight Homelessness', Fringes, S1, E12, Vice Production, 2017 [https://www.youtube.com/watch?v=f0OVvi29Pm0], retrieved 20 July 2022

82. K Kelly, 'What Technology Wants', Penguin Books, New York, 2011, p.82

83. P Rapa, 'Fear of the Pandemic Reaches California's Slab City, An Off-the-Grid Desert Community', Washington Post, 8 June 2020

84. J Nalewicki, 'Inside Slab City, A Squatters' Paradise in Southern California', Smithsonian Magazine, 1 October 2018 [https://www.smithsonianmag.com/travel/inside-slab-city-squatters-paradise-southern-california-180970218], retrieved 16 June 2023

85. J Joyce, 'Ulysses', Shakespeare and Co., Paris, 1922, p.606

86. G Perry, S Foster-Conley & N Crombie, 'All in the Best Possible Taste with Grayson Perry', Simply Media, 2014

87 + 90. BP Wong & CB Tan, 'Chinatowns Around the World: Gilded ghetto, ethnopolis, and cultural diaspora', Brill, Leiden, 2013, p.272 & p.2

88. D Poston & JY Wong, 'The Chinese Diaspora: The current distribution of the overseas Chinese population', Chinese Journal of Sociology, vol.2, 6 September 2016, pp.348–373

89. C Li, 'The Politics and Heritage of Race and Space in San Francisco's Chinatown', in 'On Location: Heritage Cities and Sites', DF Ruggles (ed.), Springer, New York, 2012, pp.37–59

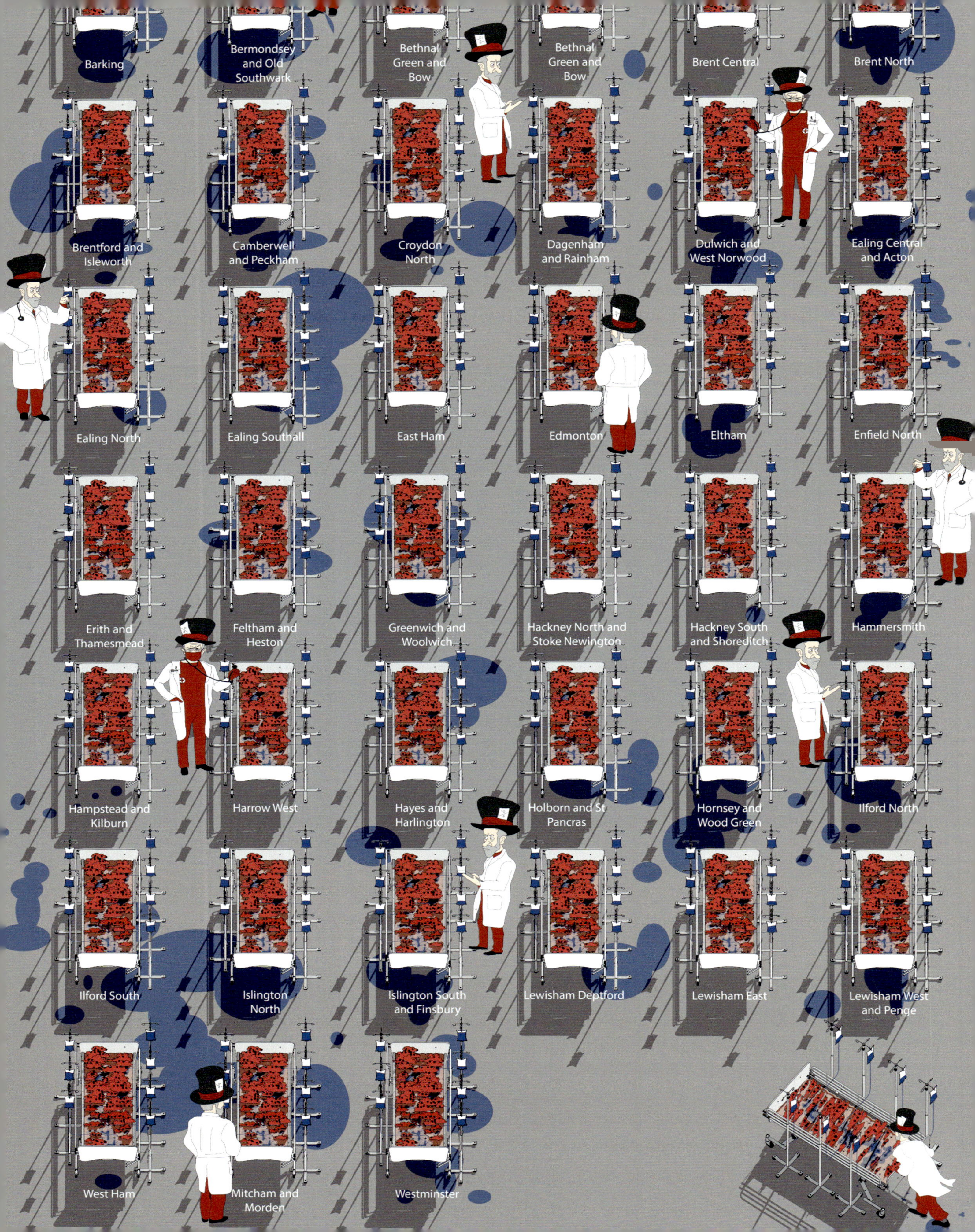
Barking
Bermondsey and Old Southwark
Bethnal Green and Bow
Bethnal Green and Bow
Brent Central
Brent North
Brentford and Isleworth
Camberwell and Peckham
Croydon North
Dagenham and Rainham
Dulwich and West Norwood
Ealing Central and Acton
Ealing North
Ealing Southall
East Ham
Edmonton
Eltham
Enfield North
Erith and Thamesmead
Feltham and Heston
Greenwich and Woolwich
Hackney North and Stoke Newington
Hackney South and Shoreditch
Hammersmith
Hampstead and Kilburn
Harrow West
Hayes and Harlington
Holborn and St Pancras
Hornsey and Wood Green
Ilford North
Ilford South
Islington North
Islington South and Finsbury
Lewisham Deptford
Lewisham East
Lewisham West and Penge
West Ham
Mitcham and Morden
Westminster

Redistribution

'A healthy city should be above all a city for all its citizens, inclusive, supportive, sensitive and responsive to their diverse needs and expectations. A healthy city provides conditions and opportunities that support healthy lifestyles. A healthy city offers a physical and built environment that supports health, recreation and well-being, safety, social interaction, easy mobility, a sense of pride and cultural identity and that is accessible to the needs of all its citizens.'

– Zagreb Declaration for Healthy Cities, 2008

Outlining the key principles and goals of Phase V of the WHO European Healthy Cities Network, this societal declaration has been systematically embedded to revolutionise the UK's National Health Service (NHS) through the curative story of 'Redistribution'. Jeremy Corbyn recognises that population health rests not only on the actions of the health sector but increasingly on diverse policies and shared values across divisions.[1] The Labour government has seized the opportunity to pioneer an audacious economic programme for redistributing capital and power – nationalisation of rail, water, and electricity companies, plus significantly higher taxes on multi-national corporations and upper classes are at the heart of funding the radical left-winger's health promises. However, the Confederation of British Industry (CBI) has rebuked that 'continual public barbs and backward-facing policy are deterring entrepreneurs and investors, at a time when we need them most. Profit and enterprise are the basis of jobs and growth, with firms paying enough tax to fund the NHS every year and much more besides.'[2] This is advice that the Labour government might find difficult to heed when Corbyn, their leader, is a devotee of capitalism's destruction, atoning for its sins at any cost regardless of consequence.

Jeremy Corbyn could be either a villain or saviour. 'If we are serious about fulfilling Nye Bevan's dream[3] of building a society that looks after everybody then we need to transform our economy so that it does not just work in the interests of a few. Men in the most deprived parts of England today will have nearly 20 fewer years of their lives in good health. There is massive inequality in even the wealthiest parts of our country. Take Kensington and Chelsea, the site of the Grenfell Tower tragedy, there, life expectancy is 14 years lower for the poorest residents',[4] said the Marxist prime minister whose first revolutionary action plan is to turn Buckingham Palace, Kensington Palace, and buildings in the Crown Estate's portfolio into social housing. A change of programme for Kensington Palace is particularly apt since it has been home to young British royal families for over 300 years. Corbyn's predecessor Theresa May admitted that young people without family wealth are 'right to be angry. Angry that, regardless of how hard they work, they won't be able to buy a place of their own', with the lack of accessibility to affordable and safe housing becoming a source of national shame.[5]

facing page: Dr. Corbyn will make sure that all his constituencies are healed and properly looked after.

1. WHO European Healthy Cities Network, 'Phase V (2009 – 2013) of the WHO European Healthy Cities Network: Goals and requirements', World Health Organisation, 2009, pp.7–11

2. C Fairbairn, 'CBI Responds to Jeremy Corbyn's Speech at Labour Party Conference', CBI, 26 September 2018 [https://www.cbi.org.uk/media-centre/articles/cbi-responds-to-jeremy-corbyns-speech-at-labour-party-conference], retrieved 12 October 2022

3. Aneurin 'Nye' Bevan was the founder of the British National Health Service, during his time as Minister of Health in Attlee's Labour government.

4. Labour Party Press, 'Jeremy Corbyn's Speech to Mark the 70th Anniversary of the NHS', www.labour.org.uk, 1 July 2018 [https://labour.org.uk/press/jeremy-corbyns-speech-mark-70th-anniversary-nhs], retrieved 12 October 2022

5. Politics, 'Theresa May: Young are "right to be angry" about lack of homes', BBC, 5 March 2018 [https://www.bbc.co.uk/news/uk-politics-43279177], retrieved 14 October 2022

0.9% Sodium
Chloride
Injection USP

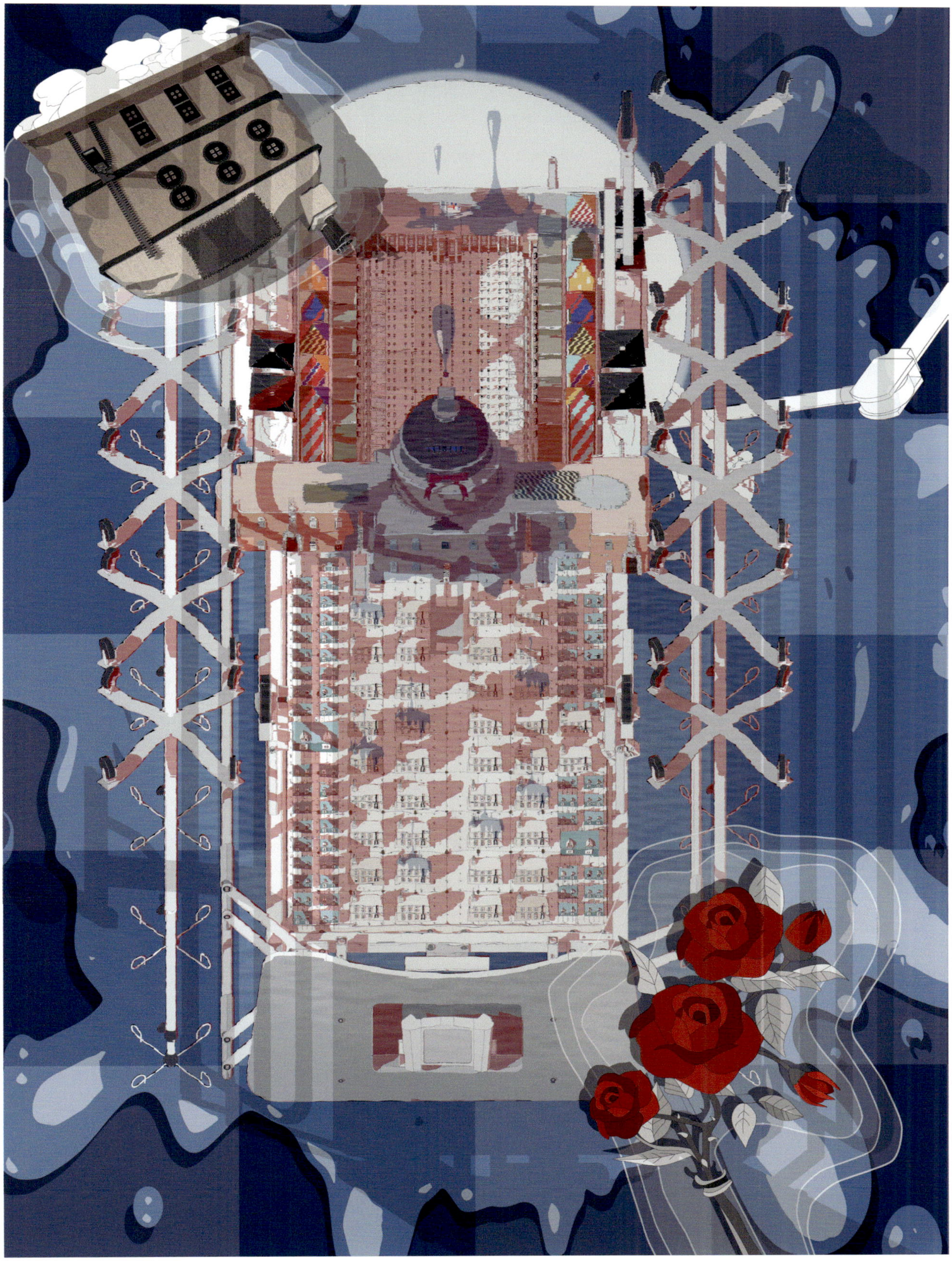

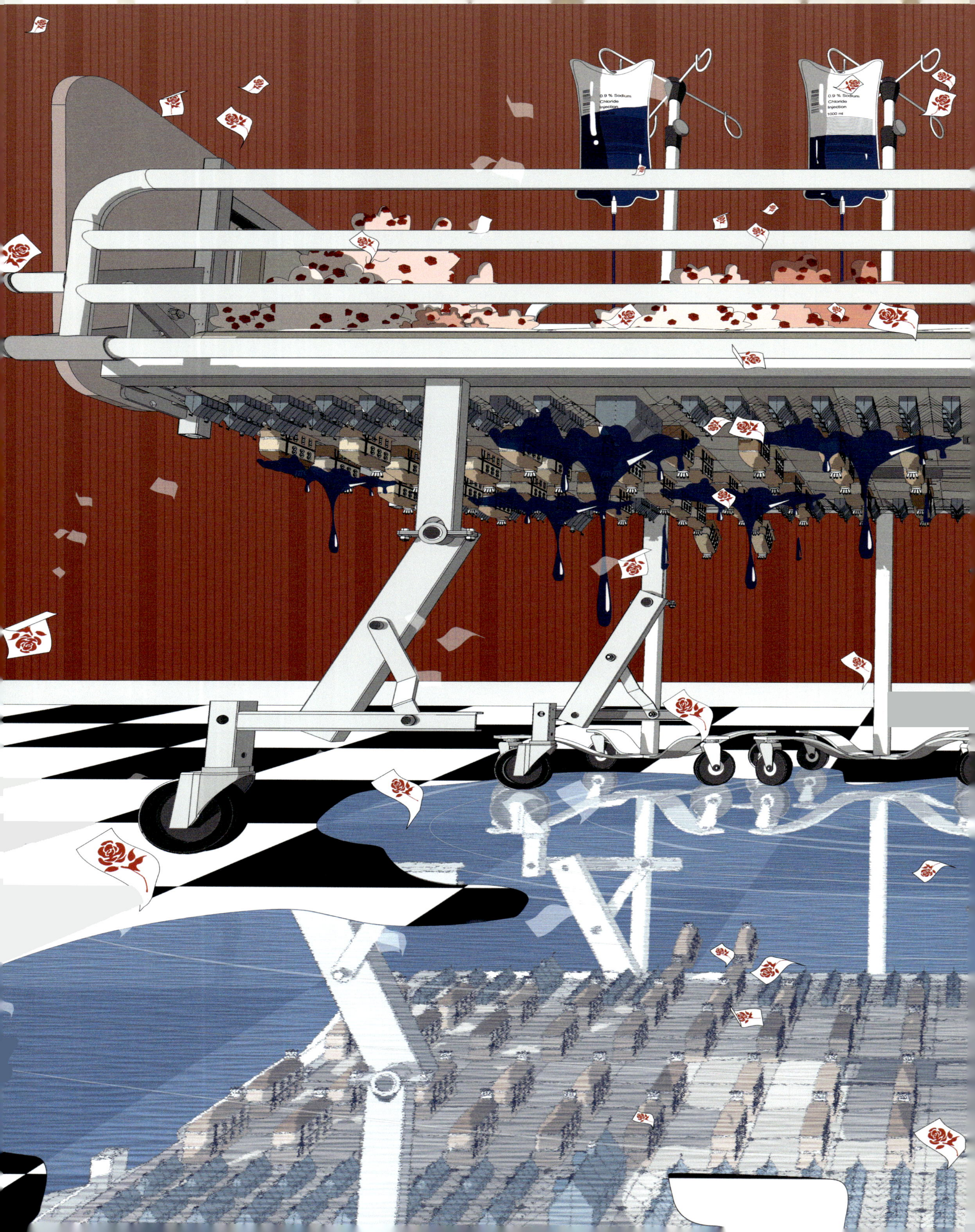
0.9 % Sodium
Chloride
Injection
0.9 % Sodium
Chloride
Injection
1000 ml

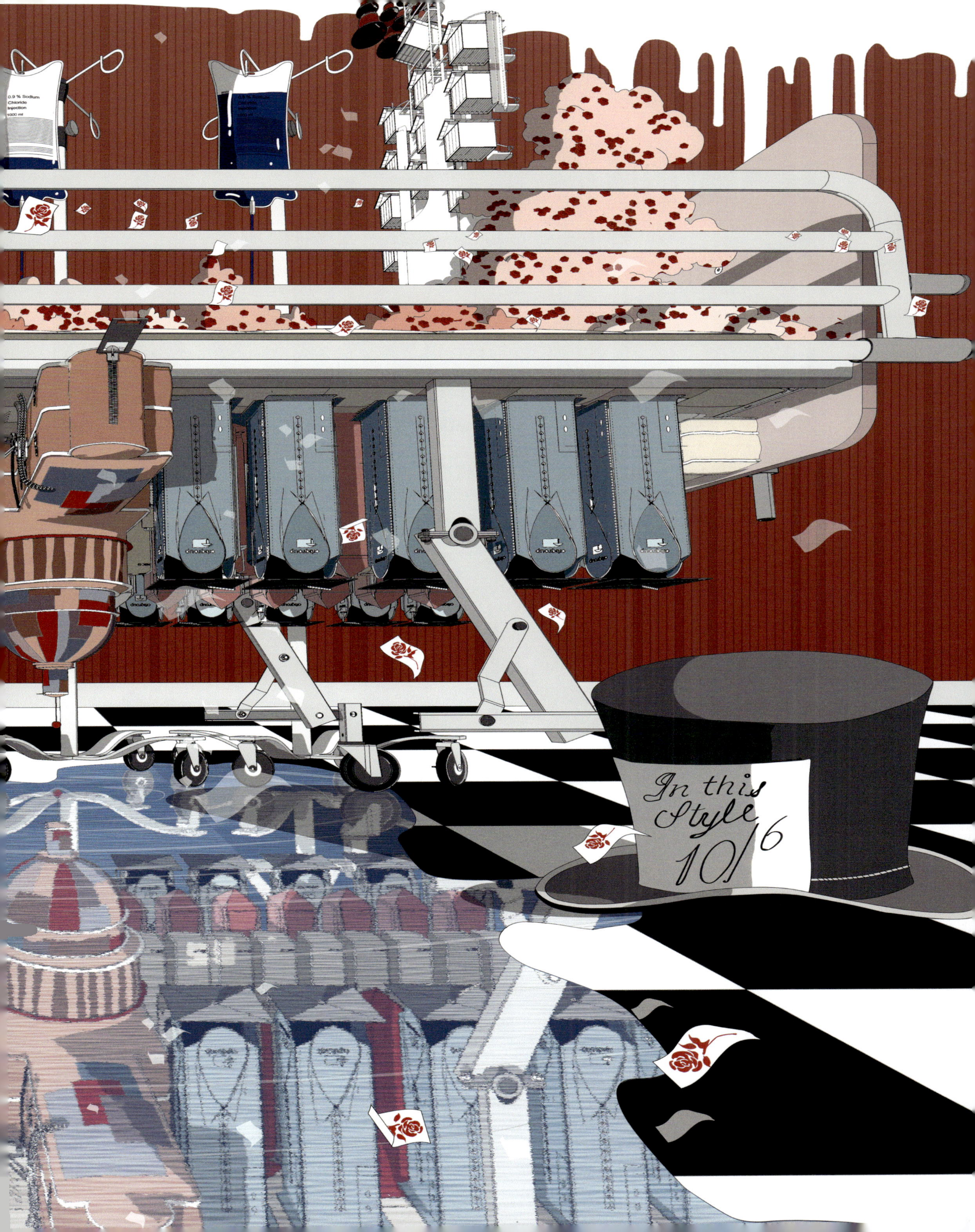
0.9 % Sodium Chloride Injection 1000 ml
In this Style 10/6

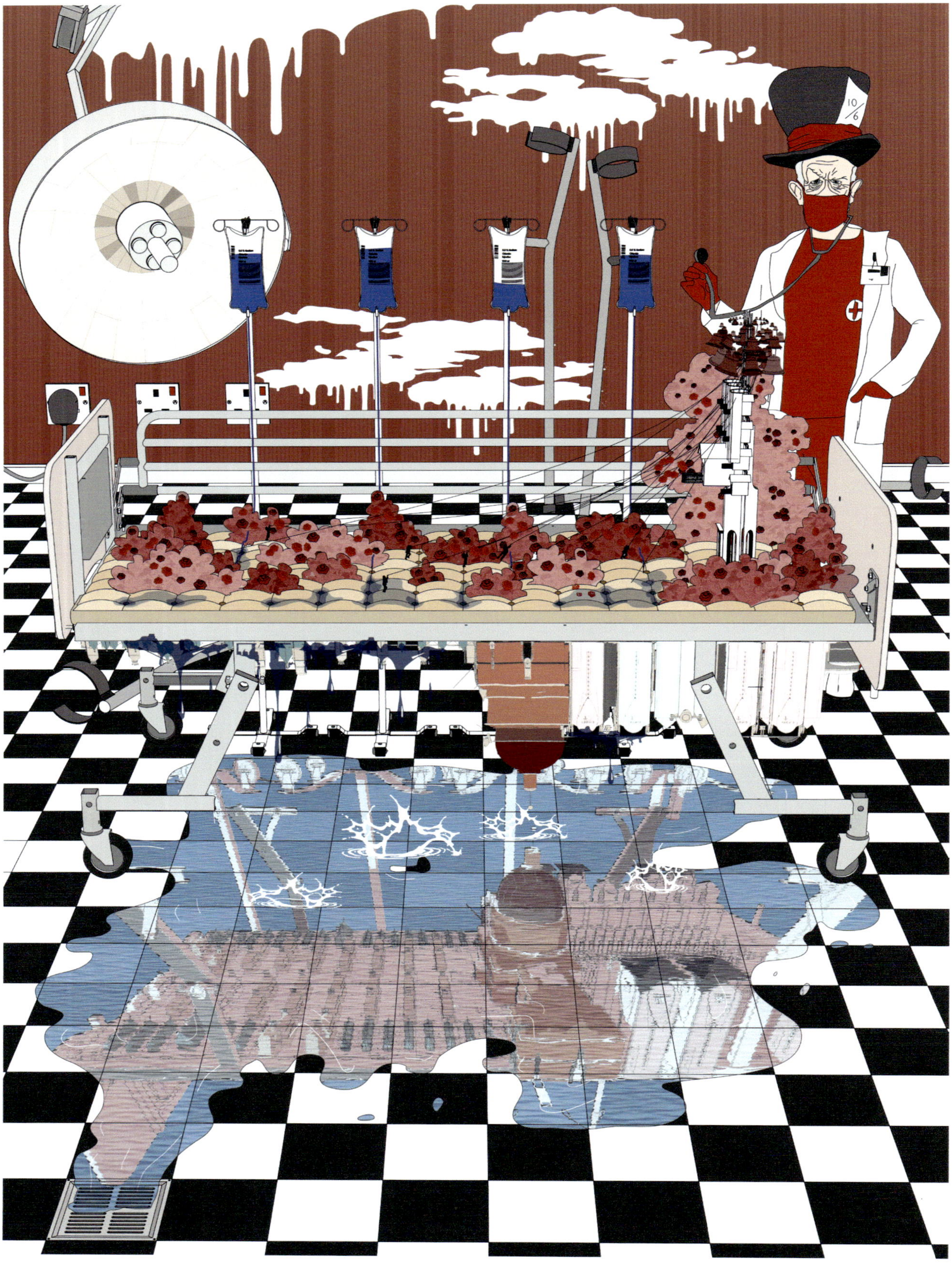
10/6

The Labour government has set out necessary political and institutional commitments to integrate the urban health implications of climate change into planning programmes for the next generation. Research by Friends of the Earth (FoE) found communities of colour are 'more than three times more likely to live in neighbourhoods with very high air pollution, putting them at disproportionate risk of heart attacks, cancer and strokes. The analysis found that air pollution also disproportionately affected lower-income areas, with half of neighbourhoods with high air pollution in the bottom 30 percent of the most deprived neighbourhoods.'[6] Transportation sectors account for over 20 percent of net greenhouse gas emissions in the UK; this air pollution in the form of carbon dioxide and methane raises the earth's temperature.[7] Corbyn, to maintain an urban advantage in health outcomes, has recruited countless flocks of swans from across the Royal Parks to mobilise transport for London and filter out pollutants, bringing to mind Santa and his reindeer zipping across the skies. By replacing more and more fossil-fuel Ubers and black cabs with swan carriages, London would limit air pollution at its source while actively restraining the warming trends that exacerbate many of the city's worst health impacts.

It is a long-accepted truism that dedication to the prevention of ill-health is better than dedication to the treatment, for which growing inequalities in society are creating so much need. On issues of 'loneliness deaths'[8] and food security, the mission of redistribution borrows from the city of Belo Horizonte in Brazil. The Banqueting House in central London, designed by Inigo Jones in the 17th century, is appropriated to play its part as 'The People's Canteen'. The public facility offers safe and nutritionally balanced meals at affordable prices for marginalised groups of the population, but everybody is welcome to use the service in an attempt to avoid stigmatisation. The ideology of 'food with dignity' ensures the human right to adequate sustenance throughout one's lifetime, and develops a sense of solidarity and connection to the environment. What has emerged is a highly effective but low-cost scheme, which reduces strain on the city's health services by affording citizens greater access to nutrition and nature. The recuperating health of the city proudly results in a continuously growing number of unused hospital beds being allocated for community rose gardens, cultivating collective representation in policy making and urban planning. Antioxidants in the rose petals can reduce the risk of heart disease, diabetes, and obesity, not to mention the rose being the symbol of socialism and the social democratic movement of the Labour party – though their buds seem to be attracting pesky flies rather than health miracles.

Feeling like a once-in-a-lifetime opportunity to focus on revitalised urban planning policies, Redistribution is especially popular amongst the young, and in the context of Brexit it is almost impossible to paint Labour's plans as risky. Then again, critics have accused the Labour government of treating public health as a political football, arguing that 'Jeremy Corbyn has not offered "credible answers" to the problems. Bandying about large-sounding increases, and saying "all will be well" is raising unrealistic expectations that will inevitably disappoint. There is a worrying mismatch between what the money will buy and what it will actually buy.'[9] Former Prime Minister Tony Blair has told the BBC's 'This Week's World' that 'it would be a very dangerous experiment for a major western country to get gripped by this type of populist policy-making'.[10] While it is fair to say that Corbyn's urban health planning efforts should recognise multidirectional unintended consequences, this is not the time for timidity. An emphasis on discursive and inclusive experimentation in the service of social learning is the only path to recovery.

previous page 122: Corbyn consulting his cabinet on the best healing strategy for the UK.

previous page 123: A masterplan of the city sewn to the underside of the mattress is reflected in the puddle of water beneath it.

previous pages: London in A&E.

facing page: Dr. Corbyn believes that the UK, and especially London, is sick. He also believes he is the only doctor properly accredited to heal it.

following page 128: Theresa May overlooking the Labour Party's expanding rose garden from her high tower at 10 Downing Street. Is someone ringing the doorbell?

following page 129: Corbyn would conscript all the royal swans to his new mad hat-bus transport system.

following pages 130–131: The army of menacing Momentum flies are lurking underneath Labour's masterplan bed and manicured rose gardens.

6. D Gayle, 'People of Colour Far Likelier to Live in England's Very High Air Pollution Areas', Guardian, 4 October 2022

7. C Waite, '2020 UK Greenhouse Gas Emissions, Final Figures', Department for Business, Energy & Industry Strategy UK, 1 February 2022, p.14

8. M Redman, 'My Loneliness is Killing Me: The Devastating Health Effects of Social Isolation', British Medical Association, 6 May 2022 [https://www.bma.org.uk/news-and-opinion/my-loneliness-is-killing-me-the-devastating-health-effects-of-social-isolation], retrieved 14 October 2022

9. C Smyth, 'NHS Leader Attacks Labour and Tories for Misleading Promises', Times, 9 December 2019

10. Politics, 'Tony Blair: Corbyn in power would be a "dangerous experiment"', BBC, 28 May 2016 [https://www.bbc.co.uk/news/uk-politics-36401105], retrieved 12 October 2022

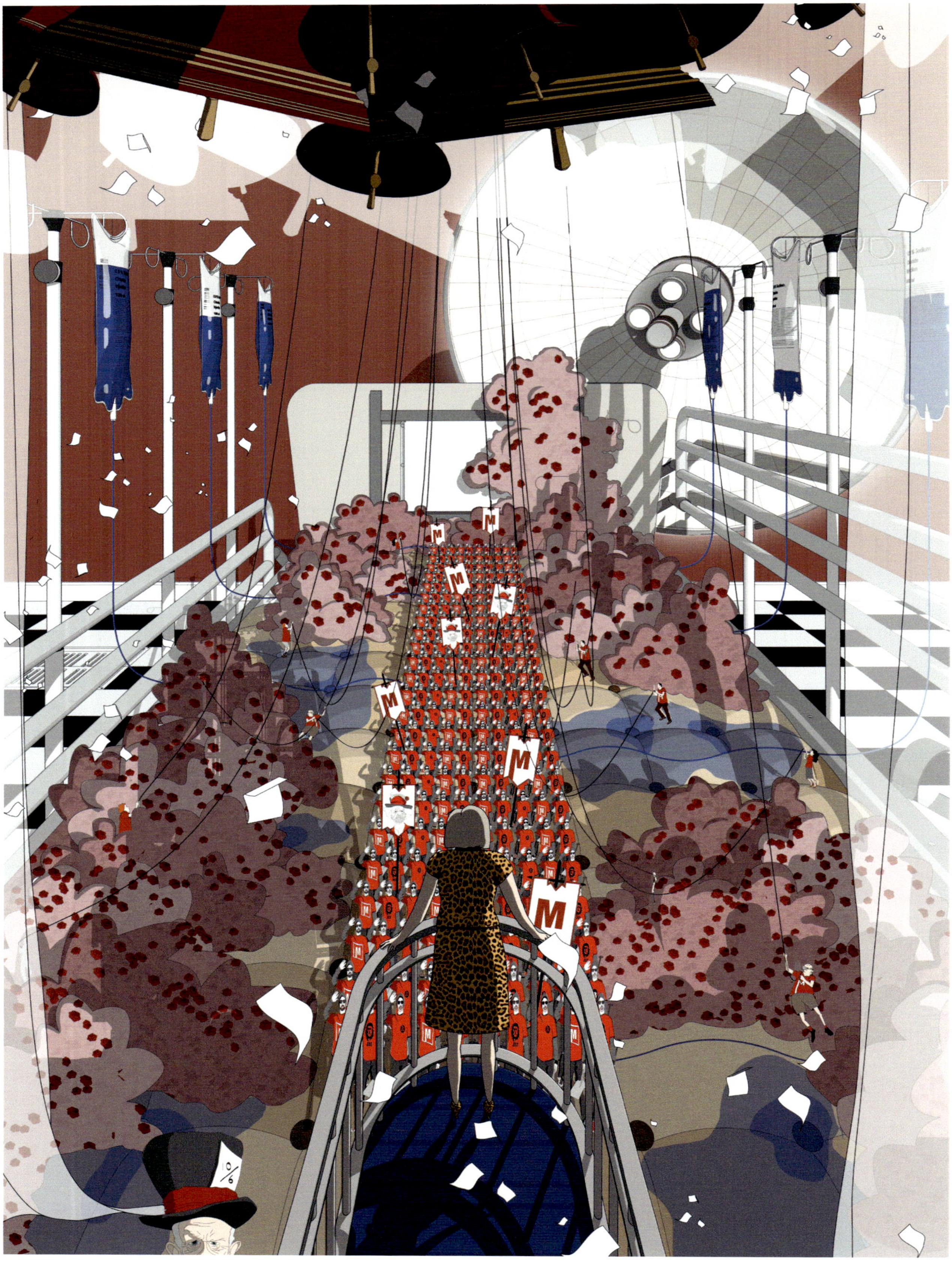

LONDON

City of Broken Promises

'I hope everyone from Weston will take the opportunity to once more stand in a puddle of murky water eating cold chips to the sound of crying children. It is just amazing having this much sarcasm in one place. It's not a swipe at Disney. I guess you'd say it's a family theme park unsuitable for children whose big theme is – theme parks should have bigger themes.'

– Banksy, Dismaland, Weston-super-Mare, 2015

A fire-ravaged fairytale Cinderella castle. A woman attacked by seagulls. An army of guides, under instruction to look miserable in pink vests. Banksy's two-and-a-half acre 'not-so-traditional seaside revolution' has brought the local economy an estimated £20 million boost in five weeks, but more importantly Weston's Local Government Association proudly reports that it helped to 'change people's perceptions and engender a new-found confidence in the town. It showed just how much is possible with ambition and imagination, and gave the town confidence to try new things and take a few risks.'[1] Traditional retirement locations by the sea such as Eastbourne and Bournemouth have managed to attract an increasingly elderly and dependent UK population, while higher education has been the catalyst for Aberyswyth, Brighton and Falmouth.[2] Margate, Ramsgate and Hastings, with their faded yet low cost and classy Victorian homes, have enticed the Zoom, flexible hours, and self-employment generation to help revive their deprived economies.

The British coast was once the ultimate summer tradition, and its rapid Victorian era urbanisation coincided with the growth in working-class free time and spending power. 'Sunburn was not considered a health risk, in fact quite the opposite. If sun tan lotion was used, it was Coppertone, otherwise baby oil and UV reflectors were used to achieve the desired deep mahogany colour that showed the neighbours you'd been away on holiday.'[3] Reversing such practices, Cancer Research UK now warns that 'getting sunburn once every two years can triple the risk of melanoma cancer, compared to never being burnt'.[4]

As the 'City of Broken Promises', Great Yarmouth reflects the adverse impact of climate change on environmental health, showing there is an imperative need for awareness, novel practices and changing attitudes around sheltering from the sun. Shadow and darkness have now become highly sought-after resources for leisure and wellbeing. After the broken promise of a new ferry connection to the city of Ijmuiden due to Brexit, it seems the city has fallen from grace only to rise again – choosing not to fight nature but to embrace the opportunities from its high annual rainfall, few hours of sunlight and all that climate change and advancing tides have to offer. The city's regeneration strategy encourages the rising sea to repurpose its urban territories on the scale of tulip fields in the Netherlands. Planned around the

facing page: Great Yarmouth, the summer holiday destination where refuge from the sun is sought after.

following pages: The Flamingo Follies, beauty parlours of promised eternal youth, reside on former urban green spaces that have since flooded.

1. Local Government Association, 'Dismaland by Banksy hosted by North Somerset Council', www.local.gov.uk, 29 March 2017 [https://www.local.gov.uk/case-studies/dismaland-banksy-hosted-north-somerset-council], retrieved 3 October 2022

2. T Challans & M Grant, 'The Rebirth of British Seaside Resorts and Coastal Towns', The Academy of Urbanism, 5 November 2018 [https://www.academyofurbanism.org.uk/the-rebirth-of-british-seaside-resorts-and-coastal-towns], retrieved 3 October 2022

3. E Castelow, 'The Great British Seaside Holiday', Historic UK [https://www.historic-uk.com/CultureUK/Great-British-Seaside-Holiday], retrieved 3 October 2022

4. About Cancer, 'How Does the Sun and UV Cause Cancer?', Cancer Research UK [https://www.cancerresearchuk.org/about-cancer/causes-of-cancer/sun-uv-and-cancer/how-does-the-sun-and-uv-cause-cancer], retrieved 3 October 2022

ideology of a company town for skin health research and zero UV beauty holidays, the city is supported by the government's plans to 'level up'[5] the country, curb carbon emissions and prevent skin cancer.

Clouds are the main protagonist of this new urban enterprise, which promises to enhance the shade level of the already gloomy skies of Great Yarmouth. Manufactured round-the-clock, the clouds demarcate several constantly shifting territories with the help of blustering sea winds. A range of cooling microclimates are managed by the Flamingo Follies in amongst dozens of mineral baths, which double up as beauty parlours. With the promises of eternal youth and 'un-kissed by sun' skin, these parlours are the heart of the thriving beauty enterprise where tourists flock in masses to avoid the aggressive sun, but without the traditional British seaside holiday miseries of uncertain weather and cold seas, not to mention grim accommodation with nylon sheets and limited hot water.

Occasionally, fragmented cloud patterns allow soft rays of sun to peek through to the fields of seaweed and lavender below, dotted within structures for mackerel fishing and skin health research units that heroically function as wave breakers. The revolutionary blueprint for joining the coasts of Great Yarmouth with the other 168 British seaside towns would result in a 31,368-kilometre-long seaweed field. Being aware of its true-blue carbon stock, Great Yarmouth is able to trade it with other UK cities and eventually other countries who want to offset their emissions. Investments for training and research into seaweed farming are key to levelling up community engagement in an industry that is also helping to fulfill the country's net-zero ambitions. Coastal ecosystems can surprisingly sequester up to 20 times more carbon per acre than land forests,[6] whereas belief in the social healing of lavender can promote urban regeneration. Research suggests that lavender oil has anti-inflammatory properties which help to heal sunburn and can also be used to treat anxiety and insomnia.[7] Seaweed and mackerel, high in omega-3s for optimal skin and hair care, along with lavender oil are all commonly used in beauty creams while being marketed as anti-ageing ingredients, another promise destined to be broken. However, there is nothing more exhilarating than frolicking in the purple-blue ocean of delicate lavender scents from mid-June to August. The resilient landscapes of hard and soft, and of little light and plenty of shadows together engage the city's traditional industry to cultivate a network of reciprocal economies. After all, it is not inconceivable that holidaymakers might swap the Costas for Cleethorpes and Sitges for Skegness if shade were preferable to sunshine.

Alas, successive governments have failed to solve systemic economic problems, leaving much of seaside Britain in the state of Dismaland but without prospects or satire. Economic hardship can fuel community tensions, and a marginalised Britain stuck in cycles of disillusionment makes an easy target for right-wing political parties and nationalist movements.[8] A report by the Office for National Statistics shows that 'between 2009 and 2018, half of the country's seaside towns saw a decline in employment, compared with 37 percent of non-seaside towns. Overall, two in every three of the seaside towns are in the higher income deprivation category compared with just over one in every three non-seaside towns.'[9] There seems to be a risk-averse inability to respond to rapid socio-economic and environmental alterations. To finally make good on promises of a sustainable future, only revolutionary strategies can simultaneously address climate change and reshape the built environment to bolster new growth.

previous pages: The lavender fields form a dynamic and sensorial edge around the city.

facing page: By embracing sea-level rise, the city has implemented a new network of productive landscapes.

following pages: Amongst the five water-saturated landscape conditions, clouds actively choreograph the poetic environment and perform as the sheltering sky to create shade and shadows.

5. A key slogan during Boris Johnson 2019 election victory, the promise to 'level up' the country will boost living standards, spread opportunity and improve public services in areas outside the traditionally prosperous London and the South-East.

6. S Hurlimann, 'How Kelp Naturally Combats Global Climate Change', Science in the News, Harvard University, 4 July 2019 [https://sitn.hms.harvard.edu/flash/2019/how-kelp-naturally-combats-global-climate-change], retrieved 4 October 2022

7. DR Wilson, 'What are the health benefits and risks of lavender?', Medical News Today, 4 March 2019 [https://www.medicalnewstoday.com/articles/265922], retrieved 5 October 2022

8. M Townsend, 'Revealed: The towns at risk from far-right extremism', Guardian, 31 October 2021

9. R Prothero & R Sikorski, 'Coastal Towns in England and Wales: October 2020', Office for National Statistics, 6 October 2020 [https://www.ons.gov.uk//articles/2020-10-06], retrieved 4 October 2022

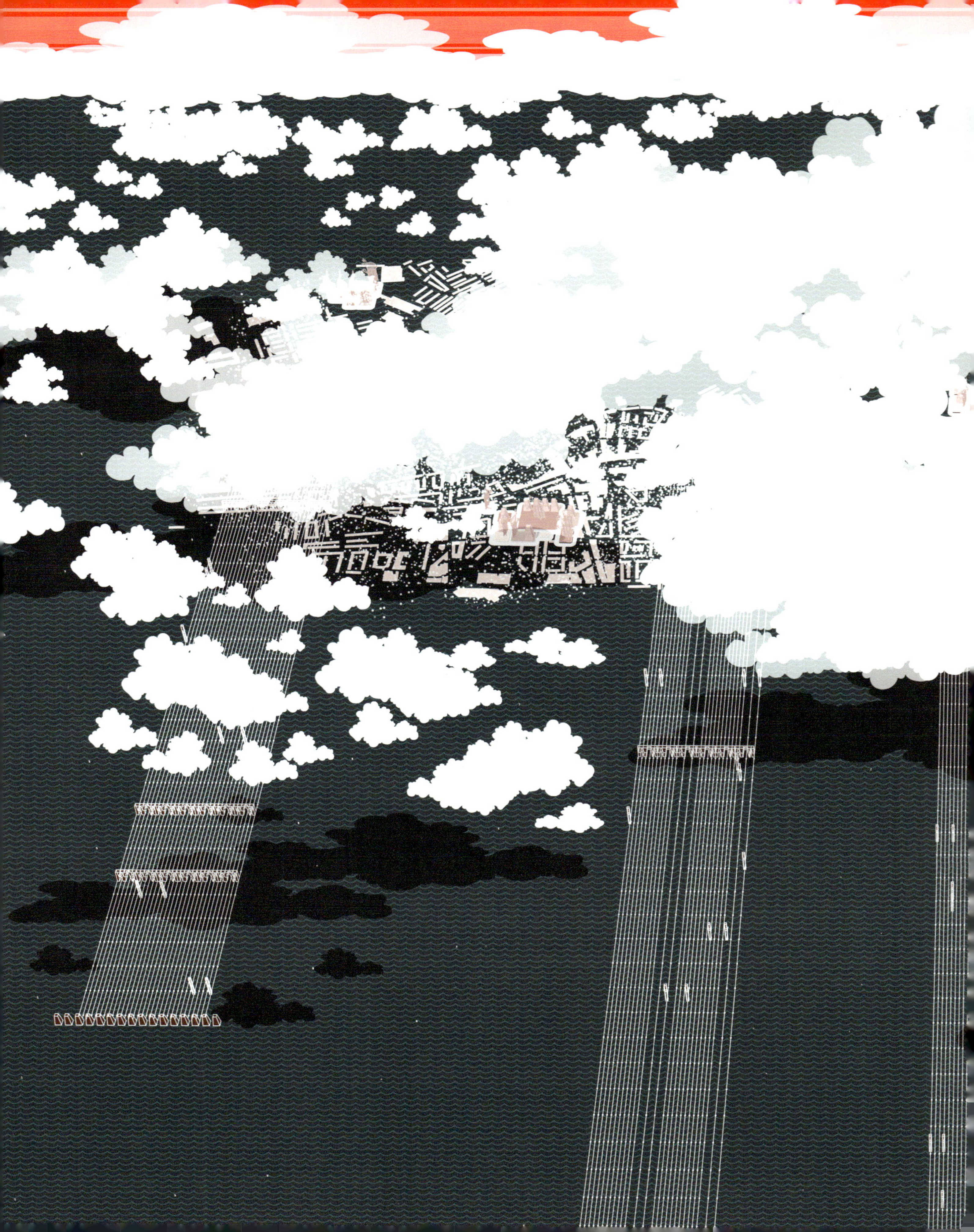

PRET A MANGER
COSTA
NERO
Marriott
SOMEWHERE OVER THE RAINBO
King's Cross St. Pancras

Rainbows Over London

'Somewhere over the rainbow, way up high. There's a land that I heard of once in a lullaby. Somewhere over the rainbow, skies are blue. And the dreams that you dare to dream really do come true...Where troubles melt like lemon drops away above the chimney tops. That's where you'll find me. Somewhere over the rainbow, bluebirds fly. Birds fly over the rainbow; why, then, oh, why can't I?'

– Harold Arlen & Yip Harburg, 'Over the Rainbow', 1939

Judy Garland's rendering of the ideological lullaby speaks to young and old alike, always promising better times to come against a backdrop of yearning that resonates with ordinary people's dreams and disillusions of affordable homes. The narrative of social housing provisions by the state presents alternative histories of every city in the UK – from prime minister Lloyd George's 'homes for heroes' built after World War I to the modernist tower blocks of the 1960s, in architectural designs ranging from art deco to brutalist. As the promise to have trees in view of every window deteriorated into grim concrete havens of decay and anarchy, housing rose to the centre of British politics, provoking media antagonism and often public indifference. Thatcher's 'right-to-buy' in the 1980s led to drastic depletion in social housing stock, and a virtual pause on new building has resulted from successive governments' refusal to invest. According to the UK Land Promoters and Developers Federation's report 'Housing Emergency: The new lost generation', young people are giving up on the dream of home ownership as prices soar, interest rates rise and the cost of living crisis hits their spending power.[1] Besides this generational unfairness and growing despondency, the UK's Crisis homelessness charity wearily appeals that 'EU nationals are almost twice as likely to experience homelessness and almost three times as likely to experience rough sleeping'.[2]

A revolution in house building is urgently needed, particularly in cities like London where half the hospitality and construction workforce are EU nationals. With W. Heath Robinson's 'How to Live in a Flat' (1936) in mind, 'Rainbows Over London' is a socio-political critique on domestic spatial impossibilities and speculative planning strategies for housing. Having the legal ability to manipulate rights and develop unused airspace would remove the key barrier to expand housing stock in city centres. Based on the '500 feet rule' recommended by Civil Aviation's 2005 regulations,[3] the Rainbow housing revolution develops across four stages up to boundaries set by the highest fixed obstacle for normal overflying aircraft.

Stage One: Propaganda. Following the famous dictum that 'Well Begun is Half Done',[4] the dawn of the revolution adopts iconic everyday urban elements including umbrellas, posters and newspapers to infiltrate society. A selection of the red telephone boxes and red post boxes that grace the streets of

facing page: 'Rainbows Over London' is a socio-political critique of urban housing inequality.

1. Land Promoters & Developers Federation, 'Housing Emergency: The New Lost Generation', www.lpdf.co.uk, August 2022 [https://www.lpdf.co.uk/housing-emergency-the-new-lost-generation], retrieved 12 October 2022

2. Crisis, 'Home for All: Why EU Citizens Are More Likely to Experience Homelessness – and Why It Matters', www.crisis.org.uk, November 2021. p.14 [https://www.crisis.org.uk/media/246341/home-for-all-why-eu-citizens-are-more-likely-to-experience-homelessness-and-why-it-matters-crisis.pdf], retrieved 12 October 2022

3. 'The Rules of the Air (Amendment) Regulations 2005', Civil Aviation, no.110, www.legislation.gov.uk [https://www.legislation.gov.uk/uksi/2005/1110/made?view=plain], retrieved 10 October 2022

4. R Stevenson, 'Mary Poppins', Walt Disney Productions, 1964

TELEPHONE
ROYAL MA
Evening Standard
REVOLUTION

THE GREAT BRITISH BAKE OFF
RAINBOW
ROAD
RAINBOW
BROMPTON ROAD STATION
CITY ROAD
RAINBOW
DOWN STREET STATION

BROMPTON ROAD
BROMPTON ROAD
BROMPTON ROAD
SUGAR COLLECTION POINT
FLOUR COLLECTION POINT
LEMON SEEDS
THE TEA PARTY

London are reappropriated with blue paint, the colour of security and responsibility. Instead of collecting mail, the post boxes print posters which disseminate propaganda similar in tone to World War II adverts supporting the Allied efforts, encouraging readers to participate in the revolution. The ubiquitous design of the telephone boxes is synonymous with ordinary people attaining extraordinary abilities to fight evil and injustice. Just as the socially inept nerd Clark Kent morphs into Superman, the passive protests of the housing activists come in the form of yellow umbrellas within the liminal protection provided by blue telephone boxes. Concurrently, newspaper headline-stands mysteriously appear in front of abandoned tube stations across London to disseminate the propaganda of injustice. The newspaper's crossword section invites discerning readers to the next clandestine gathering – the Tea Party. Stage Two: Possession. According to paragraph 1 Schedule 6 of the Land Registration Act of 2002, anyone who occupies registered land without permission from the owner and treats it as their own for 10 years is entitled to apply to be registered as owner. The Tea Party is a tool for this form of adverse possession as it occupies abandoned London stations through methods which take courage from another revolution, The Boston Tea Party of 1773 in colonial Massachusetts. In opposition to the Tea Act, every defiant attendee of the Party gathering is required to bring flour, sugar and lemons – ingredients to fabricate construction materials for the Rainbows. York Road, St Pancras, City Road, Shoreditch, Mark Lane, Waterloo, Brompton Road, Down Street, Charing Cross, Aldwych, Holborn, and Euston stations are selected as key locations for interventions.

Stage Three: Preparation. This penultimate stage reimagines The Great British Bake Off (GBBO), the reality show that has the attention of 10 million Britons whatever their political persuasion and faith. The tasks for the contestants (in this case EU hospitality workers) have become more architectural in nature, a competition where socio-political urban issues matter more than the rising of sponges or having a 'soggy bottom'.[5] Round the clock, a virtuous supply-and-demand cycle for optimism sustains the production of fresh bakes required to construct the Rainbows. The constant aroma of baking cakes permeating throughout London is probably the most powerful propaganda weapon of all. Stage Four: Participation. Elitism and social differences give way to common purpose when assembling the Rainbows. In economically bleak times with nothing but negativity on the news, watching GBBO where social solidarity in action constructs this most ambitious of tasks in record time reminds us that perhaps humanity still exists in this utopian Britain. Under the supervision of Mary Poppins[6] (Mary Berry[7] was unavailable), clouds of lemon drops and recycled poster 'origami bluebirds' graciously combat pollution to ensure the skies are blue. Poppins can mend souls and fix any structural cracks with water-proofing layers of lemon curd, ensuring resilience against another year of wet British weather.

Over the rainbow and beyond the radical imaginings of diverse stakeholders, addressing London's housing crisis requires determination and investment from the government, not more scapegoating of migrants who are struggling as much as UK citizens to afford a roof over their heads. As historian John Boughton stressed, 'we need state regulation and oversight to protect us from commercially driven agendas. And we need its idealism – that aspiration to treat all its citizens equitably and decently.'[8] Rainbows over London urges the cultivation of faith in the form and principle of high-rises that have provided decent homes to many and continue to form a vital component of the social housing stock.

previous page left: Stage One of the revolution adopts iconic everyday urban elements to disseminate propaganda.

previous page right: Stage Two involves taking adverse possession of abandoned London stations to repurpose them as urban bakeries.

facing page: Stage Three is all about the preparation of fresh bakes required for the Rainbows' construction.

following page left: Stage Four brings together volunteers who participate towards the common purpose of assembling the Rainbows.

following page right: Addressing the housing crisis requires investment by the government and imagination from stakeholders.

5. Coined by Mary Berry in 'The Great British Bake Off' (GBBO), the ubiquitous term 'soggy bottom' indicates that the bake is under cooked with a wet base.

6. Mary Poppins is the magical nanny of P.L. Traver's fictional books of the same name.

7. Mary Berry is considered the doyenne of baking and the judge of GBBO television series.

8. J Boughton, 'Municipal Dreams: The rise and fall of council housing', Verso, 2018, pp.5–6

SOMEWHERE OVER THE RAINBOW
ONCE IN A LULLA
BLUE BIRDS FLY
COSTA

TRUMP
THE TRUMP BEER
TRUMP
TEQUILA
THE TRUMP BEER

Ignorance + Hubris

'I believe we can build a community that more people will talk about and come to look at than any other area in the world – and with your cooperation, I'm sure that this experiment prototype community of tomorrow can influence the future of city living for generations to come.'

– Walt Disney, EPCOT Film, 1966

Modesty, compassion, and tolerance are often sidelined by visionaries of outlandish hubris and intractable power. They are emphatic, but not necessarily empathetic; incredibly driven, but with single-minded and often ignorant interpretations. Elevating dreams through political conviction or imposed values, they build self-contained worlds insulated from judgement. But despite their best attempts, one cannot be human alone. 'Ubuntu' reminds us that an authentic identity can only be found in connection to others. This beautiful African philosophy emphasises mutualistic values, limiting self-centredness and delusions of grandeur to beget a 'more significant relational, communal, societal, environmental and spiritual world'.[1]

facing page: The hubristic nature of 'The Wall of Cards' in case study 10 has been greatly emphasised in an attempt to 'Make America Great Again'.

Cecil John Rhodes is one of those rare individuals to have had an entire country named after him, and certainly the only one to have two – Northern and Southern Rhodesia. Other colonists have been remembered with eponymous territories, mountain peaks, and 'discoveries' of all kinds. With the city of Livingstone in Zambia, one can simply presume the origins – also familiar might be Mount Everest, named after Surveyor General of India Sir George Everest, or the South Pacific's Cook Islands for Captain James Cook. To be the 'first' to see something on a mission of scientific endeavour is one thing, but to enter an existing context with extreme prejudice and attempt to re-write history is quite another.

Commemorated for his many imperial accomplishments, Rhodes was a white supremacist whose endemic hubris manifested in delusions and belief in conspiracy theories. As he was dying, he claimed the ascendancy of Anglo-Saxons as 'the first race in the world'[2] was of benefit to humanity, wishing his name to be 'coupled with the object of England everywhere and united' with 'one language throughout'.[3] His racist mind was unwilling to accept that traditional African populations had a nuanced culture and sophisticated civic life, capable of building complex city settlements clearly evidenced in archaeological sites like Great Zimbabwe. Rhodes instead chose to believe that the Ancient Greeks had been responsible for its monuments, financing an archaeological expedition to prove his prejudicial delusions.[4] This ignorance underpinned devastating consequences. De Beers, his infamous diamond company, enforced slavery in 'Close Labour Compounds'[5] whose practices caused the abandonment of more than 2,000 football fields of mines, leaving them unrehabilitated and environmentally compromised forever.[6]

1. JR Mugumbate & A Chereni, 'Now, The Theory of Ubuntu Has Its Space in Social Work', African Journal of Social Work, vol.10. no.1, p.V, 20 September 2020

2. C Rhodes & WT Stead, 'The Last Will and Testament of Cecil John Rhodes', Review of Reviews Office, London, 1902, p.58 & p.68 [https://archive.org/details/lastwilltestamen00rhodiala/page/58/mode/2up], retrieved 20 April 2022

3. C Rhodes & WT Stead, 'The Last Will and Testament of Cecil John Rhodes', Review of Reviews Office, London, 1902, p.68 [https://archive.org/details/lastwilltestamen00rhodiala/page/68/mode/2up], retrieved 20 April 2022

4. C Mwandayi, 'Death and After-life Rituals in the Eyes of the Shona', University of Bamberg Press, Bamberg, 2011, p.39

5. R Turrell, 'Kimberley: Labour and compounds 1871–1888', in 'Industrialisation and Social Change in South Africa: African class formation, culture and consciousness 1870–1930', S Marks & R Rathbone (eds.), Longman, 1982, pp.45–76

Rhodes also concocted an unrealised 'Cape to Cairo Railway' to consolidate colonial powers across the continent. The infrastructure might have come to fruition following a key exchange of territory between Germany and the British Empire, but economic factors and the onset of war stalled construction. As Africa was gradually decolonised, the dream of a single spine-like connection to control its length was abandoned.[7] Instead, funds from the imperialist's estate were used to establish the Rhodes Scholarship fund and create a new building for Oriel College Oxford. The benefactor's statue has become a key site for international backlash against his racism and political legacy.[8]

Hubristic visions lead to abuses of the general population who are often exploited for the timely production of longstanding structures. To build the Great Wall of China, emperor Qin Shi Huang forcibly conscripted peasants, soldiers, and convicts to connect the disparate rammed earth walls of the pre-unification Warring States Period.[9] Indifferent use of forced labour transformed common conceptions of the Great Wall through the centuries, and it gained a reputation as a site of incredible suffering. Succumbing to hunger or exhaustion, the corpses of countless workers line its foundations in adjoining mass graves. The monument understandably retains a mixed legacy, viewed by the local population as a symbol of tyranny and oppression.[10] At the height of tensions with the Soviet Union in 1969, Mao Zedong ordered the creation of a similar protective structure known as the 'Underground Great Wall', this time built beneath Beijing. Labour practices under Mao's regime were seldom better than those of the empire as the subterranean shelter was 'hand-dug by 300,000 citizens, including children',[11] and is now used as a storage site for nuclear ICBMs.

Designed as tombs for the mummified remains of monarchic pharaohs rather than slaves, the spectacular reliquaries of wealth defended by the Great Pyramids were constructed piecemeal over the course of the 26th century BC. Remarkably, each of the massive structures was completed in single stretches of under 30 years. On such a timescale, workers would have had to lay one multi-ton stone every three minutes of a 12-hour working day to assemble the millions required to complete a single pyramid.[12] This incredible pace combined with a lack of detailed artefacts to reveal the secrets of how such enormous edifices were constructed has become the subject of countless conspiracy theories involving aliens, time travel, or lost technologies. As with the Great Wall, mass-slavery has been the traditional explanation for how this enormous manpower was assembled and effectively deployed. However, recent archaeological evidence implies that the pyramids were instead made by skilled workers and 'that their hard labour and sacrifice were rewarded – had these workers been slaves, they would not have received such honourable burials'.[13] Properly fed and well-provided with shelter near the sites of construction, engineers are now thought to have orchestrated virtuosic feats of strength, organising thousands of workers to cart massive stones across the desert on wheelless sleds. The sheer volumes of stone quarried and transported, presumably by the bare hands of generations working toward a single goal, is indicative of the Pyramids' compelling nature as monuments. That they were 'constructed to house the dead, not provide an environment for the living'[14] only underscores the psychological commitment of an entire civilisation to their celestial vision.

Ignorance is Bliss

In his radical narrative confession 'Notes from Underground' (1864), Fyodor Dostoyevsky makes a powerful argument for the eternal influences of irrationality and contradiction on the human condition. 'It is just his fantastic dreams, his vulgar folly that he will desire to retain, simply in order to prove to himself – as though that were so necessary – that men still are men and not the keys of a piano, which the laws of nature threaten to control so completely that soon one will be able to desire nothing but by the calendar.'[15] The inferiority complex-laden ramblings of his 'Underground Man' presaged the growing canon of disaffected dystopias populated by the alienated and atomized, from 'The Metamorphosis'

(1915) to 'Taxi Driver' (1976). While Thomas Gray likewise claimed that 'ignorance is bliss',[16] it is a major cause for dismay when applied to cities and countryside alike. Ignorance breeds an uncertainty open for exploitation, a state in which we find much of the world's leadership tragically competing for dominance. Donald Trump pledged to build a border wall between America and Mexico under the guise of preventing illegal immigration, drug trafficking, and cross-border crime. Its symbolic effect, however, has been a demonstration of Trump's ignorant and hyper conservative politics garnering few admirers outside his narrow-majority electorate. The wall aspires to make a fortress of the USA within which erroneous visions to 'Make America Great Again' can be cultivated without interruption. Like the presidency's other salacious claims and reactionary gestures, Trump's border-building rhetoric is an inflammatory marketing tactic taking advantage of mass media to erect walls in the minds of a disoriented populace. While quibbling erupted over structures that would never be realised, the quieter, more insidious work of passing policies to attack the interests of the disenfranchised could continue in earnest without meaningful pushback from higher authorities. In this unsettling example of modern statecraft, we see the built environment co-opted for the purposes of a political gimmick, a fragment in a larger narrative tapestry carefully designed to entangle, manipulate, and enrage.

As early as 1486 when his monumental treatise 'On the Art of Building in Ten Books' was published, architect Leon Battista Alberti wrote forthrightly that 'no city was ever free of civil discord when divided naturally either by a river or by being sited on several hills, or if it was partly on hills and partly on a plain. The best means of dividing a city is to build a wall through it.'[17] Enclosed settlements are nothing new – many of antiquity's greatest cities relied on barriers for protection. From the ancient stone borders of Jericho, Constantinople, Damascus or Sumer to concrete perimeters around the modern slums of Rio de Janeiro and 'the city of walls'[18] in São Paulo, this typology has been synonymous with urban life throughout history. In the earliest architectural treatises both Vitruvius and Alberti took it as given that any permanent settlement would necessitate a border wall. Alberti presents a series of possibly satirical arguments in 'De re aedificatoria', equal parts spatial and political. Cities ought to be divided in order to be peaceable because 'the smaller the parts into which a body is divided, the easier it is to govern and keep united'.[19] Focusing on social stratification, segregation, and strategic military implications, many believe Alberti to be playing to the cruel political sentiments of his time[20] when endorsing walls. Vitruvius simply observes that they 'should be laid out not as an exact square nor with salient angles, but in circular form, to give a view of the enemy from many points'.[21]

Influenced by the earlier writings of Aristotle and Plato, Alberti accepted that the foremost means for organising a society was through division. He quotes Plutarch, who 'tells us that Theseus divided the Commonwealth into two Ranks, one that made and expounded the Laws, both Humane and Divine, and the other that follow'd manual Occupations'.[22] The same beliefs are traced in Solon, Romulus, Caesar, and Hippodamus. This division of the classes is used to justify the articulation of building types for each part of the state. Book IV, 'Of the several Divisions of humane Conditions, whence arises the Diversity of Buildings',[23] studies architectures directed to this purpose. Here the rationalising principle of division provides the seed of the architectural profession, inasmuch as it expresses power, importance, and difference through the design of differentiated spaces.

6. H Matthews, 'Diamond Mining in South Africa' [https://hayleymatthews-diamondmining-southafrica.weebly.com/environmental-impacts], retrieved 23 April 2022

7. P Ball, 'The Cape to Cairo Railway Dream', The Heritage Portal, 21 November 2015 [https://www.theheritageportal.co.za/article/cape-cairo-railway-dream], retrieved 23 April 2022

8. W Hutton, 'Cecil Rhodes Was a Racist, But You Can't Readily Expunge Him from History', Opinion, Observer, 20 December 2015

9. 'The Great Wall of China', National Geographic Society [https://education.nationalgeographic.org/resource/great-wall-china], retrieved 31 July 2022

10 + 12. J Glancey, 'DK Eyewitness Companions: Architecture', DK Publishing, 2006, p.167 & p.56

11. J Glancey, 'How to Read Towns & Cities: A crash course in urban architecture', Bloomsbury, London, 2019, p.209

13. D Muller, 'How Were the Pyramids Built?', www.veritasium.com, 5 November 2014 [https://www.youtube.com/watch?v=lotbZQ55SgU], retrieved 31 July 2022

14 + 18. J Kotkin, 'The City: A global history', Modern Library, New York, 2005, p.38 & p.173

15. F Dostoyevsky, 'Notes from Underground', C Garnett (trans), Hackett, Indianapolis, 2008, p.47

16. T Gray, 'Poems', J. Dodsley, London, 1768, p.25 [http://archive.org/details/poems03graygoog], retrieved 31 July 2022

17, 19, 22, 23, 24 + 25. LB Alberti, 'On the Art of Building in Ten Books', J Rykwert, N Leach & R Tavernor (trans.), MIT Press, Cambridge, p.118, p.73, p.217 & p.236

20, 26, 29 + 30. G Fontana-Giusti, 'Walling and the City: The effects of walls and walling within the city space', Journal of Architecture, vol.16, issue 3, July 2011, pp.309–345, p.316 & p.317

Focusing an entire chapter on the 'Form and Disposition of Walls and Fortifications', Alberti considers physical barriers essential to the city's proper functioning. As with the classes and the buildings they inhabit, the urban realm is less prone to internal strife when divided appropriately into areas of public or private use for the aristocracy, principal assistants, and commonality. According to his counsel, a wise ruler should 'design the Walls of their Town with abundance of religious Rites and Ceremonies',[24] taking auspices repeatedly before yoking a bull and cow together to trace foundations, 'the Cow being placed on the Inside, and the Bull without'.[25] Directions for wall-building practices bleed into satire for the cities of contemporary tyrants in the Italian quattrocento. Alberti's intentions remain obscure, but he distinguishes the ideal town characterised by freedom of movement against cities ruled over by dictatorial sovereigns. In the latter, walls no longer serve an aesthetic purpose and are designed only to be defensible from either side, keeping the lower classes at bay within whilst protecting against aggressors without. Not only does Alberti frame the city primarily in terms of strategic division for the defence of powerful positions, but as a tool 'for offence and the waging of wars in general'.[26] In the architect's experience, it is not just the explicitly aggressive battlements and border walls which serve military conquest, but the city itself. Mirroring Alberti's buildings in their play of fortress-like interiors against paper-thin facades, the city becomes a tool of projection, exploitation, and securitisation. Situated in the perspective of martial concerns, the ultimate aim of this early urbanism becomes advancement of the mightiest political interests.

Ruling elites have favoured the creation of divisive structures to generate anxiety in the populace, attracting attention as a reliable means of raising revenue. Walls fulfil fantasies of a ready-to-build solution while remaining ambiguous in their real-world effects, becoming a blank screen for the generalised anxieties of a state and its people. Despite inevitably draining a country's finances, they 'show the government is taking action, a vote-seeking strategy that can prove very effective in the short term'.[27] Lewis Mumford reads an ego-driven possessiveness in the typology, collective expressions of the walled city preserving and transmitting a paranoid psychical structure.[28] He warns that 'fortifications do not create a feeling of security among citizens, but rather the opposite', paranoia generating a 'distorted perception about the need for further militarisation… as fear breeds fear and more walls'.[29] The consequences of this ideology 'have never deserted Western societies, their cities and the legacy of their spatiality', instead passing 'into the patterns of life, into a set of unwritten rules understood as common sense'.[30]

Notions that dividing walls are positive and even necessary go deeper still as the modern meaning of 'paradise', the Old English word for the Biblical Garden of Eden, is etymologically linked to 'walled enclosure'.[31] Traced back to the old Avestan root pairidaeza-, 'a wall enclosing a garden or orchard', is composed of pairi-, 'around', and daeza- 'wall'. Pairi is likewise related to the equivalent Greek word 'peri', as in perimeter. Xenophon, a Greek mercenary soldier who spent some time in the Persian army and later wrote histories, 'recorded the pairidaeza- surrounding the orchard as paradeisos',[32] which was then adopted to refer to the most favourable environment ancient imaginations could summon. Similarly, the Norse myth of 'The Master Builder' is concerned with the construction of a wall to protect Asgard, the realm of the gods. Loki, the troublemaker, makes a bargain with a strange 'master builder', whose name, translated from the Poetic Edda (c. 1220), is a precursor to that of the modern-day architect's. Tricking this builder into the impossible task of constructing a wall 'so high and so thick it would take many years'[33] with the time limit of a single winter, the gods lure this earliest of architects to complete its foundations without compensation when he fails to meet their deadline.

As with Babylon, Ávila and Quebec, every large city built before the modern age was fortified, and it was only in recent years that military advances made the shedding of physical defences possible. The possibilities of air raids, bombing runs and, later, nuclear strikes, encouraged the decentralisation of cities which quickly switched forms, stolid barricades limiting free movement giving way to efficient traffic networks facilitating evacuation. Shifting methods to address fundamental threats created novel urbanisms, one of which is codified in 'Life' magazine where cyberneticist Norbert Weiner published the influential article 'How U.S. Cities Can Prepare for Atomic War' (1950). Arguing that breakdowns of transportation and communication lines could potentially cause more panicked devastation than the effects of an explosion itself, 'the plan called for the construction of exurban "life belts" – infrastructural networks in radial patterns around every major American city'.[34] These were 'designed to control and direct the flow of traffic toward safe areas at the urban periphery during the hours immediately following a nuclear detonation'.[35] From highways to suburbs, the agents of change which would have the greatest spatial impact on 20th-century cities can easily be read in this proposal.

Modern spatial innovations brought about secret enclaves and protected enclosures of their own, from mountainside military bunkers to geographies separated from the corrupting influence of the outside world. In their infamous Manhattan project, the US army and federal government created entirely new cities in isolated locales to conduct the ground-breaking research which facilitated that deadliest of national defence programmes. Oak Ridge Nuclear Estate, first known as 'The City Behind the Fence' for its protected surroundings and later as 'The Atomic City' for its hand in the nuclear device that ended World War II, was not placed on state and national maps until 1949.[36] John O. Merrill, founding partner of SOM, moved to eastern Tennessee to direct the creation of the town and design housing in the form of prefabricated 'victory cottages' for its 75,000 residents, seemingly having arrived overnight in 1942.[37]

With homes made from boards of the asbestos-laiden wonder-material 'Cemesto', the ideal planned community was laid out as a loose grid of roads and dead-end lanes whose names progressed alphabetically from east to west.[38] These accessed schools, theatres, restaurants, and supermarkets along with a host of classified facilities including the world's largest building at the time, the half-million square metre K-25 plant for producing enriched uranium.[39] All the while, residents laboured in ignorance with no clue as to the nature of their work, but any uncertainty was combatted by the comforting presence of the secured boundary which ensured the hopeful self-importance of insiders and outsider curiosity. Sealed-off from the world within an atomic-research facility, the psychological importance of the wall to its caged community must not be forgotten. As Mumford wrote of the fortress-like city, its 'enclosure helps create a feeling of unity as well as security. It is significant – and a little disturbing – that the protected inhabitants of the town grew to value the "secure" life within, free from any sort of foreign invasion or even unauthorised approach – though it meant that their own comings and goings were under constant military surveillance and control.'[40]

Reflecting on the manifestation of these impulses in the infrastructure of earlier ages, he further elucidates the long history and seemingly inexorable continuation of urban partitioning. 'Not merely did the walled city give a permanent collective structure to the paranoid claims and delusions of kingship, augmenting suspicion, hostility, non-cooperation, but the division of labour and castes, pushed to the extreme, normalised schizophrenia... That structure is still visible in our own day, though the outer walls

21. V Pollio, 'The Ten Books on Architecture', HL Warren (ed.), MH Morgan (trans.), Dover Publications, New York, 1960, p.22

27. E Ganivet, 'Border Wall Aesthetics: Artworks in border spaces', Transcript Verlag, Bielefeld, 2019, p.9

28, 40 + 41. L Mumford, 'The City in History: Its origins, its transformations and its prospects', Secker & Warburg Ltd, London, 1961, p.39, p.304 & p.46

31. 'Origin and Meaning of Paradise', www.etymonline.com [https://www.etymonline.com/word/paradise], retrieved 2 August 2022

32. AC Madrigal, 'Good News, Facebook! The Root Word for "Paradise" Originally Meant "Walled Garden"', The Atlantic, 20 July 2012 [https://www.theatlantic.com/technology/archive/2012/07/good-news-facebook-the-root-word-for-paradise-originally-meant-walled-garden/260140], retrieved 2 May 2023

33. N Gaiman, 'Norse Mythology', Bloomsbury, London, 2017, p.55

34 + 35. R Martin, 'The Organizational Complex: Architecture, media, and corporate space', MIT Press, Cambridge, Mass., 2003, p.28

36. LA Freeman, 'Longing for the Bomb: Oak Ridge and atomic nostalgia', University of North Carolina Press, 2015, p.120

37. E. Westcott, ' Images of America: Oak Ridge', Arcadia Publishing, 2005, p.61

38. 'Mystery Town Cradled Bomb', Life Magazine, 20 August 1945, p.94

39. 'The K-25 Plant', Atomic Heritage Foundation [https://www.atomicheritage.org/tour-stop/k-25-plant], retrieved 3 August 2022

42 + 44. R Koolhaas, 'Exodus, or the Voluntary Prisoners of Architecture', in 'Perfect Acts of Architecture', J Kipnis (ed.), 2001, pp.15–33

43. W Churchill, 'The Sinews of Peace: Post-War Speeches', Houghton Mifflin Co., Boston, 1949

have given way to iron curtains.'[41] Indeed, nowhere has the self-defeating isolationism of the wall been more apparent than post-war Berlin, the divide between Soviet and Western spheres of influence severing neighbourhoods, businesses, families, and worldviews. Starting as 'some pathetic strings of barbed wire abruptly dropped on the imaginary line of the border, its psychological and symbolic effects were infinitely more powerful than its appearance'.[42] The Berlin Wall was constructed throughout the 1960s by East German authorities, progressing from insubstantial fencing to over 100 kilometres of smooth concrete to become the physical expression of Churchill's 'iron curtain'.[43] All the while it inverted the traditional symbolism of the walled city by preventing East Germans from entering the democratic enclave of West Berlin, rather than protecting those inside from threats real or imagined. The return of division in the heart of the modern city inspired Wim Wenders to dream of spaces where the most powerful walls could not reach in 'Wings of Desire' (1987). The massive barrier is the defining character in its portrayal of the city, featuring a recreation of its inaccessible no-mans-land which serves as a reminder of the not-so-distant realities of intractable conflict.

Rem Koolhaas visited Berlin ten years after the wall's construction and his observations of the spaces it defined drove the conception of a famous architectural speculation, 'Exodus, or the Voluntary Prisoners of Architecture' (1972). Imagined structures divide London creating a linear prison on the scale of a metropolis. Like Berlin, this space also inverts the process of confinement as people seek refuge within the architecture by their own initiative, the Voluntary Prisoners. Here, 'as so often before in this history of mankind, architecture was the guilty instrument of despair',[44] ultimately having more to do with separation and exclusion than liberation. 'One part became the Good Half, the other part the Bad Half. The inhabitants began to flock to the good part of the divided city, rapidly swelling into an urban exodus... After all attempts to interrupt this undesirable migration had failed, the authorities of the bad part made desperate and savage use of architecture: they built a wall around the good part of the city, making it completely inaccessible to their subjects.'[45]

Since medieval times the capital of Cyprus has been fortified by a border wall surrounding its old city. The circular plan adopted by the Venetians who constructed the Walls of Nicosia (1567–1570) was unique for the period. To achieve the perfect geometry, much of the Frankish old town had to be demolished at a time when the practice of planning was in its infancy and settlements usually expanded or contracted sporadically. While many fortresses like Palmanova in Terrafirma and Neuf-Brisach in France adopted geometrical outlines, this had never been implemented on the scale of cities 'and certainly not ones of such political importance or geographical extent'.[46] Instead of following the natural topography and haphazard boundaries of buildings at the city limits, the insistence on an iconographic plan draws upon 'the larger Renaissance project of designing the Perfect City: functional urban life protected by efficient fortifications'.[47] Derived from the theories of Vitruvius and formalised for Francesco Sforza, Duke of Milan, by the architect Filarete, the 'Sforzinda' ideal city was influential for the subsequent thought of Thomas More and other utopians seeking to create perfect societies through optimal urban designs. Here, circular form is tied to concerns with magic, astrology, and cosmic spheres, creating celestial harmony through the city's relation to the heavens.[48] There is also evidence that the radial design references St Augustine's 'Earthly City' from his treatise on 'The City of God'. Divided into spokes for the vices of pride, greed, lust, envy, anger, sloth and segments of virtue, the Earthly City is organised around worldly desires, materialism, and pleasure. Filarete contains these fallen natures in the Sforzinda's ten-storey centrepiece, the 'House of Vice and Virtue', with a brothel occupying its base and an academy of learning housed in the higher levels.[49]

A modern-day instantiation of the vices now divides Nicosia. After being granted independence from Britain in 1960, tensions quickly rose between preexisting political factions triggering a coup d'etat. The United Nations 'Green Line' established to mediate the dispute runs through the heart of the Cypriot capital, creating two sides of Greek and Turkish control which extend across the halved country.[50] Incorporating parts of the medieval walls into its structure, the path of the buffer zone illustrates how the use, conception, and construction of walls has changed over the centuries, ploughing forward instead of encircling, dividing rather than defending. Like the fence separating the land of the savages from civilisation in Aldous Huxley's 'Brave New World' (1932), the border marches 'on and on, irresistibly the straight line, the geometrical symbol of triumphant human purpose'.[51] Just 20 miles south of this demilitarised zone lies the UNESCO-protected archaeological site of Khirokitia, one of the oldest permanent human settlements to be discovered. Like Nicosia, Khirokitia is enclosed by massive stone walls indicating a nuanced understanding of urban planning and cooperative defence on the part of its builders.[52] Walled cities being the historical rule begs the question of whether contemporary proclivities for openness and freedom of movement will, in fact, prove to be an anomaly. Without the comfort of physical barriers, what defences might the future city create to facilitate the complex social hierarchies which regiment the interactions of its inhabitants?

Fear and Loathing

Fear is universal in its instinctive shaping of the city. If the depredations of human society are not enough, it can be provided in due measure by Mother Nature. In his characteristically austere narration for 'Into the Inferno' (2016), filmmaker Werner Herzog epitomises this chaotic wrath in the volcanic activity roiling just beneath Earth's crust, ready to erupt at any moment. 'It is a fire that wants to burst forth and it could not care less about what we are doing up here. Everything will melt, the stones, the trees, everything, like water...'[53] Tokyo, the world's most populous city, is sited in an especially earthquake-prone area of Japan. Its proximity to water in the Sagami Bay also makes it susceptible to the tsunamis which often follow such events. The Great Kanto earthquake of 1923 created a wave whose wholesale destruction of the urban fabric 'set in motion the first systematic attempt at reshaping Tokyo as a modern city'.[54] Rising oceans, sinking ground, and outdated dikes are once again making the world metropolises vulnerable to violent storms. Combined with incredible population density, these factors make Tokyo and Yokohama the riskiest metropolitan area in the world.[55]

Tehran, the most populous city in West Asia, is sinking a quarter of a metre per year due to subsidence from droughts.[56] Likewise, the densely populated eastern metropolis of Kolkata is projected to house the most at-risk population of any urban area by 2070, facing threats from development practices which compromise ecological flood defences like wetlands.[57] Both are at significant risk from less severe occurrences because impoverished areas with older buildings, infrastructure, and poor drainage are far less resilient. Indonesia's oceanside capital Jakarta also suffers regular flooding and severe subsidence affecting millions. The problem has been exacerbated by urban sprawl whose concrete coverings prevent aquifers from being replenished despite torrential rain. To avoid these environmental challenges, the government is moving its capital from the low-lying island of Java to the purpose-built city of Nusantara on Borneo.[58] Faced with the opposite problem, Minqin China is trapped between two fast expanding deserts. Akin to water-diversion catastrophes perpetrated by central planners on the Aral Sea and Lop Nur Lake, both now completely dried up, Minqin's water supply relies on a single river which is becoming increasingly strained. With the county's population fleeing, provincial officials were forced into action

45. R Koolhaas, 'Exodus, or the Voluntary Prisoners of Architecture', in 'Perfect Acts of Architecture', J Kipnis (ed.), 2001, p.16

46 + 47. D Cosmescu, 'Nicosia', Fortified Places, 12 July 2015 [https://web.archive.org/web/20150712185027/http://fortified-places.com/nicosia], retrieved 5 August 2022

48. S Kostof, 'The City Shaped: Urban patterns and meanings through history', 1st North American ed., Little, Brown and Co., 1991, p.187

49. S Lang, 'The Ideal City: From Plato to Howard', Architectural Review, vol.112, 1952, pp.91–101

50. L Graham, 'The Turkish Invasion of Cyprus', History Daily, 20 July 2022 [https://www.historydaily.com/the-turkish-invasion-of-cyprus], retrieved 14 June 2023

51. A Huxley, 'Brave New World', Harper & Brothers, New York, 1946, p.46

52. Pre-History Podcast, 'Episode 21: Cyprus goes the way of the Khirokitia culture', Apple Podcasts [https://podcasts.apple.com/gb/podcast/episode-21-cyprus-goes-the-way-of-the-khirokitia-culture/id1535005292?i=1000542233385], retrieved 14 June 2023

53. W Herzog & M Moses, 'Into the Inferno', Werner Herzog Filmproduktion, 2016

54. J Hammer, 'The Great Japan Earthquake of 1923', Smithsonian Magazine, May 2011 [https://www.smithsonianmag.com/history/the-great-japan-earthquake-of-1923-1764539], retrieved 6 August 2022

55. H Tabuchi, 'How Tokyo Is Preparing for Flooding Beyond Anything We've Seen Before', Independent, 18 October 2017

56. 'Tehran Facing Serious Risks of Natural Disasters', Tehran Times, 14 August 2019 [https://www.tehrantimes.com/news/439242/Tehran-facing-serious-risks-of-natural-disasters], retrieved 6 August 2022

after realising the loss of agricultural output would have dire consequences for a neighbouring city of two million.[59] They have since reformed water distribution rights, created a new transfer system, and spurred tree planting initiatives to combat soil degradation, but there are no guarantees on the fate of Minqin.

Almost the entirety of the Netherlands lies below sea level and is only kept from disaster by a vast infrastructure of levees and dikes which keep its cities on dry land. This engineering marvel has been maintained for 700 years by an extremely organised social structure whose frugality and foresight are now pitted against the prospect of rising sea levels.[60] By contrast New Orleans, also partially built on a flood plain, has been devastated by ocean storms in past decades. While such catastrophes can be framed through the lens of a chance natural occurrence, corruption in Louisiana's political system encourages the cutting of corners; dikes are engineered by the Army-Corps to withstand hundred-year storms rather than the ten-thousand-year storms used in specifications by the Dutch. As a result, much of the resources which could have been invested in flood infrastructure were diverted, costing its society more in the long run by allowing the combatable forces of a natural disaster to overrun structures that were well below the threshold of technical capability.

Riskier still are the cities which sit on hotbeds of seismic activity. Death-defying residents accept lives under threat of building-toppling earthquakes against which certain engineering measures are taken, or at the base of active volcanos from whose eruption there can be no conceivable protection. These contexts affect the built fabric in a binary of contradictory manners; causing either a build-up in protective measures like wall-bracing and beefier foundations by those wishing to fight against the agents of chance, or an acceptance of temporary structures which rest lightly on the landscape by those who recognise the futility of their resistance. In Los Angeles, the San Andreas Fault system runs directly under its metropolitan centre of 13 million.[61] While advances in suspended foundations have 'proofed' modern buildings against earthquakes and ordinances have required mandatory retrofitting for older, at-risk structures, a severe seismic event could still cause considerable damage. Experts have been warning about the next 'big one' for decades – Southern California has experienced major earthquakes every century on record, and little can be done about the fact that much of the urban fabric would be powerless to withstand the incredible forces of a once-in-a-lifetime calamity.

The capital of Guadeloupe, Basse-Terre, was inexplicably settled as a commune in the shadow of the Soufrière volcano. In 1976, volcanologists announced an imminent eruption and more than 70,000 inhabitants were evacuated.[62] Such prompts were readily obeyed as the nearby city of Saint-Pierre had vanished under similar circumstances in 1902 when Mount Pelée killed all but one of its residents. Saint-Pierre's annihilation was forecast by significant eruptive activity, but the mayor insisted people remain on the island for an election.[63] This time, locals on Basse-Terre were not taking their chances and the entire population left, with the exception of three rogue farmers devoted to their life on the island, its animals, and God's will. Some, perhaps sensibly, refused to return. La Soufrière never did erupt, though its settlement's ghostly condition persists having remained semi-abandoned for decades. To this day the population has only recovered to about half its original size, a memory of an inevitable catastrophe which never took place.[64]

Monuments to Hubris

John Milton's epic poem 'Paradise Lost' (1667) sees the Devil himself putting forth a powerful rationalisation for hubris. His explanation hinges on the paradoxical motivations of rulers tempted by power, heeding the clarion call of despotic desire to seek triumph over Creation. 'A mind not to be chang'd by Place or Time. Can make a Heav'n of Hell, a Hell of Heav'n. To reign is worth ambition though in Hell: Better to reign in Hell, than serve in Heav'n.'[65] Despised the world over,

Adolf Hitler was nonetheless one of the most adept leaders of all time. After becoming the chancellor of Germany in 1933, he spearheaded the greatest economic and military expansion ever seen, with an ideology priding itself on efficiency and orderliness. Rejected from Vienna's Academy of Fine Arts,[66] Hitler was careful to enlist the architectural services of Albert Speer in his political programme, dreaming up hubristic visions for the designs of a glorious Germanic nation to fulfil his former aspirations. The Nazi regime was meticulous in its propaganda and planning, harnessing the elements of light, sound, and space like none before in brilliant displays of spatial organisation. Foreshadowing today's use of spectacle-supporting city infrastructures as instruments of national power, Hitler officiated ceremonies at the 1936 Olympic games hosted in Berlin.[67] His National Socialist government would sponsor architecture on an immense scale, employing a classical reinterpretation of German culture with Speer instrumentalising countless elements associated with the Roman Empire.

Germania now exists only as blueprints and architectural models, but the ideal capital of the Third Reich was once as much a political reality as any current European parliament. Had the Axis powers won the war and Germania come to fruition, the skyline of Berlin would be dominated by the enormous dome of the 'Volkshalle'. Designed to accommodate some 180,000 spectators attending the addresses of the Führer, its interior encompassed enough volume that clouds would have formed in its upper reaches. Explicitly modelled on Hadrian's Pantheon in Rome scaled up by hundreds of times, the massive marble edifice was to be sited at the culmination of the six-kilometre-long 'Avenue of Splendors'. Reorganised along this perfect north-south promenade, Berlin would have become an exaggerated facsimile of Paris's Champs-Elysées with a gateway dwarfing the Arc de Triomphe opposite the Volkshalle's imposing dome. What appears today as historical absurdity was, during wartime, in the process of being realised, entire districts disappearing in anticipation before resources were diverted to the military.

Architectural megalomania was not limited to perennial structures, as Nazi gatherings were feats of design in their own right. The Nuremberg rally grounds designed by Speer remain some of the largest stadia ever constructed and images of his 'Cathedral of Light', projected through massive lamps above the Zeppelinfeld, are hauntingly powerful. To promote the symbolism of purifying flames rallies were often held under cover of night, obscuring what was truly underway with darkness while retaining the anonymity essential to the Nazi's 'mass-culture'[68] experiences. The delusions of grandeur which Germania's planning sought to realise are best encapsulated by the symbol that topped the dome of the Volkshalle and frequently appeared on Hitler's tribunal; an eagle with a globe clutched in its talons, the architectural representation of an autocratic movement seeking to subject the world to its reality.

Tempelhof Airport also embodied the National Socialist ideology and was one of the few buildings which remained standing in the war's aftermath as an important American outpost. Among the first world leaders to make frequent international trips, 'Hitler understood the power of associating himself with flight',[69] and his airfield was designed to resemble the Nazi eagle when viewed from the skies. Paired with imperial classicism, the thrilling modernism of political celebrity and the machine-age were appropriated by the Third Reich to construct a symbolic and highly compelling architectural identity. Leon Krier, famous for his promotion of classical revival and collaborations with King Charles III, has

57. S Sengupta, 'Kolkata: A city on the brink of climate disaster', Irish Times, 11 August 2018

58. R Radcliffe, 'Indonesia Names New Capital Nusantara, Replacing Sinking Jakarta', Guardian, 18 January 2022

59. Y Yuan, 'Island in the Sand', SixthTone, 17 December 2019 [https://www.sixthtone.com/news/1004964/island-in-the-sand], retrieved 6 August 2022

60. R Steves, 'The Netherlands: Dikes and a rising sea', 2013 [https://classroom.ricksteves.com/videos/the-netherlands-dikes-and-a-rising-sea], retrieved 5 August 2022

61. J Glancey, 'How to Read Towns & Cities: A crash course in urban architecture', Bloomsbury, London, 2019, p.214

62 + 63. Werner Herzog, 'La Soufrière', Werner Herzog Filmproduktion, 1977

64. 'Historique Des Populations Communales', Insee, 29 December 2022 [https://www.insee.fr/fr/statistiques/3698339], retrieved 5 August 2022

65. J Milton, 'Paradise Lost', J. W. Lovell Co., New York, 1884, Lines 221–270

66. WL Shirer, 'The Rise and Fall of the Third Reich: A history of Nazi Germany', Secker & Warburg Ltd, London, 1960, p.15

67. RJ Evans, 'The Third Reich in Power, 1933–1939', Allen Lane, London, 2005, p.573

68. SW Semes, 'Albert Speer: Architecture 1932–1942', The Classicist, no.11, 2014, pp.80–82

69. 'Germania: Architecture in a fascist utopia', Podcast, Listen Notes, 27 June 2019 [https://www.listennotes.com/podcasts/nice-try/germania-architecture-in-a-kAQzCbK40Y6], retrieved 6 August 2022

come under fire for his views on the aesthetic value of Nazi architecture. In a book dedicated to the masterworks of Speer, Krier rails against the legacy of modernists like Le Corbusier and the damage wreaked through industrial processes leading to Germany's Marshall Plan.[70] More controversially, he argues that Speer, like Wernher von Braun and other Nazi scientists spared prosecution and co-opted for the US space programme, should have been allowed to spread his design genius in the building of post-war cities.[71] This opportunity could have averted the excesses of modernity – a sin apparently more heinous than perpetuating the myth of Speer as an evil man nonetheless capable of creating great art, or worse, an ignorant bystander caught in the apparatus of the Nazi machine he so assiduously helped to design.

Interestingly, Speer was shifted from his role as the Party's chief architect to Minister of Armaments when the Reich suffered its first major defeats, overseeing the 'secret-weapon' rocket programs on which von Braun made many of the innovations later coveted by NASA. Launched into major cities from London to Moscow, German V-2 rockets played an important role in shaping the urban landscape of Europe after replacing the less efficient Luftwaffe bombing campaigns which rained thousands of tonnes of explosives on population centres. The Architects' Department of the London County Council kept detailed records of the bombardment's effects, creating hand-coloured damage maps that give disturbing clarity to the destruction's scope. This iconic, 'multi-layered source for London's experience of war conveys complex survey data in the tradition of Leake's Great Fire map, Milne's land use map, Mylne's geological maps and Booth's poverty maps'.[72] These documents were referenced extensively by Patrick Abercrombie and John Henry Forshaw in creating 1944's Greater London Plan which guided rebuilding efforts in the capital, but certain areas retain memories of the events in the form of visible scars. Smithfield Market, St. Clement Danes Church, and the Tate Britain all feature markings from shrapnel on their walls that can be seen today. Escaping the network of ordinary latitude and longitude, these remnants reveal new dimensions of historic narrative and their 'maps begin as dreams, pass through a finite life in the world, and resume as dreams again'.[73] In a melancholy moment, Braun likewise asserted, 'nature does not know extinction; all it knows is transformation. Everything science has taught me, and continues to teach me, strengthens my belief in the continuity of our spiritual existence after death.'[74]

In their damaged state, cities 'offer an entirely new possibility for understanding the origins of both space and habitation'.[75] Through depictions of Sarajevo after its siege, Lebbeus Woods sought to address the relationship between war, political revolution, and architecture. His speculative reconstruction drawings of a district devastated by unpredictable forces both human and natural illustrate visions of adaptable designs, existing within the scars wrought by urban ruination.'The spirit of invention that makes survival possible under the extreme conditions created by destruction makes possible the new ways of living in a city that will, in a sense, always remain in a paradoxical state of destruction and construction.'[76]

For decades housing has been built to expand Israel's territory into illegally occupied land. Separated from Palestine by a slew of border-wall checkpoints, these communities are strategically placed throughout areas under military control to displace neighbouring populations. Over 600,000 people currently live in at least 250 illegal settlements in the West Bank and East Jerusalem.[77] For Palestinians, these settlements are testament to an ongoing campaign of annexation, repression, and replacement, the most vivid example of a cultural conflict that has persisted for generations. Just a few yards from the Israeli separation wall in Bethlehem, Banksy's 'Walled Off Hotel' playing on the famous Manhattan Waldorf documented in 'Delirious New York' (1978)[78] has attracted hordes of tourists in a controversial bid to raise awareness. Proponents think the hotel is transforming a conflict area characterised by despair and suffering into a haven of art, tourism, and information. This juxtaposition does not sit well with numerous critics, some of whom accuse the work of profiting off tragedy.[79] Regardless of its propriety, most can agree with the assertion that the building probably owns 'the worst view of any hotel in the world'.[80]

Organised Ignorance: Illusions of the future

Deep within an endless maze of convoluted hallways beneath cavernous administration buildings, Joseph K. struggles against a morass of conspiratorial forces that appear to pervade the minds and actions of every person he encounters. '"You haven't got lost, have you?" asked the usher in amazement. "Come with me," said K., "show me the way, I'll miss it, there are so many different ways here." "It's the only way there is," said the usher, who had now started to sound quite reproachful.'[81] Ever since Cervantes's Don Quixote reimagined a field of windmills as giants,[82] the idea of shared fiction and illusory architectures as refuge for the human mind became an explicit potential for designers. The most engaging examples of such manipulative environments not only curate spaces but the experiences within them. Relying on mass delusions perpetuated through behavioural cues, misleading graphics, and the often-disguised materiality of construction, they shape new and peculiar versions of reality. The telos of this architecture is deception posed as sincerity, cultivating a directed ignorance to its own ends. As the ancient builders knew all too well, and as present-day practitioners are re-asserting 'architecture, as a discipline, can itself be used to tell stories... complete with elaborate plots supplied for no other reason than to explain why a particular building should exist or require designing'.[83]

One of the great architectural stories of antiquity is that of the labyrinth. From its origins in Knossos where Theseus traversed a maze of passageways laying down string to guide his escape, the mythological form of the labyrinth has been progressively internalised in collective spatial experiences. From the subterranean catacombs beneath nondescript European cities to the tile mazes on the floors of French cathedrals and parallel networks of hedges in palace gardens, these deliberately complicated objects produce a unique form of spatial ignorance by purposefully withholding their true configurations from all who enter. Nowhere is the metaphysical anguish caused by labyrinthine architecture better portrayed than in Franz Kafka's masterwork, 'The Trial' (1925). The psychological experience of protagonist Joseph K., indicted for mysterious offences he cannot remember committing and for which no records exist, is reflected in the endless passageways and nameless offices of an enormous bureaucracy. Architecture becomes a metaphor for the inhumane social order of the industrial metropolis which, like the depictions of its buildings 'are confused, self-connected, and inconsistent with themselves'.[84]

Dream-like spaces unique to the modern city confront all of Kafka's protagonists; confounding networks of crowded streets, dingy apartments, oppressive workspace crammed with filing cabinets of uninterpretable documents, and kangaroo courtrooms where absurd proceedings entertain nameless onlookers. Unfeasibly vast bureaucratic institutions are always permeated by the omniscient presence of a nameless, ambivalent authority enlisting the help of complex contraptions to persecute its unfortunate residents indiscriminately. These spatial visions embody Kafka's characteristic themes – entrapment, frustration, incomprehensible motivations – and are unaffected by the building typology in which they occur. Whether it be cramped urban tenements, or transatlantic steamships, the experiences are 'always somehow impossible, made up of surprising overlaps between law, religion, and civil society'.[85]

70. '58 – The Reactionaries – 3/3 – The Empire Strikes Back', Podcast, Listen Notes, 19 August 2019 [https://www.listennotes.com/podcasts/about-buildings/58-the-reactionaries-33-the-qGJ6mbaROkl], retrieved 6 August 2022

71. MZ Wise, 'Hitler's Words Into Stone', Wall Street Journal, 12 April 2013 [https://online.wsj.com/article/SB10001424127887323296504578398542977265774.html], retrieved 6 August 2022

72. 'London County Council Bomb Damage Maps', City of London [https://www.cityoflondon.gov.uk/things-to-do/history-and-heritage/london-metropolitan-archives/collections/cityoflondon.gov.uk/things-to-do/history-and-heritage/london-metropolitan-archives/collections/london-county-council-bomb-damage-maps], retrieved 6 August 2022

73. T Pynchon, 'Against the Day', Penguin Press, New York, 2006, p.276

74. W von Braun, 'Why I Believe in Immortality', in 'The Third Book of Words to Live By', W Nichols (ed.), Simon and Schuster, 1962, pp.119–120

75 + 76. 'Lebbeus Woods: Radical reconstruction, 1997', History of Our World (blog), 18 November 2009 [https://historyofourworld.wordpress.com/2009/11/18/lebbeus-woods-radical-reconstruction], retrieved 6 August 2022

77. Editorial, 'Israel Approves More than 4,000 Settlement Homes: Rights group', 12 May 2022 [https://www.aljazeera.com/news/2022/5/12/israel-approves-nearly-4500-settler-homes-in-occupied-west-bank], retrieved 6 August 2022

78. R. Koolhaas, 'Delirious New York: A retroactive manifesto for Manhattan', Oxford University Press, New York, 1978

79. H Ellis-Petersen, 'Banksy Walled Off Hotel in Palestine to Sell New Works by Elusive Artist', Guardian, 7 September 2017

80. E Graham-Harrison, '"Worst View in the World": Banksy opens hotel overlooking Bethlehem Wall', Guardian, 3 March 2017

When Peter the Great established a fortress for national defence on a desolate island in the Gulf of Finland, it would have required an exceedingly active imagination to envision the lavish architectural gem-turned-imperial capital that it would evolve into. Unlike more ancient European political centres, St Petersburg benefited from the lack of context and restrictions granted by a vacant marsh, along with the conscripted serf labour which allowed construction to take place in such remote environs. By the end of the 18th century, enterprising architects with abundant craftsmen at their disposal had given 'visible shape to dreams of untrammelled splendour'.[86] Following the Russian Civil War, the capital was moved to Moscow and St Petersburg was renamed 'Leningrad', concealing ties to the pre-revolutionary czarist era. The leadership of the Soviet Union created a break from its history, developing a cult of personality around Lenin by associating his name with the opulence of edifices like the Winter Palace and federal buildings lining the Nevsky Prospect. This influence is still found in surviving Stalinist architecture, from culture palaces to residential Stalinkas, constructed across the vast Soviet bloc before the cutbacks of Khrushchev demanded uniform efficiency from new buildings.

The ultimate in curated urban experiences is undoubtedly provided by Walt Disney and his renowned theme parks in the southern United States. Opening in Anaheim, California, Disneyland Park (1955) was the first attempt by America's arch-storyteller to capture the whimsical nature of his animated classics in built form. Seen as a great success for the returns it brought developers, the project was praised by planner James Rouse in a 1963 speech at Harvard University. Rouse made a shocking claim to the Ivy League audience – that Disneyland was 'the greatest piece of urban design in the United States' and that he found more to learn in it 'than in any other piece of physical development in the country'.[87]

Indeed, the park achieved all the aims it set out to accomplish usefully, unselfconsciously, and most importantly, profitably. As Disneyland grew to the Anaheim property's edge, it was boxed in by a construction boom with low-rent motels and opportunistic businesses poaching its customers. Frustrated by these goings-on, Disney became obsessed with quelling what he saw as the problems of free and open urbanity. He imagined a model community that would address the social ills plaguing city life, from poverty to congested roads. Ironically, Disney brought his dream to Robert Moses, the man who did more than anyone to tacitly perpetuate the many flaws of mid-century American cities through ruthless highway belting. Both believed that they would be able to create the first accident-free, noise-free, and pollution-free city through dictatorial top-down methods. Conflicted about the public image he had created as an entertainer, Disney set his ambitions against what he saw as the more serious accomplishments made by titans of industry like John D. Rockefeller and Henry Ford. Desirous of a legacy that could rival such men in its contributions to the Great American Society, he started groundwork for a planned community that would affect the lives of people the world over.

Disney was able to acquire swathes of empty land in central Florida for a pittance, a geography which could be moulded to the single-minded pursuit of business interests. The company embarked upon the creation of a Petersburg for the commercialism of the 20th century, an urban masterpiece meant to exceed the legacy of its animated output. Drainage canals to de-water the vast site gave way to multi-lane roads and open expanses of packed earth emptied of plant and animal life. What would become one of the world's most visited destinations was carved out of a marshy wilderness twice the size of Manhattan with the ambition of conjuring a gigantic and evolving future industrial city from thin air. At its centre, the 'Experimental Prototype Community of Tomorrow' (EPCOT) was planned on a radial footprint, with spokes stretching from a dense core to greener residential areas in an arrangement reminiscent of Ebeneezer Howard's Garden City. Reacting to the strained transportation networks in California, traffic became a priority in the functional layout of the community, its mitigation the great strategy which would 'translate one man's fanciful notion into a sprawling reality'.[88]

EPCOT was to have the first town-spanning communication network, keeping track of all the properties' functions from utility management to pollution control. These ambitious planning efforts were a precursor of current day 'smart cities', aiming at new heights of efficiency and coordination by blending capitalism with urbanism. Every resident had to be employed according to their ability, and the community would not accept retirees. Rushing to set an authoritative course for the development, Disney's demands became increasingly grandiose and outlandish, his desperation brought about by failing health. In his 1966 film advertising the project, he states that 'in EPCOT, there will be no slum areas because we won't let them develop. There will be no landowners and therefore no voting control.'[89] A special district was created which granted the project unique administrative powers and freedom from any county and state oversight. Loopholes to avoid interference over land use laws from various political levels were paired with plans to dissuade the population from organising and self-governing. Such measures illustrate the company's desire to exercise control not only over the design of the city, but its residents' lives. Walt Disney would pass away just over a year after announcing the development, and today the park is only a pale shadow of the preposterous masterplan that might have been constructed had the man gotten his way. Though he never saw his full vision completed, Disney World remains the ultimate example of an ideologically motivated space, its hubristic design tailored to incredibly specific sets of behaviours and forms of social existence.

Rhodesia went through a series of gradual breaks and eventually was liberated from imperialism. However, Rhodes and other totalitarians had sowed the seeds of perennial distrust into the socio-political mindset of what became independent Zimbabwe. These precepts inspired the African Nationalist liberator Robert Mugabe to hold his own extreme perspectives towards oppressors, clouding the vision of a leader which led the nation down another treacherous path.[90] As for Great Zimbabwe, the medieval ruins have been irrevocably desecrated. Richard Nicklin Hall, the British archaeologist appointed to preserve the site instead became transfixed with removing the 'filth and decadence'[91] of African occupation. With incredible hubris, he tore away four metres of precious history in search of evidence that a European builder had been responsible for the structures – he found none. Ill-planned reconstruction efforts have been the cause of further degradation, poor management losing out in a vain struggle against the damage done by time and multiplied by tens of thousands of clambering tourists.[92]

To some extent the world's population is living by the dreams and disillusions of individuals or small collectives; and as political currents change so do the sources of their visions. Human beings are susceptible to herd mentality, behaviours that have led to enslavement, brainwashing and manipulation. The consequences of submitting to the desires of others will certainly result in sometimes aggressive ego-urbanism, sometimes arrogant vanity infrastructures, and sometimes ill-conceived architectures to compensate self-esteem. In awe or in abhorrence, these projects will last thousands of years into the future, into a time where humanity will have either eradicated itself or grown to embrace totally unrecognisable cities and cultures. If a watchful eye is kept over the often wayward and hubristic visions of leaders, planners, and architects, a possibility remains that the built environment's atrocities could be minimised.

81. F Kafka, 'The Trial', Victor Gollancz, London, 1925, p.36

82. M de Cervantes Saavedra, 'The History and Adventures of the Renowned Don Quixote', T Smollett & OM Brack (eds.), University of Georgia Press, Athens, GA, 2003, p.58

83, 84 + 85. G Manaugh, 'The BLDGBLOG Book', Chronicle Books, San Francisco, 2009, pp.17–18

86. R Hare, 'IV. St. Petersburg – Petrograd – Leningrad: Russian architecture, yesterday and to-day', Journal of the Royal Society of Arts, vol.112, no.5094, 1964, p.440

87 + 88. S Gannawey, 'The Original E.P.C.O.T – Walt & Epcot Master Plan' [https://sites.google.com/site/theoriginalepcot/essays/walt-epcot-master-plan], retrieved 17 June 2023

89. P Williams, 'Introduction', The Original E.P.C.O.T [https://sites.google.com/site/theoriginalepcot/overview/the-florida-project], retrieved 17 June 2023

90. T Mangena, 'Rhodes, Mugabe and the Politics of Commemorative Toponyms in Zimbabwe', Geopolitics 25, no.4, 7 August 2020, pp.1015–1036

91 + 92. M Koutonin, 'Lost Cities #9: Racism and Ruins – the Plundering of Great Zimbabwe', Cities, Guardian, 18 August 2016

Flathead
Trump
High Voltage
Crater
Wanted
$$$
BROADCASTING

The Wall of Cards

'I declared a state of emergency and was the first governor to openly advocate for the National Guard at the border; yet, I have refused to agree that a wall by itself is an answer. As I often say, "You show me a 50-foot wall, and I'll show you a 51-foot ladder."'

– Janet Napolitano, US Secretary of Homeland Security, 2007

Napolitano is just one of many US senior officials that have presaged the illusions, the false sense of security, and the futility of constructing border walls. It came as no surprise in 2022 when Nick Miroff of 'The Washington Post' reported that, during the 2019 to 2021 fiscal years, Trump's 458-mile 'impenetrable and beautiful'[1] border wall was breached more than 3,000 times. Over the same three-year period, the federal government spent US$2.6 million on repairs according to unpublished US Customs and Border Protection maintenance records.[2] In 2021, the El Paso Sector announced the 'Fence Cutter Initiative' in collaboration with the government of Mexico which 'seeks the prosecution of individuals caught damaging the border barrier with the intent of smuggling people and contraband into the United States'.[3] In its first year, the effort resulted in two prosecutions with modest fines but not jail time.

The preservation of nations does not lie in prosecution and separation. Instead, it should necessitate visionary immigration reforms that address the fundamental human requirements to protect, to provide and to participate. A border should be a mutually beneficial space connecting cultures and communities, economies and ecologies, which practices a collective empathy and security that rehabilitates wounded politics and policies. Among the growing numbers who recognise this necessity, it is widely held that the meandering boundary between the United States and Mexico could become a vital and constructive component of the global economy. Prompted by recent supply chain upheavals and the escalation of animosity with China, American companies are once again seeking suppliers on the same continent as their customers. Fabricators and logistics investors shifting their businesses to the border also boosts manufacturing in America, as 'components for advanced equipment including electronics and medical devices are being made in Mexico and sent to factories in the US for final assembly and distribution'.[4]

Unintended consequences are the protagonist of this spatial narrative. Trump's hubris has offered up hundreds of ready-made infrastructural framework miles to the reshoring of manufacturing and supply chains from Asia, and the surge in demand for border facilities has fuelled development of company towns along the wall. In turn, this has encouraged a return of many thousands of illegal immigrants to the Mexican border, eager to participate in new opportunities and join an expanding workforce in what becomes decades of growth in trade between the neighbouring countries. Life as an illegal immigrant,

facing page: 'The Wall of Cards' aims to humanise and bridge socio-economic gaps across the border fence that has been designed to reject and divide.

following pages: Whilst the former president had campaigned on the 'impenetrability' of his wall, its hubristic legacy has enabled the world's largest endorsement of democracy at the Mexico-US border.

1. D Trump, 'Arizona Election Rally Speech', Politics, Washington Post, 31 August 2016 [https://www.washingtonpost.com/video/politics/trump-says-he-will-build-impenetrable-physical-tall-powerful-beautiful-border/2016/08/31/34eceacc-6fb6-11e6-993f-73c693a89820_video.html], retrieved 18 October 2022

2. N Miroff, 'Trump's Border Wall Has Been Breached More Than 3,000 Times By Smugglers', Washington Post, 2 March 2022

3. El Paso Sector, 'Fence Cutter Initiative Delivers Consequences', US Customs and Border Protection, 11 November 2021

4. J Rogers, 'Warehouses Boom on Border as Manufacturing Moves to Mexico', www.globest.com, 10 February 2023 [https://www.globest.com/2023/02/10/warehouses-boom-on-border-as-manufacturing-moves-to-mexico], retrieved 18 October 2022

TRUMP
Tahoe

TRUMP
Trump
JetCrater
High Voltage

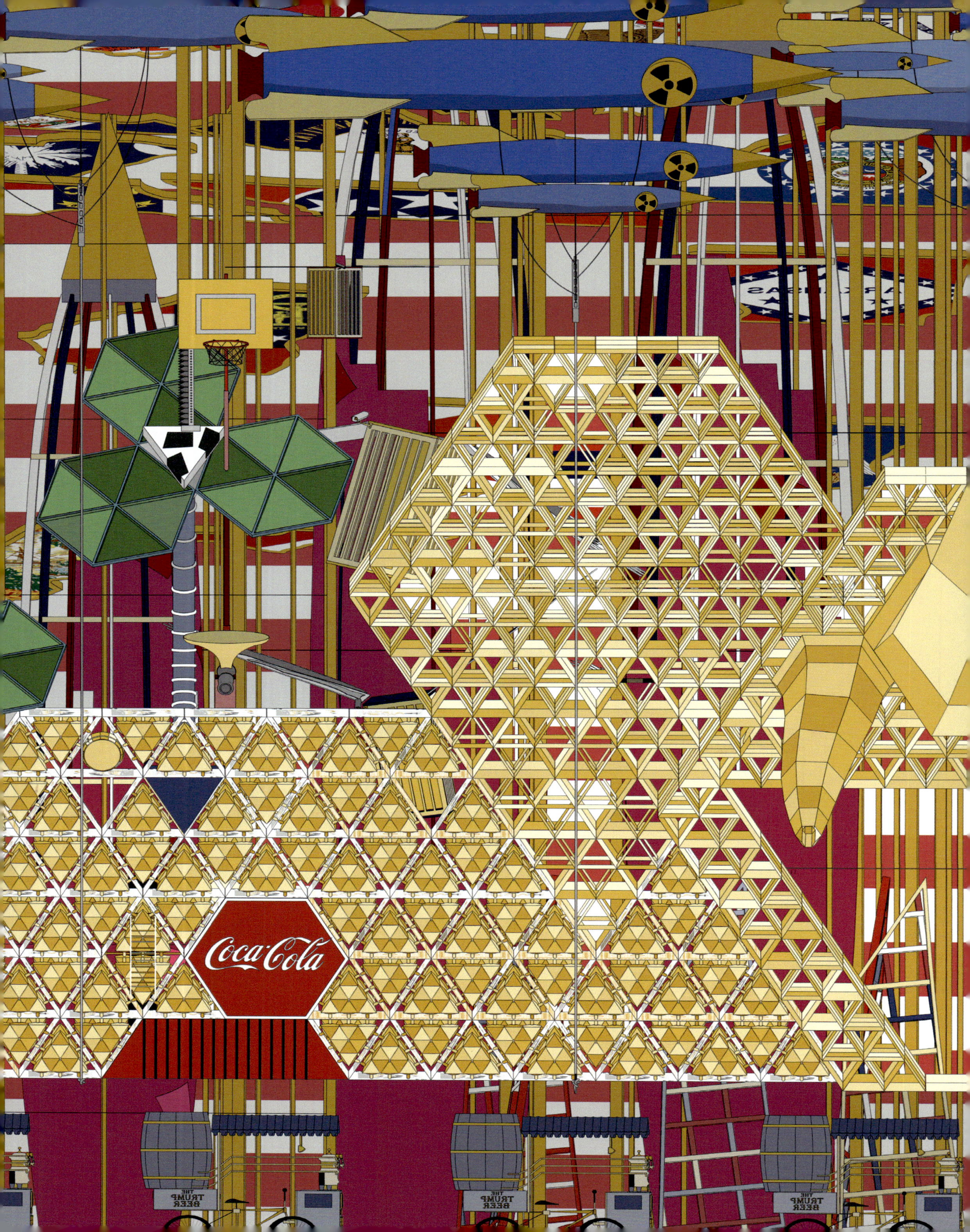
Coca-Cola

THE TRUMP BEER
THE TRUMP BEER
THE TRUMP BEER

Crater

without the right to equal protection in the US and characterised by discrimination, persecution, and exploitative labour conditions, becomes a thing of the past. This fast-growing linear city gives agency to the countries' ever-changing shared history of frequent misunderstandings and cultural collaborations – Americans, in time, able to see Mexico and Mexicans as solutions to America's woes.

A binational live-work-play district with joint law and order provides a special economic zone with tax incentives for individuals, Mexican-US companies, and international investors. This large conceptual shift has propelled the two countries towards forging a true partnership. With its revised policies, the 'Fence Cutter Initiative' trains and mobilises thousands of returning Mexican immigrants, smugglers and asylum seekers to adapt the wall. Developments for new manufacturing spaces and homes within 24 feet on either side of Trump's wall do not require planning permission; the dimension taken from a typical 48-foot ranch house. Using angle grinders, demolition saws, and other inexpensive construction tools widely available at hardware stores, they cut-stack-and-fill the barrier like a pack of cards to accommodate life, work, and play.

The expansion of the linear city has spurred the biggest housing boom in the US since Boulder City, Nevada in the 1930s. Conceived as an ongoing project adapting the ideology of 'Quinta Monroy'[5] (2003) by Alejandro Aravena, the residents are provided with the basic legal requirements for low-income housing, allowing incremental self-expansion depending on time and the resources of families. Dozens of restaurants, shops and schools fill the adapted wall at any five-mile section, along with impressive signage announcing the presence of world-class manufacturing and logistics companies. While driving for hours to work is no longer a prerequisite of better employment, equestrian travel is common. Bustling logistics riders on horse-back are reminiscent of the entrepreneurialism found in the early frontier towns of the Wild West.

previous pages: The elephant is the symbol for the Republican Party, and in 'The Wall of Cards' the elephant's trunk grows with each political lie.

facing page: The bustling logistics riders on horseback reinterpret the entrepreneurialism of the Wild West's early frontier towns.

following pages 172–173: Happy days in the Western saloon as the city is surging with employment opportunities and high wages, while offering a low cost of living.

following pages 174–175: The linear city boasts a resilient dream. Airborne US flags covered with solar cells harvest energy while inflatable 'Trump' signages absorb moisture from the atmosphere.

Despite the harsh location and desolate weather, the linear city boasts a resilient dream of energy, water and food security. Airborne US flags covered with solar cells take advantage of the abundant sunlight, while inflatable 'Trump' signages harvest moisture from the atmosphere which feeds directly down into agricultural and marigold fields. Meanwhile, an homage to the official symbol of the Republican Party takes shape in the 'elephant' reservoirs. The marigold flowers emit a smell to deter mosquitoes, and when their rich yellow pigments are added to the paint for the newly built forms within the wall, it gives an illusion of gold coverings – a reference to the gaudiness of Trumpian architecture. Every day, the flags and signage generate a reliable stream of ever-shifting spatial conversations on offer to residents and workers, signalling a metaphor of protection and community.

Trump's wall, stretching from the Pacific Ocean in the west to the Gulf of Mexico in the east, bordering six Mexican states and four US states, and running 18 to 30 feet tall, is no longer racist, ignorant, and unnecessary. After a joint 21st-century urban and architectural policy makeover between the disputing nations, the wall has become a brilliant dream. The ultimate irony of Trump's administration carrying out the cruellest anti-migration policies in decades is that their hubristic legacy enables the world's largest endorsement of democracy and entrepreneurialism at the Mexico-US border.

5. R Moore, 'Alejandro Aravena: The shape of things to come', Architecture, Guardian, 10 April 2016

Crater
Wanted
Preferbly Alive
$$$
Preferbly Alive
$$$
Preferbly Alive
$$$

TRUMP
Coca-Cola

Tahoe

Narcissus

'What kind of gaze does the city license? What is this object of desire, at once near and ungraspable, fascinating and repulsive, attractive and intractable, necessary and unbearable, intimate and impenetrable, that it is... for those who inhabit it and those merely passing through it, for anyone who knows that it is a labyrinth but nonetheless allows himself to remain trapped in it?'

– Hubert Damisch, 'Skyline: The narcissistic city', 2002

Is it possible to 'imagine the fable of Narcissus taking place in the urban context? What kind of gaze, not only is the subject able to turn on itself, but does the city-machine turn on itself through the intermediary of said 'subject'?'[1] Caravaggio's painting of Narcissus (1597–1599) gives visual form to the mythological tale of a handsome youth who falls in love with his own reflection in a pool of water. Trapped under the spell of his own admiration, the eponymous figure dies of his passion, his narcissism persisting even as he crosses into the underworld over the River Styx. A popular subject matter amongst late Renaissance and early Baroque painters, Damisch has reprised the importance of identifying narcissism in architecture through his line of inquiry. For traits associated with narcissistic ignorance, psychoanalyst Sandy Hotchkiss lists arrogance, grandiosity, envy, shamelessness, and entitlement,[2] all of which could be used to describe the modern built environment and its profession.

facing page: Life in the sky focuses on humanity repenting for the sins of its past consumerism.

following pages: With varying prismatic profiles, the Canal of Frugality functions as the main urban water reservoir while simultaneously refracting sunlight into rainbows which connect every living cluster.

Cities are besieged by narcissistic discourses which inspire actions that threaten human flourishing and ecological survival. 'Clean' and 'green' have long been illusions peddled by disingenuous developments whose litter-free streets and thirsty, perfectly manicured vanity plantings create unique forms of urban entitlement. Irrespective of high costs and water scarcity, daily washing of streets and watering of green walls, private lawns and luxury parks carries on.[3] Initiatives to increase rainwater storage capacity with large-scale reservoirs are attempting to appease such practices, yet many countries remain just as dependent on water imports from neighbours as they do for food. The European Commission has stressed the need for supply chains in cities to become more resilient, pairing down reliance on global provisions of food and energy whose costs have been exacerbated by socio-political turmoil from military conquest in the Slavic breadbasket of Ukraine.[4] For some cities, entitlement descends into shamelessness when unwanted recyclables are shipped to poorer developing countries. Steeped in irony and internal contradictions, their offshore high carbon footprints are hidden behind the veneer of sustainability to produce envy amongst competitors.

Consumerism props up endless architectural exuberances, and in turn has fed an indefensible appetite for urban grandiosity and arrogance. The colossal imports of sand to construct new islands

1. H Damisch, 'Skyline: The narcissistic city', Stanford University Press, Redwood City, CA., 2002, p.19

2. S Hotchkiss & JF Masterson, 'Why Is It Always About You? The seven deadly sins of narcissism', Free Press Publisher, New York, 2008

3. T McDonald, 'The Cost of Keeping Singapore Squeaky Clean', Worklife, BBC, 29 October 2018 [https://www.bbc.com/worklife/article/20181025-the-cost-of-keeping-singapore-squeaky-clean], retrieved 3 May 2023

4. European Commission, 'Commission Acts for Global Food Security and for Supporting EU Farmers and Consumers', 23 March 2022 [https://ec.europa.eu/commission/presscorner/detail/en/ip_22_1963], retrieved 5 May 2023

have continuously erased natural shorelines for hubristic land reclamation projects, leaving behind degraded ecologies. Like unsustainable foundations built on sandy ground, many cities' operations are inseparable from shifting imports of cheap labour. Millions of domestic helpers and low-wage workers in manufacturing and construction fill the gaps in undesirable jobs that are integral to the beautification of the city skyline and functioning of countless households.[5] Exploitation has kept their existence largely hidden, and their importance undervalued. Like reflections in Narcissus's pool, these observations of ignorant urbanism are not isolated to a particular city. Instead, they reflect upon collective actions, the everyday behaviours that impact ways of life and influence the ethics of space making at a global scale.

Narcissus, the city and the painting, share a moral concern with the unintended consequences of urban vices and the weaknesses of humankind. A new linear settlement floating above an existing city, Narcissus has the conceptual ambition of rebalancing social, ecological, and spatial politics. By encouraging regret, it allows the populace to recognise and repent their sins. As inhabitants move away from the ground, nature starts to reclaim the urban realm, wild animals roam empty streets and carbon emissions fall dramatically. To commemorate each human migration from ground to sky, one of the Gardens of Sighs exhales a seed-cloud of relief. Transitory winds take the legion of seed clouds across the skies in search of breaks, cracks and nooks to sow and rewild the harsh edges of the city. Higher still, the Memory Palace continuously pumps like a pair of lungs to harvest past narcissism, which is filtered into the essence of regret before being released into the Canal of Frugality and its associated pools. Drifting along the river, solar-powered 'Halos' thoughtfully remind citizens of their pasts in the consumerist city that once existed below.

facing page: The feather-like tectonics form interlocking spatial puzzles which, depending on wind directions, rotate around the Halos to form walkable park connectors.

following pages 182–183: The Memory Palace collects and filters narcissism into the essence of regret before releasing it into the Canal of Frugality and its associated pools.

following pages 184–185: Every so often the Garden of Sighs releases a cloud, the symbol of repentance for past extravagance, wastage and irresponsible consumption.

No part of Narcissus touches the ground except for long filigree stilts, thus allowing the warmth of the sun to gently caress nature and its reclaimed space. Its collective structures compost organic waste and filter grey water to fertilise, irrigate and cool the earth 24/7, by proxy desperately repenting and seeking atonement for the environmental sins of the old city. Water and food security are no longer concerns as past extravagances, wastage and irresponsible consumption are dissuaded. Narcissus instead promotes frugality as the new religion. Virtuous foods cultivated in the canals are banked at the Piggy Commissaries, where residents living in inflatable clusters cook and eat together. In contemplating their long absence, humanity looks back to the ground where regret for past indulgences is now repented for by newly cultivated natural wealth. Whether forthrightly compelling or another alluring hypocrisy, Narcissus is an attempt to uncover the reality of greenwashing and climate resilience agendas being paraded in cities across the world.

Whilst the darkness surrounding Caravaggio's solemnly beautiful painting suggest that reality exists only inside the self-regarding figure, the metaphoric gaze of ignorance and hubris will always be directed towards the city irrespective of its attempts at virtuous programming. As with the population of Baucis in Calvino's 'Invisible Cities', there remain three hypotheses about what drives the groundward attention of the inhabitants of Narcissus; 'that they hate the earth; that they respect it so much they avoid all contact; that they love it as it was before they existed and with spyglasses and telescopes aimed downward, they never tire of examining it, leaf by leaf, stone by stone, ant by ant'.[6]

5. MZ Lim, 'Migrant Workers Important to Singapore Economy', Straits Times, 27 May 2020

6. I Calvino, 'Invisible Cities', W Weaver (trans.), Secker & Warburg Ltd, London, 1974, p.77

Dante's Trees

'The restoration of forested land at a global scale could help capture atmospheric carbon and mitigate climate change. Ecosystems could support an additional 0.9 billion hectares of continuous forest, 25 percent increase in forested area including more than 200 gigatons of additional carbon at maturity, and has the potential to store an equivalent of 25 percent of the current atmospheric carbon pool.'

– Jean-Francois Bastin et al., 'The Global Tree Restoration Potential', Science, 2019

The headline-grabbing publication in the journal 'Science' is flawed,[1] and 'we need to understand not only whether it's possible to do such a thing, but whether we should do it'[2] cautions NASA's global carbon dynamics expert Sassan Saatchi. Whilst appearing logical, many well-meaning environmental campaigns fall short of delivering the benefits they promise and even fuel deforestation. In the journal 'Nature', researchers found no evidence that India's investments in tree planting over the past 50 years have secured substantial carbon mitigation or benefits to livelihood. Their article advocates shifting focus to discerning long-term forest management practices, restoring diversity in degraded ecosystems, and empowering the local communities best positioned to care for such landscapes through subsidiarity.[3]

'Dante's Trees' explores possibilities for China's investment in the 'Great Green Wall for The Sahara and the Sahel Initiative' (GGW),[4] intended to support development in Djibouti. Attempting to mitigate desertification and climate change, this 780-million-hectare continent-spanning green belt is endorsed by the African Union and blessed by the United Nations. However, both tree planting and the wider environmental agreements supporting it have recently received political scrutiny. In the context of neo-colonialism, economic imperialism has been used to influence broader policies in developing countries – accusations of similar suspicious incentives in the China-Djibouti relationship are inevitable.

The allegorical plot of hubris and ignorance in Dante's Trees originates from the 19th-century painting 'Paolo and Francesca' by Jean-Auguste-Dominique Ingres. While she reads the Arthurian romance of Lancelot and Guinevere, Paolo attempts to kiss Francesca. At just that moment, Gianciotto, the deformed brother of Paolo and husband of Francesca, enters and prepares to draw his sword against them. The painting is one of many interpretations of circle two, canto five, in poet Dante Alighieri's 'Inferno' (1314), where the illicit lovers are condemned to an eternity in hell. The ethos of Dante's Trees parallels the mixed emotions of lust and betrayal in Alighieri's cautionary tale with added cynical humour. Djibouti takes the role of the poet's titular sinner, China the seducer Paolo, and Gianciotto the French colonial power. Like the deadly sins defined in the epic poem, the project provides satirical interpretations of the seven recommendations for success in the GGW from the UN's Food and Agriculture Organisation.

facing page: The allegorical tectonics reinterpret the scene from 'Paolo and Francesca' (1819) by Ingres.

following page 188: Flotillas of Chinese wedding boats bearing fresh water gifts seek the betrothal consent of Djibouti.

following page 189: Cupid's arrows are shot into the sky using ballasts, touching down on the landscape where they unfold to form a gridded system of continuous lust.

following pages 190–191: Expanding the GGW, the blossoming landscape of love is actually hiding the inevitable end of the tragic relationship.

1. G Popkin, 'Catchy Findings Have Propelled This Young Ecologist to fame – and Enraged His Critics', Science, vol.365, issue 6448, 5 July 2019, p.76

2. A Buis, 'Examining the Viability of Planting Trees to Help Mitigate Climate Change', NASA, 7 November 2019 [https://climate.nasa.gov/news/2927/examining-the-viability-of-planting-trees-to-help-mitigate-climate-change], retrieved 8 October 2022

3. EA Coleman & B Schultz et al., 'Limited Effects of Tree Planting on Forest Canopy Cover Nad Rural Livelihoods in Northern India', Nature Sustainability, vol.4, November 2021, pp.1001–1002

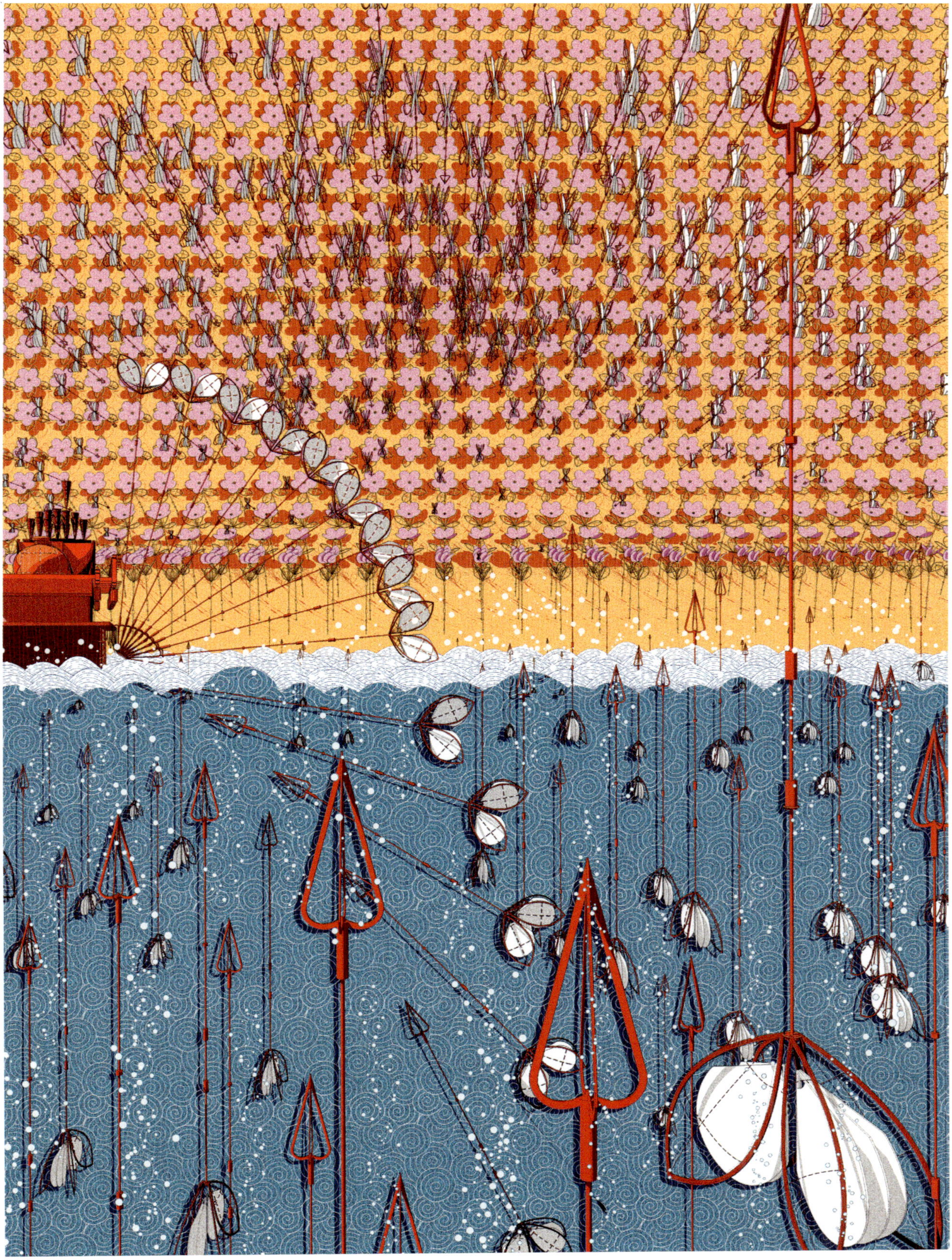

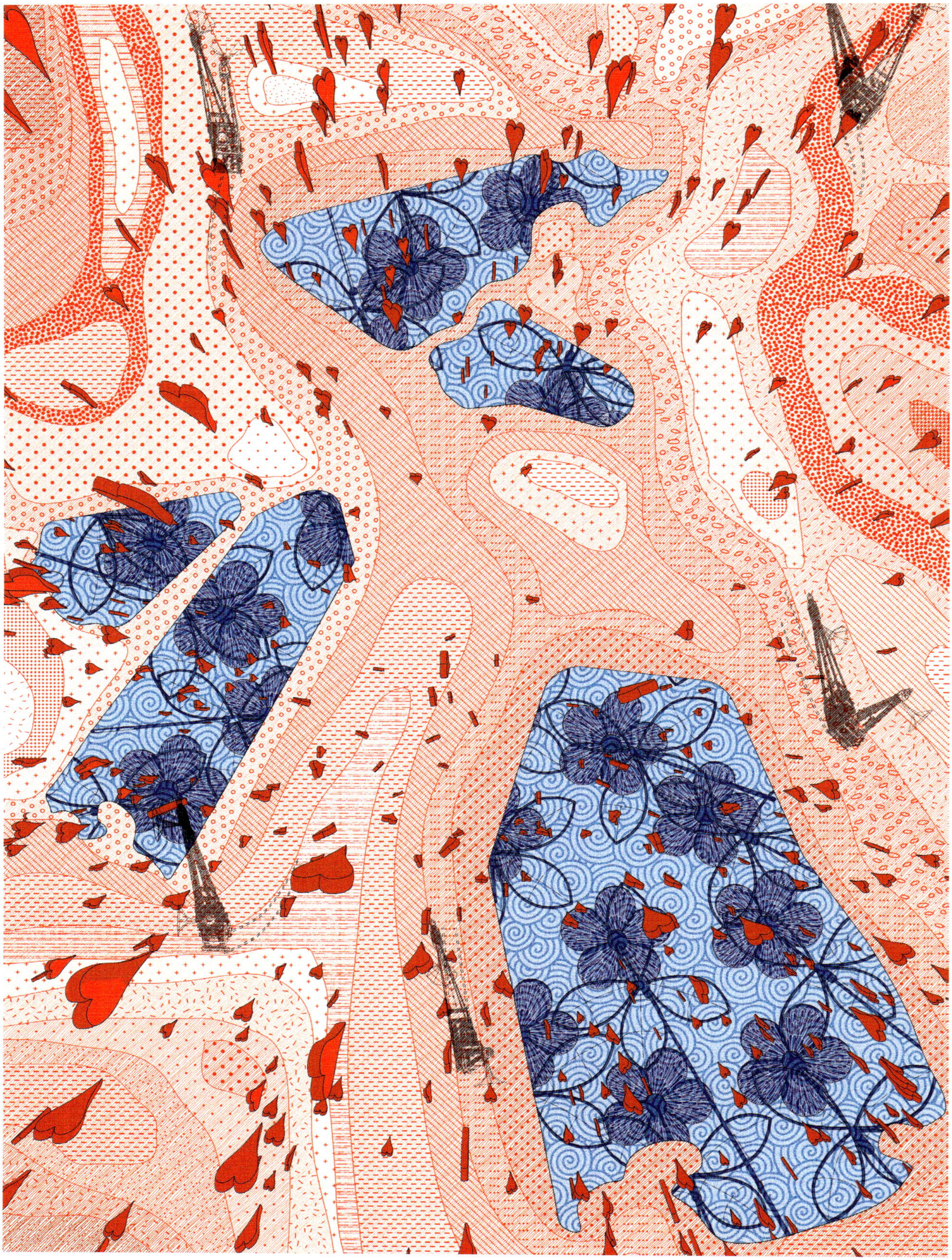

One: 'Assessing existing land uses and production systems for opportunities'. The traditional Chinese custom when seeking betrothal consent is to send 'pinli' gifts including wine. Djibouti's seduction begins with the arrival of a flotilla of red Chinese wedding boats bearing rice wine barrels of fresh water, a highly valued resource in the region. Acceptance of the gift is a symbolic promise of opportunity, but not necessarily commitment. Two: 'Developing value chains that benefit local communities and green economies'. Whilst the interlocking geographies of Lake Ghoubet and the sea are developed as a series of coastal embraces, Djibouti and China are betrayed by the unintended reflections of the opened Gates of Engagement, as with Francesca's shining ring in Ingres's painting. Cherishing the landscape's riches, the wedding boats patiently wait to be filled with valuable treasures for their return.

Three: 'Mobilising well-adapted species to build ecological resilience'. Cupid fires arrows of repurposed sails to ignite passion, forming a continuous grid of lust. Djibouti is blinded by their anchored blossoms which are covertly testing equipment for gold exploration. Four: 'Fighting sand encroachment by establishing and protecting native vegetation'. The rose-tinted GGW initiative protects lust and greed, hiding them in plain sight under the envious colonial power of France. Like the Hollywood disguises built atop WWII military bases whose camouflage 'rested in tricking the mind through the manipulation of visual form and cultural expectation',[5] the 'curtain' of blossoms fools more than the eye.

Five: 'Investing in large-scale land preparation and enrichment planting'. Masquerading as the symbol of romance, the Eiffel Tower sheepishly mines the rocky terrain with inflatable wheels. These turn a blushing red colour on contact with the earth, inspired by Paolo's trembling puffy lips. The suitor's love for Djibouti is founded only upon exploiting its wealth of minerals. Six: 'Building inexpensive participatory information systems'. The soaring embassy 'Swords' with prying-eyed telescopes are a metaphor for the betrayed husband, built for the old colonial powers to oversee implementation of the GGW. At night, their solar balloons nuzzle between the blossoms, unaware of any clandestine infidelity and exploitations.

Finally, seven: 'Promoting continuous natural regeneration'. Just as Paolo betrays Francesca, the China-Djibouti affair ends when the wedding boats depart with their ill-gotten resources. Connecting the Red Sea to the Gulf of Aden, Djibouti's strategic location blesses it with the agency to re-write its own narrative, becoming a formidable transit port for the region by discarding charity and victimhood to follow Francesca's triumph over damnation. Historian John-Paul Heil has reasoned that the major figures of Romanticism, prizing emotion above logicality, transformed Francesca from a sinner into an exemplar of female agency. 'From composers Tchaikovsky and Rachmaninoff to artists Rossetti and Rodin to writers Hunt and Byron, creatives used Francesca to challenge the cultural mores of their day.'[6]

East or West and regardless of the country, addressing the complex issues of climate change and colonisation will never be straightforward. Mass tree planting initiatives are no atonement for decades of carbon sins, and 'greenwashing' companies or states with otherwise poor environmental records only fuels ignorance. Embroiled in disputes and hubristic rhetoric, 'today's green urban dream is too often about bringing a technologically controlled version of nature into the city and declaring the problem solved, rather than looking at the deeper causes of our current environmental and urban discontents'.[7]

previous pages 192–193: The kiss is initiated when the blushing machines with inflatable 'puffy-lip' wheels start to dig and navigate through the difficult landscape.

previous pages 194–195: Allegories for the husband Gianciotto and his sword, ambassadors of the old colonial countries float high above to oversee progress on the GGW but are unaware of what is lurking underneath. By day, the ambassadors adopt a constant state of ignorant self-congratulation.

facing page: Beneath the landscape curtain, the romantic affair disguises exploitation of Djibouti's mineral wealth.

following pages: The GGW affair ends in tears leaving Djibouti with a scarred landscape.

4. N Berrahmouni & L Laestadius et al., 'Building Africa's Great Green Wall', Food and Agriculture Organisation of the United Nations 2016, p.2 [https://www.fao.org/3/i6476en/i6476en.pdf], retrieved 8 October 2022

5. J Weems, 'Los Angeles: Camouflage and contestation', KCET Artbound Series, 2012, p.6

6. JP Heil, 'Before Romeo and Juliet, Paolo and Francesca Were Literature's Star-crossed Lovers', Smithsonian Magazine, 3 November 2021 [https://www.smithsonianmag.com/arts-culture/before-romeo-and-juliet-dante-immortalized-paolo-and-francesca-as-literatures-star-crossed-lovers-180978911], retrieved 5 October 2022

7. W Graham, 'Op-Ed: Are we greening our cities, or just greenwashing them?', Los Angeles Times, 6 March 2016

chapter five

Sins + Excess

'To generations of Americans, Las Vegas is a code for self-indulgence and sanctioned deviance. It is a town of fun, of excess, where anything and everything is possible and for sale... Las Vegas is the place that you promise your mother you'll never go, then break that promise with a wink and a leer. No place in the United States gives permission like the Las Vegas of myth.'

– Hal Rothman, 'Neon Metropolis: How Las Vegas started the twenty-first century', 2002

Like the jewel-encrusted and miserly mirror cities which comprise Italo Calvino's Beersheba,[1] Las Vegas and Boulder City were built on a crossroads dividing a stolid workman's town from an escapist paradise. Later becoming the Strip and I-15 highway,[2] this interstate artery is now infamous for holding a funhouse reflection up to America's aspirations for capitalist expansion, typified by sparkling casinos and neon signs. The Strip's distinct brand of illusion has been caricatured throughout pop-culture by its own excesses – bright lights and architectural opulence – but is the long-held reputation as the world's most notorious city of sin warranted? Las Vegas is a relatively safe place to visit with strict gambling laws and policing, whilst other cities rank far higher in crimes like unsanctioned betting rings.[3] It is interesting that the place's appeal allows us to admit that we want the sins, albeit in a safeguarded environment of excess. From vagrant workers of the Great Depression to Hunter S. Thompson, gonzo author of 'Fear and Loathing in Las Vegas' (1971), wanderers and wayfarers of all kinds have descended on Nevada to chase their American Dreams. Established for the families of labourers constructing the Hoover Dam in the 1930s, prohibitionist Boulder City followed an opposing course of development, its government exercising authoritarian control over the area's planning and its residents' conduct. There was an absolute ban on gambling, prostitution, and liquor, in return for security and respite from the tumult of its nearby twin city. Only in 1969 was the sale of alcohol finally permitted and gambling remains illegal to this day,[4] though the ostentatious Vegas strip can be reached in a half hour by car.

Both cities emerged in what seemed the middle of nowhere, founded along the railroad linking Los Angeles and Salt Lake City in the Mojave Desert. After the enormous Hoover Dam was completed, abundant provisions of water, electricity, cheap land, and loose laws all but necessitated opportunistic construction, catapulting the relatively unknown area into the limelight during the second half of the 1900s. Springing from emptiness was not unique for a city in the North American context, however. Nearly a century before the urbanisation of Las Vegas, the California Gold Rush likewise drew massive urban influx to sites which were little suited to human inhabitation. Despite the danger and bloody rivalry of prospectors, gold mining was highly profitable, and the gold rush towns were breeding grounds for greed, excess and a plethora of sins. An invigorated economy and rapidly increasing population turned

facing page: A clandestine night where the colonial ambassadors hide in amongst 'Dante's Trees', 'for everyone who does evil hates the light, and does not come to the light, lest his deeds should be exposed' (John 3:19–21).

1. I Calvino, 'Invisible Cities', W Weaver (trans.), Secker & Warburg Ltd, London, 1974, p.63

2. H Rothman, 'Neon Metropolis: How Las Vegas started the twenty-first century', Routledge, New York, 2002, p.297

3. JS Albanese, 'The Effect of Casino Gambling on Crime', Federal Probation 1985, vol.49, 1985, pp.39–44

4. F McCabe, 'Boulder City: Built by the dam, for the dam', Las Vegas Review-Journal, 6 October 2014 [http://www.reviewjournal.com/nevada-150/boulder-city-built-dam-dam], retrieved 2 August 2015

California into a statehood almost overnight, transforming San Francisco into a booming city of tents and abandoned ships. The hundreds of vessels which brought prospectors were repurposed as makeshift homes, hotels, brothels, saloons, churches and even prisons. When torrential rains fell, the city was described as becoming 'one vast fathomless sea of mud. Its character is heterogeneous, its character antipellucid, its adhesive qualities immense and antagonistic to a composed state of nerves. Its ingredients are dust and water, egg shells, cabbage leaves, potato parings, onion tops, fish bones, and other articles too numerous to mention... sober or muddled, a man is sure to put his feet in it.'[5] The combination of a slippery quagmire ground, flammable structures, lack of street lighting, and plenty of inebriated prospectors unsurprisingly led to the many fires of the city.

Perhaps the most widespread driver of spatial sin, alcohol and its associated institutions have a history of changing the urban fabric for the worse. Striking historical examples are found in William Hogarth's illustrations, especially 'Beer Street' and 'Gin Lane'. The set of prints was issued as a piece of political propaganda to support the so-called Gin Act of 1751 through which the Parliament of Great Britain sought to assuage the ongoing debauchery of the 'gin craze'. Gin Lane's engraving depicts the parish of St Giles, the eras most notorious West London slum. It is estimated that a quarter of the area's residences doubled as gin shops, and some offered further services from coordinating prostitution to black-market trading.[6] In the illustration's crowded streets a scene of madness, suicide, starvation, reckless abandon, and societal decay is taking shape. Death and destruction are fueled by the growing industry of non-professional distillers and the newly popularised gin is sold by the aptly named 'Kilman' storefront. This edifice is haphazardly propped up behind a swathe of alcoholic residents, either violently rioting and selling their possessions for a drink or huddled in a post-binge stupor aside neglected children. By contrast, its Beer Street sister engraving shows the relative merits of drinking the less-potent, traditional English ale which is distributed alongside nourishment to an industrious and healthy group beneath the steeple of St George's Church in Bloomsbury.

In the wake of such campaigns, the beer-drinking culture of pubs became widely accepted and even prominent in industrialising cities. A new century saw population centres which fostered an increasingly secular and socially autonomous working class seeking any momentary respite from their crowded surroundings. The oft-repeated saying that English cities possessed 'a church for every week of the year and a pub for every day'[7] demonstrates the significance which taverns, pubs, and alehouses held for the country's expanding urban environments. 'The World of the Tavern' (2002) explores how public drink houses served as multifunctional architectures and wayfinding landmarks, becoming a new kind of social infrastructure. Pubs slowly began undergirding the common institutional and cultural centres of life throughout Europe, a role that was traditionally understood as the domain of the Church. In its place, a complex set of social forces and new requirements for more informal and accessible spaces of public gathering were making the tavern 'the principal communication hub of premodern society'.[8] Indeed, urban specialisation had been in the process of transforming cities since ancient times 'whereby functions that once were united in the village household – sleeping, drinking, eating, talking, mating, educating – in time were sorted out, magnified, and segregated in definite buildings and quarters'.[9] Like the brothels designated for the proverbial 'oldest profession in the world', the pub and tavern participated in a diffusion which saw the city magnified into a collective household, differentiating the spaces of public and private life into a web of social architectures that serve as neither home or workplace. As their ornate signs and glowing windows offered points of gathering or landmarks for orientation, lending character to the streetscape, the pub itself served the role of group companionship broker. Additionally, informal interiors were perfectly suited to the programme of a local newscaster disseminating vital information and gossip to its constituents, all for the price of a pint.

Fast forward to the 21st century and the sin is not so much in the consumption of alcohol but the mass demise of pubs and the communities they sustain. This trend is fuelling a crisis of isolation of epic proportions in cities across the UK. While reducing the health impacts of excess drinking is a positive step, author Thomas Thurnell-Read argues that 'places with strong working class communities feel particularly fragmented now in all the swirling social and economic change. The result is a nagging sense of loneliness, with a boarded-up pub becoming one of the most visible manifestations of a community changing – and leaving you behind.'[10] With a quarter of pubs shut down since 2000, weakening human connections are ironically cultivating 'cities of loneliness' amongst anonymous populations of millions.

Catch Me if You Can?

Although gambling and other sins are legally sanctioned in places like Las Vegas, the urban environment has frequently been interfaced through outright criminality. Rather than the predations of alcohol-fuelled speakeasies or glittering betting halls, it has been argued that 'burglary is the original sin of the metropolis.'[11] Within the workaday elements of the urban realm there exists a thinly veiled potential for exploitation, a bypass installed in certain structures like a Trojan horse, and 'if you look closely, from just the right angle, every city implies the crimes that will someday take place there. Burglary is designed into the city as surely as your morning commute.'[12] In 'A Burglar's Guide to the City' (2016), Geoff Manaugh reminds readers that 'burglary and heist films are in fact the most architectural genre of all',[13] the only movies where scenes of characters gathered around a set of floor plans or architectural models constitutes acceptable entertainment. But this connection between the criminal thriller and the architectural profession is not a simple creation of Hollywood.

George Leonidas Leslie, an architect by profession, had already conducted one of the most spatially astonishing crime sprees in US history at the outset of the Gilded Age, decades before the phenomena of heist films would come to prominence. Leaving the University of Cincinnati for New York, Leslie would misuse his professional acumen to access key structural drawings and blueprints of vaults and private safes, compiling a compendium of illicit spatial knowledge to gain 'a backstage pass to the entire metropolis'.[14] Full-scale spatial facsimiles of robbery targets in Brooklyn warehouses allowed Leslie and his accomplices to inhabit a parallel dimension, projecting themselves across the East River where crimes could be rehearsed to perfection. Such ingenious approaches to understanding Manhattan have been reinterpreted in Charlie Kaufman's 'Synecdoche, New York' (2008) where a life-size microcosm of the megalopolis is remade as the set for a theatre production which contains ever-multiplying copies of itself ad-infinitum.[15] More recently, innocuous apartments and local bars are recreated as exact twins without the aid of computer graphics in Nathan Fielder's 'The Rehearsal' (2022), the assiduously detailed duplicates used to host 'practise' simulations of high-stakes social interactions.[16]

In a less fanciful vein, the concept of 'Forensic Architecture' pioneered by Eyal Weizman uses architectural technologies to investigate instances of state violence, war crimes, and violations of human rights in conflict zones around the world. Formed as a research project at Goldsmiths, University of London, it formulates methods for addressing modern phenomena from the urbanisation of warfare, erosion of trust in evidence proffered by governments, and the proliferation of open-source media and smartphone

5. G Kamiya, 'The Year San Francisco's Mud Was So Bad, It Swallowed Horses', San Francisco Chronicle, 12 June 2020

6. MD George, 'London Life in the Eighteenth Century', Penguin Books, Harmondsworth, 1976, p.41

7. W Kett, 'A Church for Every Week of the Year and a Pub for Every Day of the Year.....', Shine A Light, Norfolk Museums Service (blog), 21 May 2013 [https://shinealightproject.wordpress.com/2013/05/21/a-church-for-every-week-of-the-year-and-a-pub-for-every-day-of-the-year], retrieved 28 August 2022

8. B Kumin, 'The World of the Tavern in Early Modern Europe', Department of History, University of Warwick [https://warwick.ac.uk/fac/arts/history/students/modules/hi390], retrieved 28 August 2022

9. L Mumford, 'The City in History: Its origins, its transformations and its prospects', Secker & Warburg Ltd, London, 1961, p.105

10. M Twigg, 'The Pub Closures at the Heart of Britain's Loneliness Epidemic', Health & Fitness, Telegraph, 21 September 2023

11, 12 + 14. G Manaugh, 'A Burglar's Guide to the City', McClelland & Stewart, Toronto, 2016, p.11, p.12 & p.8

13. G Manaugh, 'A Burglar's Guide to the City: On architecture and crime' Lecture, The Berkman Klein Center for Internet & Society, 14 April 2016 [https://www.youtube.com/watch?v=iSlgtqxfWkk], retrieved 29 August 2022

15. C Kaufman, 'Synecdoche, New York', Sidney Kimmel Entertainment, 2008

16. N Fielder, 'Orange Juice, No Pulp', The Rehearsal, s.1, e.1, HBO, 2022

footage in the documentation of crimes.[17] Forensic Architecture further engages witnesses and victims through the use of models and visualisations, aiding the memories of traumatic or violent experiences often clouded by the confusion of war. Mentally reconstructing and embodying these spaces encourages the recollection of key details, mapping the built environment through memory to uncover important pieces of evidence.

Organisations like militaries, police and firefighting departments, and even municipal service bodies furnish their members with extraordinary knowledge of a city's sanctioned spaces, glimpses of internal secrets allowed by virtue of their privileged positions. For this reason, many believe it was a disgruntled group of public workers who infiltrated Los Angeles' water network, using expert knowledge of underground sewers as an unexpected means of accessing a First Interstate Bank vault in Hollywood.[18] LA's storm drain infrastructure is impossibly complicated, a catacomb of concrete pipes encasing former creeks and streams which ran through the valley before the city was established. By tunnelling off these drains directly below the bank, the perpetrators showcased an exceptional knowledge of geology, engineering, and spatial reasoning, using long-forgotten county maps to successfully navigate the liminal infrastructure as though it were everyday public space. While some may consider the heist to be miraculous or even admirable, from the perspective of the law the city's storm sewer network was sinfully manipulated beyond its intended purpose, supposedly limited to hosting plumbing lines for the transport of water and waste. Manaugh cautions on the ethical peril of condemning or embracing the creative approaches found in such morally dubious practices. At the same time, for those referenced in his book, it is conceded that often 'the best way to commune with an architectural space was by breaking into it'.[19]

On the other side of the coin, lawmakers have continuously been enlisting the built environment to assist in the maintenance of order with designers frequently criticised for their engagement. Stemming from the ethical belief that incarceration is not an appropriate solution to the complex social problems at the foundation of many crimes, it is argued that the perpetuation of prison infrastructure by politicians and architects alike simply feeds a broken system in which sprawling industrial jails have become a grim reality. While more often associated with the US where such institutions are run on a for-profit basis and create undue incentive for arrests, the pattern has spread throughout the globe. It now afflicts supposedly enlightened European regions from Scandinavia to the UK, with 10,000-cell mega-prison projects slated as part of a £2.5bn 'plan to crackdown on violent crime'.[20] Such developments represent the antithesis of community building that could affect positive, lasting change. In place of this, a disturbing regime of disciplinary force is being installed whose projects are best summarised by the prophecy 'if they build it, they'll fill it'.[21] Revealing the unjust nature of carceral government models, this architecture fuels duplicitous relationships between private contractors and cities intent on consolidating control through prisons run as businesses.

Cities of Incarceration

The Carceri d'Invenzione, a set of 16 prints by the Italian architect Giovanni Battista Piranesi, introduced the 18th-century imagination to the terrifying power of the sublime. Depicting labyrinthine masonry structures of an apparently endless penitentiary, the vertiginous drawings provoke visceral reactions to this day. It remains 'extraordinary to imagine a space that appears architectural, yet would be nearly impossible to traverse. The interiors of the Carceri are great subterranean gorges, suggesting Tolkien landscapes or the passes of China's Huangshan, edged by tiny boardwalks.'[22] Piranesi's creations dwarf their subjects and seem to prophesise the projections of power and surveillance that would consume regimes in following centuries. The foreboding ideology of the newly formalised mass prison is given architectural expression, intertwined with the fantastical urban fabric of Rome. In this way, the engravings double as a play on the baroque tradition of imagined 'capriccios' in works by Tiepolo, Canaletto, and Bellotto. These artists created worlds of pure invention arrived at by recombining illusory landscapes and the relics of antiquity, injecting compositions with personal fantasies. In these heightened realities unbelievable spaces are rendered alongside recognisable buildings, seeming altogether real despite their impossibility.

Seen in this historical context, the Carceri are part of a broader trend coming to the fore in the 18th century wherein imaginary architectures began to hold more power in defining taste and driving discourse, what serves as the foundation for the 'paper architecture' tradition that continues to the present moment. Characterised by illustrations of implausible constructions conceived on a truly megalomaniacal scale, Piranesi's inventions were mirrored by contemporaries like Étienne-Louis Boullée and his delirious proposals for cenotaphs, churches, and libraries whose correspondence to physical reality were as doubtful as the Carceri. What did exist in the real world was the truly enormous Albergo dei Poveri (1751), which Piranesi was no doubt familiar with through his regular visits to Naples. This five-story internment facility stretches for hundreds of metres along the city's walled edge and was intended to house 10,000 criminals and innocent inhabitants including the poor, infirm, insane, and elderly.[23] Built in precisely the same years Piranesi was designing his prison etchings and Hogarth published his Rake's Progress series, the Albergo and the works it inspired envision the outcasts of society brought together into an alternative world, their lives mediated by an all-encompassing architecture. Such examples were taken to heart by English architect George Dance who designed Newgate Prison in London (1777),[24] a functional but more importantly symbolic edifice that adopted high masonry walls to create an imposing facade, a sublime object of deterrence against crime whose message was concretised out of the Piraneisan nightmare. Their awe-inspiring depths notwithstanding, the Carceri are best viewed as a warning against the capacities of unbridled architecture, its power easily passing from compelling magnificence into horrifying oppression.

Another fantasy of the built environment sharing the same time and spirit as the Carceri was the English vision of prison reform dubbed the 'Panopticon'. Conceived by the political theorist and utilitarian social reformer Jeremy Bentham who, like Dance, would have been exceptionally familiar with the work of Piranesi, the Panopticon has come to stand for the idealised archetype of a prison made up of a central watch tower surrounded by a hollow cylinder of cells. The arrangement is such that occupants of the cells are permanently in the sightline of the tower and therefore never able to tell whether they are being observed or not. No one may see inside the tower, and they may not know who, if anyone, is looking where and at what times. Scholars have asserted that this model pioneered modern notions of surveillance and its influence can be traced in today's maximum-security jails.[25] Bentham put forward the concept as a means of optimising the social function of prisons and other programs requiring oversight from authorities like military barracks, hospitals, and schools.[26] Under such conditions 'the Panopticon is a marvellous machine which, whatever use one may wish to put it to, produces homogeneous effects of power.'[27] This was recognised and popularised in the text 'Discipline and Punish' (1975) where philosopher Michel Foucault uses the notion of 'panopticism' to condense his ideas on technologies of control into an idealised spatial metaphor, highlighting their role in creating a 'disciplinary society'[28] where the threat of authority is visible and yet unverifiable.

17. R Mackey, 'Video Analysis of Fatal West Bank Shooting Said to Implicate Israeli Officer', New York Times, 24 November 2014

18 + 19. G Manaugh, 'A Burglar's Guide to the City', McClelland & Stewart, Toronto, 2016, p.50 & p.10

20. 'Government Announces Plans to Build Four More Mega-Prisons', Corporate Watch, 1 July 2020 [https://corporatewatch.org/newprisons], retrieved 31 August 2022

21. B Walker, 'The UK's Mega Prison: If they build it, they'll fill it', Screenshot, 25 January 2022 [https://screenshot-media.com/politics/human-rights/uk-mega-prison], retrieved 31 August 2022

22. J Comaroff, 'Horror in Architecture', ORO Editions, Novato, 2013, p.173

23 + 24. J Marciari, 'The Imaginary and Eternal Prisons of Piranesi', First Friday Film Lecture, San Diego Museum of Art, 7 June 2013 [https://www.youtube.com/watch?v=6bNMavWXj1Y], retrieved 31 August 2022

25. D Jensen & G Draffan, 'Welcome to the Machine: Science, surveillance, and the culture of control', Chelsea Green Publishing, White River Junction, VT., 2004, pp.4–5

26. J Bentham, 'The Works of Jeremy Bentham', vol.4, William Tait, London, 1843, p.39

27 + 28. M Foucault, 'Discipline and Punish: The birth of the prison', A Sheridan (trans.), Allen Lane, London, 1977, p.202 & p.209

Michael Radford's film adaptation of George Orwell's 'Nineteen Eighty-Four' (1949) features a set modelled after the panopticon while the novel itself remarks on the insidious nature of power structures capable of maintaining an unbroken supervision through the eerily familiar technology of the telescreen. As protagonist Winston Smith recounts, there was 'no way of knowing whether you were being watched at any given moment... you had to live – did live, from habit that became instinct – in the assumption that every sound you made was overheard, and, except in darkness, every movement scrutinised'.[29] Likewise in The Truman Show (1998), the panoptic 'OmniCam Ecosphere' reveals just how corrupted notions of privacy and autonomy have become in the era of mass media broadcasts. Its narrative views modern society as so embedded in the illusions of the entertainment industry that such conditions no longer carry associations of threat or punishment but rather serve as a form of amusement, pleasure, and liberation.

Foucault connects the earliest emergence of the panoptic principle to the plagues of Europe when authoritative measures had to be taken, requiring the close observation of populations for the collection of relevant data to identify, sequester, and quarantine the infected. The strict spatial partitioning which followed was of inestimable impact on the urban morphology of future centuries, in many cases defining and distinguishing the different quarters of cities.[30] As Manaugh and Twilley write, such examples are 'a useful reminder that government programmes enacted during times of quarantine and plague often become permanent features'[31] of both the social and spatial environment. On pain of death, these early quarantines required citizens to imprison themselves and, at the end of their sentence, their residences are purified with a flammable perfume. A form of natural chaos in their own right, humans, like the plague, are 'met by order; its function to sort out every possible confusion'.[32] Such desires to account for and document human action by fiat lead to the mechanical drive for a spatial unity which makes possible constant viewing and immediate recognition. Out of these developments the panopticon is born as the perfect solution to the problem posed by the prisoner, where 'the arrangement of his room, opposite the central tower, imposes on him an axial visibility; but the divisions of the ring, those separated cells, imply a lateral invisibility. And this invisibility is a guarantee of order.'[33] Like the prisoners of Rem Koolhaas' Exodus, anxious inhabitants in the vicinity of the panopticon watchtower voluntarily modify their behaviour, the only means of survival in an all-encompassing and perfectly designed urban trap. Their suppressed environment recalls the walled city within a fictional London, where 'papers are banned, radios mysteriously out-of-order, the whole concept of "news" ridiculed by the patient devotion with which the plots are plowed; the surfaces are scrubbed, polished, and embellished. Nothing ever happens here, yet the air is heavy with exhilaration.'[34]

Gilles Deleuze goes further still in his 'Postscript on the Societies of Control' (1990) where he examines the emerging phenomenon of surveillance and its spatial effects, arguing that technological advancements have rendered disciplinary societies obsolete, and have been replaced with what he calls 'societies of control'.[35] Here the notion of the panopticon is etherealised as modern surveillance obfuscates the need for physical enclosures. Schools, factories, prisons, and office buildings no longer require actual structures or envelopes, and can instead be managed through flows of information, functioning as panoptic machines in a digital realm capable of automating governance.

Decadence and Desire

Just as viewpoints on lawful use and unlawful manipulation of the city are constantly disputed, cultural attitudes towards sex and prostitution have varied tremendously throughout time. As the urban condition became ever more pervasive and anonymous throughout history, altogether unexpected forms of human interaction became not only possible but commonplace. 'In the city, strangers and different cultures could meet as never before, sparking new forms of adventurous and even intoxicating delight, whether high-spirited dance halls, illicit shebeens or assignations in public parks, along with streets and alleyways of unbridled seduction.'[36] From Egyptian fertility rites to the temple prostitutes of Ancient Sumer who played important roles in sacred rituals like the hieros gamos,[37] as well as ceremonies in Ancient Greece and Rome, sex has been a central concern in the spatial hierarchies of urban environments. As recently as the Middle Ages and parts of the early modern period, looser attitudes were the norm in European society. Social conventions were drastically shifted by the advent of syphilis. This horrifying affliction of 18th- and 19th-century urban populations fuelled the extreme repression and properness of the Victorian era which still defines status-quo etiquette across much of the western world. The sex industry, an eternal element of the city, has been perennially sidelined and driven underground by such developments.

Before its moral purification via a late 1970s cleanup campaign, the London borough of Soho was a bohemian stronghold effectively zoned for the sex trade.[38] A series of ambiguous laws dating back to the Chamberlain administration provided loopholes for enterprising venue owners to exploit, creating a hub of semi-legal businesses concentrated within a few blocks. The progressive reputation of the 'swinging' city made it a magnet for visitors from the surrounding countryside, mainly boisterous groups of out-of-towners, along with a steady supply of local regulars. For ordinary women drawn to the new enclave, Soho provided bountiful opportunities to make better livings in labour which they saw 'as a step up from menial jobs that were neither inspiring nor rewarding'.[39] Regardless of its emancipatory potential, however, the revolutionary attitudes cultivated were destined to return to the margins from which they arose. The forces of the free-market economy along with the mass-production and distribution of pornography quickly transformed the areas risqué appeal into a less comfortable honey-wagon for sleaze. The strip explosion of a supposedly permissive 1960s society proved, on closer examination, yet another illusion formed by the many obscure and complex interactions of city life. While workers and patrons alike lived within a shared dream of tolerant, metropolitan ideals, in actuality 'very little had been actively permitted – by the law, by the police, by public authorities or even by public opinion'.[40]

Similar areas exist in more-or-less censored conditions in cities around the world. With its network of alleys comprised of one-room cabins lining hundreds of ground floor subdivisions, Amsterdam's famous Red-Light District 'De Wallen' is widely known for its continuing openness and serves as an attraction for tourists from all manner of restrictive environments. 'Sin city' quartiers like Patpong in Bangkok and Kabukicho in Tokyo also persist as testaments to the cross-cultural universality of commercialised sex trade in the city. The inverted expectations of these environments have been immortalised in the writings of James Joyce who explored the outlandish goings-on in Dublin's Nighttown, a red-light district centred around the disorderly brothel house of Mrs. Bella Cohen at 82 Tyrone Street Lower.[41] Under the influence of absinthe and through the warped perspective of his broken glasses, Stephen Dedalus weaves a delirious account of overindulgence and rollicking conquest. The surreal atmosphere and heightened drama of the events which take place evoke an episode in the Odyssey of Homer where Odysseus's men are turned into swine by the goddess Circe,[42] the streets of Nighttown serving as sets for distorted spatial dramas which, like Circe's Island, become places of transformation, enchantment and limitless temptations.

29. G Orwell, 'Nineteen Eighty-Four', Penguin Books, London, 2008, p.5

30, 32 + 33. M Foucault, 'Discipline and Punish: The birth of the prison', A Sheridan (trans.), Allen Lane, London, 1977, p.195, p.197 & p.200

31. G Manaugh & N Twilley, 'Until Proven Safe: The gripping history of quarantine, from the Black Death to the post-Covid future', Pan Macmillan, 2021, p.269

34. R Koolhaas, 'Exodus, or the Voluntary Prisoners of Architecture', in 'Perfect Acts of Architecture', J Kipnis (ed.), 2001, p.33

35. G Deleuze, 'Two Regimes of Madness: Texts and interviews 1975–1995', Semiotexte, New York, 2007, p.321

36. J Glancey, 'How to Read Towns & Cities: A crash course in urban architecture', Bloomsbury Publishing, London, 2019, p.36

37. SM Kramer, 'The Sacred Marriage Rite: Aspects of faith, myth, and ritual in ancient Sumer', Indiana University Press, Bloomington, 1969, p.18

38, 39 + 40. J Davis, 'Waterloo Sunrise: The life of London from the sixties to Thatcher', Princeton University Press, Princeton, 2022, p.70, p.60 & p.64

41. 'Ulysses: Summary and Analysis Chapter 15', CliffsNotes [https://www.cliffsnotes.com/literature/u/ulysses/summary-and-analysis/chapter-15], retrieved 21 July 2022

42. Homer, 'The Odyssey', B Knox (ed.), R Fagles (trans.), Penguin, New York, 1997, p.162

Capitalising on the alienation which large metropolises engender, the revolutionary technology of light in the city became intertwined with changing attitudes towards traditional modesty and propriety. Indeed, street prostitution and the accompanying phenomenon of so-called 'red-light' areas exist in virtually all cities throughout the world.[43] The shining crimson bulbs illuminating the architectures of commercial love in De Wallen's harbour front district have, in collective cultural understanding, become synonymous with areas of sex trade from London to Bangkok. Initially De Wallen was forbidden ground for married men and priests apt to be tempted by sin around each corner. As the area modernised, its reputation changed to that of a harmless tourist attraction and visitors have been given cause to walk past hundreds of prostitutes beckoning from behind sealed windows on their way to the new sex museum.[44] In the era of globalisation and cheap air-travel 'the existence of well-organised red-light districts is an important element attracting tourist trade in many parts of the world, particularly for richer tourists visiting poorer countries'.[45] A broader trend of commercialisation across entertainment quarters is further strengthening the link between red-light districts and international tourism, as increasingly marginal components of the city are brought under the umbrella of merchandisable spectacle for foreign visitors. Like the optical manipulations of commercial fashion outlets or food retailers, the advertising of sexual services has made appeals to consumer choice through brightly lit ground-floor window displays that capitalise on vernacular elements while offering 'the chance to be seen without actually being on the pavement and thus liable to arrest'.[46]

Despite growing acceptance, red-light districts maintain an air of transience as ambiguous laws and conflicted planning policies place arbitrary constraints on the ever-prevalent urban tradition of sex work. West Germany, like Amsterdam, was one of the first areas to officially license brothels. Even so, street prostitution remained prominent in the spaces zoned for sex trade, one of the better-known cases being Berlin's Kurfurstendam where acceptable entertainment functions along the avenue's front end merge into an area of streetwalkers. Even with regulations being liberalised, the prevalence of prostitution cannot be wholly controlled by local authorities. It remains highly concentrated in specific liminal areas resistant to oversight, endowing them with a distinctive character and the potential to set up reciprocal relationships with other activity clusters. The situation presents unique land use planning problems and is no different in Paris, the world-capital for romance, where street prostitution occupies the lowest rungs on a hierarchy of sex marketplaces. Upper levels in more visible locations are occupied by sanctioned peepshows, massage parlours, and escort agencies or call-girl systems perceived as classier and easier to regulate by big business gatekeepers, now formalised and tolerated as part of Paris' tourist attractions.[47]

In the illustrious French Quarter, backdrop to New Orleans' Mardi Gras carnival, such attractions have remained highly illegal despite their persistent legacy. When it first sprang up, the Quarter was renowned for grand buildings with distinctive wrought-iron balconies, but as New Orleans grew and wealth fled to its perimeter, the area devolved into a rabbit warren of brothels, hotels, and gut-bucket joints. By the end of the 19th century, this transformation had concentrated illicit activities within America's most notorious red-light district. Where earlier times saw the houses of ill repute scattered throughout the city, 'at the urging of the reformer Alfred Story, they had been relocated in a defined district, a neighbourhood of once grand houses gone to seed'.[48] The finest buildings, colonial mansions with front porches and plush parlours, fronted the district on Basin Street while farther back bordellos gave way to single rooms with windows for girls to beckon from. Farther into the district, performances took place in hallways and even entrance thresholds. Despite their illegality, many of these informal attractions were charted in underground publications collectively known as 'Blue Books', while on most official maps of the city the entire footprint occupied by the district remained blank.[49]

In the graphic novels of 'Sin City' (1991–2000), Frank Miller's expressive brush strokes and strict black and white colour scheme invoke the 1950s hard-boiled film noir plots which inform the series' ambience and aesthetic. Narrative elements from detective fiction like Raymond Chandler's 'The Long Goodbye' (1953) and Dashiell Hammett's 'The Maltese Falcon' (1930) are easily read in the gritty low-life tales of sex, intrigue, and violence in a fabricated Western US city only shown under the cover of darkness. The artist heightens this effect with creative use of value inversions and negative space, generating interest by remaining alluringly minimal and leaving most elements to the imagination. Rain and snow effects frequently streak across the darkened pages creating a sense of reality and immersion through a distinctive portrayal of the weather.[50] In the night-time atmosphere, intense lighting is played up to the nth degree with extreme blown-out contrasts, stark silhouettes, and complex scenes reduced to plays of pure forms. These mimic the low-keyed photo exposures and patterned shadows of the best noir film cinematography, nodding to Hollywood while extending chiaroscuro and expressionism from historic art movements into the commercialised medium of the modern age comic.

As with the heightened neo-noir aesthetic of a silver screen era long departed, the classic trope of the femme fatale is played up to an absurd extreme. Prostitutes and their allies rule Old Town, Sin City's own red-light district, with absolute authority, becoming the agents of their own liberation by keeping the space completely off-limits to police. Scantily clad women characters are frequently depicted in dominating positions, wielding weapons and endowed with autonomy. This polarising portrayal, often dismissed as cartoonish, objectifying, and pornographic, has alternatively been viewed as an empowering model of femininity 'appearing through the murderous capacity of females in the plot, miles away from images of vulnerability'.[51] While Miller's fantasy inverts traditional understandings of sex work and forges a new paradigm for the 21st-century superhero, the ethical gloom of the source material is always maintained, mirrored by the visual darkness of the artwork and framed through the encompassing corruption of the lawless city. The pervasive sense of despair and unpleasantness are summarised in the statements of two characters found lying in a filthy street next to garbage cans and expressing their hatred for 'this rotten town... it soils everybody it touches'.[52]

The American Disillusion

Famously sardonic comedian George Carlin summarised countless works of extensive cultural criticism into a single line, both astute in its purpose and succinct in its delivery: 'It's called the American Dream because you have to be asleep to believe it.'[53] Disillusionment with the world superpower has only increased since these sentiments were first broadcast in the early years of the millennium, and in the decades which followed similar questions of urgent relevance would need to be addressed. Is Donald Trump's career and presidency the 'failure of the left'[54] personified? Or is it that his qualities align with some prevalent devotion that citizens have thoughtlessly absorbed into their lives night and day, the highest ideology of excess resulting in disillusionment with 'The American Dream'. Philosopher Slavoj Žižek believes that 'the function of ideology is not to offer us a point of escape from our reality but to offer us the social reality itself as an escape from some traumatic, real kernel.'[55] We cannot escape ideology, even in our dreams. According to Žižek, it is 'exactly when we think we escape', when we believe that reality is firmly within our grasp, 'at that point we are within ideology'.[56] He charges us with

43, 45, 46 + 47. GJ Ashworth, PE White & HPM Winchester, 'The Red-Light District in the West European City: A neglected aspect of the urban landscape', Geoforum 19, vol.19, issue 2, 1988, pp.201–212

44. J Glancey, 'How to Read Towns & Cities: A crash course in urban architecture', Bloomsbury, London, 2019, p.37

48. R Cohen, 'The Fish That Ate the Whale: The life and times of America's Banana King', (1st ed.), Farrar, Straus and Giroux, New York, 2012, p.13

49. EE Landau, 'Spectacular Wickedness: Sex, race, and memory in Storyville', Louisiana State University Press, Baton Rouge, 2013, p.243

50. F Miller, 'Frank Miller's Sin City Volume 1: The hard goodbye', (4th Edition), Dark Horse Comics, Milwaukee, 2021

51. C Gelly, 'Genre and Gender in Sin City', in 'Women Who Kill: Gender and sexuality in film and series of the post-feminist era', C Maury & D Roche (eds.), Bloomsbury Academic, London, 2020, pp.78–96

52. R Rodriguez & F Miller, 'Sin City: A dame to kill for', Dimension Films, 2014

53. 'G Carlin: Life Is Worth Losing (2006) – Transcript', Scraps from the Loft (blog), 28 December 2020 [https://scrapsfromtheloft.com/comedy/george-carlin-life-worth-losing-transcript], retrieved 26 August 2022

54. R Hoffman, 'How the Left Created Trump', POLITICO Magazine, 20 November 2016 [https://www.politico.com/magazine/story/2016/11/how-the-left-created-donald-trump-214472], retrieved 26 August 2022

55. S Žižek, 'The Sublime Object of Ideology: The essential Žižek', Verso Books, London, 2008, p.45

56. S Fiennes,'The Pervert's Guide to Ideology', Zeitgeist Films, 2012

being uncritical of how ideological systems, the dreams and disillusions of others, affect our values and actions, which are inevitably translated into the very fabric of our infrastructure, urbanism, and architecture. If this book could stress a single point, then this is it.

If part of the American Dream is the ownership of one's own house with a private backyard, then it is either the cause for or symptom of suburban sprawl. Conniving property developers have supplied the dream and capitalised upon it in a self-reinforcing, cyclical pattern. The WWF have evidenced that suburban sprawl and its automobile accomplice are the main causes of massive ecological damage, with current patterns of consumption becoming increasingly unsustainable. According to 2015 data, the world's population now uses more than one and a half planets worth of the resources that Earth can sustainably provide. If trends continue, three planets' worth of resources will be needed by 2050,[57] and this amount would already be required if global populations were to use as much as England and Scotland.[58] Worse still, if everyone on the Earth lived in America with its unique brand of inefficient urbanism hostile to alternative modes of transport and literal growth Ponzi-scheme of suburban housing development,[59] it would demand the use of five planets.[60]

None predicted the pitfalls of excess with more troubling accuracy than F. Scott Fitzgerald in 'The Great Gatsby' (1925), a novel which ironically eluded recognition and sales for decades. 'Gatsby turned out all right at the end; it is what preyed on Gatsby, what foul dust floated in the wake of his dreams that temporarily closed out my interest in the abortive sorrows and short-winded elations of men.'[61] In short, the erosion of altruistic virtue and sometimes outright destruction, the foul dust which accompanies constant striving for success and wealth is, to Fitzgerald, the ultimate downfall of social orders produced by an unworthy dream. The architectural and urban promises of the American Dream have lured many into an ideology where the image masquerades as substance and material ostentation pretends to emancipate or elevate the individual, family or a whole community. Suburban sprawl influences and even creates its own politics as presented in Tim Burton's 'Edward Scissorhands' (1990), either stubbornly defending or lamenting the environmental, social and urban consequences of this thoroughly flawed model. Red roses and white picket fences abound in filmic portrayals of the suburban American Dream from 'Desperate Housewives' (2004) to 'American Beauty' (1999). The former makes ingeniously subtle observations through the medium of a serialised show which uses the suburbs as a stage-set, elevating the mundanities of neighbourhood barbecues and lawn care into the realm of high drama. Evincing a more overt critique, the latter focuses on the apathy and frustration of its family-man protagonist, corrupting the symbolism of bucolic beauty and suburban rosebushes at every turn. Understandings of the home are similarly contaminated. Spaces which on their face are designed to provide comfort and safety become traps, the supposed freedoms of a single-family house forming the confines of a monolithic culture requiring the adoption of a predetermined set of identities.

'American Beauty' in particular presents preconceived notions of life in the United States filtered through the perspective of outsider British director Sam Mendes. Breaking from standard Hollywood formulas, the film reveals deeper insights into a controversial substrate which fuels suburbia's quiet desperation, where beneath a 'zen-like tranquility lurks something wounded... and dangerous'.[62] Even the film's title, itself the name of a type of rose,[63] is revealed to be a contradiction in terms. The ugly realities of the suburban nightmare more closely resemble a prison, a facade, a cause of great stress and sadness, and, despite outward appearances, serve as the context of overwhelming sins. Likewise, David Lynch's 'Blue Velvet' (1986) performs a complete inversion of the arcadian family neighbourhood, twisting expectations to reveal a seedy underbelly, a deeply unsettling parallel world inhabited by shadowy characters. As the local fireman waves from his passing truck and dogs dash through garden sprinklers, the uncanny sense that a profound form of outright evil lurks just beneath the surface pervades the film, a feeling that is made explicit when the camera pans beneath the perfectly green grass to reveal a dark mass of writhing insects.[64] It is in this domain of chaotic and decomposing nature that a severed human ear is only moments from being discovered, setting up the thread which propels the unveiling of a disturbing criminal underworld.

Illusions, Fakery and Spatial Lies

In the current urban condition, what kind of inscrutable city has replaced the older fabric of 'that sweet monotony where everything is known and loved because it is known'?[65] Italo Calvino replies that 'it is a city made only of exceptions, exclusions, incongruities, contradictions. If such a city is the most improbable, by reducing the number of elements, we increase the probability that the city really exists. So I have only to subtract exceptions from my model, and in whatever direction I proceed, I will arrive at one of the cities which, always as an exception, exist. But I cannot force my operation beyond a certain limit: I would achieve cities too probable to be real.'[66] Many have taken the sceptical position that Marco Polo never undertook extensive travels abroad, and the legendary cities he visited are lies from his very fertile imagination. A lie is a declaration meant to fabricate an alternative reality, and by definition in Ethics 4 the Philosopher, 'lying is wicked in its own right and to be avoided, whereas telling the truth is good and praiseworthy'. Hence, as Saint Augustine likewise claims in 'Contra Mendacium', every instance of lying is a sin. Polo's tales are no more sinful than the countless spatial lies of the built environment: Junction City, an Iraqi town where US troops simulate fighting insurgents in the middle of California's Mojave Desert; Tianducheng, the suburb of Hangzhou, China modelled after Paris with a one-third height replica of the Eiffel Tower; and to impress Catherine the Great, the mobile Potemkin Villages along the banks of the Dnieper River with fake carboard buildings disassembled, placed on carts, rushed downstream and re-created anew. If only the current crop of architects and planners had the same fervour for design falsehood, no longer would the canons of sin cities be limited to the predictable vices of gambling, prostitution, and organised crimes.

Throughout history, the fictive cities consisting of real buildings on the sets of various film studios have played leading roles in the construction of new kinds of spatial lies. So dramatically have expectations for the French city been built up that so-called 'Paris Syndrome' has become a widespread phenomenon. The term refers to the feeling of disappointment many visitors experience when the city of their imaginings, informed by years of media appearances and secondary images, does not live up to expectations. As noted by Mumford, historic cities have often found their peak existence in the realm of collective memory, captured by authors and storytellers in infinitely variegated narratives of dramatic falsehood. This is certainly true of Calvino's Venice which, like an amalgam of every documented city, is at once eminently real and yet fictional, all-encompassing and imperceptible. In the middle of 'Invisible Cities', Polo reveals this hidden truth when he says, 'every time I describe a city I am saying something about Venice... memory's images, once they are fixed in words, are erased'.[67]

Cities can also take on more subtle, even distorted characters in their appearances on the movie screen. Films like 'Richard III' (1995) and 'Children of Men' (2006) break and reconfigure the traditional understanding of London and its buildings through clever disguises creating a form of heightened

57. 'WWF Report: By 2050 we will need 3 planets', UPI, 15 May 2012 [https://www.upi.com/Science_News/2012/05/15/WWF-report-By-2050-we-will-need-3-planets/85601337117734], retrieved 26 August 2022

58. R Dixon, 'Three Planet Living', Friends of the Earth Scotland, 7 January 2020 [https://foe.scot/three-planet-living], retrieved 26 August 2022

59. 'Why American Cities Are Broke – The Growth Ponzi Scheme [ST03]', Strong Towns Series, Not Just Bikes, 11 January 2021 [https://www.youtube.com/watch?v=7IsMeKl-Sv0], retrieved 26 August 2022

60. 'Introduction to WWF's One Planet Living Site', oneplanetliving, 13 January 2008 [https://www.youtube.com/watch?v=IRNEEb_uBrI], retrieved 26 August 2022

61. FS Fitzgerald, 'The Great Gatsby', Charles Scribner's Sons, New York, 1925, p.4

62. S Mendes, 'American Beauty', Dreamworks Pictures, 1999

63. C Quest-Ritson, 'American Rose Society Encyclopedia of Roses', 1st American ed., Encyclopedia of Roses, Dorling Kindersley, New York, 2003, p.30

64. D Lynch, 'Blue Velvet', Universal Studios, 1986

65. G Eliot, 'The Mill on the Floss', Harper & Brothers Publishers, New York, 1860, p.32

66 + 67. I Calvino, 'Invisible Cities', W Weaver (trans.), Secker & Warburg Ltd, London, 1974, p.69 & pp.86–87

reality. In the latter's production, set designers co-opted rougher-looking areas of East London along with industrial icons like Battersea Power Station, dressing them down to create a dystopic future police state. Richard III takes further liberties with its filmic portrayal, creating an entirely unfamiliar reality. A reinterpretation of the Shakespeare play, it transposes the original setting of medieval courts to the non sequitur backdrop of 1930s Britain, a concept which allows recognisable landmarks to be given unconventional programmes and alternative histories in the film's narrative. Among others, St Pancras Railway Station is reimagined as the divergent future's seat of government instead of Westminster. Again, Battersea Power Station takes on new life as a damaged military base while Bankside Power Station, now the Tate Modern, doubles as a prison.[68] The film's production designer Tony Burrough confesses: 'We're using thirties architecture – the Shellmex Building, the art deco terminal at Shoreham Airport. Richard of Gloucester's car is a 1936 Bentley. The style of the picture, however, is heightened reality. By that I mean we haven't been slavish to period detail. We haven't been frightened to use something which might not be accurate, but looks perfect in the context. That's the great thing about movies. You can cheat.'[69]

Founded on the singular vision of a dogmatic leader, industrial company towns have provided an archetypal wellspring for the fictions of writers, artists, and directors. The digital world of 'BioShock Infinite' (2013) is set in the floating city-state of Columbia, named after the female personification of the United States and inspired by the Chicago World's Fair of 1893. Drawing heavily on religious allegory, the hypothetical city's backstory claims it is the product of visitation by an archangel who delivers a true vision of urban perfection, the leading example of a Godly American society. In a similar vein, novels have used the historically charged setting of the 'White City' to comment on the hubristic quest for perfection in puritanical Belle Epoque society. With the era's ignorance to the disasters of the first World War 'looming just a few years ahead, it is a time of unrestrained corporate greed, false religiosity, moronic fecklessness, and evil intent in high places.'[70] The trope of the company town recently appeared in 'Severance' (2022), shot in New Jersey where Eero Saarinen's Bell Labs Holmdel Complex plays the headquarters of a sinister corporation. Protagonist Adam Scott lives in subsidised housing developed for the company's dependent town of Kier, named after its revered founder. Updated for the 21st century, corporate urbanism exercises an even more totalising command over the lives of its employees by offering a 'severance' medical procedure where a brain chip allows for the dissociation of work and non-work memories. The Holmdel campus is especially apt as a filming location for such a premise – as headquarters of Bell's R&D operations until the turn of the century, it was filled with thousands of the flannel-suited 'organization men' who diligently set the groundwork for an ever-expanding network of technologically arbitrated corporate spaces. This architecture has come to dominate the everyday environment, responsible for mediating what Reinhold Martin calls 'the organizational complex'.[71]

'Impostor Cities', the Canadian pavilion at the 2021 Venice Biennale, was a project dedicated to the study of cities playing alternate roles in film. It is a little-known fact that many Canadian cities are used in the production of movies from Hollywood blockbusters to low-budget independent pieces. Big American studios are incentivised to work abroad partially because of economics and tax breaks, but more importantly for the anonymous visual backdrop supplied by the subtle character and aversion to grandiosity found in Canadian architecture. Vancouver is surprisingly the third most popular filming location in North America. Unlike its competitors New York and Los Angeles, it has the uncanny ability to play hundreds of cities in wildly divergent contexts – but never itself.[72] Speculating on the ramifications of the Canadian city's nondescript spatial character, curator David Theodore put forward the notion that 'it's about identity, and it's about faking it'.[73] What does it mean for architecture to be read so broadly when architects often champion a project's specificity to its place, climate, political backdrop, economic situation and more; what are the implications for an industry which designs for the cultural specificities of its context to have buildings read so generally and yet accurately? Echoing the slippery cultural identity of Canada as a country, seeking to advertise itself as the first 'postnational state',[74] the impostor city being built in our collective imagination is a chameleon with no discernible characteristics, able to blend into the semblance of any place it desires to become.

To this day, the excesses of Vegas remain the most visually recognisable example of sinful architecture. As new cities grow, morph, and compete with its precedent, the tactics deployed to create glittering illusions spread to increasingly innocuous places, soaring advertisements and electronic billboards occupying ever more real-estate in population centres the world over. The tricks and spatial lies of these new environments harken back to episodes at the dawn of modernity, where architects were devising unthinkable forms of inhabitation and authors like Mikhail Bulgakov were grappling with the unsteady ground upon which urban futures were being manufactured. In his best-known work, 'The Master and Margarita' (1928–1940), the Devil and his accomplices visit Moscow to wreak havoc in the halls of the federal offices, asylum yards, and train stations, materialising chance accidents and mass delusions which corrupt public trust in the city's soundness.

Beyond contemporary cities, the suburbs are no less susceptible to ideological sins, becoming spaces where endless picayune differences must be negotiated. Though people are, by nature, distinct from one another, wanting different things and acting in different ways, the society of suburbia adds and magnifies differences where they do not belong, categorising its constituents in unnatural and negative ways. Seen through the lens of Lynch or Mendes, the excessive difference this model produces is not just unnecessary, but also evil, leading to selfishness and overt decadence by centring every aspect of life around surplus. Žižek identifies the ability of constructs like the suburb to perpetuate themselves long after their animating principles fade into irrelevance as the great sin of capitalist dynamics, what is called 'the inertia of the real'. Always pushing forward new commodities, this force produces tremendous waste and prompts an inherent reaction to somehow conceal, obfuscate, or lie about its failures. Nothing gives a better sense of this predicament than post-apocalyptic scenes from pop-culture, the many excesses of human environments – once-manicured lawns, empty high-rises, food rotting on shelves, failing infrastructure and abandoned automobiles – all overtaken by natural growth. New understandings and alternative visions can only be reached through observing these projections of failure, portrayals of a collapse which wipes the illusion clear.

The dream of explosive movements from Occupy Wall Street to the protests in Taksim and Tahrir Square was the restructuring of this failing global order. While crowds opposed to the overwhelming sins of corrupt leaders and reckless development bore witness to the hidden potential for a different future, there is no guarantee that change will arrive, no set path to reach the promised land. Lasting change depends on collective will, on the individual choices and human interactions which are shaping the built environment every day. Now lost to history, the promise shared by former revolutions begins with 'some utopian dreams' which 'take place, they explode, and even if the actual result of a social upheaval is just a commercialised everyday life, this excess of energy, what gets lost in the result, persists not in reality but as a dream haunting us, waiting to be redeemed'.[75]

68. I McKellen, 'Fotos: Richard III', Ian McKellan Photo Galleries [https://mckellen.com/m/galleries/60.htm], retrieved 16 June 2022

69. I McKellan, 'Richard III: Screenplay by Ian McKellan and Richard Loncraine' [https://mckellen.com/cinema/richard/screenplay/001.htm], retrieved 16 June 2022

70. 'New Thomas Pynchon Novel to Be Released', TODAY.com, 20 July 2006 [https://www.today.com/popculture/new-thomas-pynchon-novel-be-released-wbna13959469], retrieved 16 June 2022

71. R Martin, 'The Organizational Complex: Architecture, media, and corporate space', MIT Press, Cambridge, Mass., 2003, p.233

72. T Zhou & T Ramos, 'Vancouver Never Plays Itself', Every Frame a Painting, 13 September 2015 [https://www.youtube.com/watch?v=ojm74VGsZBU], retrieved 16 June 2022

73. A Gupta, 'STIRring Together: David Theodore & Thomas Balaban on Impostor Cities', STIR, 15 May 2021 [https://www.youtube.com/watch?v=eouk4BGsdaA], retrieved 13 June 2022

74. G Lawson, 'Trudeau's Canada, Again', New York Times, 8 December 2015

75. S Žižek in S Fiennes,'The Pervert's Guide to Ideology', Zeitgeist Films, 2012

Network of Virtuous Mobility

'The 20th century was about cities building airports. The 21st century will be about airports building cities.'
– John D. Kasarda, 'About the Aerotropolis', www.aerotropolis.com

The revolutionary prototype of the 'aerotropolis', perching atop skyscrapers in urban cores to 'save time now lost journeying to and from airports',[1] was conceived by New York commercial artist Nicholas DeSantis for the November 1939 issue of 'Popular Science'. Whilst 18th-century seaports, 19th-century railways and 20th-century highways boasted the distances of their connections, the aerotropolis focuses on the excesses of speed and efficiency. Reprised by air commerce researcher John D. Kasarda, this 21st-century infrastructure creates a new kind of city centred on the airport with amenities developing concentrically around integrated roads. The aerotropolis could also be imagined as a form of sanctuary for the marginalised: Iranian refugee Mehran Karimi Nasseri spent over 17 years in Terminal One of Paris' Charles De Gaulle Airport where he ate, slept and bathed in the departures lounge.[2] Prominent throughout history, the concept of sanctuary stems from the Old Testament where God instructed Moses to establish six Cities of Refuge providing the right of asylum in the Promised Land of Canaan.[3]

facing page: Referencing paintings 'The Fall of the Damned' by Rubens and 'The Triumph of Christianity Over Paganism' by Dore, 'The Rise of the Virtuous' shows the network of seven aerotropolises surrounded by planes in concentric rings akin to angels.

following pages: Based on the triptych painting 'The Garden of Earthly Delights' by Bosch, 'Network of Virtuous Mobility' depicts all seven virtues with their associated aerotropolis in the middle and left side of the composition. The right side portrays the sinful aspects of the city, including rising pollution levels, waste and commercialism.

'Network of Virtuous Mobility' is premised on the sanctuary – a protective threshold for refugees as an alternative to the EU Summit's 2018 proposal for detention centres in Africa.[4] Referencing Cedric Price's 'Potteries Thinkbelt' (1966), the network of aerotropolises connects the air space of seven European cities and their cathedrals within a loop system: the Vatican City, Szeged, Krakow, Prague, Cologne, Paris, and Madrid, together forming a united states of freedom. Convinced that stationary architecture could not serve a transforming society, Price embraced individual and infrastructural mobility as the only recourse.[5] Just as pilgrims seek enlightenment on the Camino de Santiago, the refugees within the network would rebuild a life with hope, responsibility, dignity and purpose in the participating cities. The main protagonist of each aerotropolis is an aircraft runway, integrating both the city and its aspiration for social mobility. Propitiating the sins of history, the cathedral remains at each runway's heart and anchors the seven virtues: charity, humility, kindness, temperance, diligence, chastity, and patience.

The Cathedral of Charity: Vatican City. St Peter's Basilica is extended by a three-tiered oval ring hovering above St Peter's Square. Visible from around the city, the brightly illuminated runway highlights the virtue of charity, and utilises Via della Conziliazione and St Peter's Square as the arrivals hall and turning space for airplanes, respectively. The cable car system radially reaches out to the city in response to Rome's disconnected transport system, where heritage protection disrupts urban developments. Each cable car acts as the arrival check-in space – the commencement of the pilgrimage.

1. C Dienstbach, 'Skyscraper Airport for City of Tomorrow', Popular Science Monthly, vol.135, no.5, November 1939, pp.70–71

2. S Wavell, 'Memoir: The terminal man by Sir Alfred Mehran', Sunday Times, 5 September 2004

3. Deuteronomy 19:2–9

4. J Rankin & J Henley, 'EU to Consider Plans for Migrants Processing Centres in North Africa', Guardian, 19 June 2018

5. S Hardingham & K Rattenbury, 'Supercrit 1: Potteries Thinkbelt', Routledge, London, 2007

GIFTS
WORLD

KFC
DUNKIN' DONUTS
KFC
Gaffel
Kölsch

500
400
300
200
100
9

Arrivals
charity
charity
charity
charity

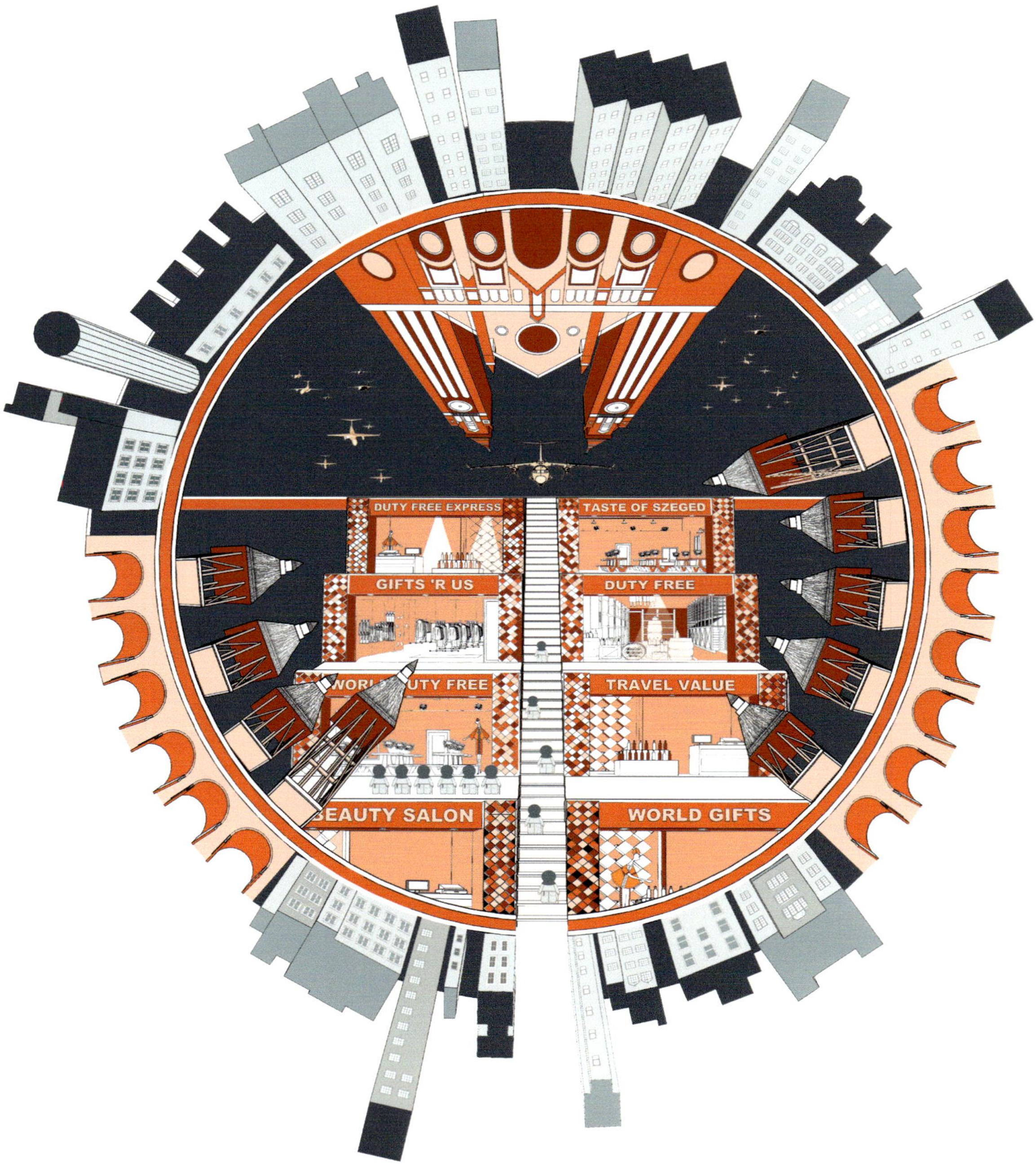
DUTY FREE EXPRESS
TASTE OF SZEGED
GIFTS 'R US
DUTY FREE
TRAVEL VALUE
BEAUTY SALON
WORLD GIFTS

The Cathedral of Humility: Szeged. The circular runway, inspired by the conceptual designs by H.T. Hanson as depicted in 'Popular Science Monthly',[6] connects the Cathedral and Votive Church of Our Lady of Hungary via an inhabited stairway comprising a duty free retail hall. An affirmation to the virtue of humility, the runway is fitted with workshops to train a new generation of skilled labour in carpentry and construction to maintain the tradition of Hungarian vernacular architecture.

The Cathedral of Kindness: Kraków. St Mary's Basilica is on a 45-degree angle to the city's grid structure. The aerotropolis follows this urban decree and is accompanied by inverted housing towers at intervals which respectfully reference the existing cathedral's spire while reaching out into the city below. A glass runway, symbolising the virtue of kindness, integrates environmental sustainability and employment opportunities to ensure food security.

The Cathedral of Temperance: Prague. The runway at St Vitus Cathedral provides an underground link with continuous lightwells of holy motifs to both the crypt beneath the cathedral and the airport's baggage claim space. Allied to the runway and referencing the Plecnik Lookout, the crescent formations of tenancy provisions criticise the abstinent nature of planning and social housing in the city.

The Cathedral of Diligence: Cologne. The elevated runway follows the train tracks leading to and from Cologne's main station, located directly next to the Cathedral Church of Saint Peter. The runway, which extends from the floor plan of the original cathedral, embodies the virtue of diligence where the architecture facilitates atonement and the restoration of trust in humanity and state.

The Cathedral of Chastity: Paris. The rhythm of the flying buttresses connects Cathedrale Notre-Dame de Paris to Memorial des Martyrs de la Deportation, extending the remembrance dedicated to the 200,000 French citizens who died in Nazi concentration camps, and emphasises the significance of sanctuaries. The runway-cum-food hall simultaneously offers employment opportunities and cleans the River Seine against the effects of polluted runoffs from the urban environment, emphasising the virtue of chastity.

The Cathedral of Patience: Madrid. Two runways lead to and from the main square between the Almudena Cathedral and the royal palace. Fan-shaped solar decks supply green energy for the entire air-borne mobility network. The sustainable agenda responds to Europe's energy crisis following sanctions brought about by Russia's invasion of Ukraine. With the dark history of Catholicism, the environmental activism is not only a form of repentance for inhabitants but for the Church – patience is the ultimate virtue.

The ideology of the aerotropolis network echoes the resilience of West Berlin when the city was surrounded by the barbed wire and machine-gun turrets of Soviet-controlled East Berlin and East Germany. For years, the authorities in the East fabricated propaganda to quash West Berlin's 'island of freedom' persona. With constant food shortages under communism, the images of children in the enclave eagerly anticipating the daily sweet deliveries via small parachutes from Western Allies only reinforced West Berlin as the symbol of freedom and excess,[7] an emotion perfectly captured in Herbert Smagon's painting 'The Fall of the Berlin Wall' (1989).

previous pages: The Cathedral of Charity has runways in the form of a cross. Refugees are employed as stewards to guide passengers to the next destination on their pilgrimage.

facing page: The staircase of the Cathedral of Humility leads up to the runway past cafés and duty free shops.

following page 222: The Cathedral of Kindness features a glass runway enclosing greenhouses which simultaneously cultivate food to reduce the environmental impact of imports.

following page 223: In the Cathedral of Diligence, security checkpoints are operated by the refugees.

following page 224: The Cathedral of Chastity boasts an efficient yet grand food hall with long tables, referencing regimented airplane seating.

following page 225: The Cathedral of Patience features ceiling and floor radar screens showing the flight positions of planes which are piloted by the refugees.

following pages 226–227: 'The Congregation of the Blissful' depicts mobility as the highest form of aspiration and references 'The Wedding at Cana' (1563) by Veronese.

6. C Dienstbach, 'Roosts for City Airplanes', Popular Science Monthly, vol.94, no.6, June 1919, pp.72–73

7. C Heins, 'The Wall Falls: Oral history of the reunification of the two Germanies', Grey Seal Books, London, 1995, p.32

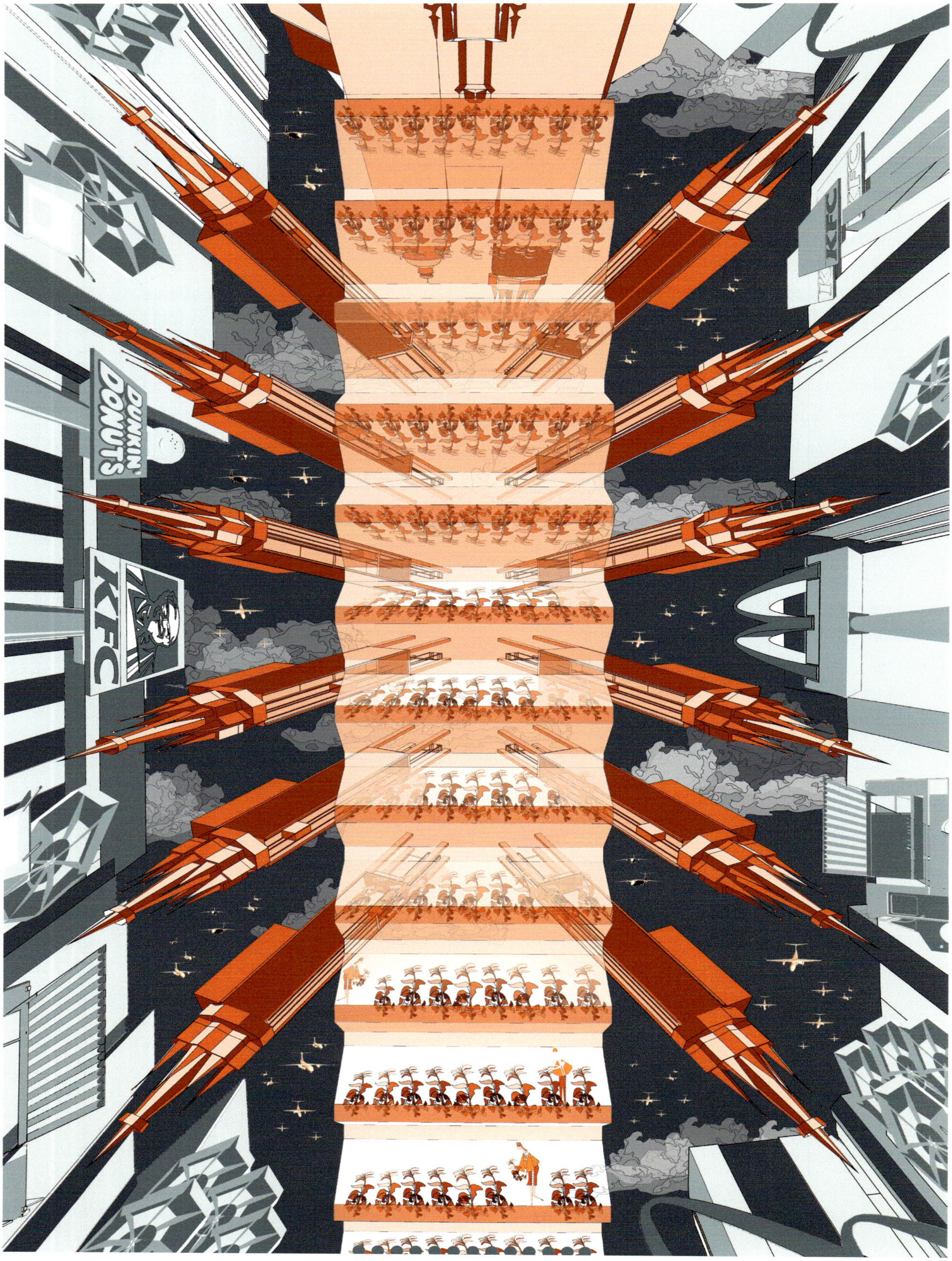
DUNKIN' DONUTS
KFC
KFC

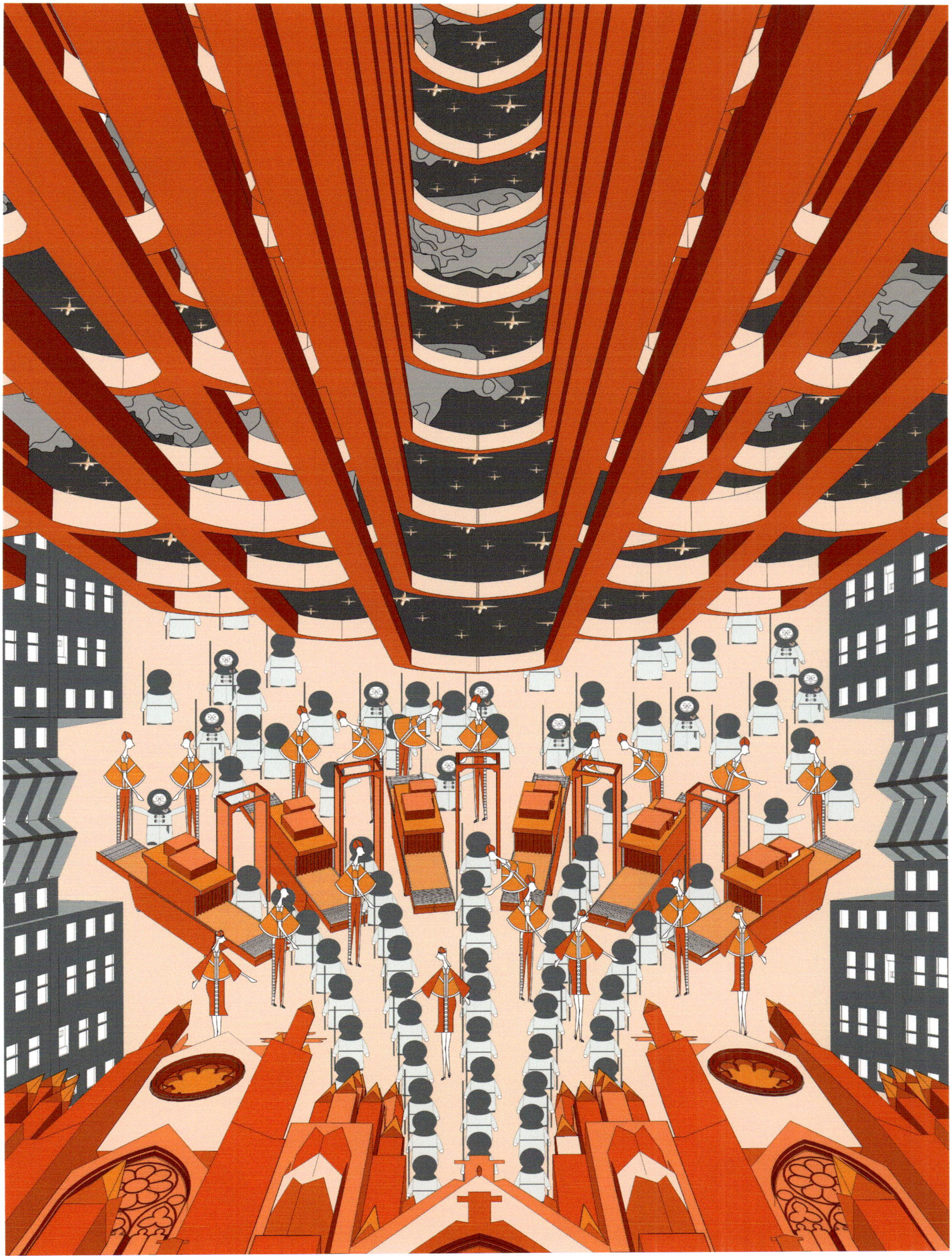

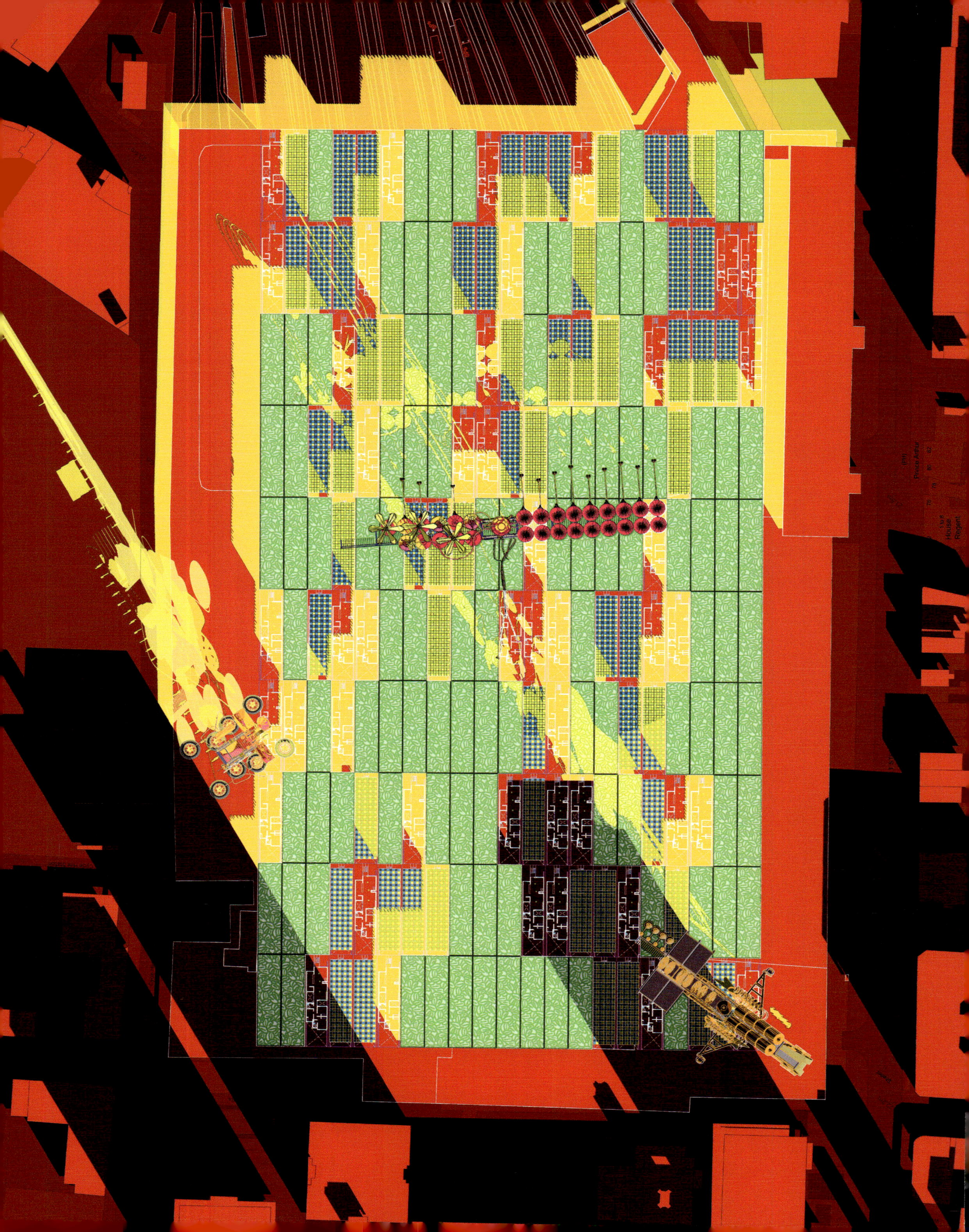

The Domestication of the Shrew

'...how complacently Nature accommodates violence; Nature loves it and needs it to such an extent that the wardens of Canada's national parks, in the absence, these last seventy years, of enough natural forest fires, had taken to setting them, to initiate regeneration and encourage biodiversity. Diversity – why do we all assume it's so good, when it is uniformity that makes us comfortable?'

– John Updike, 'The Widows of Eastwick', 2008

Amidst the excesses of a 21st-century world often focused on the pursuit of sins, how can the concepts of tolerance and pride be repositioned in the built environment? Referencing Marc Cherry's portrait of domestic life on Wisteria Lane in 'Desperate Housewives' (2004) and William Shakespeare's 'The Taming of the Shrew' (1594) whilst performing a narrative reversal of gender roles, this case study addresses the underlying subject matter of class and social identity with spatial allegory. Through detached perspectives rooted in sarcasm and irony, the often-maligned conventionality of suburban idealism and its material culture become the agents for diversity and emancipation within the city. Drawing inspiration from Cherry's characters, a series of mobile tectonics with transforming personalities set about taming the non-idealised urban 'shrews'. Disguised in garbs of hedges, picket fences, picnic blankets, and other suburban canonicals, these unlikely embodiments of tolerance and pride bring life to neglected spaces born of sinful planning practices and offer commentary on the domestic bliss of conformist community structures depicted in Updike's novel.

facing page: Newly cultivated spaces redefine the suburban ideal by coopting its canonical elements. Smiling neighbours amongst other domestic comforts tame the unlikeliest of areas within the urban environment.

following pages: Each Wisteria Lane character is an allegory to address the underlying subject matter of class, social identity, and spatial politics.

As seen in Wisteria Lane, the strongest associations, emotions and biases for reappraising tolerance and pride are to be found in the domestic sphere.[1] By relating urban issues to spaces of the individual and their most intimate interpersonal relationships, these concepts can simultaneously transcend socio-political boundaries and geographical borders. The bed is seen as the ultimate domestic theatre where every aspect of privacy, safety and care can be accommodated. What are the implications, then, when sleeping spaces move beyond the private bedroom and into the unlikely realms of museums, bookstores, and increasingly public areas? Mobile sleeping spaces reflect the modern longing for impermanence, extending domesticity to wider realms. The typical workplace likewise has a complex relationship with domesticity. Should professional environments be purely oriented towards productivity, or can the mundanity and boredom of office life be co-opted as an unlikely realm of security, engagement, and enlightenment? Upon closer inspection, the conventional window, generally regarded as a tool for framing a view and bringing natural light into another space, actually possesses more intrigue within the shallow area defined by the portal itself. Its threshold of gossip mediates the contradictory relationships between people, context and divisive situations taking place outside the protected interior.

1. S Mallett, 'Understanding Home: A critical review of the literature', The Sociological Review, vol.52, issue 1, 2004, pp.62–89

9 8
5 6

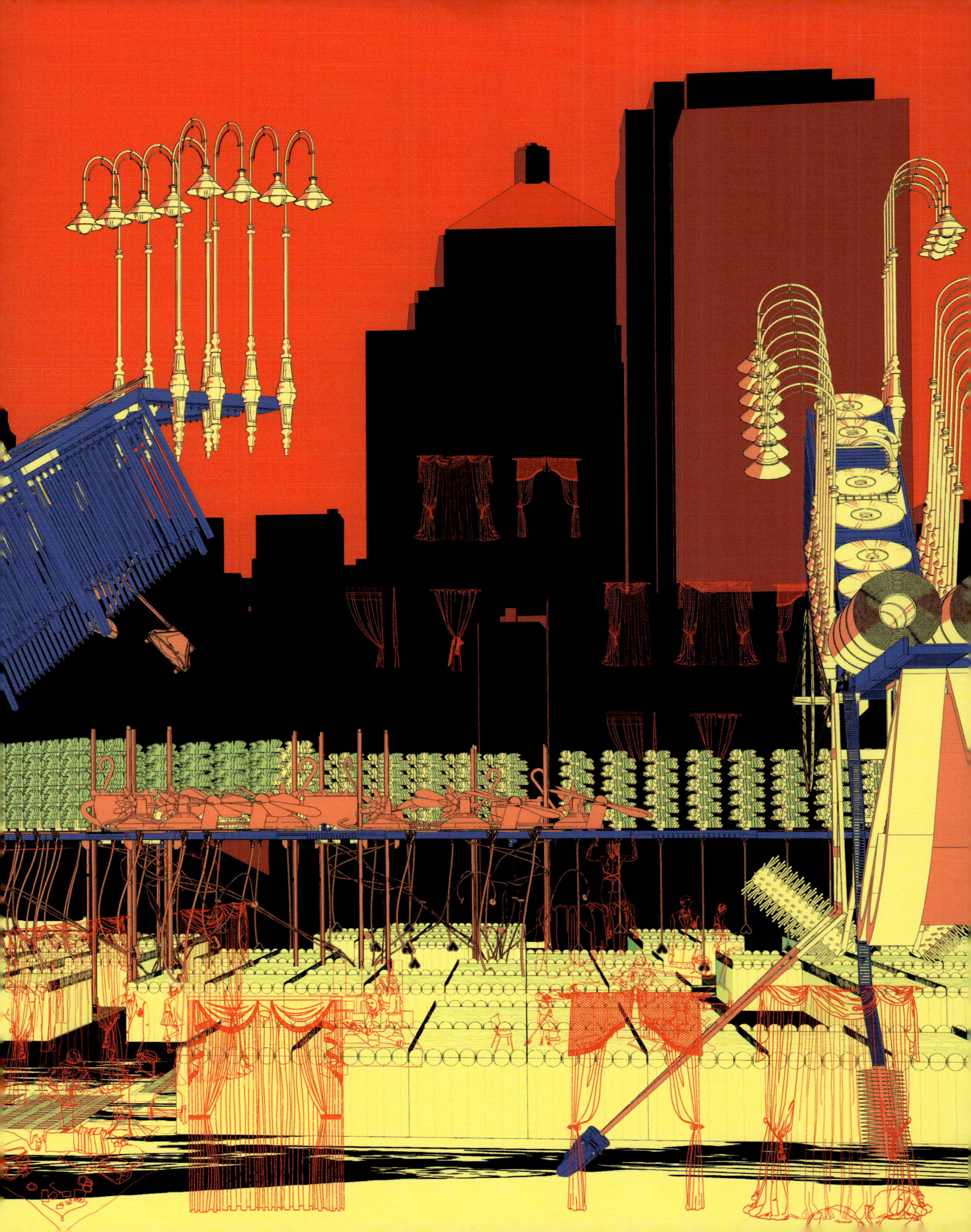

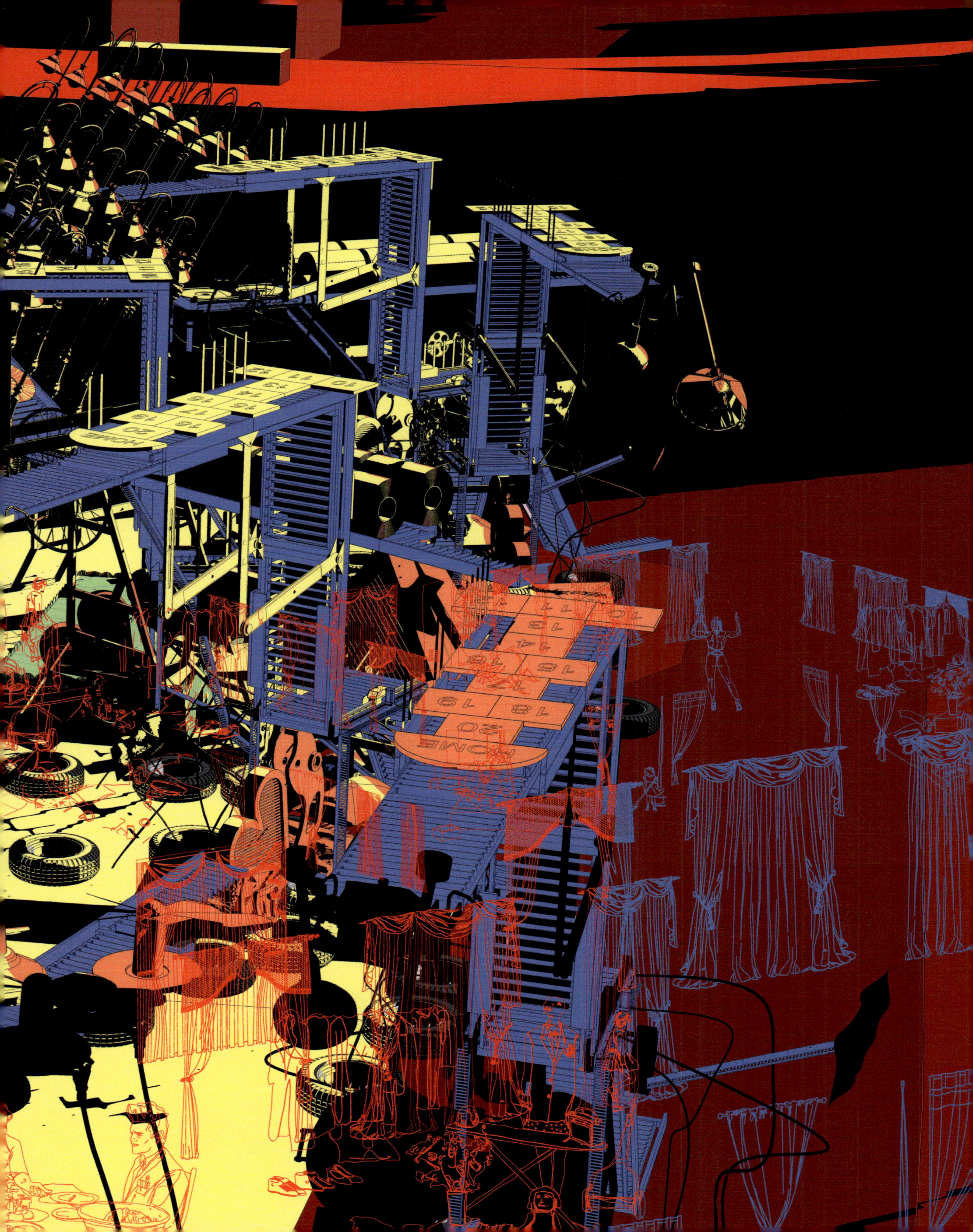

In the observations of poet Robert Frost, 'good fences make good neighbors'.[2] Imagining new forms of boundaries, the ideal 21st-century house no longer serves the role of a fortress but is now seen only through a series of unconventional interactions between dispersed tectonics. The lawn, often perceived as the ideal of openness and freedom,[3] is employed instead to define areas of privacy, while porous hedges flirt with the irony of no longer being the 'cozy symbol of conservatism'.[4] In each taming location, from bridges in London to Montreal car parks, the grid layout of the newly planted hedge is determined with reference to the average plot dimensions of a suburban home. Carved out by the tectonic allegories, these hedge spaces are available for varying periods of time as the growth process fills them in, or as colder weather removes their foliage. Seasonal variations are curated such that inhabitable spaces and yields from the plants are available year-round in shifting locations throughout the metropolis.

The network of urban voids-turned-suburban idyll offers a new interpretation of the values and capabilities of public use infrastructures. Unwanted city corners are linked through the tectonic satires which inherit the peculiarities of individuals from Wisteria Lane, ultimately unifying to shape a holistic urban narrative. Bree, who cannot take her husband suffering from a heart attack to the hospital without the bed being made, is the highly strung lawn trimming tectonic. Seeking to create the unattainable suburban perfection of her dreams, she combs, manicures, and straightens the unruly grasses. Lynette, the career woman turned stay at home mom, tries to manage the excitement and wildness of her children while ferrying them around with a caring embrace. In similar fashion, the tectonic is used to provide roof access between spaces and straightens out to a path when the urban shrews are behaving properly, but twitches upward into a protective position when noise levels and traffic get out of hand. The Edie and Susan tectonics are inherently linked, much like their characters in the series. Their seductive allegories take inspiration from a car wash scene which adds fuel to the fire between Edie and Susan. Edie uses water as her main seduction technique, a quick method instantly attracting people on a hot summer's day. Fold out wings attached to her watering cans allow for the use of solar cells to generate electricity. Susan has a slower approach to seduction – she is in it for the long game. Using a form of entrapment, Susan sows seeds within an inflatable pool to produce inviting greenery and attract insects. The final tectonic takes inspiration from Gabrielle, the fun and flirty, but selfish friend. Fully unfurled, she helps to sow seeds while fertilising them with nitrogen constantly harvested from the air. She busies herself further by filtering out pollutants and spraying sugar water in her attempts to entice butterflies.

Referencing the Shakespearean play, these acts of subversion rearrange and recontextualise the unused urban shrews. They redefine both the sins of spatial planning and socio-political understandings of the domestic needs for security and friendship as the new urban ideals. Through their distortions of gendered aesthetics, materials and construction methods alongside their production of ambience in architecture and urbanism, the spaces defy societal expectations. The domestication of the shrews results in green enclosures, open stretches of lawn, clean air, and freedom from noise and disturbance – a homely 'getaway', whether this be respite from the stifling surroundings of multi-generational parental houses in Rome,[5] or the anonymity separating social classes in Santa Monica. The urban shrews, once viewed as harsh and cantankerous, aid the true use of these cities and are chosen with the intention of creating a sense of tolerance and pride, raising awareness of the intricacies and apathy of urban life.

previous pages: Expanses of shrubs on the roofs of carparks and shopping centres throughout the city are carved into diverse interpretations of suburban idealism.

facing page: Upon disturbance from noise, light pollution, and anti-social behaviours, Lynette twitches into an upright position to protect inhabitants.

following pages: The tectonic allegories defy societal expectations in their distortions of gendered aesthetics, materials and construction methods alongside their production of ambience in architecture and urbanism.

2. R Frost, 'Mending Wall', Poetry Foundation [https://www.poetryfoundation.org/poems/44266/mending-wall], retrieved 28 November 2022

3. C Borrelli, 'How About Rethinking a Cultural Icon? The Front Lawn', Chicago Tribune, 7 October 2017 [https://www.chicagotribune.com/entertainment/ct-ent-lawns-20171002-story.html], retrieved 28 November 2022

4. P Ross, 'How Hedges Became the Unofficial Emblem of Great Britain', Smithsonian Magazine, November 2020 [https://www.smithsonianmag.com/arts-culture/history-hedges-scotland-england-180976023], retrieved 28 November 2022

5. A Vogt, 'Third of Italian Adults Live with Their Parents, Report Finds', Guardian, 19 September 2012

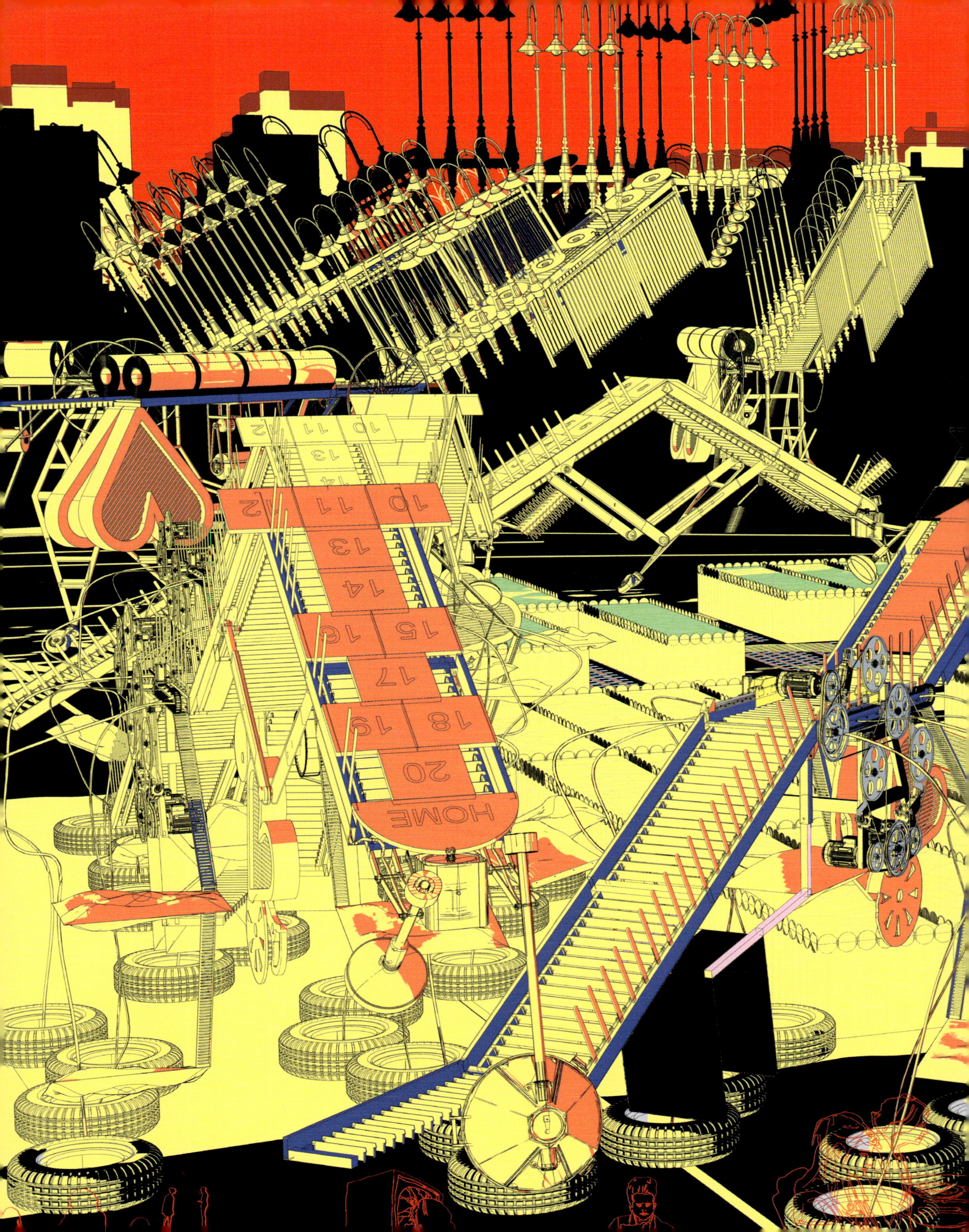
10
11
12
13
14
15
16
17
18
19
20
HOME

left: The tectonics aim to subvert, rearrange, and recontextualise given programmes to suit the domestic needs of care, friendship, and security.

following pages: Pride and tolerance guide the subtle art of embracing diversity and change in the built environment, creating care as the intended and unconditional consequence.

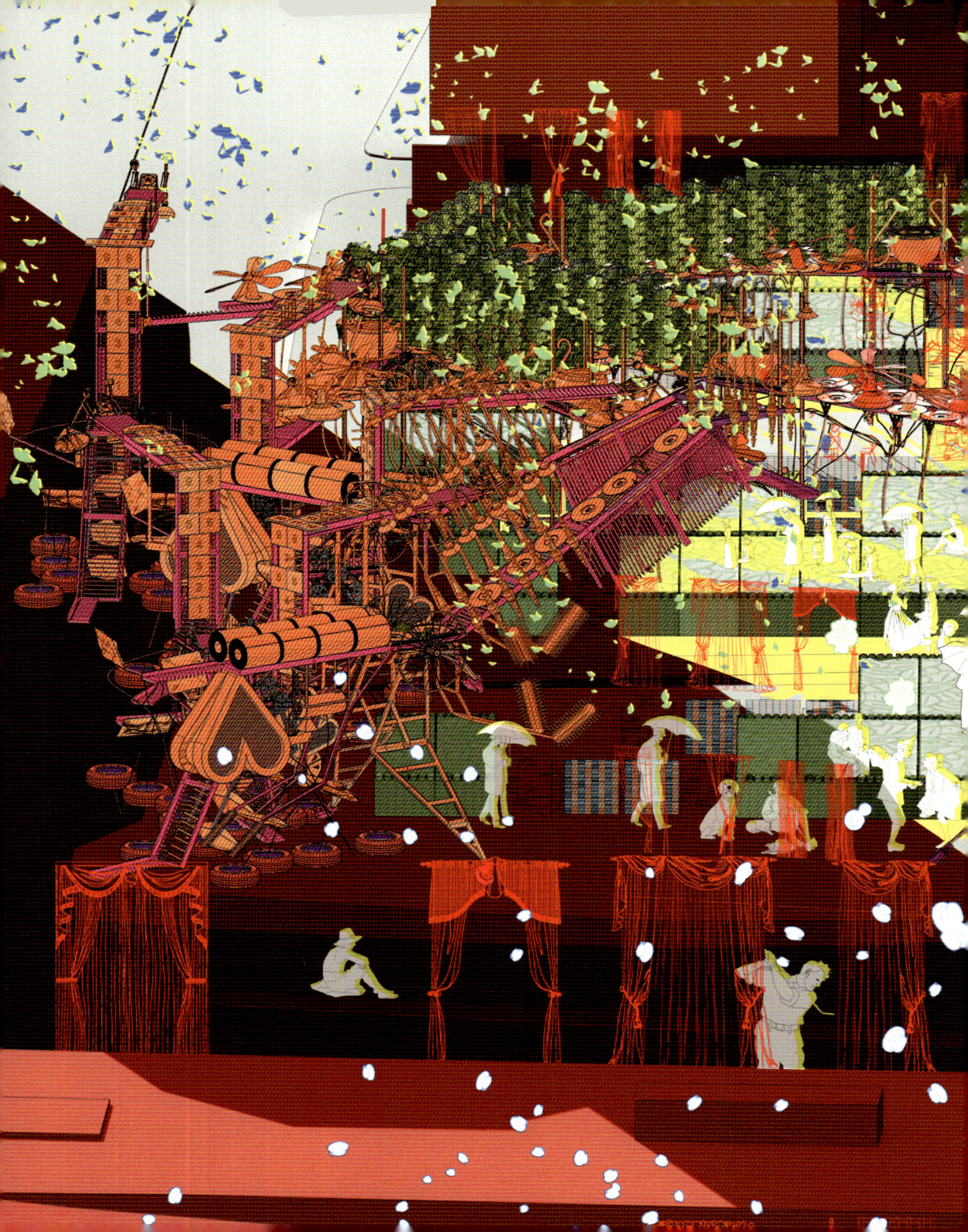

Forgiveness

'The 1913 Natives Land Act restricted black people from buying or occupying land. The apartheid government began the mass relocation of black people to poor homelands and to poorly planned and serviced townships. This marked the beginning of socio-economic challenges the country is facing today such as landlessness, poverty and inequality.'

– South African Government, 'Land Reform', www.gov.za, 2019

Although President Nelson Mandela enshrined the basic rights to equality for all South Africans and passed laws prohibiting the 'arbitrary deprivation of property',[1] the legacy from Apartheid's original sin of racial segregation still colours the political and socio-economic landscape today. Tackling South Africa's land question has likewise proceeded at a dawdling pace. In 2018, 'The Economist' reported that 'the government promised to transfer at least 30 percent of white-occupied farm land by 1999; most estimates reckon it has only transferred 10 percent. And it is sitting on as many as 4,000 farms that it bought but not yet handed over to black owners. As much as 70% of the estimated eight million hectares of land transferred by the state since the end of apartheid is now fallow.'[2]

These statistics, compounded by the African National Congress's lack of financial investment, represent fertile ground for populist politicians and the manifestation of an unstable socio-economic climate.[3] Land reforms can salve open wounds, if only they are as well managed and supported as 'The Rainbow Community', a steep valley in the middle of an arid desert located 20 kilometres south of the Orange River on the Namibian border. Through an intensified education-incubator programme, a new generation of skilled black female farmers can expunge the failings of their predecessors and re-assert their legitimacy amidst on-going gender inequality and contestations over land. South African women are already an integral part of the unskilled agricultural workforce, both permanent and seasonal. Men, in comparison, are more likely to occupy positions that require a higher level of physical strength and technical skill, which result in higher pay grades.[4] These inequalities stem from a fundamental geo-cultural outlook, where women have traditionally been impelled to fulfil gendered expectations. UNICEF laments a study of 24 sub-Saharan countries which 'revealed that when the water collection time is more than 30 minutes, an estimated 3.36 million children and 13.54 million adult females were responsible'.[5] By contrast, a Tanzanian study showed 'a 12% increase in female school attendance when water was available in 15 minutes of home'.[6]

Regrettably, many of the farms transferred in this cross-generational handover have failed due to new landowners lacking the agricultural skills required to operate commercially. In response, the Rainbow

facing page: The symbolism of female empowerment is manifested at different scales within the vast landscape.

following pages: Land reforms can salve open wounds, if only they are well managed and supported.

1. Special Report, 'Land Reform Will Continue To Be One of South Africa's Biggest Problems', The Economist, 25 April 2019 [https://www.economist.com/special-report/2019/04/25/land-reform-will-continue-to-be-one-of-south-africas-biggest-problems], retrieved 10 October 2022

2, 3 + 7. Middle East & Africa Editorial, 'South Africa is Getting Land Reform Wrong', The Economist, 25 January 2018 [https://www.economist.com/middle-east-and-africa/2018/01/25/south-africa-is-getting-land-reform-wrong], retrieved 10 October 2022

4. International Finance Corporation, 'Afrifresh – Fresh Produce (Export), South Africa', September 2016, p.5 [https://documents1.worldbank.org/curated/en/586891511419987163/pdf/121532-WP-PUBLIC-ZA-afrifresh-v2-PUBLIC.pdf], retrieved 11 October 2022

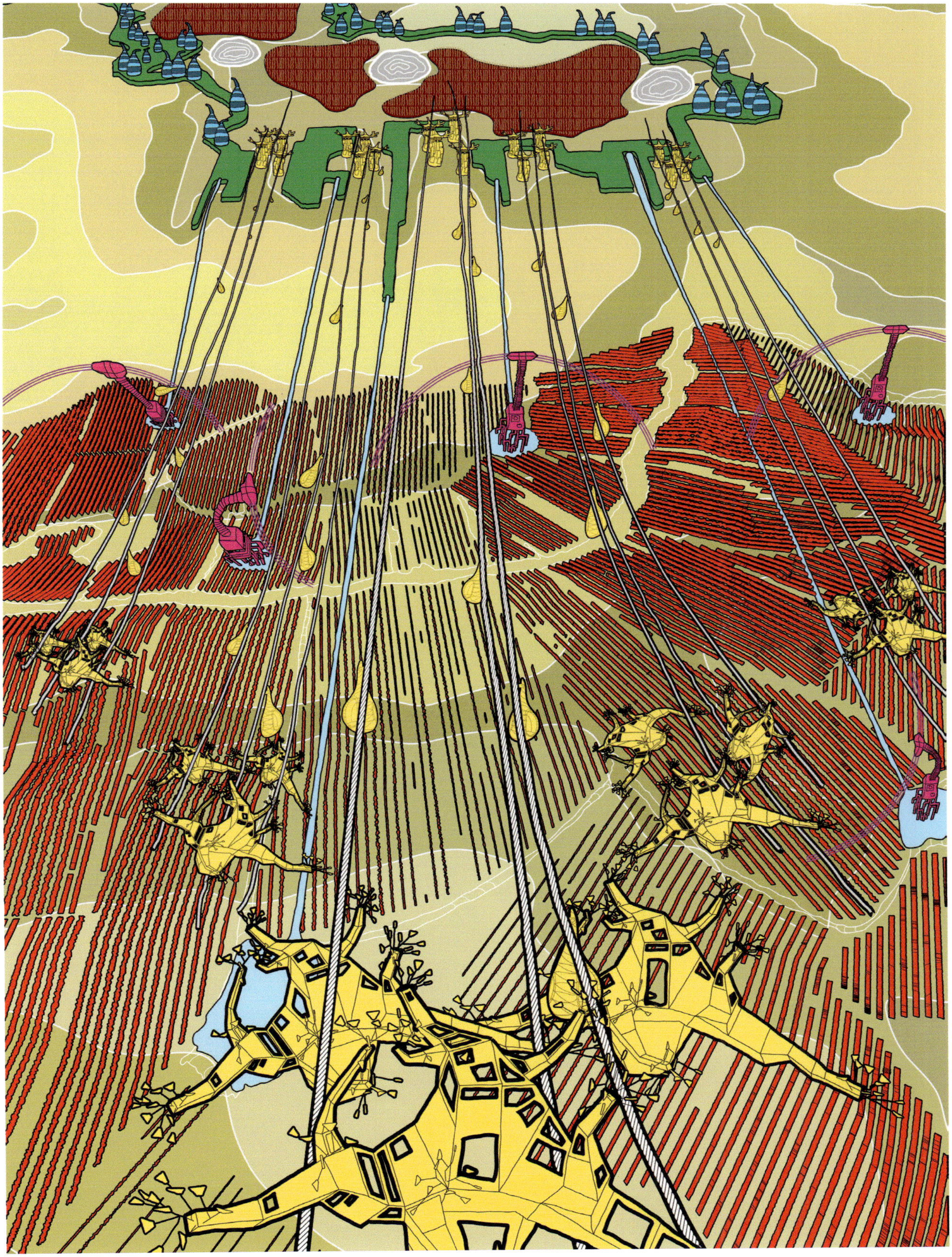

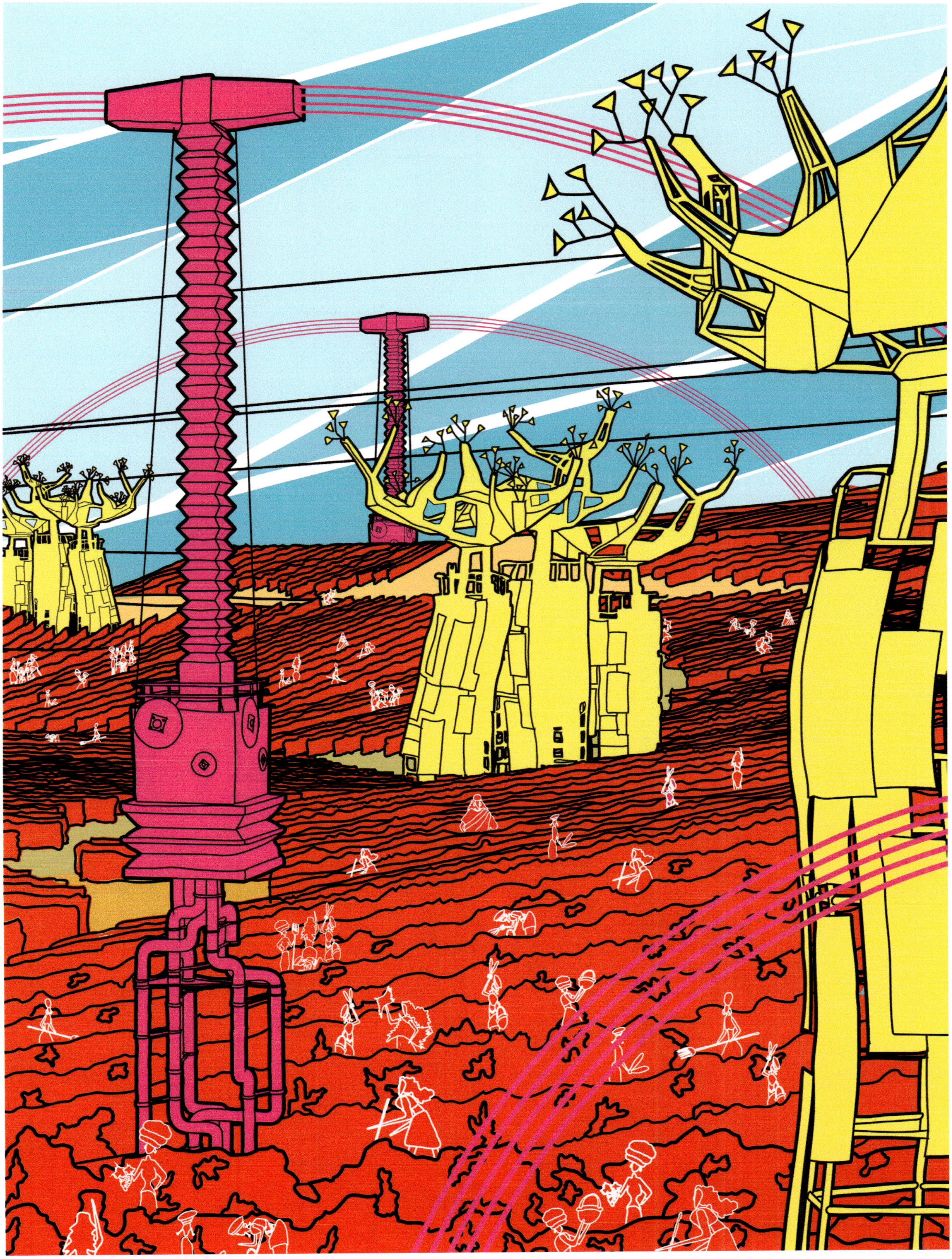

Community has adopted the 'Integrated Programme of Land Redistribution and Agriculture Development' (IPLRAD), offering a kibbutz-style collectivism which brings together black and white farmers with the common goal of agri-centric education and production. Andrew Braithwaite, a fifth-generation white South African farmer has engaged in this collectivised ownership scheme and can see its benefits: when workers become co-owners, 'they feel they have something to lose. It adds to the stability of the nation'.[7] At the same time, the community embraces the blessings of Mbaba Mwana Waresa, the Zulu goddess of rainbows, rain and agriculture. The symbolism of female empowerment manifests at different scales within the vast landscape. Each element references a colour in the rainbow and an indigenous flora: combined, the assemblage of togetherness is designed to reaffirm the goddess's protective spirit.

In the punishing heat and scarcity of rainfall which makes the site inhospitable to most forms of life, the initial phasing of the Rainbow Community begins with a seemingly simple and yet profoundly empowering element – water. The procurement of this life-giving resource comes in the form of the Guardian Angels, replications of the South African Adenium Obesum bloom. Doubling as individual housing units, these water seers draw in moisture from warm air and pass it down into the cooler ground, condensing it to liquid form. Water not only shifts the composition of the land – it also challenges the unequal patterns of public infrastructural investment and land improvement in large-scale commercial farms which are predominately influenced by colonial and post-colonial economic policies. The community's second phase introduces sand dams to preserve the procured water year-round. These technologies abolish the need to travel miles in search of water and combat evaporation in the desert environment while simultaneously advancing female empowerment and geological boundary protection.

The agricultural cultivation of the Rainbow Community is primarily concerned with the production of wine. Thriving vineyards symbolise biblical forgiveness as well as offering economic independence. Collective entrepreneurialism reimagines the traditional role of the 'home-maker', offering the opportunity for South African women to become the 'bread-winner' instead. Independence presents itself when surplus water from the sand dams is transferred across the valley, and mangrove-like structures send droplets high into the sky using an extendable billowing 'trunk'. As productivity grows, so too does the settlement's population and the need for accommodation. The communal housing, taking a figurative reference from endangered Baobab trees, is a forum for knowledge sharing and promotes traditional values.

Sarah de Villiers argues that the Rainbow Community's speculated implementation of high economic yield wine farming as a major subsistence practice arouses difficult historical memories, black labourers often being paid with liquor as a form of enslavement in the past.[8] But importantly, 'the project takes a bold stance toward the critical issue of addressing quality of land, so that land which might be redistributed is good quality and has higher viability of economic restoration'.[9] Cultivated through its engagement with nature, the resilient landscape brings forth female independence and economic equality to move the nation towards a form of unconditional forgiveness. In forgiving, the community reaffirms that 'God does not punish a new generation for the sins of a former generation. But God does hold children who don't learn from their parents' mistakes accountable. It is the responsibility of every generation to not repeat the mistakes of those that came before them.'[10]

previous pages: The cultivation of equality and forgiveness is reflected by patterns of land ownership.

facing page: Technology abolishes the need to travel miles in search of water as a form of female empowerment.

following pages 250–251: Referencing the endangered Baobab trees, the communal housing also functions as the forum for knowledge sharing and traditional values.

following pages 252–253: The architecture is animated by the spirit of Mbaba Mwana Waresa, the Zulu goddess of rainbows, rain and agriculture.

5. UNICEF, 'Collecting Water is Often a Colossal Waste of Time for Women and Girls', www.unicef.org [https://www.unicef.org/press-releases/unicef-collecting-water-often-colossal-waste-time-women-and-girls], retrieved 11 October 2022

6. K Myers, 'Women, Water & the Cycle of Poverty', United Nations Office for the Coordination of Humanitarian Affairs, 10 August 2017 [https://reliefweb.int/report/world/women-water-cycle-poverty], retrieved 11 October 2022

8. E Arungadade, 'The Names We Give: Narrative of identity and positioning of the "helpers" in Pofadder', University of Cape Town, 2012, p.72

9. S de Villiers, 'Making Rainbows: Landscapes for negotiation' in 'Radical Architectural Drawing', N Spiller (ed.), AD, no.4, vol.92, 2022, 2012, p.59

10. BibleProject Team, 'The Sins of Our Fathers', BibleProject, 2020 [https://bibleproject.com/articles/the-sins-of-our-fathers], retrieved 20 November 2022

chapter six

Seasons + Climate

'Suddenly, I heard ringing and a quivering bong, as if I were up in a belfry. That puzzled me because there wasn't a single bell anywhere around... First it was just the sound of a big bell from the deep, then little bells chimed in, and then a choir started singing the Hymn of the Cherubim.'

– 'Bells from the Deep', Werner Herzog Filmproduktion, 1993

facing page: In case study 16, 'Dear Van Gogh', profound feelings associated with the passing of seasons prepared the artist to reinterpret the built environment with particular emotional significance.

Standing on the edge of a nondescript Siberian lake amongst the pine trees and snowdrifts an elderly pilgrim, the devoted Maria Pavlovna, describes her supernatural encounters with apparitions from a sacred landmark which is nowhere in sight. Each winter when Lake Svetloyar in the Novgorod Oblast of central Russia freezes over, groups of pilgrims can be found crawling on the translucent surface to glimpse the sunken remains of the lost city of Kitezh. At least, this is what we are told in Werner Herzog's documentary 'Bells from the Deep' (1993). In one of its most salient scenes two prostrate men are filmed inching along the ice, faces pressed to its surface, intermittently rising to cross themselves.

Long ago, residents of the Great City of Kitezh implored God to redeem and protect their settlement from invasion by the Mongol ruler Batu Khan, cousin of Kublai, who had just burned Kiev forcing the historic shift of Russian national life to Moscow.[1] God answered their prayers by sending down an Archangel to plunge the city into a fathomless lake where it survives to this day in bliss. Its monasteries, The Elevation of the Cross, The Assumption of Mary, and The Transubstantiation of the Lord, were transformed into the three surrounding hills, one of which is said to have opened on a winter's night and revealed a grand cathedral. People make pilgrimages looking for these buildings, praying, asking for blessings, and traversing the banks of the lake on hands and knees before touching its purifying waters.

Considering its 100-metre elevation above sea level and location northeast of the Volga, Lake Svetloyar is a geographical anomaly. Its perimeter is almost perfectly circular and geological evidence suggests that implosion, volcanic activity, or a meteor strike could have been responsible for the land subsidence which created it. Scientists have dated its formation to the same period as the Batu Khan invasion,[2] further muddying the relationship between historical reality and folklore. Said to be without a bottom, its waters are far clearer and colder than surrounding lakes and are noticeably barren of fish, who frightened by the observation that 'there seemed be just water under the surface of the earth',[3] fled to adjoining rivers. Though many come searching for signs of the city or to hear notes from submerged church bells, the mystery of the lake often escapes visitors; according to popular beliefs, God opens it to those worthy only. Frustrated by attempts to apprehend its holy significance, people nonetheless travel great distances to bathe in its invigorating waters and hang icons upon the surrounding branches.

1. A Tikkanen, 'Batu: Mongol ruler', Britannica [https://www.britannica.com/biography/Batu-Mongol-ruler], retrieved 2 September 2022

2. MM Barinov, 'The New Worlds of Underwater Archaeology – Diving into the Past', UNESCO Courier, 1972 [https://unesdoc.unesco.org/ark:/48223/pf0000078276_fre], retrieved 2 September 2022

3. W Herzog, 'Bells from the Deep', Documentary, Werner Herzog Filmproduktion, 1993

When the frozen lake was filmed behind Maria Pavlovna, cold temperatures had driven away any real visitors. Herzog recounts: 'I wanted to get shots of pilgrims crawling around on the ice trying to catch a glimpse of the lost city, but as there were no pilgrims around I hired two drunks from the next town and put them on the ice. One of them has his face right on the ice and looks like he is in very deep meditation. The accountant's truth: he was completely drunk and fell asleep, and we had to wake him at the end of the take.'[4] Shifting weather conditions paired with a shrewd manipulation of the filmic medium here combine to present a poetic reality about the city, a fictional construct that reveals what Herzog calls an 'ecstatic truth'.[5] Like a parable out of Italo Calvino's 'Invisible Cities' (1974), this is not a realistic, fact-based description of a place as it exists but instead a deeper, more profound narrative of layered truths. Recordings of bells from a faraway church play over shots of the pretend city-seekers. Their tones and the pilgrims' apparent engrossment are illusions crafted to entice the imagination, to construct visions of what might be appearing through the ice.

'Bells from the Deep' does not 'strive to report facts about Russia, like an explicitly ethnographic documentary might do. This sounds like someone who reads a poem by Holderlin where he describes a storm in the alps claiming, "Ah, here we have a weather report back in 1802..." In a way, the scene of the drunken city-seekers is the deepest truth you can have.'[6] Just as the poetry of Calvino amasses details from imaginary realms to communicate profound truths about the dream city of Venice, the film uses seasonality to validate the illusion of the mythical sunken city, a place that we, like the pilgrims, can only approach through an understanding of complex ritual frameworks, beliefs, and fleeting moments of time captured by the movie camera. In fact, the opera which served as Herzog's source material describes Kitezh as the first invisible city.[7] Novels steeped in local folklore depict it as a place seen only by the faithful, who 'on a quiet summer evening can see walls reflected in the water, churches, monasteries, princely mansions, courtyards of townspeople' and 'can hear the dull, mournful ringing of the Kitezh bells'.[8] To all others it is invisible – we cannot see its beauty.

Also predating the publication of 'Invisible Cities' is a 1963 collection of 20 short stories, five for each season, in which Calvino's quixotic everyman-character Marcovaldo is entangled by a series of bewildering interfaces between day-to-day life and the ever-accelerating advance of industrial environments. While this condition is presented as pervasive and all-consuming, each narrative is permeated by inconspicuous elements of seasonality which, despite its extravagant modern conveniences, the city remains uniquely susceptible to. From a patch of mushrooms poking through the concrete encrusted soil next to a bus stop in the heart of the city to a southward flight of birds over a street's slice of sky, the subtle indications of seasonal change never escape the attention of Marcovaldo 'who always walks with his nose in the air'.[9] It is revealed that he possesses 'an eye ill-suited to city life: billboards, traffic-lights, shop-windows, neon signs, posters, no matter how carefully devised never arrested his gaze'. At the same time, this eye never fails to miss 'a leaf yellowing on a branch, a feather trapped by a roof-tile';[10] these are always worthy of remark and consideration.

As the artifices of modern architecture encroach ever further, seasonality and its effects are diluted. Traditional harvests are rendered unpalatable and even dangerous, progressing from misidentified mushrooms to fish poisoned by the runoff of a paint factory and an escaped lab rabbit injected with some terrible disease.[11] Meanwhile city lights, airplanes, and flashing radio towers come to replace the constellations of the night sky and, in greater concentrations, the moon. What formerly would have provided an unwavering connection to the natural world and its cyclic phases is lost to a hyper-novel, never repeating 'universe of capitalistic semiotics'.[12] While it is true that 'advertising, like fruits and flowers, has its seasons',[13] its relationship to human needs proves far more alienating and incapable of providing enduring meaning, relying on hollow manipulation rather than ritual fulfilment. This can be seen most clearly in the final story, where the corruption of even the most sacred season is presided over by the Society for the Implementation of Christmas Consumption. While jaded Saint Nicholas impersonators are preoccupied with ice-encrusted sidewalks, delivering gifts which keep the engine of industry turning, a birds-eye view makes the chaos of the winter city appear smaller, contained and collected 'in a luminous vessel, buried in the dark heart of a forest, among the age-old trunks of the chestnut trees and an endless cloak of snow'.[14]

Temporal Cities

Mirroring the fragile duality of cyclic seasons, the invisible city of Sophronia consists of two halves which form a mercurial embrace. 'One of the half-cities is permanent, the other is temporary, and when the period of its sojourn is over, they uproot it, dismantle it, and take it off, transplanting it to the vacant lots of another half-city... Here remains the half-Sophronia of the shooting-galleries and the carousels, the shout suspended from the cart of the headlong roller coaster, and it begins to count the months, the days it must wait before the caravan returns and a complete life can begin again.'[15] Constantly changing by definition, complex systems like the climate and the anomalous weather it creates are always affecting human engagement with architecture and patterns of inhabitation. In reaction to uncertainty, participation in repetitive traditions such as seasonal pilgrimages or celebrations have helped to develop and retain the ineffable character of cities through time. These often engage transitory elements, leveraging the broader environment through its flora and fauna, weather and human inhabitants to create fleeting spatial dreams of colour, texture, smells and adrenaline.

Since medieval times the 'Palio de Siena', a daredevil bareback horserace with riders representing different 'contrade', city-wards, has reconstructed Siena's shell-shaped Piazza del Campo on an annual basis.[16] The stone square is covered in a layer of clay and sand while a mass of spectators standing in its centre create a physical barrier which forms a track between the ring of surrounding buildings. This crowd also served as the stage set for a chase sequence in the film 'Quantum of Solace' (2008), which uses the precarious social infrastructure of the seasonal race to mirror the stakes and danger of a 007 mission. Even more daring is the now famous 'Running of the Bulls' in Spain, held to honour Pamplona's patron saint during the festival of San Fermines.[17] The 'encierro', or bull running, started in obscurity during the early 14th century. As the transporting of bulls from the countryside into Spanish cities became necessary to support expanding populations, it was gradually formalised into a summertime spectator sport. Remaining relatively unknown until the publication of Ernest Hemingway's classic novel 'The Sun Also Rises' (1926) which prominently features bull fighting and the running itself,[18] the subject would go on to inspire paintings by Picasso and Francis Bacon.

The occasion has become a major draw for tourism with international participants making the once localised festival a broader celebration of human folly in the era of global connectivity. Pamplona's architecture serves as a flexible accommodation where pedestrian balconies and cobblestone streets are transformed into the racecourse for an impulsive spatial drama at the drop of a hat. Alleyways are barricaded by gateposts demarcating the route while storefronts place boards along their windows to prevent damage. Onlookers again define the space of spectacle by lining enclosed paths while experienced runners attempt to 'stay on the horns'.[19] The run culminates at a circular arena in the

4, 5 + 6. W Herzog, 'Herzog on Herzog', Faber and Faber, London, 2002, pp.252–253

7. N Rimsky-Korsakov, 'The Legend of the Invisible City of Kitezh', Koch Schwann, 1905

8. 'Kitezh/Lake Svetloyar – Russian Atlantis – Russian Federation', Ermak Vagus Guide [https://ermakvagus.com/Europe/Russia/kitezh/kitezh.html], retrieved 3 September 2022

9, 10, 11, 13, 14 + 15. I Calvino, 'Marcovaldo or The Seasons in the City', W Weaver (trans.), Picador, London, 1983, p.13, p.1, p.53, p.92, p.120 & p.63

12. MM Cantarin & MC Marino, 'Post-War Ecosophic Intuition: About the (Im)Possibility of Ecological Coexistence in Marcovaldo, or The Seasons in the City by Italo Calvino', Humanities, vol.7, no.3, 2018, p.64

16. J Glancey, 'How to Read Towns & Cities: A crash course in urban architecture', Bloomsbury, London, 2019, p.96

17, 18 + 21. E Hemingway, 'The Sun Also Rises', Project Gutenberg, 1926, p.98, p.111 & p.164

19. J Ilundáin-Agurruza, 'Between the Horns: A dilemma in the interpretation of the running of the bulls – Part 1: The confrontation', Sport, Ethics and Philosophy, vol.1, no.3, 1 December 2007, pp.325–345

city centre where the bulls are summarily killed in a ritual, echoing the ancient tale of Mithras.[20] This is acted out in a dramatised fight where, provoked by the red 'muleta' cape of the costumed matador, bulls are allowed to level charges at their assailant's head on before the swords are drawn.[21]

Just as cities take new forms during specific parts of the year, seasonal celebrations evolve to reflect the concerns and preoccupations of a populace. Since the early 20th century, the June streets of Monaco have transformed into a coliseum of speed for the Formula One Grand Prix, a spectacle that redefines the spatial organisation of the city in terms of glamour, adrenaline, competition, and skill.[22] Less densely populated geographies can also play host to vehicular theater. Every summer hundreds of people are drawn to the salt flat remains of Lake Bonneville, Utah for so-called 'Speed Week'. One of Earth's most spectacular landscapes becomes so creased with tire treads that the change is visible from outer-space. Here, humanity projects the realisation of temporary spatial dreams on a truly grand scale. Participants often lacking professional sponsorships spend their own money on equipment, putting their financial and even physical well-being on the line.[23] In risking the dangers of the figurative frontier of speed, they follow in the footsteps of earlier generations of Americans who dreamt of adventure and fortune in the geographical frontier of the Wild West. More informal rearrangements also take place through enterprising individuals who appropriate swathes of tarmac for their own spatial tribute to speed. This unique mechanical flare undertakes visual and acoustic expression through sparkling enamel designs and deleted mufflers, as in the musical 'Grease' (1978) which depicts a drag race between rival gangs. Greased Lightnin', a car scrabbled together with used parts is driven by lead John Travolta on a makeshift racetrack provided by the concrete spillways of the Los Angeles River. Essential to the initial design and functioning of the city before becoming completely subject to the process of human engineering and encased in concrete, the dried-up waterway is further subverted by the film's mid-century American dreams of vehicular autonomy and individualism.

Ironically, the concrete riverbed created by the US Army Corps of Engineers to protect from seasonal flooding in the 1930s is today undergoing a new transformation focused on returning the site to its earlier function as a natural formation of the environment. Led by a team of designers at Gehry Partners LLP, the 'LA River Masterplan' (2020) envisions a future park system centred on evolving ideals of democratic access to open spaces, air quality, and safety.[24] Often compared with the greening of New York's 'High Line', the river is attempting to change expectations for how infrastructure which overlaps with nature or reacts to the seasons is designed, managed, and made available to the public.[25] Despite shifting priorities, however, maintaining flood management capabilities requires the river's concrete walls to remain indefinitely. This limits the scope of revitalisation and feeds greater disillusionment with Los Angeles's urban policies and approach to water management, where corrupt interests have historically prevented the realisation of any meaningful progress.

Water and its legal, economic, and infrastructural implications have long been contentious subjects given their association with political operations that determine the design of cities. The shroud of mystery surrounding such exploits serve as the central plot device in Hollywood classic 'Chinatown' (1974). Set in 1937, the corruption foregrounded by the film's story was drawn from real events in Los Angeles's history which came to be known as the 'Water Wars'.[26] These were just a small part of a broader pattern in the American Southwest where water was revered as the most sacred and scarce commodity, often determining whether a settlement would fail or succeed. As the rapidly growing frontier town began to exhaust available water resources, powerful officials and businessmen manipulatively procured rights from poorer rural populations in the surrounding Sierra Nevada mountains and Owens Valley, using a series of exceptions and loopholes perpetuated by outdated laws based on 'the miner's code of first in use, first in right'.[27] Paired with healthy doses of deception and bribery, profits were syphoned from investments brought in to construct the 233-mile-long LA Aqueduct. This enormous infrastructure project of dubious legal standing depleted groundwater aquifers and effectively destroyed any hopes of viable yields for agricultural interests in the region. Water was treated akin to the precious non-renewable mineral wealth that drove the Gold Rushes which established western metropolises like Los Angeles in the first place, serving as a means for enrichment rather than a vital source of life and essential component of a successfully functioning city.

As numerous commentators including politicians like Barack Obama have been quick to point out, the Los Angeles Water Wars never really ended. The true costs of ill-conceived projects like the Aqueduct are still being revealed as 20th-century dreams of controlling or reshaping nature have undermined resilience in the face of an increasingly erratic climate. While LA usually experiences an 'eternal spring' with some of the most pleasant weather conditions in the world, spurious environmental policies starting with its approach to water management have continued with egregious planning practices that virtually invented the wasteful trend of urban sprawl. With its opulence and penchant for creating alternative realities, nowhere may have escaped the ineluctable effects of seasons and climate better than the City of Angels. Using its infamous network of traffic-ridden freeways, bumper-to-bumper lineups of airconditioned automobiles connect similarly insulated spaces in an endless web of fake environments.

In distinct contrast to Los Angeles and its increasing reliance on spatial technologies to separate inhabitants from their surroundings, music festivals rely on infrastructure that is both temporary and transportable, out of necessity creating efficient and unobtrusive architectures that are nonetheless capable of accommodating large numbers. Built each year during the June solstice, Glastonbury festival's informal, radial grid layout is akin to Burning Man with its plays of organisation and chaos. Notwithstanding being held in a cloudier and more rain-prone part of the world, the festival momentarily transforms farmers' fields into a pop-up city with more than 200,000 residents. Along with the hallowed 'pyramid stage',[28] a permanent building which serves as a cowshed for most of the year, a battery of over 150 structures are resurrected annually, housing performances in what amounts to a seven-week logistical miracle.[29] Equally transient accommodation is provided by tents of all sizes, some small enough to be carried by individual attendees for sleeping quarters and others large enough to host their own concerts. Despite mandatory 'fallow' years-off and the contingencies of heavy rainfall which have transformed grassy landscape to mud puddles on more than one occasion, the festival has established a unique architectural energy with 'green fields acting as a stage for the most imaginative minds to create alternative worlds, visions of utopia, escapist universes, and political theatres'.[30]

Still more architecturally impressive is the 55-day gathering of Hindus and Buddhists that occurs every 12 years at the confluence of the Ganges and Yamuna rivers. To accommodate pilgrims seeking spiritual liberation, a megacity springs up as the architectural setting of the Kumbh Mela religious festival. Constructed with only five materials, bamboo, rope for binding, nails or screws, and skinning materials of corrugated metal, fabric, or plastic, ephemeral buildings provide every convenience one would expect to find in a permanent metropolis of equal size. The modular simplicity of these elements makes possible their aggregation into extensive structures of any proportion for any programmatic requirement – and

20. LA Campbell, 'Mithraic Iconography and Ideology', EJ Brill, Leiden, 1968, p.12

22. 'The First Grand Prix of Monaco, 1929', Motor Sport Magazine, May 1929

23. J Embry, 'The Last Amateur Sport: Automobile racing on the Bonneville Salt Flats', Americana: The Journal of American Popular Culture (1900–present), vol.2, issue 2, 2003

24. JM Henson & M Hanna, 'The Los Angeles River Reimagined: 51 miles of connected public open space', Landscape Architecture Frontiers, vol.9, no.3, 2021, p.58

25. County of Los Angeles, 'Master Plan 2020', LA River Master Plan [https://larivermasterplan.org], retrieved 4 June 2022

26. 'What Were the LA Water Wars', DailyHistory.org [https://dailyhistory.org/What_Were_the_LA_Water_Wars], retrieved 6 September 2022

27. R Nadeau, 'The Water War', American Heritage', vol.13, no.1, 1961, p.30

28 + 30. V&A, 'Glastonbury Festival Stage Design', Victoria & Albert Museum [https://www.vam.ac.uk/articles/glastonbury-festival-stage-design], retrieved 6 September 2022

29. 'Glastonbury Returns – And So Do Our Temporary Structures!', Danco [https://www.danco.co.uk/blog/temporary-structure-at-glastonbury-festival], retrieved 6 September 2022

with the economies of scale inherent to such an approach what is built in 10 weeks is completely disassembled in one. Out of necessity, these constructions rest lightly on the landscape using no foundations and leaving no permanent marks.[31] As water levels drop, city street-grids are laid out on flat sandbanks that comprised a submerged riverbed just weeks prior to their creation. Adjustable pontoon bridges connect the constantly shifting streams that separate the different areas of dry lands, dependent on rainfall and the chance path which the water takes. Seven million inhabitants reside there for the duration of the festival and another hundred million visitors pass through, with daily attendance sometimes rising above 30 million on a site of just 30 square kilometres (half a Manhattan Island). Clearly, much can be learned from this fully functioning yet temporary settlement, offered back to the river at each festival's close.

Such case studies fall under what Rahul Mehrotra labels 'ephemeral urbanism'[32] in a corpus of research projects looking at unlikely typologies which are nonetheless deeply embedded in the seasonal operations of cities. From Christmas markets to food stalls in parking lots or floating on canals, mining towns lasting on the scale of months or years, and military encampments, the spatial phenomena of temporal cities can all add an imaginative dimension to planning discourse. Elements that appear and disappear have some of the largest impacts on the productivity of the urban economy as they are uniquely positioned to engage vast numbers of people with minimal overhead costs. As Mehrotra argues, 'urban design today is in a place between the city of the "captive globe" as represented by Rem Koolhaas – an intuitive exploration premised on architecture perhaps as the sole instrument of representation – and Archigram's "Instant City" premised on temporality, between formalism and functionalism, between the temporary and informal, in the space of transition because the simultaneous validity of both these conditions is what we should accept'.[33]

Along with the previous examples of impermanent architecture, this realisation should inspire a change in priorities and redefine the allocation of resources in current urban paradigms. Like the abandoned shopping malls littered across suburban intersections or Olympic stadiums that are often left vacant, how much of what is being built today with aspirations of immutability will not be relevant in coming years? As with the constant changing of the seasons and the daily variability in sun, cloud, rain, and wind, perhaps cities and their architecture should aspire to flexibility and ephemerality, fostering structures that can be usefully deployed and reabsorbed as conditions dictate. This notion becomes especially pertinent when considering the flux which increasingly characterises climate and the unique challenge this poses to urban areas, demanding that infrastructures soften and become more accommodating instead of continuously confronting natural change through heavy-handed and ineffective approaches.

Engaging the Elements

Even in their opus mapping of urban delights, the protagonists of 'Invisible Cities' were sure to recognise the cardinal truths behind the disillusions of architecture. 'Contemplating these essential landscapes, Kublai reflected on the invisible order that sustains cities, on the rules that decreed how they rise, take shape and prosper, adapting themselves to the seasons, and then how they sadden and fall in ruins.'[34] Time and the higher principalities which govern movement, growth and decay blur static paradigms and make mockeries of expensive, brittle solutions. From Babylon to Chernobyl once great and since permanently abandoned cities litter the archaeological record. Like organisms they are born, and thrive, decline, or die based on environmental factors like water supply and natural disasters like earthquakes, or else political decisions which determine the economic fates of entire regions. Any of these incidences can be chalked up to pure chance, but if cities are to survive and remain resilient having the capacity to roll with the literal and metaphorical seasons helps considerably. Vernacular tradition varies from region to region, continent to continent. One of the most apparent rationales for this variation is the formal influence that climate and seasonality has on built form. In recent centuries, the wisdom of vernacular architecture has been sidelined for the experiments of avant-garde design ideologies or faulty political motives. It would be foolish of these forces to forget that urban and architectural morphology not only protects from the sun, the wind or the rain, but can work with them in an extremely efficient manner without any form of complex technology. Since labeled the world's first air conditioners, windcatchers have defined the skylines of cities in Afghanistan for thousands of years. They comfortably ventilate interiors by harnessing crosswinds through architectural form, calling into question the modern reliance on energy-intensive equipment. Likewise in the early 20th century as the densification of urban cores was underway in cities across Europe and North America, the phenomena of window-mounted 'baby cages' became a widespread means of providing much-needed fresh air and sunlight to those born into crowded high-rise life.[35]

Before the Aswan Dams were constructed, the River Nile was subject to yearly floods which had dramatic effects on the ancient civilisations living within its vicinity. For Egyptians of earlier millennia, the flooding was poetically described as the tears of Isis, spilled in sorrow following the slaying of Osiris by Seth, and the mythical occurrence is still celebrated as an annual holiday. Prior to installation of the dam infrastructure in the 20th century, flood heights could reach nearly 14 metres at Aswan[36] and the lands inundated by these massive volumes of water were used by the earliest Egyptians as fertile agricultural plains. Using a method of basin irrigation whereby canals and dykes diverted floods into prepared areas whose soil was left to saturate with moisture and mineral-rich silt, the productivity of farming endeavors was drastically increased. When the floods co-operated, crops were bountiful enough to support populations higher than 10 million. However, colonial powers and industrialists sought to control and fundamentally reshape the Nile's functions. Completed in 1902, the first dam serviced the world's largest alluvial system in upstream Sudan, compelling the agricultural practices of surrounding areas to transition into reliance on perennial irrigation.

The Great Mosque of Djenne in Mali, West Africa responds to the constant changes wrought by rainy seasons in an altogether different way. In preparation for the inevitable erosion caused by monsoons and flooding, each year sees the recurrence of an epic one-day Crepissage. Hundreds of locals volunteer to re-plaster the mosque's exterior with thick coats of mud, climbing on the wooden pegs which ornament the edifice's every facet. Ostrich egg pinnacles atop the mosque's minarets are also said to protect from water damage.[37] The immense undertaking causes the shape of the mosque along with the town's traditional adobe homes to alter ever-so slightly each year and has experienced widespread fame. Popularised by a United Nations World Heritage designation, the restoration process is now funded by the Aga Khan foundation, though financial support has been far from an unencumbered good. The inherent friction between aspirations for development and simultaneously maintaining 'authenticity' to please the sensibilities of visitors has made preserving the building's cultural character difficult.[38]

The Yemeni walled cities of Shibam and Sana'a also feature mud as a primary building material. The former has been called 'the Manhattan of the Desert'[39] featuring skyscrapers that reach 30 metres, as tall as the first steel-frames to be given that moniker in Chicago. Both possess densely packed mud

31. R Mehrotra, 'The Architectural Wonder of Impermanent Cities', TED Talks, 29 August 2019 [https://www.youtube.com/watch?v=Kc6hkHGHQQc], retrieved 26 June 2022

32. R. Mehrotra & F Vera, 'Ephemeral Urbanism: Does permanence matter?', List–Laboratorio Internazionale Editoriale Sas, 2017

33. 'UD 50 Lectureship in Urban Design: Rahul Mehrotra MAUD '87', Harvard GSD, 18 November 2015 [https://www.youtube.com/watch?v=LL1i4S_ZD0c], retrieved 6 September 2022

34. I Calvino, 'Invisible Cities', W Weaver (trans.), Secker & Warburg Ltd, London, 1974, p.122

35. 'Put Your Baby in a Bird-Cage', Times Dispatch, 14 September 1913, p.53

36. EA Wallis, 'The Nile: Notes for travellers in Egypt', T Cook & Son (Egypt) Ltd., Cairo, 1905, p.46

37. JL Bourgeois, 'The History of the Great Mosques of Djenné', African Arts, vol.20, no.3, 1987, pp.54–92

38. N MacFarquhar, 'World: The Great Mosque of Djenné', New York Times, 11 January 2011 [https://www.youtube.com/watch?v=aghKLgfPQcs], retrieved 7 September 2022

39. 'Mud Houses in Sanaa in Yemen: The world's ancient skyscraper cities', The Balkantimes Press, 5 October 2021 [https://balkantimes.press/en/mud-houses-in-sanaa-in-yemen-the-worlds-ancient-skyscraper-cities], retrieved 7 September 2022

40. Vitruvius, 'The Ten Books on Architecture', HL Warren (ed.), MH Morgan (trans.), Dover Publications, New York, 1960, p.23

brick structures that undoubtedly rank as some of the world's oldest high-rises, though exact dating is difficult because, like the Mali mosque, the buildings must be constantly added to by workers dangling from pulleys. These adaptable construction techniques employ natural materials in a manner perfectly suited to the specificities of local climate. The unbaked earth used to maintain walls has exceptional thermal mass making it an ideal ingredient for buildings which resist the Arabian desert's beating sun, especially in the context of concentrated group typologies. Throughout the day, heat is absorbed by the heavy walls keeping interiors at a relatively comfortable temperature that is sustained throughout the night as accumulated thermal energy is gradually released.

Vitruvius wrote that 'one who professes himself as an architect should be acquainted with astronomy and the theory of the heavens'.[40] Historical evidence of architecture and urban planning with sophisticated relations to solar and celestial phenomena have long been studied as indicators for advanced systems of engineering and theology in ancient societies. Prominent archeological sites such as Stonehenge, Abu Simbel, and Machu Picchu are 'oriented so sunlight falls on or enters monuments on the sunrises or sunsets of the solstices and equinoxes'.[41] The earliest societies 'identified earth-sun relationships as significant markers for the annual march of seasons and their related growing cycles' which 'evolved into days of worship and benchmarks for yearly events, holidays, and religious rites'.[42] In the earthen mound tomb at Newgrange, Ireland, the entrance is positioned such that sunlight floods into the inner chamber on the rise of the winter solstice. Likewise, the rock-cut temples of Abu Simbel, Egypt, possess vaults that are only illuminated on the shortest day of the year. The great portal of the Mayan Dzibilchaltún temple in Yucatán, however, aligns with sunrises during the equinoxes. Built to worship nature and especially the life-giving sun, Machu Picchu fell dormant after Spanish conquest of the Americas eradicated much of its native population. Hidden 2,400 metres above sea level in the Andean mountains, the remarkable city was only rediscovered in 1911 due to its remoteness, and with no road capable of servicing the site it has remained relatively untouched, one of the few well-preserved remnants of the Inca Empire.[43] Its miraculous construction features precisely cut rocks that had to be carried absurd distances along steep terrain.

Among the fantastic structures which remain is the Temple of the Sun which features trapezoidal windows to frame the June solstice by day and various Incan constellations by night. Believed to anchor the sun to its path through the sky, the Intihuatana stone points directly towards the winter solstice and is positioned such that it casts no shadow when the sun reaches its zenith at midday of 14 February and 29 October.[44] Constructed at the mouth of a nearby cave, Intimachay is the most architecturally significant structure at Machu Picchu and was likewise 'designed to admit the light of the rising sun only for a brief period before and after the December solstice'.[45] This interest in astronomy served both the practical purpose of timekeeping, regulating the schedules of agricultural production as well as important civic events, and religious beliefs which prescribed the buildings orientation towards the sun god Inti. The completely inconvenient geography for such an impressive construction project may have something to do with its unique position relative to the solar cycle, in a context of natural formations provided by the Andes that themselves align with astronomical events.[46]

Masdar City, the most socially and technically ambitious urban dream of the 21st century, worships at the altar of the same sun but uses a new form of scientific sacrament. A futuristic masterplan in the Arabian desert complete with solar farm and driverless cars, its architect Norman Foster embraces the inevitability of global climate disaster arguendo. From this perspective Masdar harshly evaluates the wastefulness of status-quo cities by assiduously preparing, researching, and formulating possibilities for impending cataclysms. Initially conceived as a new urban typology leading the way to a net-zero future, the eco-city adjacent the Abu Dhabi airport represents a first attempt to build on the new beliefs in environmentalism first addressed by author Rachel Carson. In opposition to the urban desiccation wrought by the free proliferation of highways and cars, Masdar has implemented a subterranean network of egg-like electric pods which run along key lines of transport.[47] Automated and driverless, this transit infrastructure is reminiscent of the network of solar craft seen in the City of Domes from the 1976 sci-fi dystopia 'Logan's Run'. As Gökçe Günel, author of a book on Masdar's urbanism states, 'despite the utopian ambitions there is something deeply conservative about the imagination and the design of the project'.[48] It shares aspects of prior models from oil-company towns and Special Economic Zones to the knowledge capitals centred around university establishments, though its pursuits involve developing green technologies rather than accumulating wealth or academic merit.

Interestingly, MIT played a key role in the image and marketing of Masdar, which houses a graduate research institution for renewables. This promises to transition Abu Dhabi's oil-centric economy into one based on knowledge work, akin to the start-up haven that MIT has produced around the Boston area.[49] Citing a lack of satisfying economic returns, authorities have since reduced and in some cases abandoned aspects of the masterplan initially budgeted at $22 billion.[50] Despite technology allowing 'planners to design and build virtually any city, even self-sufficient eco-cities', the fact remains that 'even the most visionary plans must allow for change over time and, most importantly, for the needs of inhabitants'.[51] Although a city can never truly be 'completed', Masdar and other dream-like experiments raise questions around where those who build the future urban environment are placing their belief; in the vision of a sustainable and enduring environment for human life on the Earth, or in the short-term gains and profits extracted from marketing schemes and the promises of an illusory future.

Migration, Hibernation and Prosperity

From parched plains exploding into desert blooms after rainfall, to landscapes miraculously transformed by flocking overnight arrivals, to low-lying habitats fallen dormant under cloaks of insulating snow, all manner of natural environments exult in the joyous spontaneity of seasonal weather. Learning from these examples, cities that take in migratory birds become more connected to seasonality, as in the so-called 'Stork Villages' that incorporate existing habitats lost to urbanisation by encouraging nesting on all manner of structures. Accommodating themselves to the birds' presence, these cities are reshaped by yearly migration cycles, preserving an age-old connection between sub-Saharan landscapes for wintering and breeding grounds in the northerly reaches of Europe. Resident stork colonies are celebrated by many communities, as in Cheshinovo-Obleshevo district of North Macedonia where 'their arrival is the reminder that work in the field needs to begin', their 'nesting success is a sign of a good year, and the date they leave is part of religious festivities'.[52] This relationship has fostered a mutual respect and a rooftop nest has come to symbolise luck and happiness. Through this social convention, stork populations are able to coexist in landscapes transformed by houses and featherless inhabitants. If humans instead subscribed to the values of an avian migratory society, urban perceptions of habitats and communities would alter and in turn present alternative understandings of land ownership and sovereignty. Whilst advocacy for human rights and for democratisation are gradually unravelling the legacy of borders, more radical desires are required to terminate the neurotic confinement and conservative mindset which characterise architecture and planning in regard to these issues.

41 + 42. C Angel & T Paradise, 'Nabataean Architecture and the Sun', Esri, 6 February 2019 [https://www.esri.com/about/newsroom/arcuser/nabataean-architecture-and-the-sun], retrieved 7 September 2022

43 + 47. J Glancey, 'How to Read Towns & Cities: A crash course in urban architecture', Bloomsbury, 2019, p.88 & p.232

44. D Scherrer, 'Ancient Observatories, Timeless Knowledge', Stanford Solar Center, 2008, p.44

45. DSP Dearborn, KJ Schreiber & RE White, 'Intimachay: A December solstice observatory at Machu Picchu, Peru', American Antiquity, vol.52, no.2, 1987, pp.346–352

46. J Golomb & K Hearn, 'Machu Picchu', National Geographic, 21 January 2017 [https://www.nationalgeographic.com/history/article/machu-picchu-mystery] retrieved 8 September 2022

48. G Günel, 'Spaceship in the Desert: Energy, climate change, and urban design in Abu Dhabi', Podcast, Duke UP, 2019 [https://www.scribd.com/podcast/418997279/Gokce-Gunel-Spaceship-in-the-Desert-Energy-Climate-Change-and-Urban-Design-in-Abu-Dhabi], retrieved 11 June 2022

49. G Günel, 'Spaceship in the Desert: Energy, climate change, and urban design in Abu Dhabi (Experimental Futures)', Duke University Press, Durham, 2019, p.8

50. B Walsh, 'Renewable Energy: Desert dreams', Special Report, Time Magazine, 14 February 2008

51. PD Smith, 'City: A guidebook for the urban age', Bloomsbury, New York, 2012, p.67

52. BirdLife International, 'The White Storks Have Taken Off!', [https://flightforsurvival.org/the-white-stork-has-taken-off-discover-the-stork-villages-where-it-spent-the-summer], retrieved 7 March 2023

Nature can magically alter the character and mood of the built environment – in Venice, the bitingly chilly winter, mists, and floods transform the city's bustling persona to a surreal haven of tranquility and solitude. Seasonal changes can also be affected or entirely determined by undergraduates inundating university towns where 'studentification'[53] results from high spending power concentrated in the vicinity of campuses. Indeed, areas which incorporate longstanding educational institutions in aspects of economic and social life often have better outcomes than those focused on narrow, short-lived business interests. Cultural amenities, technological research and innovative start-ups can bolster a city's resources as they have done in the quintessential academic capitals of Boston in North America and Munich in Europe. Santiago de Compostela is a unique combination of a pilgrimage destination and university town, making it an idiosyncratic example of a city sustained in large part by transient populations. The culmination of the international Camino footpath is found at its centre in a cathedral which holds the tomb of St. James and its associated shrine. An enormous fifty-kilogram incense burner can be found fiercely swinging between the cathedral's transepts during services on holy days. For visitors and pilgrims alike, this motion serves as a reminder of the constant turnover in the cultural poles of the city which shifts between tourism and education depending on the season.

Like Compostela and Venice, the Renaissance cradle of Florence has been struggling to strike a balance between a tourist-driven economy and a cultural identity reliant on locals. Capable of flooding the city with cash while bolstering job markets, the travel boom of recent decades has created enticing opportunities for growth, leaving behind the exigencies of the permanent population who are quickly being priced out of amenities, services, and homes. Much-maligned rental platforms like Airbnb stand accused of destroying the vitality at the heart of the city's fantastic atmosphere. Indeed, part of the reason for the aesthetic capital's immense appeal in the first instance is being lost, whether by calculated fiat or happenstance, leaving its architectural masterpieces lifeless and removed from the everyday experience of residents, as though behind glass in museums.

Fighting against the tide, Florence's city council has instantiated measures to reduce strain on the resources of the Unesco-protected 'centro storico'. Short term lets promulgated by Silicon Valley start-ups have been banned outright in the first ruling of its kind in Italy, while property taxes for owners offering regular leases have been waived for a three-year period. Florentine officials are even contemplating a Venice-style entrance ticket and they already charge a so-called 'tourist tax' of €5.50 per person per night. But despite these pyrrhic victories the Disneyfication of Florence appears to be a forgone conclusion. 'Small local shops have either closed or changed their business to target tourists. The bakery has become a sandwich shop, the greengrocer's is now a wine bar and the knife-sharpener sells cheap scarves.'[54] Lamenting the exodus, local advocate Camilla Speranza was quoted in headlines with this haunting utterance: 'What is a city without its people? Florence is in danger of becoming a beautiful museum with no life.'[55]

Prominent activist Patrizia Asproni dealt with similar challenges daily as former president of Florence's Museo Marino Marini. From her perspective 'everyone talks about the tourism boom, but few mention the enormous cost and strain on our resources of these millions of people passing through our city: the extra litter, the extra sewage, wear and tear on our streets and buildings, the filling-up of our A&E departments by American students in alcoholic comas. Not to mention the housing shortage and the environmental impact.'[56] And this is not the only problem which the never-do-well American youth are causing for the Tuscan capital. Affordable accommodation for students is another social substructure once taken for granted and now facing extinction. Offered at inflated prices, much of the city's limited stock of single-bed apartments are snapped up in three-month cycles by a continuous supply of 15,000-odd American scholars passing through the city on overseas study programmes. Amazingly, the spatial phenomena driven by wealthy collegiates are reaching into the realm of global influence.

In America itself, reading week celebrations see students mirroring the paths of retirees with Florida serving as one of the primary destinations. The film 'Spring Breakers' (2013) provides an excellent summary of the dream being sold by resort developers seeking to entice younger populations to seemingly paradisal estates in an uncanny impersonation of their grandparents. After all, the elderly demographic is well known for their migratory behaviour, and their economic prowess has led to entire cities being built exclusively for their use in the inviting climates of America's 'Sun Belt'. For the first time in human history, the increased prosperity and consequent good health of post-war generations made the concept of retirement a reality. Ordinary people of this age bracket are now able to fund lives beyond ceaseless participation in everyday careers, finding themselves in a modern limbo being 'too old to work and too young to die'.[57]

Sun City is situated in the Sonoran Desert of Arizona and was the first settlement of this kind. Many of the features that now typify 'active adult communities', marketed to those aged 55 and over throughout the globe, originated here. Beginning as the pet project of developer Del Webb, the master-planned seniors' paradise provided the leisurely lifestyles prized by those entering their golden years on a mass scale. The hyper-arranged 'Original Fun City'[58] first opened its doors in 1960 and an unexpected 100,000 visitors poured in to witness the concept, their interest piqued by a nine-hole golf course conveniently located moments from a neighbourhood of model homes. With the resulting 'Time' magazine cover story[59] and offerings of some of the most affordable properties and tax rates in the US, it proved to be a massive success selling thousands of lots in the first year of operation. Streets grew outwards from the central core in a radial pattern, and the communities' acclaim gave it access to untold resources. Despite being one of the hottest and driest places in the country, it now offers 11 irrigated golf courses and two man-made lakes.[60] Luckily for the locals, golf is considered an essential service by Arizona governance and hence was permitted to continue in spite of transformative lockdown restrictions during the 2020s.[61] Seasonal rentals are also sought after by the 'snowbirds' of more northern geographies, and many make the leap to move in favour of the appealing year-round amenities in the pioneering community. Like 'Disneyland for seniors', Sun City has been compared by its residents to 'living permanently on vacation, but you don't have to live out of your suitcase'.[62] Annual migration has also prompted more informal settlements, making use of RV campers and mobile trailers to transform empty swathes of land into makeshift retirement communities. When recent border restrictions prevented international travel, some constructed their own senior-friendly winter paradise. 'Domaine de la Florida' was born out of necessity in a one-mile subdivision of St Ambroise, a retirement community outside Quebec City.[63] Replete with plastic palm trees, pastel-coloured garden gnomes and pink lawn flamingoes, the community is a distant love-letter to the southern state it is modeled after, and despite sub-20 degrees Celsius temperatures and deep snow, provides an illusory semblance of the Floridian dream.

Though Sun Belt and Mediterranean geographies boast the comforts of year-round warmth, the monotony of their climate is contrasted by northern localities which benefit from the fleeting magic

53. DP Smith & L Holt, 'Studentification and "Apprentice" Gentrifiers within Britain's Provincial Towns and Cities', Environment and Planning A, vol.39, no.1, 2007, pp.142–161

54, 55 + 56. N Swallow, 'Florence is in Danger of Becoming a Beautiful Museum with No Life', The Telegraph, 20 October 2023

57. 'The Family: A place in the sun', Time Magazine, 3 August 1962 [https://content.time.com/time/subscriber/article/0,33009,896472-1,00.html], retrieved 8 September 2022

58. 'Welcome to Sun City AZ!', Sun City, Arizona [https://suncityaz.org], retrieved 8 September 2022

59. 'Time Magazine Cover: Del Webb', Time Magazine, vol. LXXX, no.5, 3 August 1962 [https://content.time.com/time/covers/0,16641,19620803,00.html], retrieved 8 September 2022

60. J Glancey, 'How to Read Towns & Cities: A crash course in urban architecture', Bloomsbury, London, 2019, p.56

61 + 62. K Brinson, 'In Sun City, America's Oldest Active Retirement Community, Joy Endures through the Pandemic', National Geographic, 28 October 2020 [https://www.nationalgeographic.com/history/article/sun-city-america-oldest-active-retirement-community-joy-pandemic], retrieved 8 September 2022

63. D Bilefsky, 'Canadian Snowbirds Find Refuge in Their Mythical Miami', World, New York Times, 20 March 2021

of endless sunlight in the summer months. Cities that experience the midnight sun span the northern reaches of Iceland, Canada and Russia, but the most accessible are likely the capitals of the Scandinavian countries where stable cultures and relatively mild climates make habitation more commonplace. The Arctic Islands of Svalbard in Norway have transformed old mining towns into high-end tourist destinations. Travelers are lured from far and wide by visions of winter wastelands transformed by 24-hour light and the promises of Knut Hamsun who, seeing the red sun dip and rise from the sea without setting, felt 'more strangely on those nights than anyone would believe'.[64]

In seasonal cities of more temperate regions like Holland, a colourful floral extravaganza reaches its height at the temporal midway point of the calendar year. The 25-mile Bloemen Route between Haarlem and Leiden hosts the densest concentration of tulip gardens in the world[65] in an area known as the Westland district. This part of the country essentially had to invent itself in the 18th and 19th centuries, raised out of flood plains through meticulous water management. Subject to the whims of nature, this precarious foundation would motivate it to become a flower production and agricultural powerhouse spurring a series of innovations in horticulture, livestock farming and the universally recognised glasshouse architecture which extends the ever-important growing season. These structures earned the Westland its current nickname 'The Glass City', an ironic title considering its largely rural geography. It recently featured in Rem Koolhaas' 'Countryside, The Future' (2020) exhibition at New York's Guggenheim Museum, where the connections between agricultural landscapes and urban development are highlighted alongside research on the 'Dutch mastery of nature in the 17th century', which is 'manifest in today's striated landscapes of big agriculture, big energy, and big data'.[66]

In 'The Botany of Desire: A plant's eye view of the world' (2001), there is an implicit recognition of the role which chance plays in the highly managed environments of agricultural production and dilettante cultivation. 'Perhaps more than most, the farmer or the gardener understands that his control is always something of a fiction, depending as it does on luck and weather and much else that is beyond his control. It is only the suspension of disbelief that allows him to wade out in the season's uncertainties.'[67] Author Michael Pollan compares these densely packed and scrupulously managed networks of plants to a city – 'the flowering garden is a place you immediately sense is thick with information, thick as a metropolis, in fact'.[68] He also highlights the Dutch genius for horticulture which started with the economic bubble of the 17th-century tulip craze and has created ephemeral landscapes of stunning colours at regular intervals each year since. The tulip bulb market in particular, once subject to the rhythms of the seasons, is now precisely choreographed. Each spring when thousands of acres of muddy fields burst to life with row upon row of colourful flowers, farmers diligently mow down the stalks of the mega bloom.[69] This sacrificial decapitation preserves the bulbs at the base of the plants which can then be sold to buyers around the world and make for transformations on a mass scale along the Bloemen Route. A large quantity of these bulbs are shipped across the Atlantic to the Canadian capital of Ottawa by the Dutch Royal Family in gratitude for having sheltered the future Queen Juliana in the years of Nazi occupation during World War II. This tribute results in the metamorphosis of the northern city's dreary canal shores into a facsimile of the Dutch countryside in defiance of its chilly climate.

From Massachusetts to Wisconsin and as far north as Quebec, hundreds of hectares of low-growing cranberry plains experience similar transformations at the end of their growth cycle. Purposefully flooded with up to 18 inches of water in the middle of autumn, fields turn into bogs of an exuberant red hue as the deluge loosens seas of floating berries from their vines. This inventive strategy allows farmers wielding booms and rakes to corral the harvest into spectacular crimson landscapes easily pumped into waiting trucks. From late September to early November, the cranberry producing regions of Wisconsin alone employ thousands of seasonal workers from Mexico. However, warmer weather with more erratic behaviour is wreaking havoc on growing seasons and crop yields while threatening these livelihoods.[70] In Canada, state regulations on closed seasons and quotas for game animals and fish also include cranberries. While regulating commons can bring ecological benefits, these laws shortsightedly extend non-indigenous authority over lands once freely used in passing down cultural practices.[71]

In a letter to his wife, Alice, one of the world's most renowned artists noted the transient nature of all things physical, emphasising the unique interaction of human perception with the qualities of nature that served as his greatest enduring muse: 'Everything changes, even stone.'[72] As in his famous haystack studies, Claude Monet's series of paintings depicting London at the turn of the 20th century made more of changing light conditions and atmosphere than the underlying architecture. Monet read the city with a different protagonist, examining nature as it appeared on the surfaces of his subject whether it was a pragmatic infrastructure or an intricate cathedral. During a stay in London, he produced 19 different renditions of the Houses of Parliament and 41 of Waterloo Bridge all painted from the exact same viewpoint. Each contain distinct variations which show that 'our perception of any object no matter how monumental it is, is actually all about the weather, the time, the light, the moment that you see it in'.[73] This obsessive practice was revolutionary in its ability to demonstrate how ethereal conditions enhance an observer's engagement with the material world, revealing a hidden collaboration between the city and its surrounding environment.

Pollan emphasises the centrality of change for an emerging paradigm of climate-focused design in both city and landscape. In coming years, sustainable and easily repurposed forms of building will grow into every facet of the architecture world, necessitated by novel climatic conditions. The same forces will drive an analogous change in the plant world where global warming promises to be 'a cataclysm that some species will turn into a great opportunity to expand their range'.[74] In Fred Hoyle's portrayal of climatic end times, 'The Dark Cloud' (1957), the speakers in Hyde Park experience an abundance of converts moved by desperation to embrace the solar deity present in the ancient teachings of Sun-worshippers. Out of crisis is born a new form of reverence for the environment and its governing bodies, reminiscent of the Inca society at Machu Picchu. During the approach of the Cloud, an ambivalent force of nature, 'all manner of religious beliefs had flourished mightily... true, Sunworship never became an established religion, for it had no central organisation, but the undertones of the ancient belief were set vibrating and were never again damped out'.[75]

A similar though reduced emotional effect might have been felt after the unprecedented December 1999 windstorm that destroyed the centuries-old plantings of André Lenotre at Versailles 'crumpling in a matter of seconds that garden's perfect geometries – perhaps as potent an image of human mastery as we have'.[76] Certainly, a less emphatically ordered garden would be able to resist and regenerate from the chaos inflicted by such an event, finding strength in the mutualistic relationships that sustain everyday wilderness. What to make of such a disaster? 'It all depends: on whether one regards that particular storm as a straightforward proof of our hubris and nature's infinitely superior power or, as some scientists now do, as an effect of global warming.'[77]

64. 'Northern Norway – Where the Sun Never Sets' [https://www.visitnorway.com/things-to-do/nature-attractions/midnight-sun], retrieved 8 September 2022

65. 'Bloemen Route', Atlas Obscura [http://www.atlasobscura.com/places/bloemen-route], retrieved 8 September 2022

66. GF Shapiro, 'Rem Koolhaas's Countryside, the Next Frontier of Urbanization', Domus, 26 February 2020 [https://www.domusweb.it/en/architecture/gallery/2020/02/26/countryside-the-future.html], retrieved 8 September 2022

67 + 68. M Pollan, 'The Botany of Desire: A plant's eye view of the world', (1st ed.) Random House, New York, 2001, p.161 & p.76

69. 'Tulip Farm Timelapse in Netherlands', Europe From Above, National Geographic UK [https://www.youtube.com/watch?v=UfS8tJ7pGkA], retrieved 8 September 2022

70. S Vittek, 'Will Rising Temperatures Force Cranberry Production to Move North?', Environment, Ambrook Research, 23 November 2022 [https://ambrook.com/research/environment/cranberry-production-massachusetts-jersey-wisconsin-climate], retrieved 18 August 2023

71. S Spike, 'Cranberry Capers: Wild harvesting in Nova Scotia, 1880s and 1950s', NiCHE, 10 December 2014 [https://niche-canada.org/2014/12/10/cranberry-capers-wild-harvesting-in-nova-scotia-1880s-and-1950s], retrieved 18 August 2023

72. C Monet quoted in 'Monument, Moment, and Memory: Monet's Cathedral in Fin de Siècle France', Bucknell University Press, 2007, p.73

73. S Sze, 'The Cathedral in Rouen by Claude Monet', Musée d'Orsay, 11 April 2021 [https://www.youtube.com/watch?v=S3gXpnFVvOY], retrieved 18 December 2022

74, 76 + 77. M Pollan, 'The Botany of Desire: A plant's eye view of the world', Random House, New York, 2001, p.123 & p.161

75. F Hoyle, 'The Black Cloud', Harper & Brothers, New York, 1957, p.77

Dear Van Gogh

'It is something to be deep in the snow in winter, to be deep in the yellow leaves in the autumn, to be deep in the ripe wheat in the summer, to be deep in the grass in the spring. It is something to always be with the mowers and the peasant girls, in summer with the big sky above, in the winter by the black fireplace. And to feel – this has always been so and always will be.'

– Vincent van Gogh, 'To Theo van Gogh. Nuenen, on or about Monday, 22 June 1885', no.509

The profound feelings of eternity evidenced by his letters prepared Van Gogh to paint the passing of seasons with particular emotional significance. 'Wheatfield with Crows' (1890) is understood to be Van Gogh's suicide note. Not only does it appear to depict the exact setting of his death, but the disarray of the crows can be interpreted as the aftermath of a gunshot. The tragic idea of death has similarly characterised the sombre monochromatic paintings of Picasso's 'Blue Period' (1901–1904). Although they never met, Picasso described Van Gogh as his 'patron saint', and felt his influence was 'not a superficial stylistic question of borrowed compositions, but a matter of deep spiritual identification'.[1]

In this exercise of historical fiction, Picasso's letters arrived when Van Gogh was in his darkest moment. Their empathetic reassurances propose Cubist dreams of nature's sensorial pleasures, spatialised as tectonic allegories of prostitutes, drunks, and the homeless. Taken from Picasso's Blue Period, these are responsible for providing care and continuously reimagining the environmental conditions of each season for Van Gogh's rehabilitation, akin to the desolation of social outsiders which brought Picasso out of his own depression. Depicted in the simplified forms characteristic of pictorial symbolism, the allegories express the core beliefs of the Symbolists who 'sought escape from reality, expressing their personal dreams and visions through colour, form, and composition'.[2]

Pheasant Island, the site situated in the middle of the Bidasoa River, is the only condominium territory to alternate sovereignty between France and Spain throughout the year. The island has been passed back and forth since 1659 and to this day it remains a powerful symbol of peace, a much-required medication for Van Gogh. Starting with autumn, the tectonic allegories create reminders of the site's symbolic and natural cycles, composing a complex set of finely choreographed placements and spatial dialogues with its strange half-year sovereignty and the assurances of seasonal arrivals.

Writing about his favourite season, Van Gogh proclaimed that he would 'sometimes yearn for a country where it would always be autumn',[3] with its bountiful harvests and figures sowing seeds in the twilight of crimson and yellow ochre. He found solace in the hazy shadows of Picasso's slender framed spatial

facing page: Van Gogh's prolific writing, captured in dated letters, reveal his dreams and disillusions as they metamorphose throughout the four seasons.

following page left top: Picasso's letters arrived in the midst of Van Gogh's darkest moment.

following page left bottom + right: Van Gogh found comfort in his favourite season – autumn.

1. J Richardson, 'The Catch in the Late Picasso', New York Review, 19 July 1984

2. N Myers, 'Symbolism', Metropolitan Museum of Art, August 2007

3. V van Gogh, 'To Anthon van Rappard. The Hague, on or about Sunday, 22 October 1882', no.273, www.vangoghletters.org [https://vangoghletters.org/vg/letters/let273/letter.html], retrieved 6 July 2022

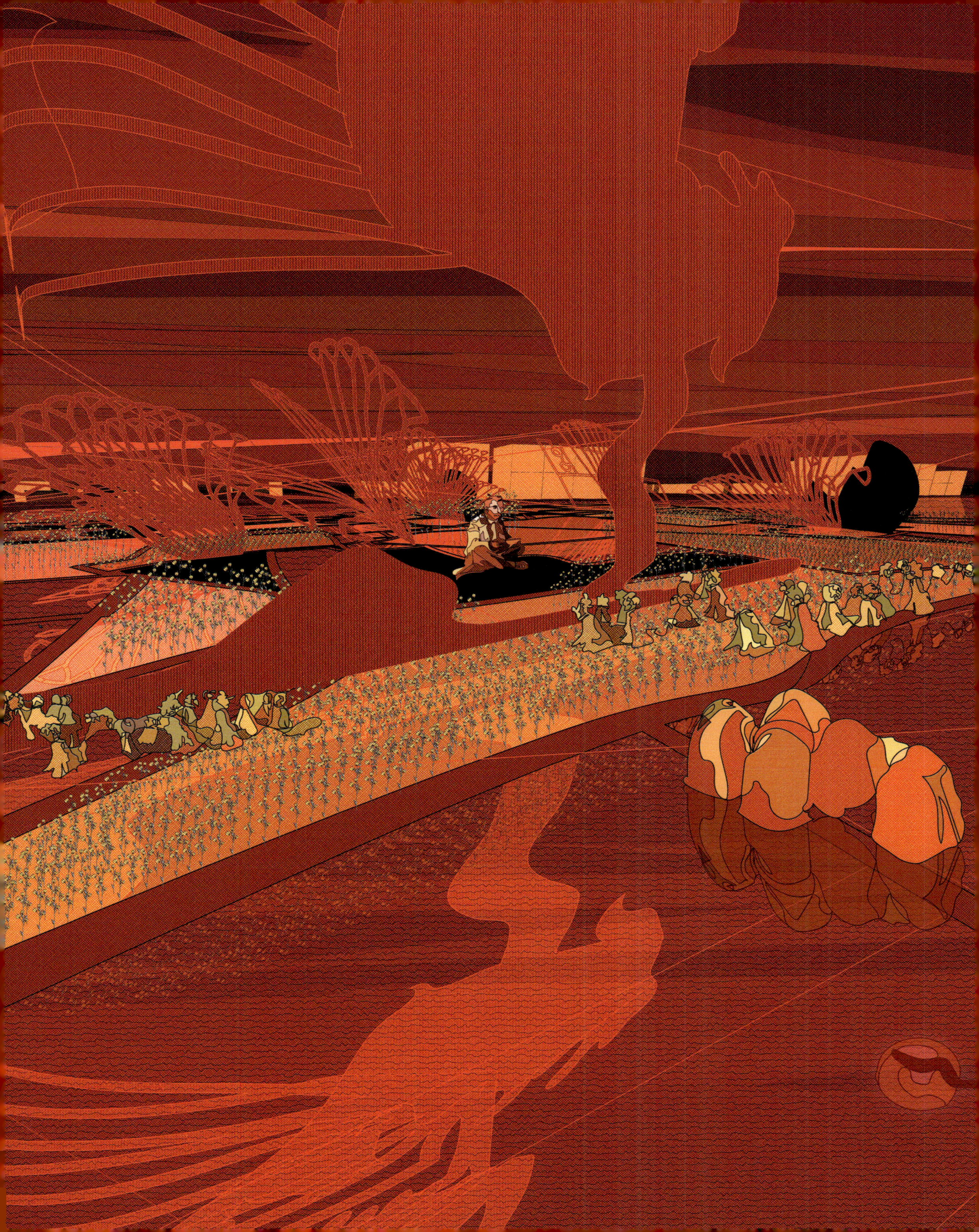

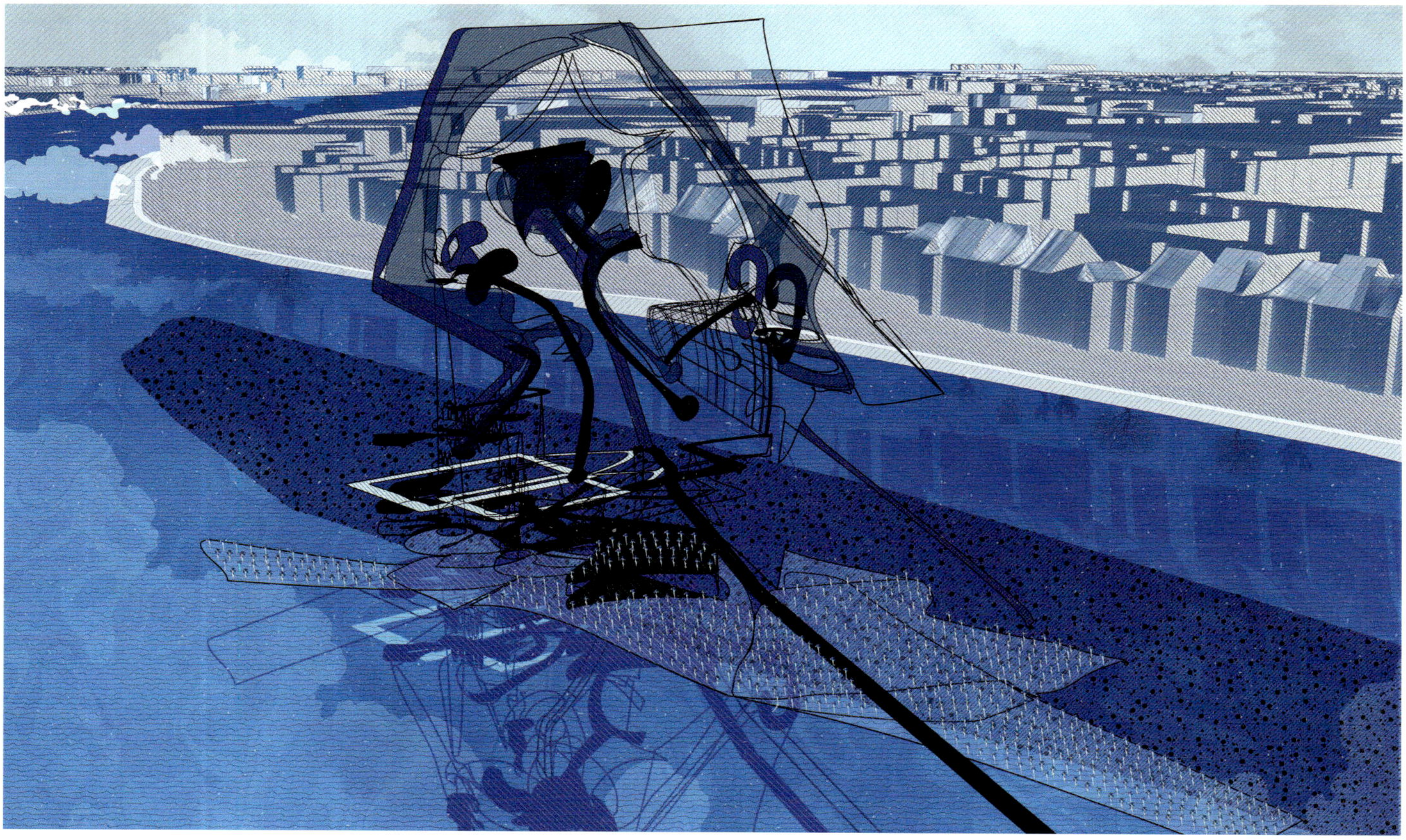

protagonist 'The Absinthe Drinker' (1902) which, along the island's accommodating waters, comes to rest on the peculiar 'Man with Fireplace' (1916). Comforted by the gently tempered light and warmth of sunflowers radiating from the Cubist fireplace, he replies to the Spanish artist, 'I thank you for sending while you yourself are so hard pressed. I need it twice as badly, because the autumn goes so quickly.'[4]

Van Gogh is already contemplating the germination of spring whilst idle ploughs remain motionless in cobalt blue frozen fields, writing 'sometimes in winter it's so bitterly cold... and one fine morning the wind has turned and we have a thaw. Comparing the natural state of the weather with our state of mind and our circumstances, subject to variableness and change, I still have some hope.'[5] Picasso, to soothe the Dutch artist's distress, offers faith and hope in the form of blue irises together with two tectonic allegories possessing a network of thick trunks which pare down to thin tangles of branches: 'Woman with Folded Arms' (1902) and 'The Weeping Woman' (1937) are respectively symbols of 'maternal protection',[6] 'hope' and 'a possible representation of new life'.[7]

In the midst of painting a spring scene with blooming orchards, Van Gogh takes notice of the ephemeral conditions which drive the unrelenting march of the seasons. 'Suddenly a tremendous wind began to blow, an effect ever seen here – and came back again at intervals.'[8] This sensation symbolises the multi-dimensional Cubist viewpoints which 'Le pigeon aux petits pois' (1911) has towards France and Spain. Meanwhile, 'La Celestina' (1904), partially blinded by the abundance of vivid green grass and lush green meadows, attempts to persuade Van Gogh to develop a more profound grasp of reality. Picasso equated blindness with a sharpening of senses, wherein the restriction of sight could provide a deeper, inward vision. Alas, even for Van Gogh with his sight unencumbered, writing to Picasso 'in a calm frame of mind presents serious difficulties, yesterday (he) wrote some letters that (he) later destroyed'.[9]

Gradually coming to terms with the difficulties of expression, Van Gogh struggles against summer's golden fields of ripe wheat shimmering under the sun's heat. He suffers for the fact that 'it isn't easy to find the effect of a summer sun that's as lush and as simple and as pleasant to look at as the characteristic effects of the other seasons'.[10] If only he could hear the sounds of summer when the flow of the Bidasoa River plays the strings of the two musical allegories of human survival, 'The Old Guitarist' (1904) and 'Girl with Mandolin' (1910) – all Van Gogh's emotions reflecting his predicament at the time might ebb away. Nevertheless, looking forward to the gentle melancholy in the falling leaves and autumn's subdued, striated light, Van Gogh mutters to himself: 'let me not leave before there's something of an autumn evening in it, something mysterious, something with seriousness in it'.[11]

Setting aside the fictional imaginings of this alternate history, Van Gogh nonetheless reveals dreams of the on-going myth-making present in seasonal cycles through his prolific letter writing. Promises of tomorrow, hinted at by inevitable mood changes, fade into disillusions with each seed of rebirth that ends in death. There is spatial healing to be found in the rhythms of nature, in seasons, in colour, in the air's smells and sounds, and in the qualities of light that change with both the time of day and the time of year. At the same time, profound meaning is formed by the greatness of nature and the existence of a higher force, experienced anew through their shifting patterns.

previous pages: The tectonic allegories come together, giving hope to Van Gogh during the bitterly cold winter months.

facing page: Van Gogh contemplating the seasons' germination into spring.

following pages: If only Van Gogh could hear the sounds of summer, the emotions reflecting his predicament might ebb away.

4. V van Gogh, 'To Theo van Gogh. The Hague, Monday, 11 September 1882', no.262, www.vangoghletters.org [https://vangoghletters.org/vg/letters/let262/letter.html], retrieved 6 July 2022

5. V van Gogh, 'To Theo van Gogh. Cuesmes, between about Monday, 11 and Thursday, 14 August 1879', no.154, www.vangoghletters.org [https://vangoghletters.org/vg/letters/let154/letter.html], retrieved 6 July 2022

6. JE Cirlot, 'Picasso: Birth of a Genuis', Praeger Publishers, New York, 1972, p.133

7. J Jones, 'Weeping Woman, Pablo Picasso (1937)', Portrait of the Week, Guardian, 13 May 2000

8. V van Gogh, 'To Theo van Gogh. Arles, on or about Wednesday, 11 April 1888', no.595, www.vangoghletters.org [https://vangoghletters.org/vg/letters/let595/letter.html], retrieved 6 July 2022

9. V van Gogh, 'To Theo van Gogh. Arles, on or about Tuesday, 3 April 1888', no.592, www.vangoghletters.org [https://vangoghletters.org/vg/letters/let592/letter.html], retrieved 6 July 2022

10. V van Gogh, 'To Theo van Gogh. Nuenen, on or about Wednesday, 2 July 1884', no.451, www.vangoghletters.org [https://vangoghletters.org/vg/letters/let451/letter.html], retrieved 6 July 2022

11. V van Gogh, 'To Theo van Gogh. The Hague, Sunday, 3 September 1882', no.260, www.vangoghletters.org [https://vangoghletters.org/vg/letters/let260/letter.html], retrieved 6 July 2022

yesterday yesterday
ALCOHOL
ALCOHOL
CIGARETTE
DRINK ME
19:53
34 %
Reception Room of Yesterday
Instagram
realkanyewest
Reception Room of Yesterday
129,306 likes
realkanyewest Look at this perfect "Texas Dip" #elegantgirl
#allamericangirl #thisishowladylookslike
#debutanteball #whiteball
3 MINUTES AGO
1

Yesterday Tomorrow

'Traditionally, the British look to the open sea, yet now, a fixed, visible link to the Continent is forcing them to turn their attention to Europe. The French are the last conservatoire of Marxist theory, a regime where the citizens serve the state and the state serves itself. The tunnel acts as a liberalising counter-balance to this philosophy.'

– André Bénard, Speech at the Opening of the Eurotunnel, 6 May 1994

Without Benard's calmness and perseverance, the dream of London and Paris becoming one would have succumbed to incessant 'spiralling costs, investor fright, government vacillation and unexpectedly difficult tunnelling conditions'.[1] In the process of realisation for centuries, this idea dates back to French Emperor Napoleon Bonaparte's horse-drawn carriage scheme for two tunnels illuminated with gaslight. Ventilated by chimneys rising above the sea, these infrastructures would have met at an artificial island in the middle of the Channel. The tunnel is much more than a means to an end in transportation terms – it is a triumph of ideology and confidence in the perpetuity of stability in Europe's political climate.

facing page: The concept of tomorrow and yesterday not only describes the island's time zones, but the state of their two countries with Russia ratifying the Paris Agreement and the US leaving.

following pages: The secret 'hot alliance' between Trump and Putin has mutual benefits, which are hidden by their ostensible 'Cold War' hostility staged to a world audience.

Contrary to the beliefs of naysayers, when cities on either side of international borders collaborate, they become significant life-adaptors, culture-cultivators, and fiscal-generators. In his book 'Cities In Evolution' (1915), Patrick Geddes refers to the incorporation of cities with large adjoining towns, industrial build-up and extensive suburban communities to form a continuous environment as 'conurbations'.[2] High population growth and physical expansion both contribute to the phenomena, but Geddes drew attention to new technologies which made the creation of a single urban economic zone or travel-to-work conurbation viable. The Oresund Fixed Link, a highway and railway line that runs along a bridge-tunnel, rekindled ties between Copenhagen and Malmö. The southern part of Sweden, Scania, in which Malmö is located was a part of Denmark for much of the Middle Ages. Dreaming, planning and politicking since the early 20th century resulted in the creation of the transnational metropolitan Oresund Region which, in its first decade, has generated more than double its construction budget and has 'more than 350 businesses in the region that employ 40,000 people, ranging from big pharmaceuticals to start-ups'.[3] There are many examples of cities which put aside political and cultural differences across borderlines to become even more formidable. The economic gap between Shenzhen and other special economic zones like Zhuhai, Shantou and Xiamen, for example, only emphasises its neighbour-with-benefits relationship to the global financial hub, Hong Kong.

For two autonomous urban systems to develop into one, there are innumerable issues and influences to consider: from anthropology, economics and environmental science to geography and history.

1. Obituary, 'Andre Benard', Times, 6 May 1994

2. P Geddes, 'Patrick Geddes: Spokesman for man and the environment', M Stalley (ed.), Rutgers University Press, New Jersey, 1972, pp.127–129

3. Reportage, 'With the Bridge Comes a Region', www.webuildvalue.com, 5 December 2020 [https://www.webuildvalue.com/en/reportage/with-the-bridge-comes-a-region.html], retrieved 23 September 2022

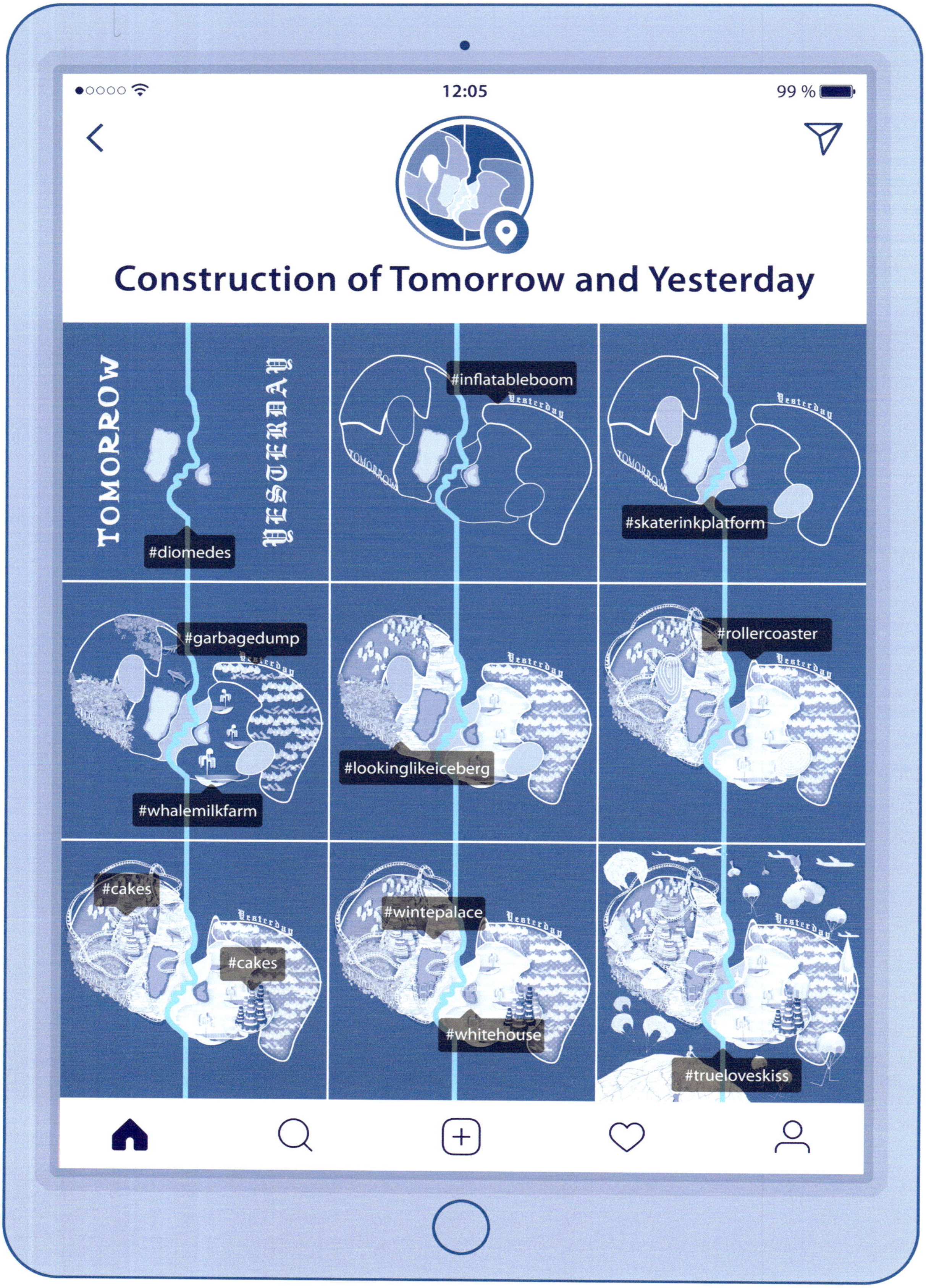
12:05
99 %
Construction of Tomorrow and Yesterday
TOMORROW
YESTERDAY
#diomedes
#inflatableboom
#skaterinkplatform
#garbagedump
#whalemilkfarm
#lookinglikeiceberg
#rollercoaster
#cakes
#cakes
#wintepalace
#whitehouse
#trueloveskiss

12:00
100 %
Islands of Tomorrow and Yesterday
Yesterday
TOMORROW
#trueloveskiss
Yesterday Station

16:18
64 %
Instagram
realvalentinamatvienko
Winter Palace
625 likes
realvalentinamatvienko Enchanting Winter Palace is ready to welcome our first debutantes! #livebeautiful #seemycity
#festivalofwinter #noclimatechange #zero
3
3 MINUTES AGO
Winter Palace
TOMORROW

16:18
64 %
Instagram
realivankatrump
White House >
176,392 likes
realivankatrump So proud of our Capitol! #whitehouse #uscapitol #festivalofwinter #noclimatechange #zerocarbon
3 MINUTES AGO
2
Instagram
realivankatrump
White House
86,658 likes
16:18
64 %
White House

the lonelyshepherd onceuponatime
@February29th
February
March
A Shepherd's Tale
February is giving away one of her days to March; cold winter breezes in the end of the month are killing the Shepherd's sheep.

Political espionage is the unsurprising motivation behind the 2021 unification of the Russian-US 'Islands of Tomorrow and Yesterday'. The speculative 'hot alliance' between Vladimir Putin and then-President Donald Trump caricatures their ostensible hostility, while concealing clandestine activities to countermeasure their respective countries' consistently high carbon emission rankings. 'The United States will withdraw from the Paris climate accord. I promised I would exit or re-negotiate any deal which fails to serve America's interests.'[4] Here, Trump's climate denialism and economic nationalism are clearly intended to play to his political base. While Putin reaffirmed Russia's commitment to the agreement, his laissez-faire conspiracy theory that global warming will 'continue anyway and anyhow' is no more assuring. From his perspective, the melting ice enables maritime passage year-round between Asia and Europe while 'climate change brings in more favourable conditions and improves the economic potential'[5] of the Arctic region.

Adamant that the climate emergency is a hoax and determined to convince the world of their position, the bilateral Russia-US collaboration fakes year-round winters at the International Date Line on the Diomede Islands in the middle of the Bering Strait. Dividing mainland Alaska and Siberia, Russia's Big Diomede Island is located only 3.75 kilometres from US military-occupied Little Diomede, nicknamed 'Tomorrow Island' and 'Yesterday Island' respectively because of their 21-hour time zone difference. The concept of tomorrow and yesterday not only describes the dates on each, but also the state of mind, with Russia keen to protect territorial interests and the US clinging to power and illusions of yesterday.

The newly reimagined 'Cold War' is the quintessential debutante ball held on the 29th of February every leap year, a reference to the folk tale where the month 'borrowed' an extra day from March in return for a lamb promised by a shepherd. The dream of consistent winters and innocent teenagers from both countries symbolically easing political tensions exists only inside the virtual space of social media; each photograph of the ball is carefully framed and curated for global dissemination. However, behind the filters and beyond the frames lie the ugly truths and debaucheries of climate fakery to veil dwindling periods of cold. The white winter backdrop is not ice or snow, but composites of garbage painted with whales' milk. Throughout the obsolescent tradition of the ball, guests deconstruct the 'White House' made with anything from white napkins to toilet paper on the Island of Yesterday, only to fill up the 'Winter Palace' on the Island of Tomorrow. Hidden in plain sight by voluminous ivory dresses, the debutantes trade in the 'contraband products of yesterday'. These accomplices to the bullish voices of Putin and Trump are the grassroots purveyors of fake news, preying on woke celebrities through social media.

Madelon Vriesendrop once described her beguiling painting 'Flagrant Delit' (1975) of post-coital Empire State and Chrysler Buildings caught in bed as an 'in-depth analysis of the possibilities provided by architecture', marking 'the moment when the rigid corset of modernism seemed to be entirely exhausted'.[6] The 'intercourse' between the Islands of Tomorrow and Yesterday evokes similar ideas of delirium – shamelessness, surrealism and satire all come together as a pop drama of our troublous times. Undoubtedly, cities are receiving ever-increasing negative sentiments for their environmental irresponsibility, but the real threat in this cautionary tale is the unthinkable destruction that could arise from unholy alliances, sometimes between seemingly antagonistic parties.

previous pages left + right: Winter Palace on Tomorrow Island; White House on Yesterday Island.

facing page: The folktale where February 'borrowed' a day from March.

following page 286: The photographs of the ball are carefully curated for social media. Behind the filters and outside the frames lie the ugly truths of faked winters and the social season.

following page 287: Debutantes trade the 'contrabands of yesterday' hidden underneath their voluminous dresses.

following pages 288–289: The pure white landscape is neither ice nor snow – transient seasonal effects have been replaced by marine debris, collected and painted with whales' milk.

4. BBC News, 'Paris Climate Deal: Trump pulls US out of 2015 accord', BBC, 1 June 2017 [https://www.bbc.co.uk/news/world-us-canada-40127326], retrieved 23 September 2022

5. S Meredith & G Cutmore, 'Climate Change Doubters May Not Be So Silly, Says Russia President Putin', CNBC, 30 March 2017 [http://www.cnbc.com/2017/03/30/vladimir-putin-russia-trump-us-climate-policy.html], retrieved 23 September 2022

6. K Leuschel, 'Sex and the City? In Architecture', Architonic, 1 February 2009 [https://www.architonic.com/en/story/klaus-leuschel-sex-and-the-city-in-architecture/7000243], retrieved 25 September 2022

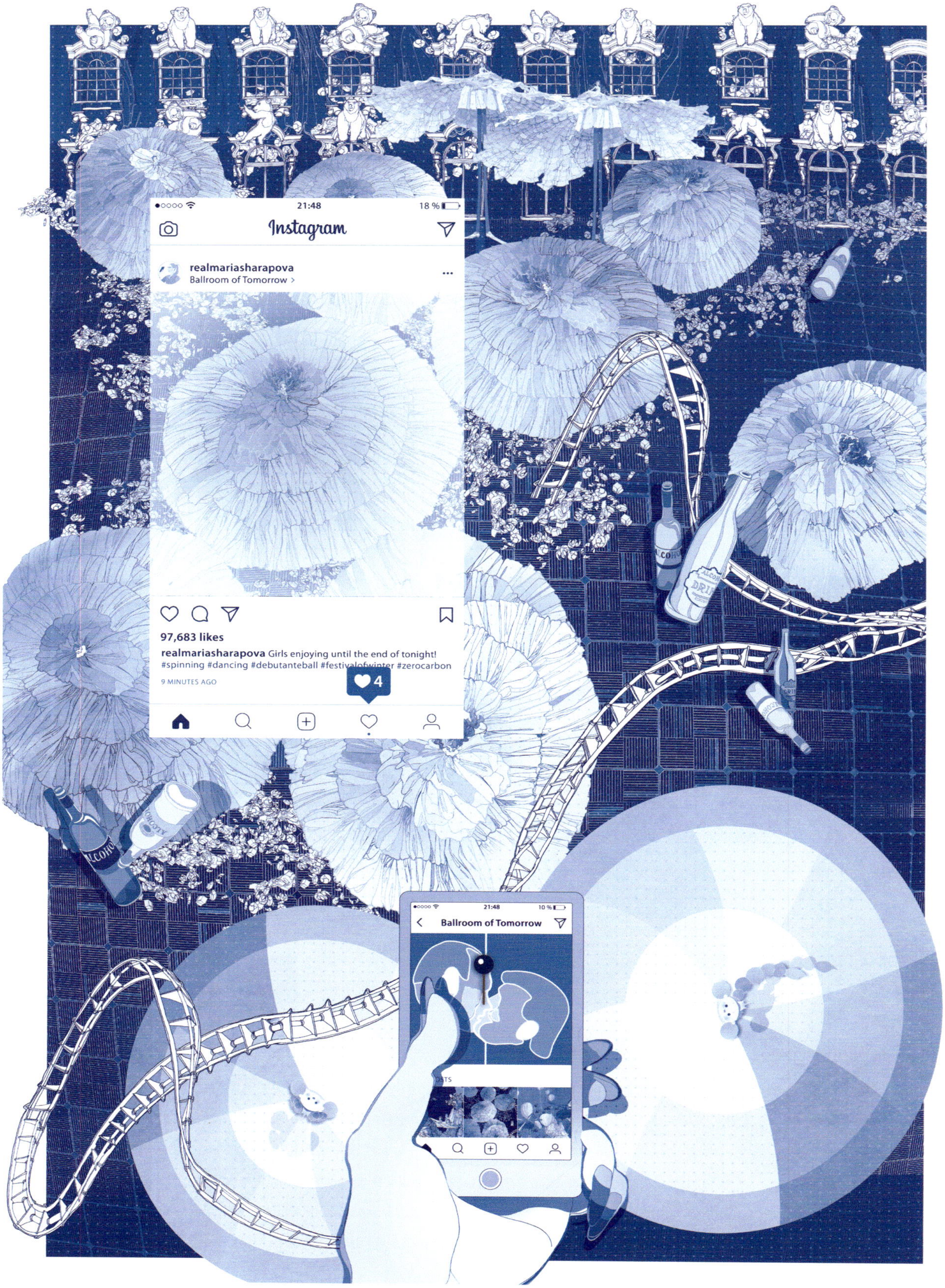
21:48
18 %
Instagram
realmariasharapova
Ballroom of Tomorrow >
97,683 likes
realmariasharapova Girls enjoying until the end of tonight!
#spinning #dancing #debutanteball #festivalofwinter #zerocarbon
9 MINUTES AGO
4
21:48
10 %
Ballroom of Tomorrow

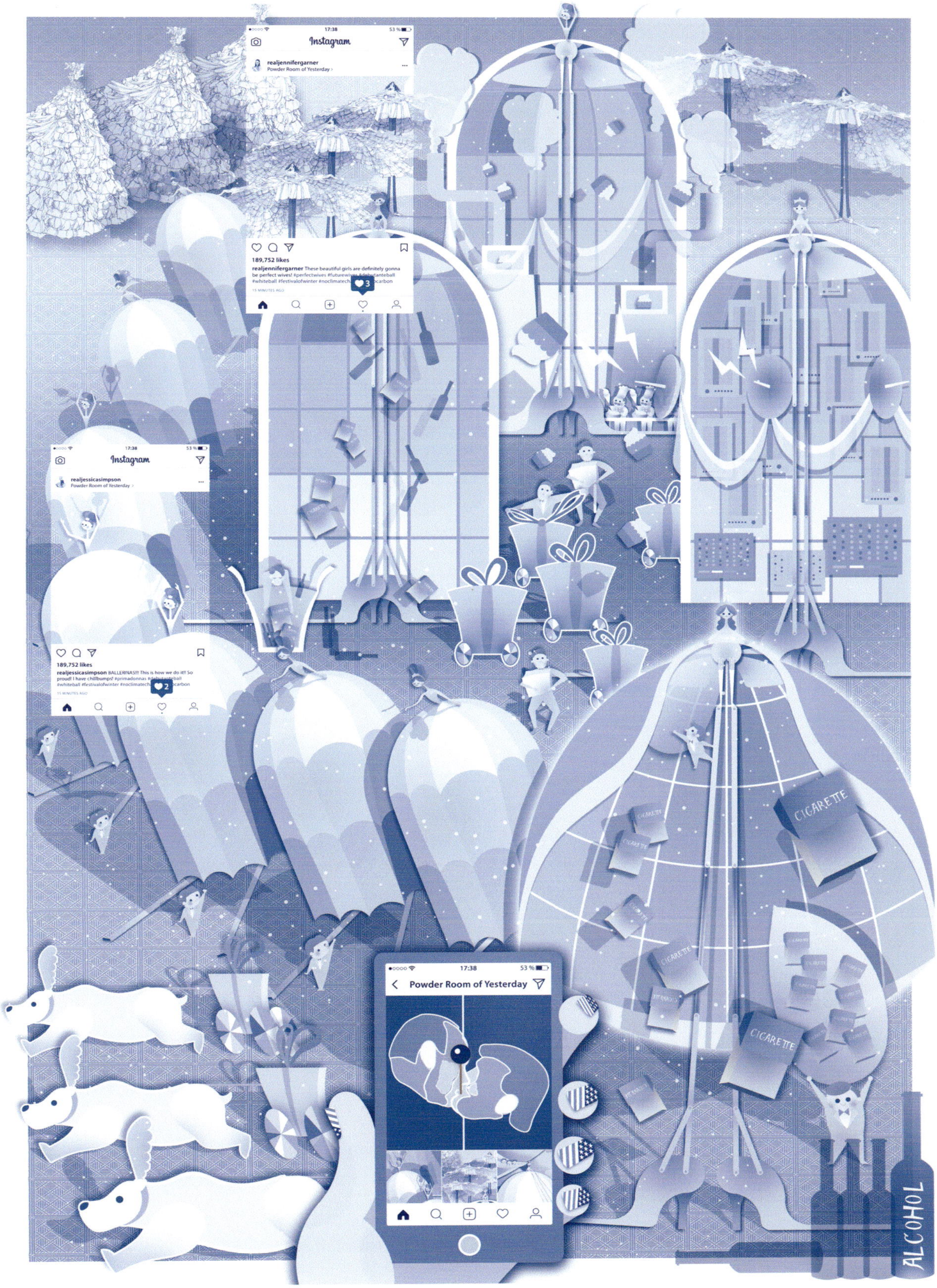
17:38
53 %
Instagram
realjennifergarner
Powder Room of Yesterday
189,752 likes
realjennifergarner These beautiful girls are definitely gonna be perfect wives! #perfectwives #futurewiv
#whiteball #festivalofwinter #noclimatech
carbon
15 MINUTES AGO
3
17:38
53 %
Instagram
realjessicasimpson
Powder Room of Yesterday
189,752 likes
realjessicasimpson BALLERINAS!!! This is how we do it!! So proud! I have chillbumps! #primadonnas
#whiteball #festivalofwinter #noclimatech
carbon
15 MINUTES AGO
2
CIGARETTE
CIGARETTE
CIGARETTE
17:38
53 %
Powder Room of Yesterday
ALCOHOL

14:34
78 %
Instagram
realmashaimedved
Island of Tomorrow›
1,463,829 likes
realmashaimedved Mishka is my best friend! He is so happy playing with the snow! #polarbear #cubs
#festivalofwinter #noclimatechange #zero
2
9 MINUTES AGO
14:34
78 %
Iceberg of Yesterday

14:34
78 %
Instagram
realleonardodicaprio
Island of Yesterday >
68,385 likes
realleonardodicaprio This iceberg makes my skin freeze again!
@sea_legacy It seemed like a pretty good ice year. #iceberg
#titanickiller #festivalofwinter #noclimate
6
9 MINUTES AGO
14:34
78 %
Iceberg of Tomorrow

Roosevelt's Yellow Submarine

'As we live a life of ease... Every one of us has all we need... Sky of blue and sea of green... In our yellow submarine.'

– The Beatles, 'Yellow Submarine', Capital Records, 1969

The 'Four Freedoms Park' located on Roosevelt Island, NY, is a celebration of President Franklin D. Roosevelt's 'Four Freedoms Speech' delivered in the State of the Union Address of 1941. In the following years and amidst the catastrophe of World War II, the United Nations was founded as the political architecture for Roosevelt's vision, promising 'the maintenance of international peace and security'.[1] The Beatles delivered a similar dream of world peace encouraging humanity to live in harmony with the planet, and in Madelon Vriesendorp's surreal pictorial narrative 'Flagrant Delit' in Rem Koolhaas' 'Delirious New York' (1978) the machismo skyscrapers of Manhattan, namely the Empire State and Chrysler Buildings, are shown in vulnerable and highly suggestive positions instead of their real world postures of dominance. What escaped this fiction was the aftermath of their affair...

In the president's wildest dreams of the future, his park and the freedoms it represents are reframed to amend injustices, both political and climatic, at the foundations of the UN's global alliance. In his state of delusion, Roosevelt has a peculiar vision that the Empire State and Chrysler Buildings made love. From their union, the UN is birthed as 'Roosevelt's Yellow Submarine', incorporating 1960s optimism with retrospective atonement and delivered into the East River by four midwives named John, Paul, George and Ringo.[2] Watched over by its towering parents, the lovechild expands to fill Roosevelt Island's extents while its amenities reach below the water's surface to accommodate over 300 UN employees from the nearby Manhattan headquarters. From the two iconic skyscrapers, the lovechild inherits the parental characteristics of the Art Deco style.

The idea of relocating the UN has a long history, from Secretary General Kofi Annan's support for the concept in 2005[3] to the vetoed 2019 proposal of a transfer outside the United States.[4] Roosevelt's four freedoms and the four buildings from the current UN Headquarters – the General Assembly, Conference Building, Secretariat Building and Dag Hammarskjöld Library – become the 'four seasons', representing ephemeral conditions to spread peace and security rather than stultifying office blocks of paperwork and loggerheads. Most of the lovechild is subterranean in audacious contrast to the regular urban development of New York, motivated by Zaha Hadid's 'Leicester Square' (1990), a futuristic city vision of inverted inhabitable infrastructures.[5] The 'earth-scraper' typology has numerous benefits that significantly reduce the submarine inhabitation's impact on the environment.

facing page: Akin to the design of submarines, the double enclosures convert water into an endless supply of fresh oxygen.

following page 292: The lovechild grows into 'Roosevelt's Yellow Submarine' under the careful watch and admiration of its two proud parents, the Empire State and Chrysler Buildings.

following page 293: On either side of its East River docking station, the UN Library forms a memory wall of environmental atonements and climate battles won.

1. United Nations, 'Maintain International Peace and Security' [www.un.org/en/sections/what-we-do/maintain-international-peace-and-security], retrieved 28 August 2022

2. John Lennon, Paul McCartney, George Harrison and Ringo Starr were members of the English band 'The Beatles'.

3. W Hoge, 'U.N. Could Move to Brooklyn While Headquarters Undergoes Renovation', New York Times, 10 May 2005

4. UN Press, 'First Committee Votes to Reject Draft Decision on Relocating Overseas', United Nations, 8 November 2019 [https://press.un.org/en/2019/gadis3645.doc.htm], retrieved 28 August 2022

5. P Schumacher & G Fontana-Giusti (eds.), 'Zaha Hadid Complete Works', Thames & Hudson, London, 2004, p.21

FRESH AIR
E=mc2

With spring commencing, the lovechild begins cleaning New York's air while filtering water and cultivating a diamond forest by extracting the atmospheric carbon particles which saturate the polluted concrete jungle. In doing so, oxygen – a product of carbon reacting with iron rich minerals during diamond formation – becomes the principal US reserve currency, creating a new world order. The wealthiest countries become those possessing the cleanest air, thus incentivising a transglobal reduction of atmospheric carbon at macroscopic, city-wide and individual scales. Throughout the summer, provisions for peace are collected as solar energy and stored within heat sinks to cool internal spaces, naturally warming them later in the year when the weather changes. Referencing the design of submarines, a double skin houses floodable spaces around the perimeter of the island and a cylindrical inhabitation hull is encased within, where colourful ribbons and long, interrupted columns now support hanging accommodation towers. In fall, leafless crystalline trees formed from collected carbon achieve optimum levels of natural lighting through shallow and deep-cut diamond configurations, refracting light either into or out of the submarine architecture to create microclimates. Security is provided in the winter months by the river's freezing, on whose surface the expanded Security Council convenes. As they gather, constituents learn that Roosevelt 'had always dreamed of stainless-steel Chryslers and flying Empire States', freed, and seeming 'almost to float, like an enchanted fairy tower'.[6]

previous pages: With the Art Deco characteristics of the parents, the inverted accommodation ribbons hang deep below the ground.

facing page: Like a scene off Abbey Road, the diamond forests 'Come Together' to serve as a growing barometer of global environmental damage as more carbon is sequestered – 'Here Comes the Sun', though everything might not be alright.

following pages: Captained by Phileas Fogg, the city of atonement journeys around the world to unite millions of people, bringing environmental awareness and peace for humanity.

Upon reaching maturity, 'Roosevelt's Yellow Submarine' sets sail as an itinerant United Nations, housing a City of Atonement in its ark-like structure to spread the gospel of climatic end times throughout the globe. The floating city's first destination – The Reform Club in London – is 'founded in the ferment of ideas, ideals and political activity',[7] where member Phileas Fogg conceived his incredible voyage 'Around the World in Eighty Days'.[8] Becoming captain of the submarine and the new UN Secretariat, Fogg makes atonement for prior generations by capturing and crystalising more carbon to create reflective structures. Implemented as trusteeships in coastal population centres, these 'diamond forests' modulate seasons with landscaped urban accretions of architectural microclimates that either concentrate or reflect the sun's rays, distributing the clean-air wealth of the new world currency. Under Fogg's leadership, areas most threatened by climate change take on the aspects of environmental resilience found in the faraway lands of Jules Verne's adventure tales, where 'there are no more seasons; climates are no more; the heat of the globe continually increases and neutralises that of the sun'.[9]

UN workers are the only permanent residents, serving as Climate Guardians aboard the yellow submarine. Critiquing the institution's past failures of stagnation and indecisiveness, the only non-permanent residents consist of youth from around the world. Inspired by the sailboat shenanigans of Greta Thunberg and the week-long migrations to Glastonbury,[10] they travel in the City of Atonement for fixed periods as it progresses from stop to stop. As UN Chief Economist Elliott Harris reiterated, 'the UN DESA's World Youth Report is clear: Young people have the potential to save the world. All we have to do is let them.'[11] By focusing on youth engagement, Roosevelt's submarine dream bypasses earlier mindsets bogged down in micro-management and divisive negotiations[12] to secure a wide range of benefits that will aid the social and educational development of a more decisive future population. Inattentive to the proverb 'All that glitters is not gold', shining forests are now sprouting around the world ...Franklin D. Roosevelt snaps awake!

6. R Koolhaas, 'Delirious New York: A retroactive manifesto for Manhattan', Oxford University Press, New York, 1978, pp.255–279

7. The Reform Club, 'History and Architecture' [www.reformclub.com/home/about/history], retrieved 28 August 2023

8. J Verne, 'Around the World in Eighty Days: The extraordinary journeys', Oxford University Press, New York, 1995, p.3

9. J Verne, 'A Journey to the Centre of the Earth', Scribner, Armstrong & Co., New York, 1874, p.276

10. 'Introduction to Glastonbury Festival', [www.glastonburyfestivals.co.uk/information/an-introduction-to-glastonbury-festival], retrieved 29 August 2022

11. United Nations, 'Youth and the 2030 Agenda for Sustainable Development', 16 February 2019 [https://www.un.org/development/desa/youth/news/2019/02/youth-sdgs], retrieved 29 August 2022

12. H Clark, 'The UN Is Failing – States Must Back off and Give Its Leader the Power to Act', Global Development, Guardian, 13 September 2017

Index

Page numbers in bold denote illustrations

case study 18: roosevelt's yellow submarine

Franklin D. Roosevelt snaps awake!